CONVERSATIONS FROM THE PRINT STUDIO

CONVERSATIONS FROM THE PRINT STUDIO

A MASTER PRINTER IN COLLABORATION WITH TEN ARTISTS

Yale University Art Gallery
New Haven

CRAIG ZAMMIELLO
ELISABETH HODERMARSKY

Distributed by Yale University Press
New Haven and London

Publication made possible by the Janet and Simeon Braguin Fund
and an endowment created with a challenge grant from the National
Endowment for the Arts.

First published in 2012 by the
Yale University Art Gallery
P.O. Box 208271
New Haven, CT 06520-8271
www.artgallery.yale.edu

and distributed by
Yale University Press
P.O. Box 209040
New Haven, CT 06520-9040
www.yalebooks.com/art

Tiffany Sprague, Director of Publications and Editorial Services
Molly Balikov, Associate Editor

Christopher Sleboda, Director of Graphic Design

Copyeditor: Molly Balikov
Proofreaders: Penelope Cray and John Mordecai

Set in Greta Text (designed by Peter Biľak in 2007)
and LL Brown (designed by Aurèle Sack in 2008)
Printed at GHP, West Haven, Conn.

Cover designed by Christopher Sleboda

Library of Congress Cataloging-in-Publication Data
Zammiello, Craig, 1955–
  Conversations from the print studio : a master printer in
collaboration with ten artists / Craig Zammiello and Elisabeth
Hodermarsky.
    pages cm
  Includes index.
  ISBN 978-0-300-17989-7 (alk. paper)
1. Intaglio printing. 2. Printmakers—Interviews. I. Hodermarsky,
Elisabeth. II. Title.
  NE1630.Z36 2012
  769.9'051—dc23
                    2012010849

10 9 8 7 6 5 4 3 2 1

Illustration, page 6: Ellen Gallagher, *So Fun* (detail), from *DeLuxe*,
2004–5

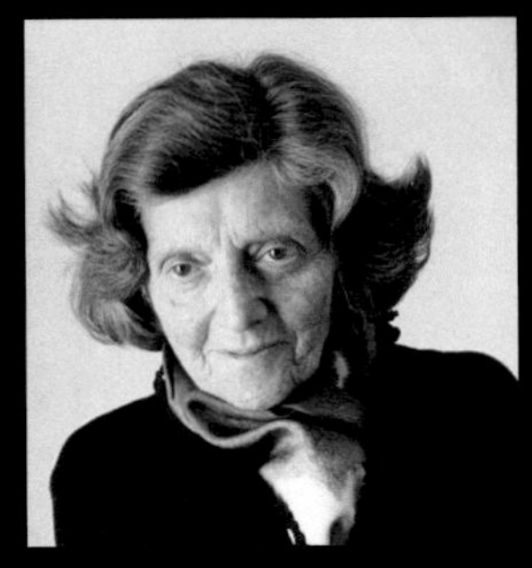

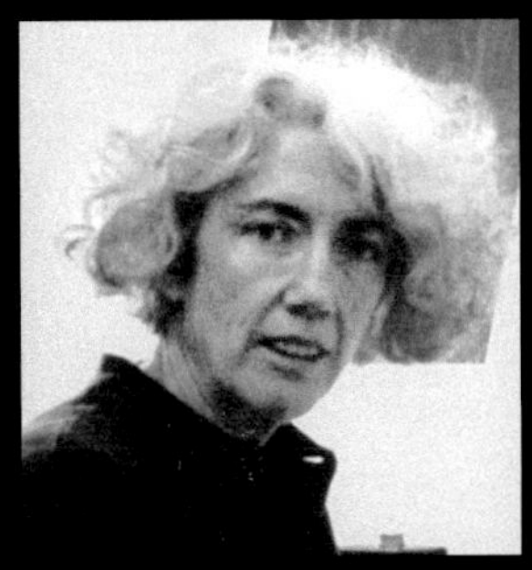

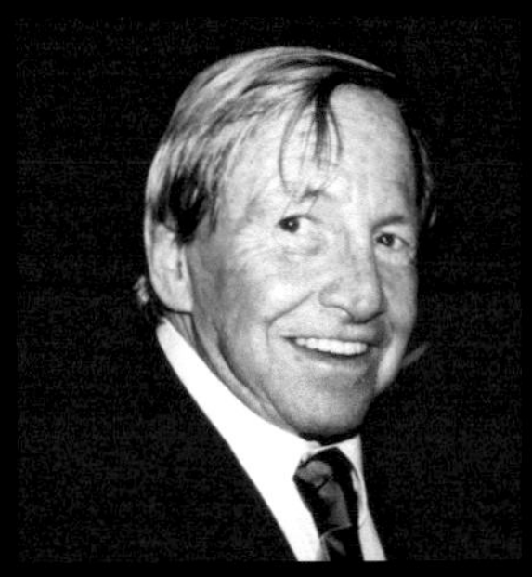

In memory of

**TATYANA GROSMAN
ELIZABETH MURRAY
ROBERT RAUSCHENBERG**

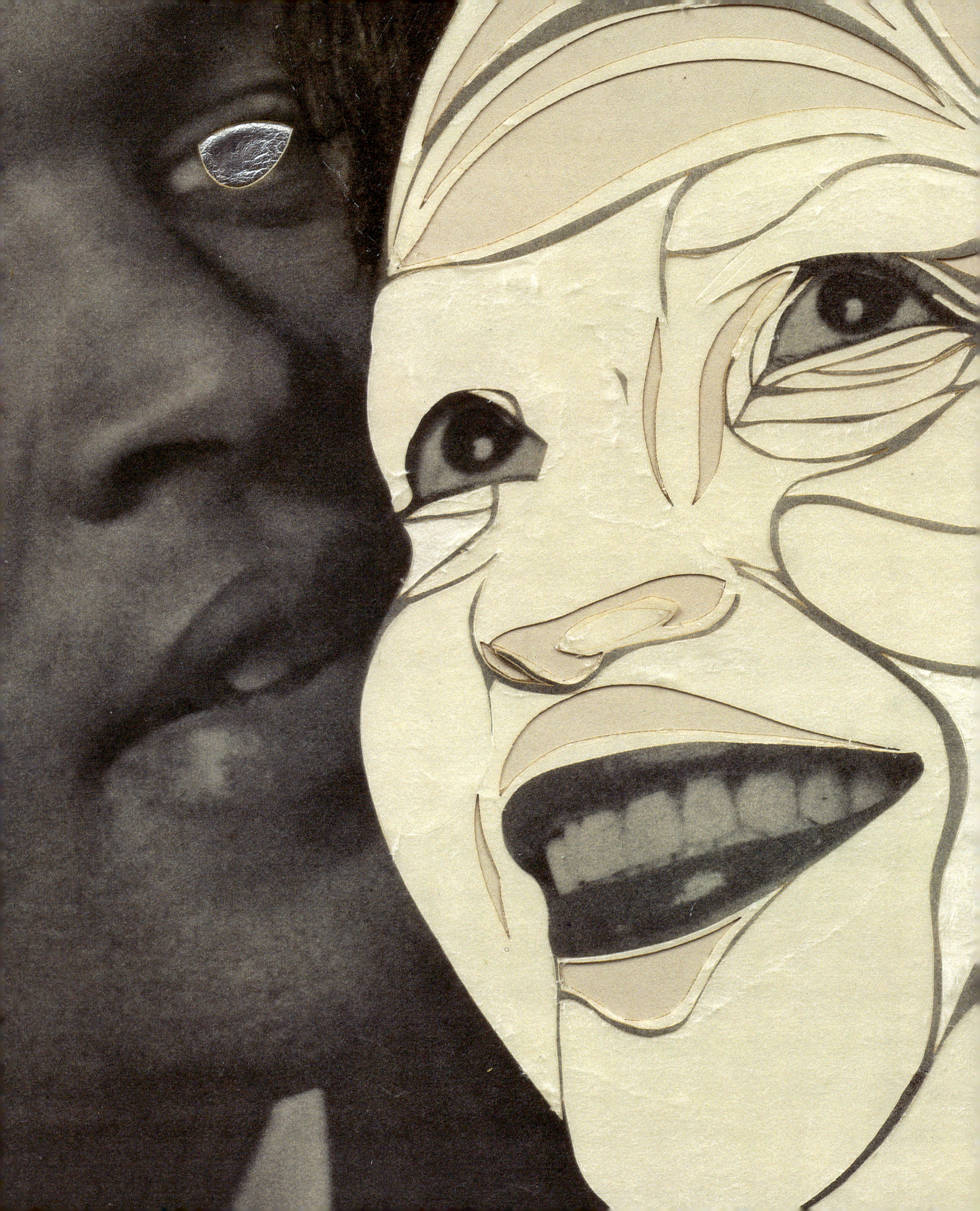

Contents

Director's Foreword

On occasion, the Yale University Art Gallery publishes books that are unconnected to any special exhibition but contribute to a particular field of art historical study or celebrate a particular artist or art collector. This publication fulfills both functions. By showcasing recent innovations in printmaking, it provides a source for technical information and ideas about contemporary printmaking processes while also championing contemporary artists and the extraordinary work currently coming out of independent print studios throughout the United States and the world. Part narrative about the collaborations that occur between artist and master printer in a modern-day print shop and part technical manual, this book describes many of the innovations Craig Zammiello (and, by implication, other master printers) have brought to bear on printmaking today.

The book is divided into ten chapters, each of which focuses on a particular print (or print series) and takes the form of a conversation between an artist, a printer, and a curator. In a compilation of lively dialogues with Zammiello and Elisabeth (Lisa) Hodermarsky, the Sutphin Family Senior Associate Curator of Prints, Drawings, and Photographs at the Gallery, each artist recounts his or her project from inception to fruition. The path is traced from the artist's initial vision, through the processes that the artist and printer chose or invented to realize this vision, and finally to the reactions of both artist and printer to the finished print. Thus, each chapter serves as both a narrative about a particular collaboration and as a technical primer of sorts on the processes and innovations employed in the realization of the final print.

In his over thirty years of experience, Zammiello has established himself as one of America's foremost specialists in intaglio printmaking. His energetic search for ways to assist painters and sculptors with the realization of their visions in print has inspired generations of artists to become devotees to printmaking, and has pushed the traditional boundaries of the intaglio medium. We are tremendously grateful to the ten artists who collaborated on this book: Mel Bochner, Carroll Dunham, Ellen Gallagher, Jane Hammond, Suzanne McClelland, Chris Ofili, Elizabeth Peyton, Matthew Ritchie, Kiki Smith, and Terry Winters—each of whom has adopted the print medium and considers it a vital part of his or her artistic production. Throughout their careers, all of these artists have served as instructor as well as student; each has embraced the rich spirit of collaborating and sharing, instructing and learning—qualities of central importance to a teaching institution such as Yale.

I wish to thank Craig and Lisa, who collaborated with these artists to record these ten very different accounts, these "adventures in printmaking." I also wish to thank Elizabeth C. DeRose, formerly the Florence B. Selden Assistant Curator in the Gallery's Department of Prints, Drawings, and Photographs, who assisted on this project. As readers of this book will learn, far from being a "lost" or "dying" art form, printmaking is very much alive and well today, and, unquestionably, some of the most innovative contemporary work is coming out of print studios across the globe. At this historic juncture between the mechanical and digital ages, we eagerly embrace the new innovations that continue to arise in print shops through the melding of the physical and cyber worlds.

Jock Reynolds
The Henry J. Heinz II Director

Preface

Artists have long gravitated to professional print shops, where master printers help them to realize their creations in print, and the medium of printmaking, with its entirely distinctive, ever-expanding lexicon of tools and vocabulary of mark-making, continues to lure new devotees. This book is a celebration of the unique relationship between artists, who are drawn to printmaking for the unique ways in which it allows them to express ideas, and master printers, who are well versed in the nuances of particular techniques and who continue to devise new processes that push the boundaries of the medium. Although this book focuses on a particular master printer and ten of the artists with whom he has worked at two East Coast presses—Universal Limited Art Editions (ULAE), on Long Island, and Two Palms, in New York—it is indicative of the tremendously exciting and innovative work being made today in print studios throughout the world.

The idea for this book began in spring 2007, following a symposium on contemporary printmaking hosted by the Yale University Art Gallery and organized by Elizabeth C. DeRose, the former Florence B. Selden Assistant Curator of Prints, Drawings, and Photographs and a contributor to this publication. That spring, Master Printer Craig Zammiello approached DeRose and Elisabeth (Lisa) Hodermarsky, the Gallery's Sutphin Family Senior Associate Curator of Prints, Drawings, and Photographs, for advice on finding a publisher for a book on recent innovations in intaglio printmaking—many of which he had himself invented or adapted. The proposed book would follow in the footsteps of John Ross's and Clare Romano's *The Complete Printmaker* (1972) and Donald Saff's and Deli Sacilotto's *Printmaking: History and Process* (1978). After extensive discussions we realized that such a specialized technical primer would not likely be considered by a publisher to be marketable. Yet as Zammiello continued to recount his fascinating stories of collaborations with artists, it became clear that a book that explored these ventures might be of interest to an art-minded public. Technical information could be woven into the narrative in a more organic way. The result is the discussions that fill this book, each exploring a particular print project from its inception to its completion from the dual perspective of master printer and artist. In these discussions, we explore the incorporation of new technologies (for example, the use of digital tools, such as the CO_2 laser, and digital film-imaging techniques for photogravure), as well as modifications or exploitations of existing tools to achieve new effects on a print matrix (for example, the integration of the vertical hydraulic press, the periphery camera, the airbrush, and the tattoo machine).

It is fitting that this book—which celebrates the collaborative spirit—is itself a collaboration. As a master intaglio printer and print curator we came at this project from two very different perspectives but with a shared passion for the endless possibilities of copper, acid, and ink, as well as for the rich and ever-expanding history of printmaking. It has been a tremendous pleasure to work together on this project—itself as much of a journey of discovery, of stops and starts, as any etching.

The artists who have participated in this project have done so enthusiastically and with no remuneration other than our paltry thanks. We wish to sincerely thank Mel Bochner, Carroll Dunham, Ellen Gallagher, Jane Hammond, Suzanne McClelland, Chris Ofili, Elizabeth Peyton, Matthew Ritchie, Kiki Smith, and Terry Winters, who embraced this undertaking and encouraged its movement to completion. We cannot adequately express to them our gratitude for their extraordinary generosity, patience, and dedication to this project.

There have been sad points along the way. Originally this book was to include conversations with Elizabeth Murray (1940–2007) and Robert Rauschenberg (1925–2008), who both tragically passed away before we were able to meet with them. It is to their memories, as well as to the memory of Tatyana Grosman (1904–1982), founder of ULAE and a primary catalyst of the postwar printmaking renaissance, that this book is dedicated.

It was Tatyana Grosman who told Zammiello, just after he started working at ULAE, fresh out of college, "You can do this. After all, you are an artist." David Lasry, the owner of Two Palms, has a similar approach. As an artist himself, Lasry embraces the fact that his printers are also artists and that there is a constant collaboration, a mutual respect, involved in the production of any print.

Lasry believes in pushing the boundaries of printmaking beyond any preconceived limits—and that if the studio environment is rife with excitement and pleasure, the art will come on its own. For this as well as for his ongoing support of this book, we wish to express our heartfelt thanks to David and his wife, Evelyn, as well as to Jessica Kreps at Two Palms. We also wish to express our sincere thanks to Bill Goldston, Jill Czarnowski, and Larissa Goldston at ULAE for their extraordinary generosity and assistance.

Each print studio is populated by a team that works as one. Craig would like to extend his deeply felt personal thanks to the many gifted colleagues with whom he has worked so closely over the past thirty years: John Lund, Douglas Volle, Lorena Salcedo-Watson, Douglas Bennett, Vanessa Viola, Matt Enger, Bruce Wankel, Hitoshi Kido, Jihong Shi, Brian Berry, Frank D'Agostino, Michael Edelson, Dan Welden, Matthew Day Jackson, Roger White, Patti Lee Becker, Hilary Harnischfeger, Amy Pryor, Georgia Küng, and countless others.

At Yale, there have been numerous champions of this project, to whom we are tremendously appreciative. First and foremost we would like to thank Suzanne Boorsch, the Robert L. Solley Curator of Prints, Drawings, and Photographs, and Anna Hammond, former Deputy Director for Programs and Public Affairs, for their early and sustained support. For her sage advice and project oversight, we are indebted to Pamela Franks, Deputy Director for Collections and Education, who inherited this undertaking. Pam, along with Tiffany Sprague, Director of Publications and Editorial Services, ushered this book along with gusto and trust—and made certain that global economic conditions did not derail, but only delayed, the book's publication. Deeply felt thanks are also due Elizabeth C. DeRose, our co-conspirator on this project and close friend, for her marvelous contributions that have helped to greatly enrich this book.

We wish to sincerely thank Molly Balikov, Associate Editor, whose arrival at the Gallery could not have been more eagerly awaited, and who immediately and energetically embraced the editing and oversight of this book. Molly's keen attention to every detail of prose and picture is deeply appreciated, as is the expert organization of Bryne Rasmussen, Administrative Assistant, and Stacey Wujcik, Editorial Assistant, in the Department of Publications and Editorial Services. Suzanne Greenawalt, Museum Assistant in the Department of Prints, Drawings, and Photographs, was as instrumental as ever in her attention over months and years to the myriad details involved in the production of this book.

To Christopher Sleboda, Director of Graphic Design, we are most indebted for his innovative and dynamic yet sensitive design of this book that so seamlessly responds to the playful, image-and-dialogue format of the publication.

Last, but in essence first, we wish to thank Jock Reynolds, the Henry J. Heinz II Director, for his immediate enthusiasm and embrace of this project, and for his continued support of such unorthodox but important ventures as this.

In the years that it has taken to write and produce this book, many other techniques and exciting developments have emerged in the print world. One need only visit a few of the innovative studios throughout America and the world to quickly realize that some of the most interesting and unique contemporary art today is being made there. This book celebrates those presses—numerous and vital— as well as the artists who frequent them and the printers with whom those artists collaborate; they demonstrate the spontaneity, brilliance, and vigor of the contemporary print scene. We honor and applaud their dedication to making quality art.

Craig Zammiello
Elisabeth Hodermarsky

Note to the reader: *Throughout the book, the measurements provided are sheet dimensions, as is the convention of contemporary print studios. For the sake of readability, the conversations have been lightly edited to avoid redundancies and to remove minor infelicities. All edits were made with the approval of the contributors.*

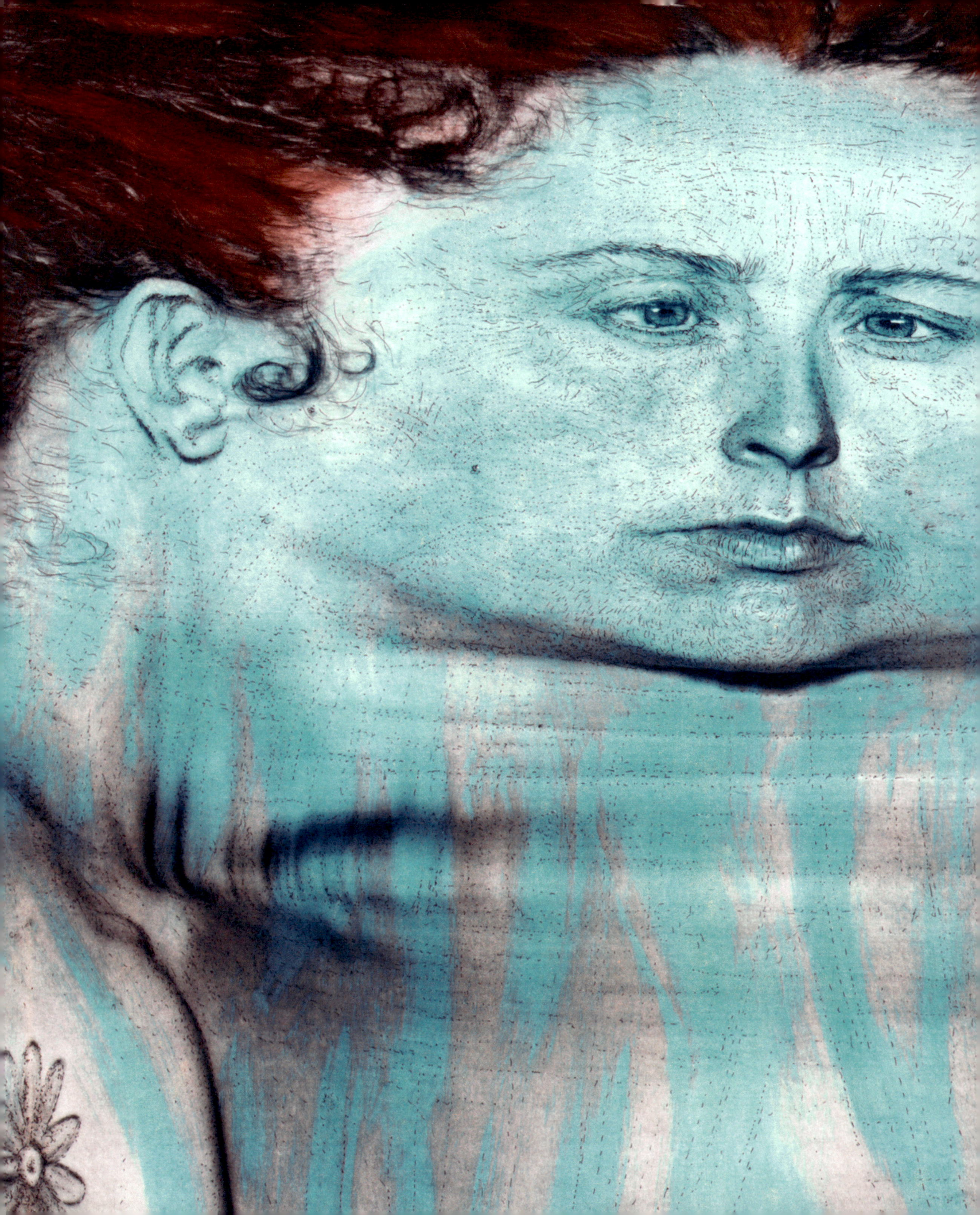

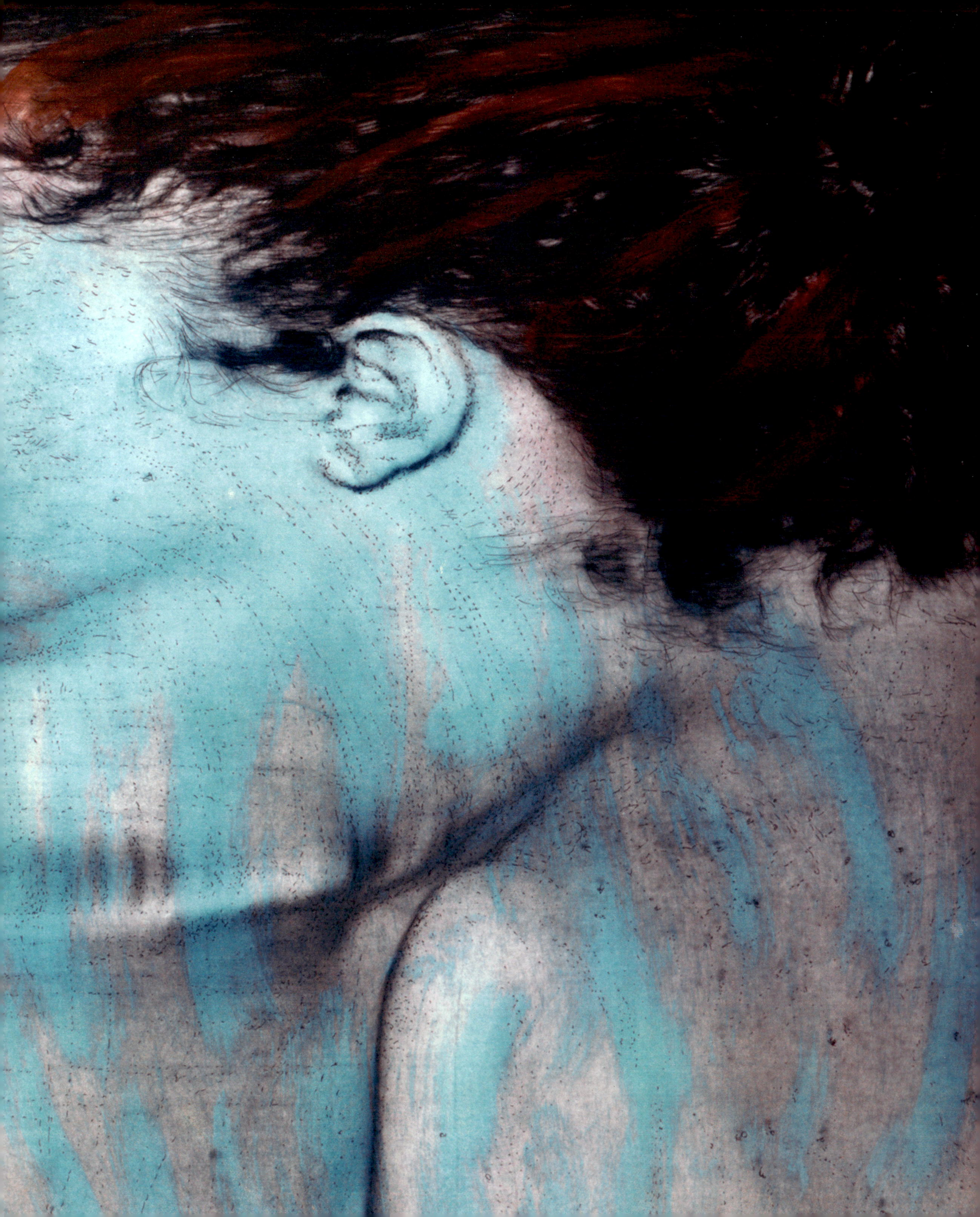

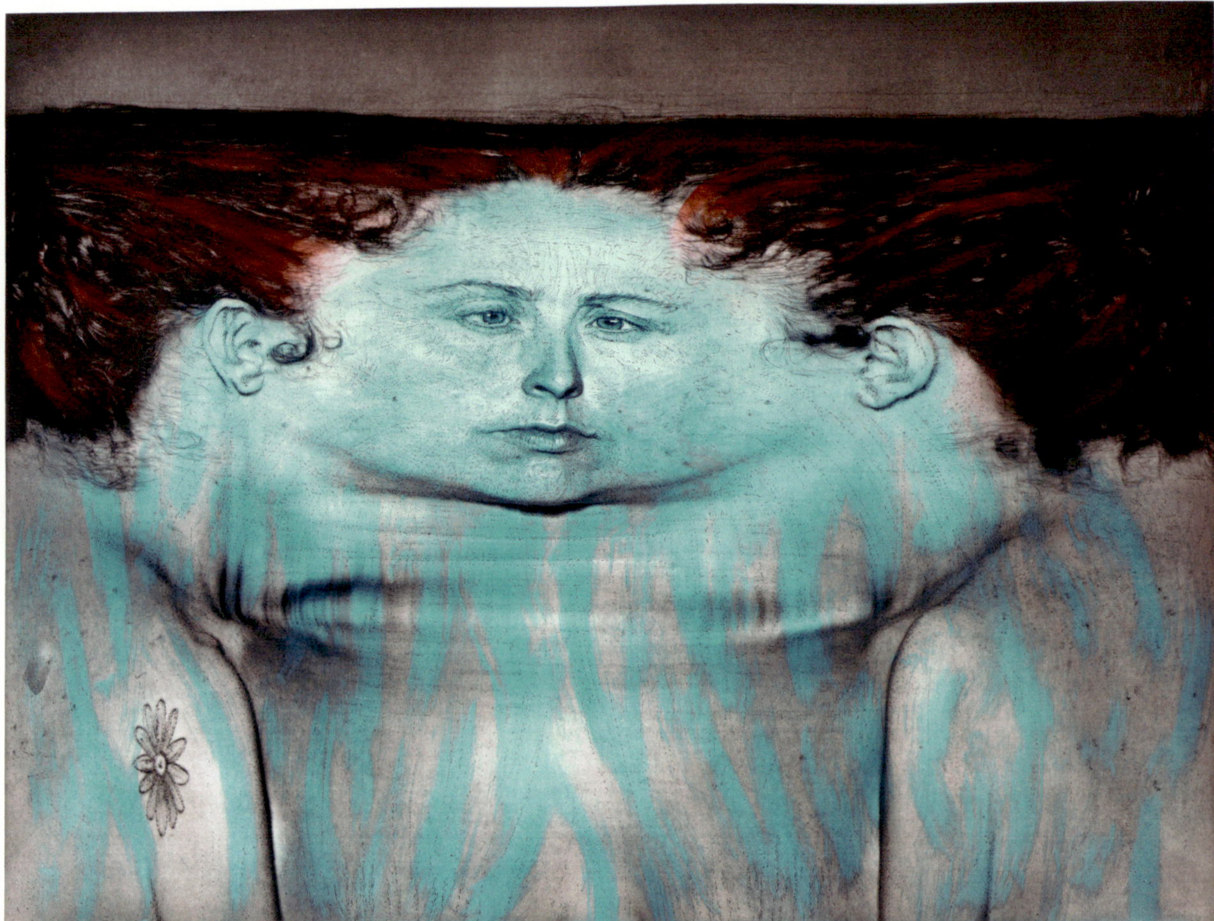

Kiki Smith
My Blue Lake, 1995

In its otherworldly distortion of the artist's face, its morphing of body and landscape, there is something deeply haunting about Kiki Smith's *My Blue Lake* (fig. 1). With its high horizon line, and its earthen-red "coastline" defined by the artist's hair engulfing the blue "lake" of Smith's exposed skin, the print becomes a sort of organic hybrid. The print's title, as well as the blue streaks (applied *à la poupée*), furthers this allusion so that one succumbs to the image's metaphor of harbor as body, body as harbor.

My Blue Lake began with Smith's desire to create a 360-degree image of her head in print. As the artist and Craig Zammiello describe in this chapter, early attempts to realize this goal led to photo shoots in which Zammiello would prop Smith on a stool and take a series of still, 35 mm images of her rotating (in the manner of primitive animation). Unfortunately, these attempts were somewhat clumsy and did not yield results of the seamless quality that Smith desired. Finally, Zammiello located a specialized "periphery camera"—a 1940s technology developed to photograph cylindrical objects—by which they were ultimately able to achieve the desired results.

Thus, one of the remarkable things that distinguishes *My Blue Lake* from other prints produced within the past twenty years—prints that have either embraced new technologies (such as power tools or digital technologies) or revisited older, "pure" processes (for example, etching, lithography, or woodcut)—is that it began with a concept that could not at the time be achieved by any existing printmaking technology. As Zammiello remarks, his initial reaction to the periphery camera was, "Oh my, high-tech, circa 1970." Today, with all the digital technologies now at the fingertips of artists and printers, *My Blue Lake* would not present the challenge it did in 1995. However, its creation was a tour de force of its time and exemplifies how existing tools can be embraced in innovative ways when adapted by a master printer to the needs of the print studio to realize an artist's vision.

FIG. 1. Kiki Smith, *My Blue Lake*, 1995. Etching with photogravure, *à la poupée* inking, and lithography on mold-made Arches En-Tout-Cas paper, 43 11/16 × 54¾ in. (111 x 139 cm). Edition of 41. Published by Universal Limited Art Editions

CRAIG ZAMMIELLO: So, Kiki, this book is about prints that I feel are important . . . that I collaborated with certain artists on. And I think this print, *My Blue Lake*, is one of the most important ones that you and I have done.

KIKI SMITH: Yes, yes.

ELISABETH HODERMARSKY: So just to get started, Kiki, perhaps you could just give a little background about your work in print prior to this project. I've read that you began making prints in the late seventies, and that you made your first print at ULAE [Universal Limited Art Editions] in 1989?

KS: I actually started making prints on my own well before 1989. I made T-shirts and printed on fabric in the early eighties. I took classes at FIT [Fashion Institute of Technology] on yardage printing and silkscreening. I was in a show at the Brooklyn Museum, where Bill Goldston saw my work and asked me to come to ULAE. I had already published one print before that with Editions Fawbush, which was a linoleum print [*Possession Is Nine-Tenths of the Law*, 1985].[1] When I went out to ULAE, I became more actively involved in printmaking.

EH: And do you remember which prints you made at ULAE before *My Blue Lake*?

KS: The first one was a lithograph, *Untitled (Hair)* [1990], and then I worked on a couple of small things that got lost. I made the group of lithographs, *Banshee Pearls* [1991], which was the first time that Craig and I worked together, because of its prominent use of photographic images.[2]

CZ: Yes, it was a print that both Matt Enger and I worked on. At the time, Matt was doing a lot of the photo work at ULAE, and then he moved on and I started taking pictures of you.

KS: It was when we first started working together.

CZ: Yes. So from the beginning, our collaborative work was based upon a model-photographer relationship.

KS: That's right. Out of *Banshee Pearls*—or the next print—I decided that I wanted to make a puppet head, a print that was two different sized puppet heads, which I'm still trying to make. For this we photographed my head 360 degrees—photographed it from different sides with me sitting on a stool, so that I could take all of those images and put them together, like a globe. I wanted to make a puppet head that was at two different scales, in black and white. In the end I made one print called *I Am* [1994; *fig. 2*]. But the puppet head never happened.

And then Craig was . . . do you want to say what you were doing? You were reading about a camera?

CZ: Well, yes. We were sort of stalled on the puppet-head project—on how to make it work—and I happened to be thumbing through the book *Advanced Photography* by Michael Langford, and I saw a portrait of a man who looked as though he had been skinned and then his flayed hide laid out flat on a surface.[3] All of his facial features were present—his ears, nose, et cetera—but were one-dimensional. The reference for the photo noted that it was taken by a periphery camera.[4] I immediately set out to purchase one, thinking it was some sort of attachment for a 35 mm camera, or, at best, a fancy novelty. And at first—my first thought was that I could go buy one of these and take a picture of Kiki, and we could print it and then make a cylinder, kind of turn the image back into a three-dimensional head. And I went around to all of these specialty camera stores and no one knew what I was talking about.[5] And it turned out that only two existed in the world. And one of them happened to be at the British Museum, where Bill Goldston located it.

KS: They were made by Shell Oil for examining cores for oil production. The British Museum had one for photographing objects like amphora—cylindrical Greek vases.[6] And Craig suggested that we go to London . . .

CZ: And Bill Goldston arranged it.

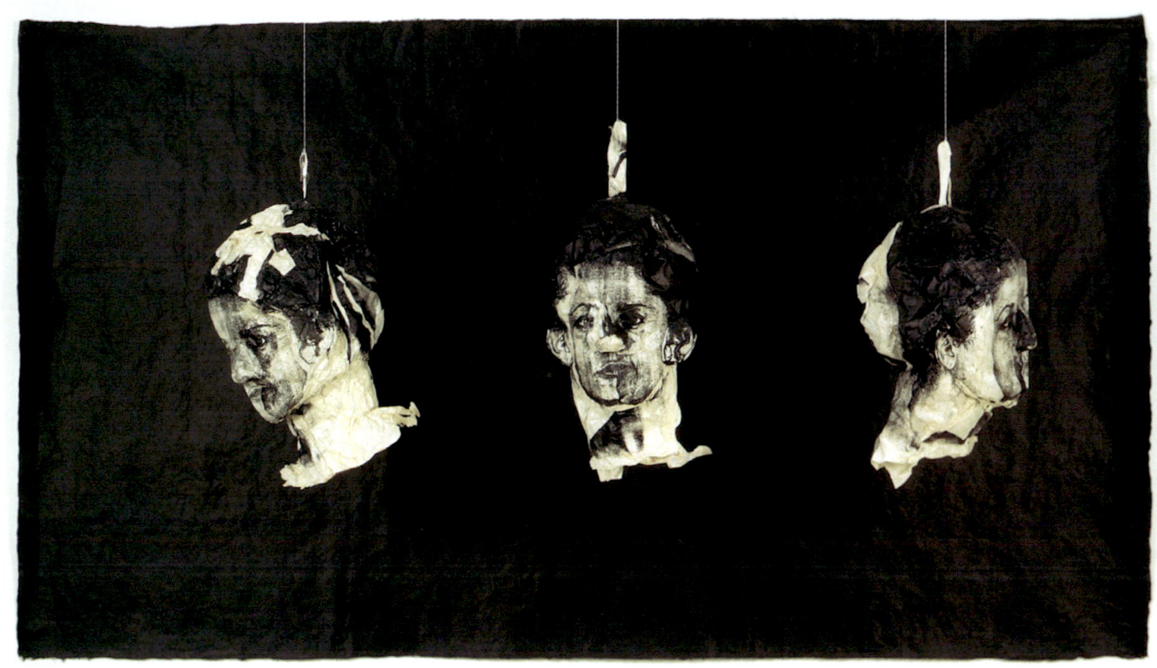

FIG. 2. Kiki Smith, *I Am*, 1994. Lithograph on handmade Japanese paper and three photolithographed heads constructed of handmade Nepalese paper suspended from strings, each head L. 21½ in. (54.6 cm); sheet 42 × 76 in. (106.7 × 193 cm). Unique print. Collection of Robert and Mary Looker

KS: So Craig and Bill and I went to London. It was a very simple procedure in a way. They had a lazy Susan that I sat on and I turned as the film moved across the open shutter. You can explain it better, Craig.

CZ: Well, actually, it was a regular view camera with a regular lens [*fig. 3*]. If you opened the lens completely, where the film is, in the back, there was a slit, about a .05 mm slit. And as the lazy Susan turntable turned, the motor on the back of this thing would bring the film past that slit at the same speed. The depth of field was achieved by adjustment to the lens aperture in relation to the distance from the object. And so what you got was a continuous exposure of film as it kept moving— achieved through the synchronization of both motors. So, as long as it didn't stop, you wouldn't get a line; you'd get an even exposure. It was basically sort of Stone Age Xerox scanning, or CCD [charge-coupled device] scanning. When I first saw it I thought, "Oh my, high-tech, circa 1970." It was a pretty ungainly apparatus.[7]

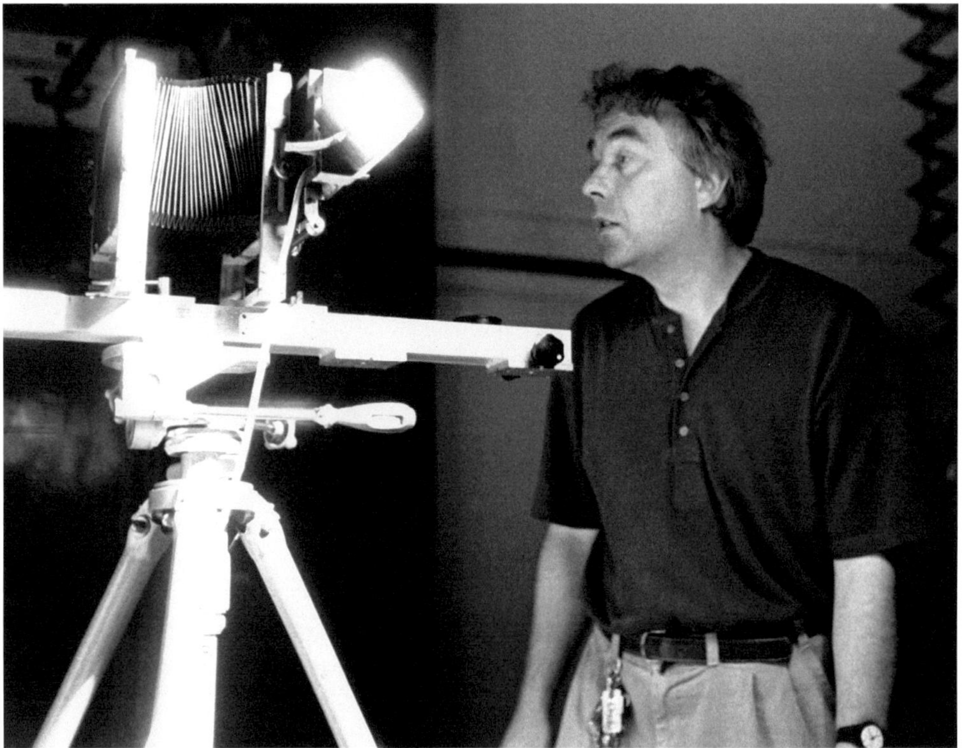

FIG. 3. Ivor Kerslake at the British Museum with the periphery camera

EH: How long did it take?

CZ: Well, Kiki, you would have to sit there for about four minutes, right?

KS: [*nodding to CZ*] It was fabulous. I mean the experience of it—to go on a mission, to go to England, to work in another country. Craig had had a lot of experience working in other countries, because he would go regularly to Belgium to teach and work.

CZ: It was kind of fun to be in the British Museum.

EH: And to be an artifact on a turntable?

KS: Yes. I was about forty, and I hadn't had so many experiences working in different places. It's a completely different experience to work in another country. I think people there just thought we were odd. They [the British Museum] had their own technicians and were used to filming cylinders.

EH: Like . . . "What are these Yankees doing?"

KS: They were really straight.

CZ: These were the guys that take pictures at archaeological sites.

EH: Did they help you or did they just sit there and gawk at you?

KS: Oh they helped. They wouldn't have us touching their stuff.

CZ: We paid them. They ran the equipment.

KS: It was expensive. And that was the great thing about ULAE at the time. As far as one needed to go, you went. Papers were handmade, sometimes very expensive papers. It was really a remarkable moment. For me it was an enormous lesson, in that you always followed the work. They had the willingness to say, "Okay, we've got to go to London." We were like spies going off to London to make images. It was fantastic, very exciting. Very satisfying.

EH: [*looking at a photograph of a female model taken with the periphery camera*] This looks so Man Ray–like to me. How did you pick the British models?

KS: I think we just asked somebody for some models, and we got these people. That's the other thing—I didn't care about their bodies. One of my early interests in the body was to make unfolded skins. I had made several sculptures this way, earlier.

EH: Like an animal hide?

KS: More like topographical maps, really. Like topographies of the body. But yes, like an unfolded skin. It is a complicated thing to do, physically. I had some different versions of success with it, so this seemed like an opportunity to try with the models. But, ultimately, for some reason I wasn't so interested in the photographs of the models.

EH: So, it wasn't necessarily going to be a self-portrait? Just an experiment with the camera and the 360-degree image? [*fig. 4*]

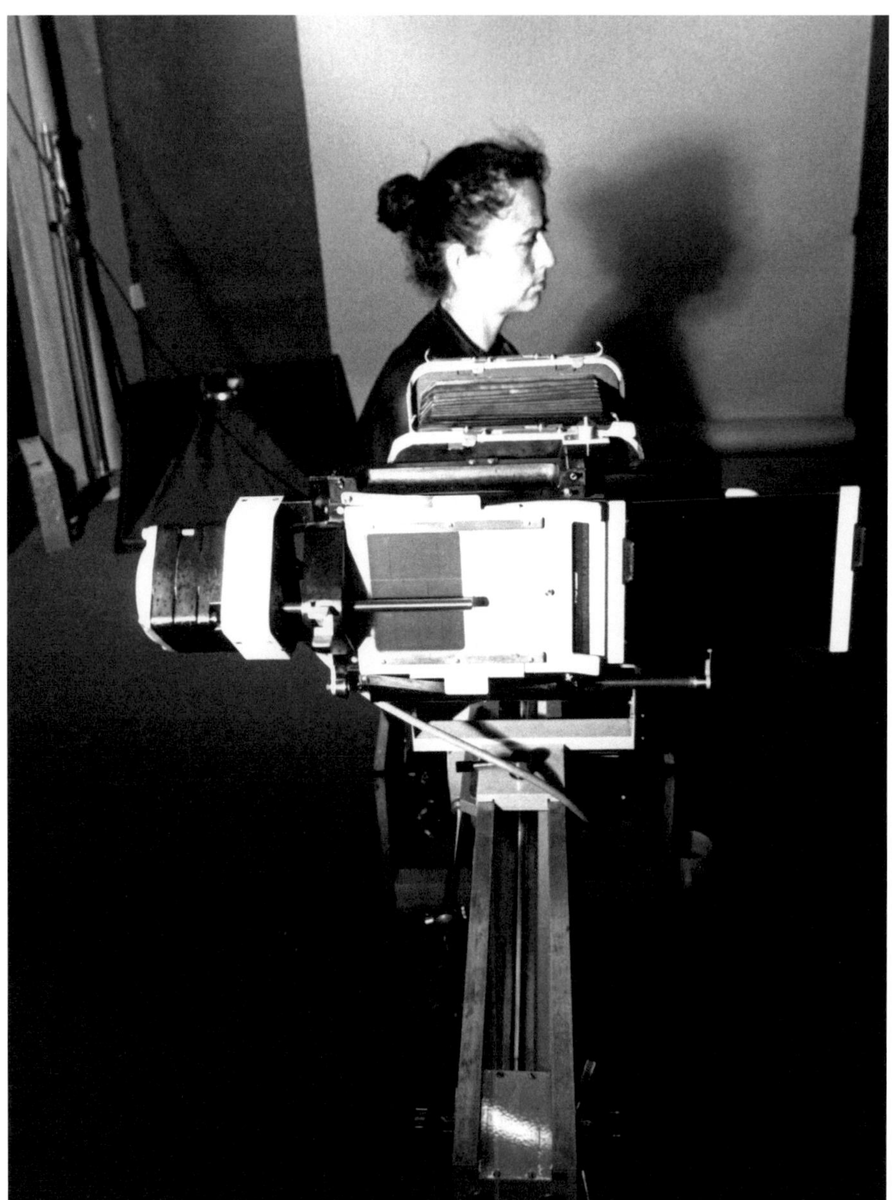

KS: Well, I was interested in the idea of the unfolded body. The one thing that's interesting about this print is that five years later you could do all of this at a computer. There are artists in Brooklyn who became well known for making photographs—a man and woman couple—for making topography photographs of the body, for unfolding the body. All on the computer. But prior to that, this was really the only way one could do it.

CZ: This was analog, this was in real time.

EH: That would have been sort of awkward too, right? If you had tried to do it in a series of still 35 mm shots. Too staccato?

KS: Well that's how we *had* done it. The ones that we pieced together. [*fig. 5*]

CZ: Yes, piecing together the 360-degree 35 mm images never quite worked out. Looking back, I think the problem was probably that we were both trying to be too literal with constructing the three-dimensional piece. We would select a nose from one photo and perhaps an eye from another and try to assemble the head in that manner. After using the periphery camera, it's quite clear that we should have cut actual full length strips out of each photo and attached them side by side to complete the 3-D transformation. This would have rendered a much more realistic representation of Kiki's entire head than the selective editing we were using. Granted, it would not have represented the topographic structure of her head in a 3-D format.

> KS: Yes, the periphery camera presents a different kind of distortion. It gives an unfolding of yourself, almost concave. Whereas with still shots, the image takes a convex, three-dimensional form.

CZ: And the periphery camera also gave different effects when it was set at different speeds.

> KS: Yes, and depending on how you moved during the shooting. And where you started the camera, which side of the body you started from. I think we liked this particular one [*looking at the photograph from which* My Blue Lake *was made*] because it was the most like a big open plain.
>
> At the time I was very interested in Egyptian mythology and the image of Hathor, which is the second manifestation of Nuit, the Egyptian sky goddess. Sometimes Nuit (as Hathor) is represented as a cow. She holds her hands to her ears, which is related in appearance to Etruscan funerary masks, which are an unfolding of the head. Jasper Johns had also made unfolded images of his head. I had also been making death-mask rubbings of my family and unfolding them into flattened, unfolding heads. So they have the look of the unfolded funerary mask where Hathor's hands are held to her ears and her ears pushed out to the side, so her hearing was amplified. I liked this one [*looking again at the photograph*], where the face is the widest and most open.

CZ: Hmm. I never knew that.

> KS: Unfolding faces is something I tend to do anyway if I draw other people, because it's an alternative to Cubism, to see things from all sides but simultaneously; to figure out how to see things from different sides at once.

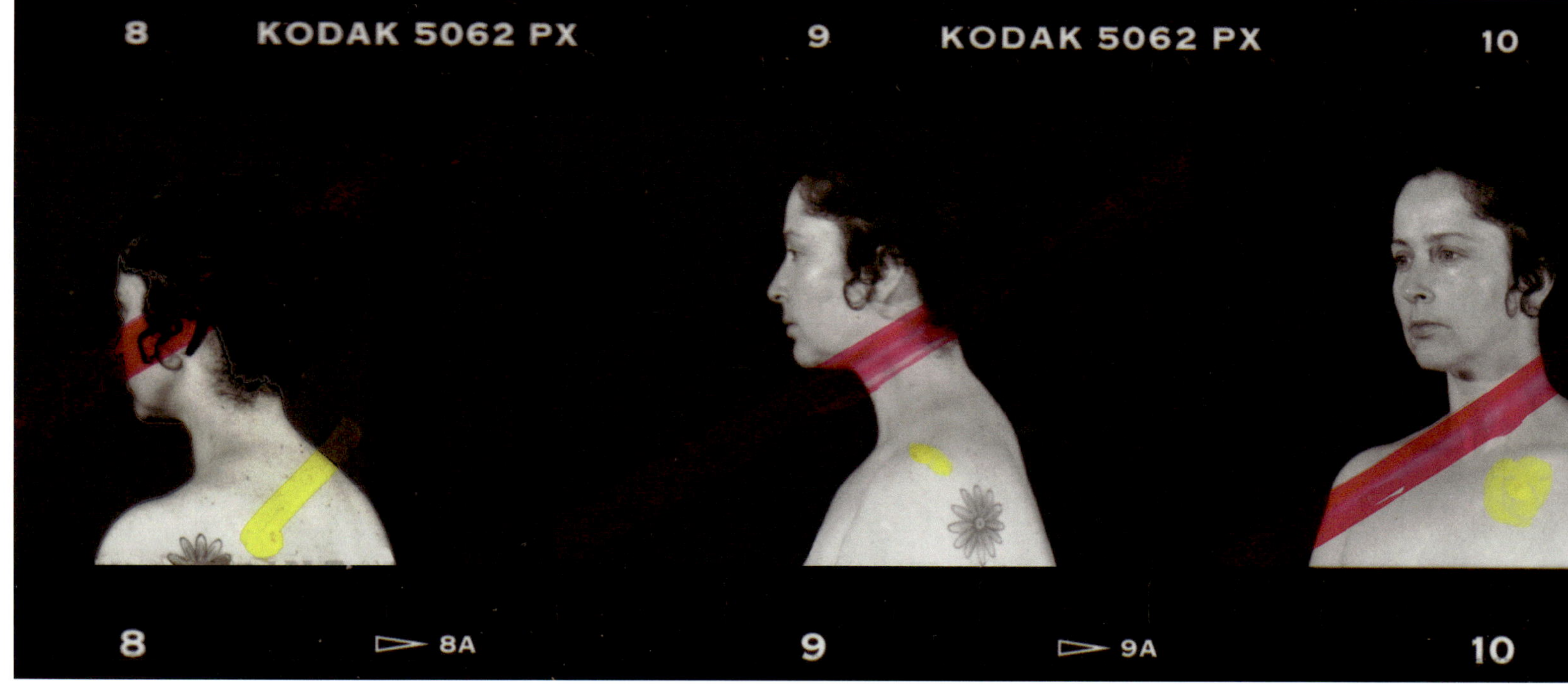

FIG. 5. Filmstrip of serial 35 mm images of Smith rotating 360 degrees

EH: [*looking at one of the periphery photos of KS; fig. 6*] This is you though, isn't it? It's so sensuous, it looks like a circle dance . . .

CZ: Yeah, that's Kiki. That's Kiki sitting like this [*demonstrating*] . . . sitting on the turntable holding her wrist, and then the speed is changed so that you get this odd stretching and so it looks like three people holding each other's arms.

[*pause*]

EH: So, once you selected the photograph, how was the print produced?

KS: We made it as a photogravure and a monotype at the same time. The plate was inked up black, wiped, then it was surface-inked up with blue and with red, then printed. This gave it the look of a landscape—like a body in a landscape, like a lake in a landscape. Each one was different. This was similar to one of my first prints, *Possession Is Nine-Tenths of the Law,* which was also something between a print and a monotype, with each impression having a uniqueness. I find this interesting in terms of printmaking.

CZ: When you did the first one, you rubbed the ink in as a monotype and then we made an impression of it. And the printer, Jihong Shi, was able to . . . he really, really worked well at capturing exactly your style as much as he could. And so

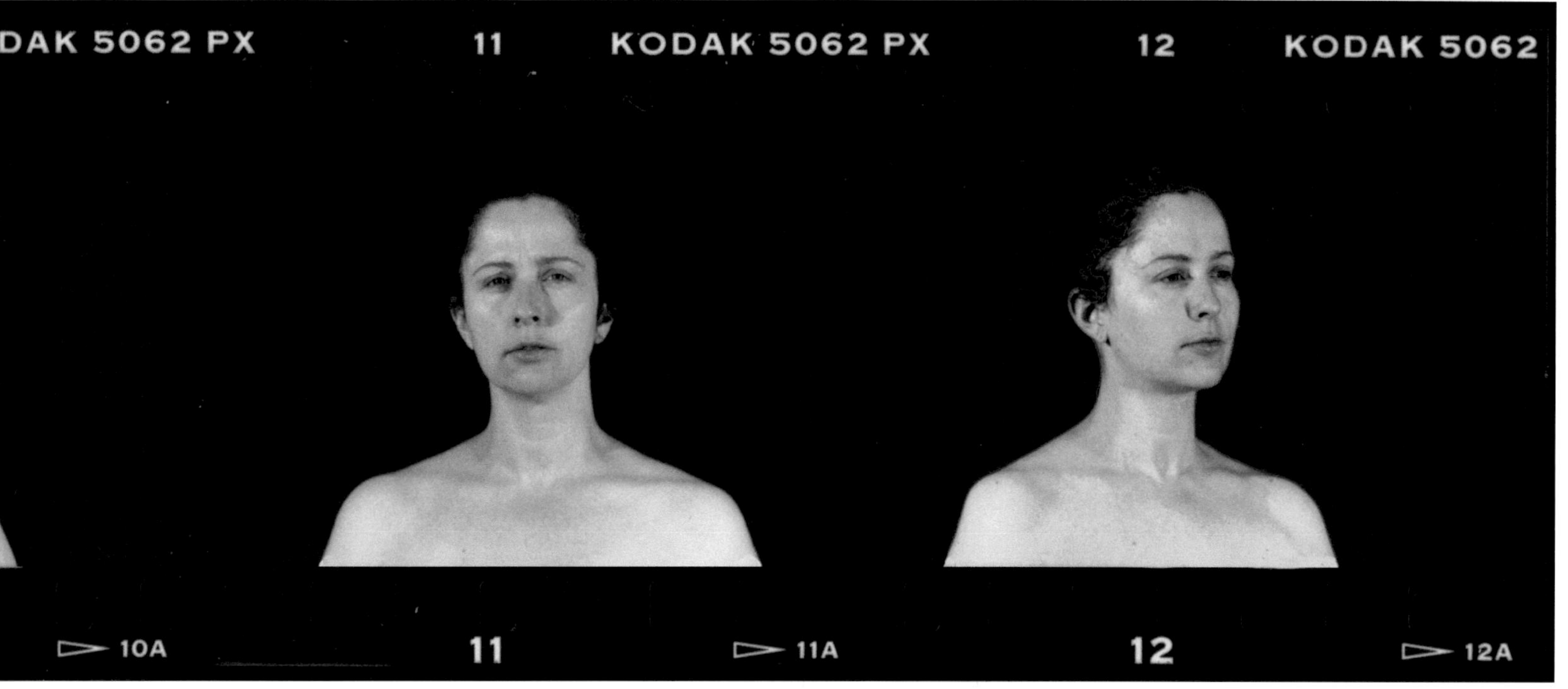

people don't realize the monotype effect. It's almost more like *pochoir*, in that the ink was put in precisely the same spot each time. He was really very good at that.

 KS: Yes, yes.

CZ: We'd call him in each time. I would ink the plate, wipe the plate, and then I'd call Jihong and he'd come in, and I'd have Kiki's BAT [*bon à tirer* proof] on the wall and he'd just go . . .

 KS: He was really amazing. Very professional, very precise.

CZ: Trained in Beijing.

EH: So, I didn't realize that each one is slightly different.

CZ: Yes, each one has its own uniqueness. I kind of forgot that, but now that you bring it up . . .

 KS: Yes, that's interesting to me in retrospect, as I still am using the possibility of repetition and uniqueness in my printmaking.

CZ: And Kiki, you also spent a lot of time drawing on top of the print for the litho . . .

 KS: Yes. I did spend a lot of time drawing.

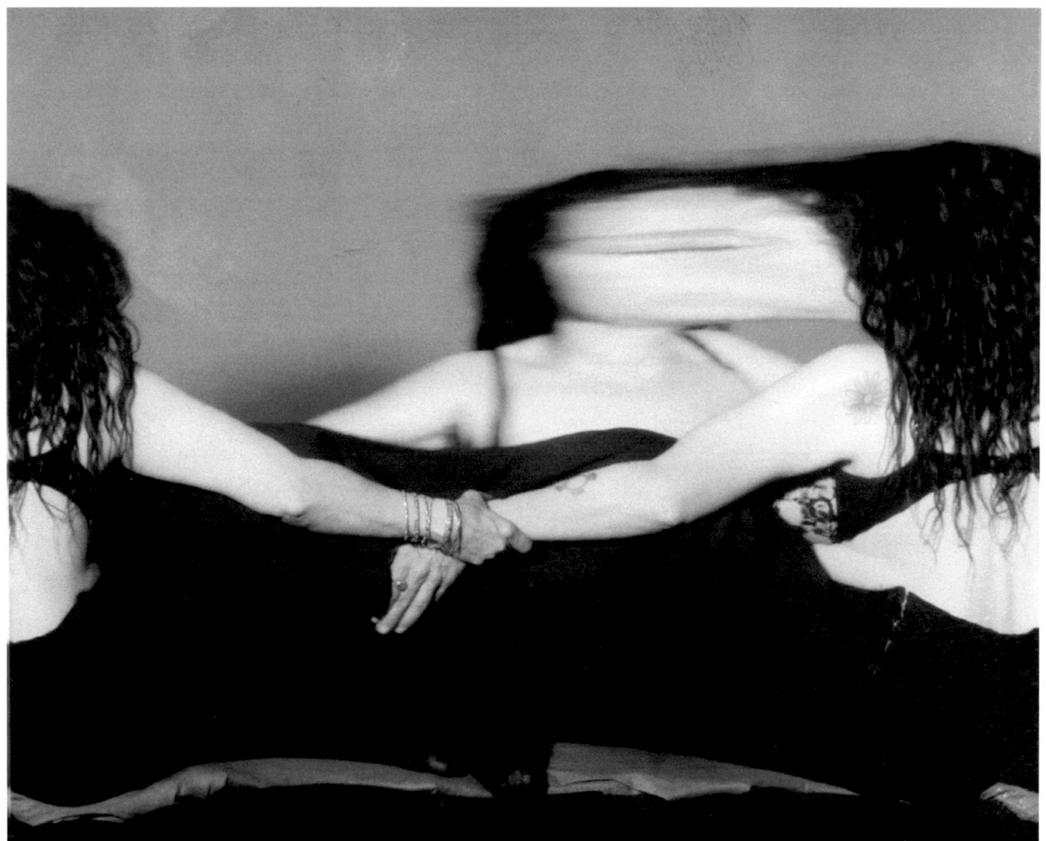

CZ: And you don't notice that in reproduction. You have to see the real print to see its incredible depth. You know, it's funny, but there's sort of a tattoo thing going on with graphite ink for the face.

> KS: I was trying to emphasize the pores. Because maybe I thought the image was a little flat, because it's a photograph, but I wanted to have the pores accentuated. The pores on the body spiral in very specific forms. I thought it was interesting to accentuate that.

EH: It's fascinating to look at all of these other periphery photographs of you that you didn't ultimately choose to use for the print. They're all so interesting.

CZ: Yes. And oh, Kiki, remember the butterfly? You went somewhere and bought a morpho butterfly, and you held it above your head? And in the final shot—which was in color—it looked like a whole bunch of butterflies, a kind of organic strip of metallic blue hovering along the top of the image?

> KS: Oh, yes, that was beautiful. I should pull those images out and use them again.

EH: You could make another print.

> KS: But this image, this is really the one we liked best because it was neutral.

CZ: Yes. This shot proved to be "the keeper" [*fig. 7*], not only for the excellent facial rendition, but also for the artifacts that fell quite nicely into place. What we came away with from the British Museum were a whole stack of four-by-five negatives, and also some four-by-five color transparencies. I contact printed all the negatives, and then, once we decided on this image, we made a full-size positive film that would be used to create the photogravure.[8]

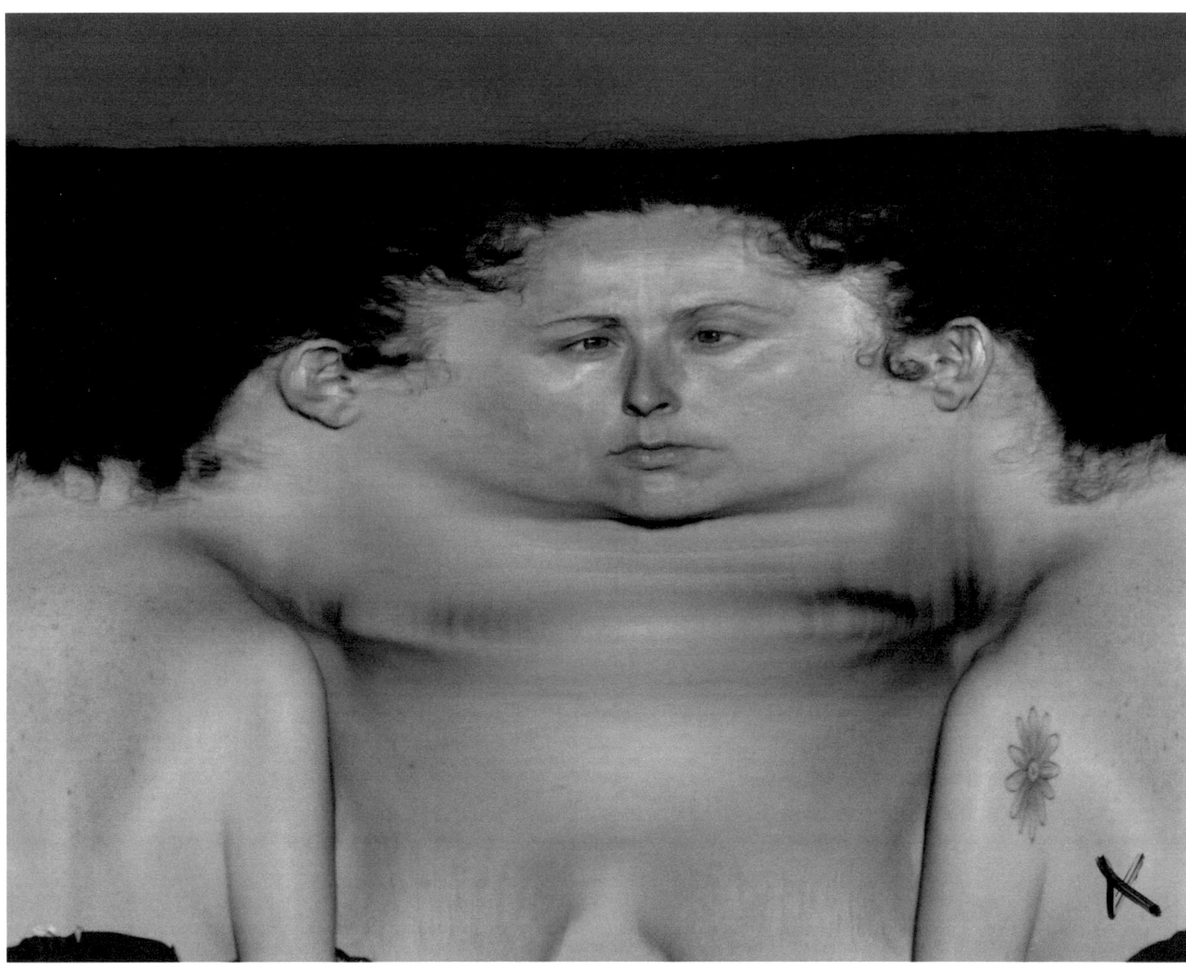

FIG. 7. The periphery photograph of Smith that is the basis of *My Blue Lake*

EH: And then plates were made from that.

CZ: One etching plate and one litho plate. The positive film was made and exposed to the sensitized carbon tissue in a vacuum frame. A copper plate was prepared with aquatint, the exposed carbon tissue adhered, developed, dried, and etched according to the traditional photogravure process. Then, a few proofs were pulled and Kiki set about drawing on a clear Mylar film placed over one of the proofs with opaque enamel pen. This tattoo-like drawing was made into a litho plate and printed in graphite ink over the final etching. The blue streaks and red areas in her hair were added à la poupée, as we've already talked about a bit. Kiki smeared ink over the gravure plate that had already been prepared and wiped in black ink. For the edition, stencils were cut out of Mylar traced from the original BAT, permitting Jihong to apply the blue and red inks in a consistent and controlled manner that imitated Kiki's inked marks as closely as possible.

EH: And so, technically, it's a fairly simple production for a rather complicated-looking print.

> KS: *Banshee Pearls* was a complicated print, and the hair print [*Untitled (Hair)*, 1990] was a complicated print, and then my first etching, *Sueño* [1992], and this print [*My Blue Lake*] were both fairly simple, in terms of the use of plates and such.[9] There was an economy to them.

CZ: It really was a pretty straightforward printing.

> KS: And I like that. The prints that I always most admire are the most economical prints, where there's not something tricky about it. The complexity is in the image.

EH: I'm interested in the water imagery here, and when you decided to title it *My Blue Lake*. Because you use fluids or fluid imagery a lot in your prints, but they are usually body fluids, right? Like urine, semen, tears, diarrhea, breast milk . . .

> KS: People are 80 or 90 percent water. Largely water. I like to think of this print as a landscape.

CZ: I always thought the title referred to the color—I thought you meant the color "lake"—the blue of the à la poupée coloring.

> KS: It's cyan blue, isn't it? Cyan blue or process blue—or process blue over cyan. I have several tattoos in those colors. They are some of my favorite colors.

EH: How long did it take from the time that you went to London to the time that this print was editioned?

CZ: Relatively quickly, I think, six months?

> KS: It always takes a long time for the printing.

CZ: I think the week we got back I had already made the film. And we had decided on the picture, and . . .

EH: And the size?

> KS: It was large. *Banshee Pearls* was bigger, but it was in components [twelve sheets]. I made a self-portrait also around that time, an image of the intestinal system [*Kiki Smith*, 1993].[10] I had brought that print out to ULAE from the

Lower East Side Printshop to work on it. All of these prints, like *Sueño* and the self-portrait have a little bit of coloring in a rough kind of manner.

EH: And this is printed on watercolor paper?

CZ: En-tout-cas. It's just a very basic white watercolor paper.

KS: Yes, it had to be a sturdy paper.

CZ: Yes.

KS: I would say that *Sueño*, the self portrait, and *My Blue Lake* were all relatively large prints at that time.

CZ: Yes. When you see them framed, they take up some space.

KS: I was influenced by artists like Carroll Dunham, working at ULAE, and Terry Winters and Bill Jensen, all of whom were working with color. I don't really understand color. I loved Dunham's wave prints.[11]

EH: Those are gorgeous.

KS: Yes. The big hammerheads, in different colors. I don't use color very much, but always when I went to ULAE I looked underneath the tables and would spy on what colors people were using. They just "get" color, they understand color in a way that's completely incomprehensible to me.

[*pause*]

EH: The hair here in *My Blue Lake*—the reddish hair—is this printed from a plate or is it hand-colored?

CZ: It's ink. That's the monotype, the à la poupée part.

KS: It's a hand-rubbing of color.

CZ: I think you took a tarlatan and picked up some color, and then you just painted right on the plate. And then Jihong, what he had worked out for the editioning was . . . you know, he had this whole system where he would take different stencils and tarletons with different colors and then just put it all together.[12]

KS: I could have never done that. I have no patience for things like that. I enjoy printmaking but am a terrible printer. I'm too sloppy. And I hate ink, can't stand touching it . . .

CZ and EH: [*laughter*]

KS: I hate the oil of it. I would have never been able to reproduce the prints the way he reproduced them. It was interesting, because like this artist couple in Brooklyn whose names I can't remember, and Paul Ramirez Juarez, who also made a piece with a panoramic camera several years later . . .

cz: The direct opposite of this sort of thing . . .

 ks: Yes.

eh: Like Chuck Close has done at Two Palms? More like an anamorphic print?

cz: There is now a computer program that one can use to make these things.

 ks: Yes. That has some relationship to this image.

eh: But those are circular, and this is flat.

cz: Well, you know, Kiki, did you ever actually take one [an impression of *My Blue Lake*] and connect it? Roll it up in a cylinder? Because we [the printers] did it, and it's perfect. And now years have gone by, and I can tell you that one day we did it. We had the proofs, because we were storing them. And John Lund and myself and Hitoshi Kido walked around the studio with your mask on.

 ks and eh: [*laughter*]

cz: I wish we had taken a photo of it.

 ks: That's hilarious. No, and it's really interesting, because this print really was made exactly at this moment, pre-computer. Keith Brintzenhoff, who was at ULAE then, was very interested in computer imaging. It was right at the moment when it was incredibly laborious, and incredibly expensive, and really only available to the very wealthy—to the film industry or advertising. Whereas something like five or ten years later it means nothing. Regardless of the technology, it still has a nice presence as an image. It's a compelling image. I wouldn't want it on my wall particularly. It's just too big for me. It's a little too much of me for me.

cz: Too much of you for you? You know, I think it's framed in John's house, John Lund?

 ks: Really?

cz: Because he had loaned it to the Corcoran Gallery of Art, so he had it framed.[13] And when it was returned he said, "Well, hell, I'm going to hang it up." And then John and his wife, Christina, came to love it. And I still have mine. It's one of the printer's proofs I won't part with. And I've had some large offers for it.

 ks: Really? I gave one to my niece, one to my sister, one or two for me to give to some museum someday. Periodically people ask if I want to sell them, and I say no. "What burns never returns." I sold something when I was young once, and it was just the stupidest thing to do. The income was gone in five seconds. John told me he just sold something to send one of his kids to school, and I was happy it was helpful.

EH: Because it's going toward something important.

KS: Yes. Something useful.

CZ: Jasper [Johns] put both my daughters through Pratt [Institute].

KS: That really is great. Whereas just selling your work for the cash doesn't do anything.

EH: Well, by not wanting to sell your proofs of this print, it means that you both must think quite highly of it and that you must remember the experience of making it quite fondly.

KS: I had the most fun working with Craig. We really did have fun because Craig is a very transgressive person, so he would always push me out. Tom Otterness is my friend like that—he kind of pushes me out the gangplank with a stick. Craig is the same. We made a lot of prints together . . .

EH: You made *Free Fall* [1994], you made . . .

KS: We made *Free Fall*, we made *Worm* [1992; *fig. 8*], and those are sort of strange prints.[14] That was only because of Craig's coaxing me. He'd say, "YES! YES!," whereas normally I'm not taking my clothes off. If you look at the people who take their clothes off in art they don't look like me. I guarantee that. But with Craig, he'd say, "Okay, let's do this," and it was not very risqué or anything, but it was playful—to photograph my stretch marks and vari-cose veins—and we used infrared film that is used for medical purposes.

CZ: Kiki was very courageous. She wanted a way to exaggerate certain physi-cal traits that one would normally want to cover or camouflage—such as stretch marks and varicose veins—to exaggerate these flaws. So one solution was to employ a red filter for use with black-and-white film, which improved the con-trast of the blue veins under her skin, revealing outlines that would not be visible to the naked eye and extremely amplifying those that were . . . so that instead of a few random veins, we now had an entire surface circulatory sys-tem at our fingertips. This is especially evident in prints like *Worm* and *Puppet* [1993-94].[15] We also did some shooting with 35 mm high-speed infrared film to record the higher radiation wavelengths generated by heat. Those infrared photos had a coarse, grainy look. *Free Fall* was created from one of those shots.

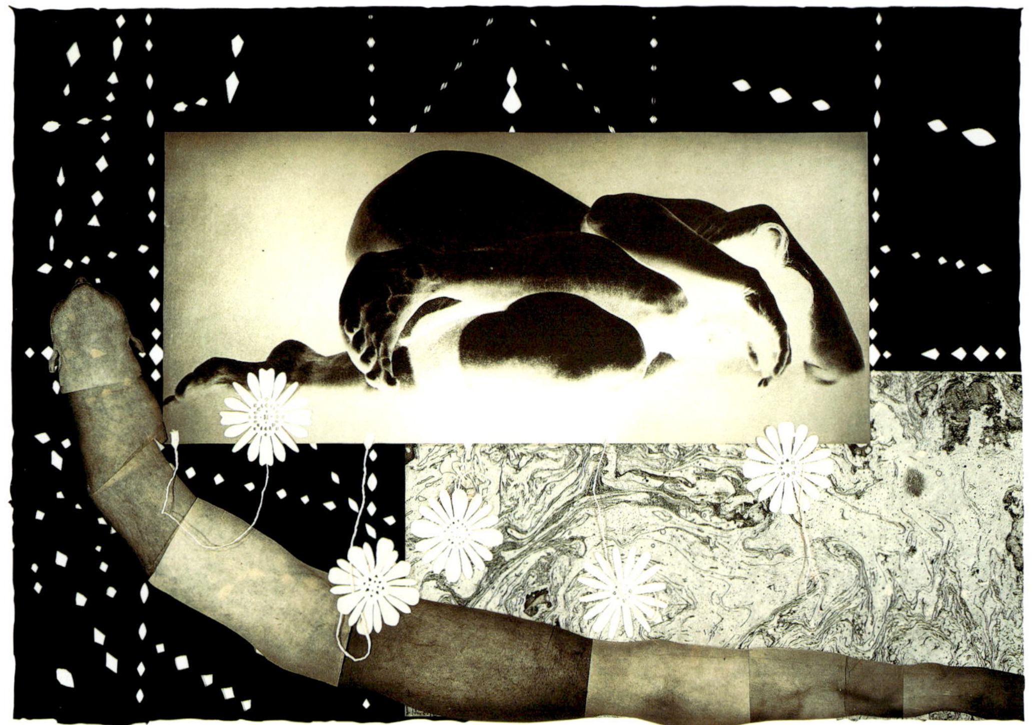

EH: So you got more and more comfortable with Craig.

KS: Yes, we had a good relationship for making photographs. We used them playfully, put them together in playful ways. I remember the print *Puppet* that I made. I brought images back from Holland of children in nudist camps. Which, of course, I was so naive; I realize now I could probably still be in jail for pornography trafficking. But I just needed some images of children. The Right in this country was trying to erase children's sexuality and young peoples' bodies from the American culture, and I thought it important to refuse this and present a more complex understanding of being a child.

EH: Were you fully naked for *My Blue Lake*?

KS: No, I didn't need to be.

CZ: Just your shoulders.

EH: Well, it's a beautiful print.

KS: I like it because it's somewhat representational, and somewhat abstract. It is also a landcape. So its abstract, and figurative, and landscape.

CZ: I never connected the landscape. And now it's so plain.

EH: The high horizon . . .

KS: I thought of Sekhmet, an Egyptian goddess in the form of a lion. There are hundreds of images of her in Karnak, around the lake, standing and sitting. I thought of this print like a lake. Just as your body, as a territory, is like a lake. It's probably one of the last prints that captures my dark hair.

EH: I love what it does optically. I mean, you can never see it all at the same time. You can't focus on the face and then simultaneously see the hair or the "lake" of the chest . . .

KS: You can flatten it out into a horizon.

EH: It's like a cove.

KS: Yes.

CZ: You can't perceive it here, but Kiki of course had to breath during this long exposure.

EH: How did you compensate for that?

CZ: Well, Kiki remained very, very still.

EH: How did you keep your eyes open throughout?

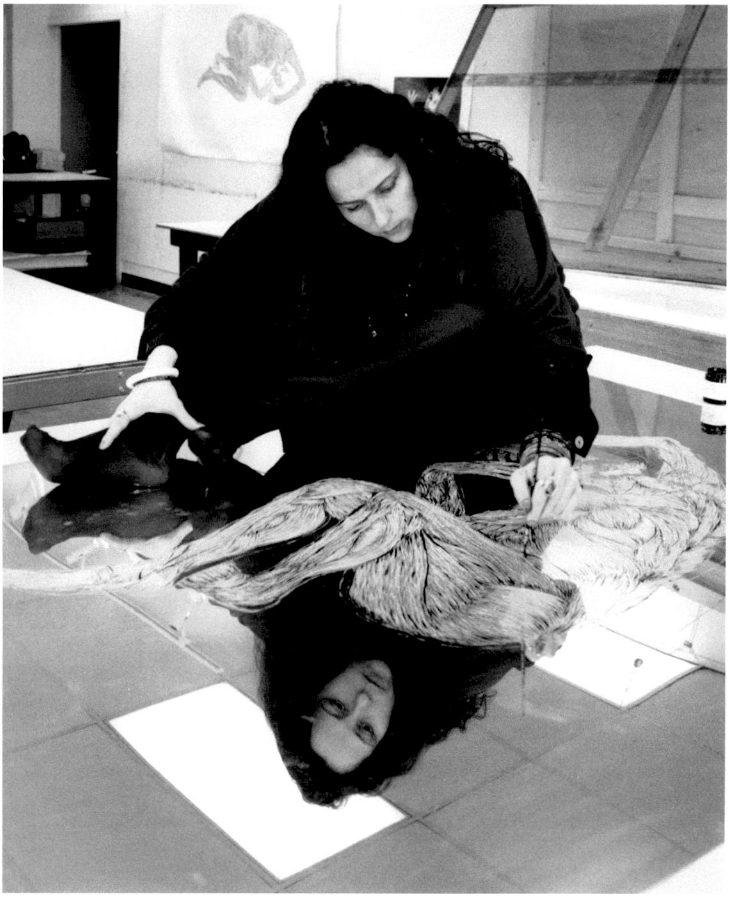

FIG. 9. Smith at work on *Sueño*, 1992, at Universal Limited Art Editions

CZ: Well, she knew she had to have her eyes open at a certain period of time in order for them to register on the film—though she could blink periodically. But the eyes look very strange here.

EH: Slightly cross-eyed too.

KS: That's because the face caves in, it goes in and out at the same time. An artist like Cindy Sherman—or Janine Antoni, to a lesser extent—and other artists make transgressive images of themselves; mutilated images, deconstructed images, or reconstructed images. To me it was a freedom to use myself as subject matter, to manipulate my body. I think for many of the prints that Craig and I made, that was the operating factor . . .

CZ: Sort of the modus operandi, with Kiki as the subject of the work.

KS: Well, that was also because of Bill [Goldston]. When I first went to ULAE he said, "Don't bring anything but yourself." I thought that was ridiculous. I had never made prints professionally. I had no idea what ULAE was, or who he was, or what any of it was. I was thinking, "I'm not getting seduced by that!" They took my coat when I came and were very gracious. And the artist always came first, and I was sort of, "Oh, I'm not getting seduced by that . . . they can't get me." But then, well, they could.

CZ: [*laughing*] "They can't get me . . ."

[*laughter*]

KS: I thought, "I'm just going to learn how to print and I'm going to get out of here." Pin, she was a . . .

CZ: That was Jihong's wife.

KS: She was an intellectual, but also a really great cook. She was temporarily cooking at ULAE. It was the only time I had a cooked meal during the week, so I was very happy to go there. I was completely seduced. I hate ink still. But I learned to enjoy collaborating with others, and working at ULAE was an enormous gift to my life.

Notes

The preceding conversation was held on January 22, 2008, at Smith's studio, in New York.

1. For an image of *Possession Is Nine-Tenths of the Law*, see Wendy Weitman, *Kiki Smith: Prints, Books, and Things* (New York: Museum of Modern Art, 2003), 58.

2. According to Douglas Volle, a master printer at Two Palms, for *Untitled (Hair)*, a wig was inked up and then pressed onto the lithographic stone. Agar casts of Smith's facial skin were also inked and transferred to the stone. For an image of this print, see Weitman, *Kiki Smith*, 74. For an image of *Banshee Pearls*, see ibid., 86–87. Images of both works can also be found on the ULAE website, http://www.ulae.com/ (accessed September 26, 2011).

3. Michael J. Langford, *Advanced Photography: A Grammar of Techniques*, 4th ed. (London: Focal, 1980), 50, fig. 3.17.

4. *Periophotography* is the term for photographing the surface of a cylindrical object. The resulting photograph is a view of the object that depicts all of its sides at once. Early attempts at periophotography date to 1849, with experiments made by William Henry Fox Talbot.

5. In Zammiello's search for the periphery camera, he located a device that operates by taking a 360-degree view from the point of the camera, which would revolve around an axis while exposing the film. This arrangement reverses that of the periphery camera, which operates by rotating the object, rather than the camera.

6. The British Museum developed a camera system in the late 1800s for photographing continuous scenes on Greek painted vases. It was referred to as the "cyclograph," and a description of it can be found in the *Journal of the Royal Photographic Society* 19 (May 30, 1895): 253. In 1961 Shell Research Ltd. designed a new, electronically operated camera system, the Research Engineers Periphery Camera, which Shell had begun developing during World War II to photograph the surfaces of pistons from test engines. Only two prototypes were made: one is owned by Shell Oil and the other by the British Museum (created in 1972), which has used it to photograph three-dimensional objects (such as Greek vases) and has also rented it to Scotland Yard for forensic investigations of three-dimensional objects such as bullets. *My Blue Lake* was made with the British Museum's camera. See the unpublished description of periophotography by Ivor Kerslake, British Museum Photography and Imaging Manager and current keeper of the retired periphery camera (4 October 1993; © Ivor Kerslake). A copy of this document is on file with Zammiello. In a May 28, 2009, email from Kerslake, Zammiello learned that the British Museum was retiring the periphery camera, due both to the considerable age of the apparatus and the advent of more efficient digital technologies.

7. The periphery apparatus was hooked to a four-by-five-inch Sinar camera mounted in a standard fashion on a tripod. Wires coming out of the camera's back led to a cobbled-together box that sat in front of the camera on the floor. This plywood box housed the motor-driven turntable, which was synced with the motor driving the worm gear that pulled the film past the slit lens in the camera's back. The British Museum's photography department had attached a three-quarters-inch-thick piece of plywood to the top of the turntable as a base, allowing large objects, such as a chair or a person, to rest on it and revolve. The actual periphery-camera setup came mounted on a fixed-rail system resembling that of a copy or reproduction camera.

8. The negative was mounted to the transmitted light box of ULAE's copy camera and enlarged to the size desired for the gravure plate. This was possible because ULAE had built a separate, freestanding vacuum back for holding film larger than that ordinarily used by its copy camera. A horizontal copy or reproduction camera usually includes a back containing the film holder; a simple, flat vacuum base; and a focusing screen (a sheet of ground glass), all of which are accessible from the darkroom. This arrangement enables the operator to load film onto the back under safelights or in complete darkness. Both the film back and focusing screen on ULAE's copy camera were limited to twenty-four-inch film. By design, the back and the focusing screen are hinged, opening and closing in the manner of a door. If you leave both "doors" open, an image is projected into the room, allowing the camera to function along the lines of a camera obscura. By building a freestanding vacuum back mounted on wheels, the team was no longer constrained by the twenty-by-twenty-four-inch film format. The back would accept roll film up to sixty-four inches tall by forty-eight inches wide. All that one needed to do was to move the vacuum frame to a set location in the darkroom coinciding with the desired film size and focus the camera. In this manner the copy camera was acting like a typical film enlarger that had been turned on its side. The large movable camera back opened up the possibilities of producing larger, seamless films resulting in an increase of larger photogravure plates produced at ULAE throughout the nineties.

9. For an image of *Sueño*, see Weitman, *Kiki Smith*, 62; or the ULAE website, http://www.ulae.com/ (accessed September 26, 2011).

10. For an image of *Kiki Smith*, see Weitman, *Kiki Smith*, 64; or the ULAE website, http://www.ulae.com/ (accessed September 26 2011).

11. Smith is referring to a series of four large prints (each 47¾ x 67⅝ in. [121.3 x 171.8 cm]) that Carroll Dunham made at ULAE: *Untitled*, 1988–89; *Wave*, 1988–90; *Point of Origin*, 1988–92; and *Another Dimension*, 1988–1995 (see Dunham fig. 6). Images of all four works can be found in Allison N. Kemmerer, Elizabeth C. DeRose, and Carroll Dunham, *Carroll Dunham Prints: A Catalogue Raisonné, 1984–2006* (Andover, Mass.: Addison Gallery of American Art, Phillips Academy, 2008), 216.

12. To reproduce Smith's marks and smudges of colored ink, the areas on the original print were traced onto a clear sheet of Mylar, then those areas were cut out of the sheet, leaving a stencil that was open where Smith's colors were to be pushed through. This stencil was then laid on top of the inked (in black) plate, and the colors were applied with tarlatans directly over the stencil into the black ink. The shapes conformed to those made by Smith in the first proof and were then wiped and gradually blended into the plate. This technique provided a very repeatable way to add color based on Smith's initial print.

13. *My Blue Lake* was included in the exhibition *Proof Positive: Forty Years of Contemporary American Printmaking at ULAE, 1957–1997*, organized in 1997 by the Corcoran Gallery of Art, in Washington, D.C., in association with Universal Limited Art Editions. An image of the print is also included in the accompanying catalogue of the same title (Washington, D.C.: Corcoran Gallery of Art, 1997), pl. 174.

14. For an image of *Free Fall*, see Weitman, *Kiki Smith*, 91; or the ULAE website, http://www.ulae.com/ (accessed September 26, 2011).

15. For an image of *Puppet*, see Weitman, *Kiki Smith*, 89; or the ULAE website, http://www.ulae.com/ (accessed September 26, 2011).

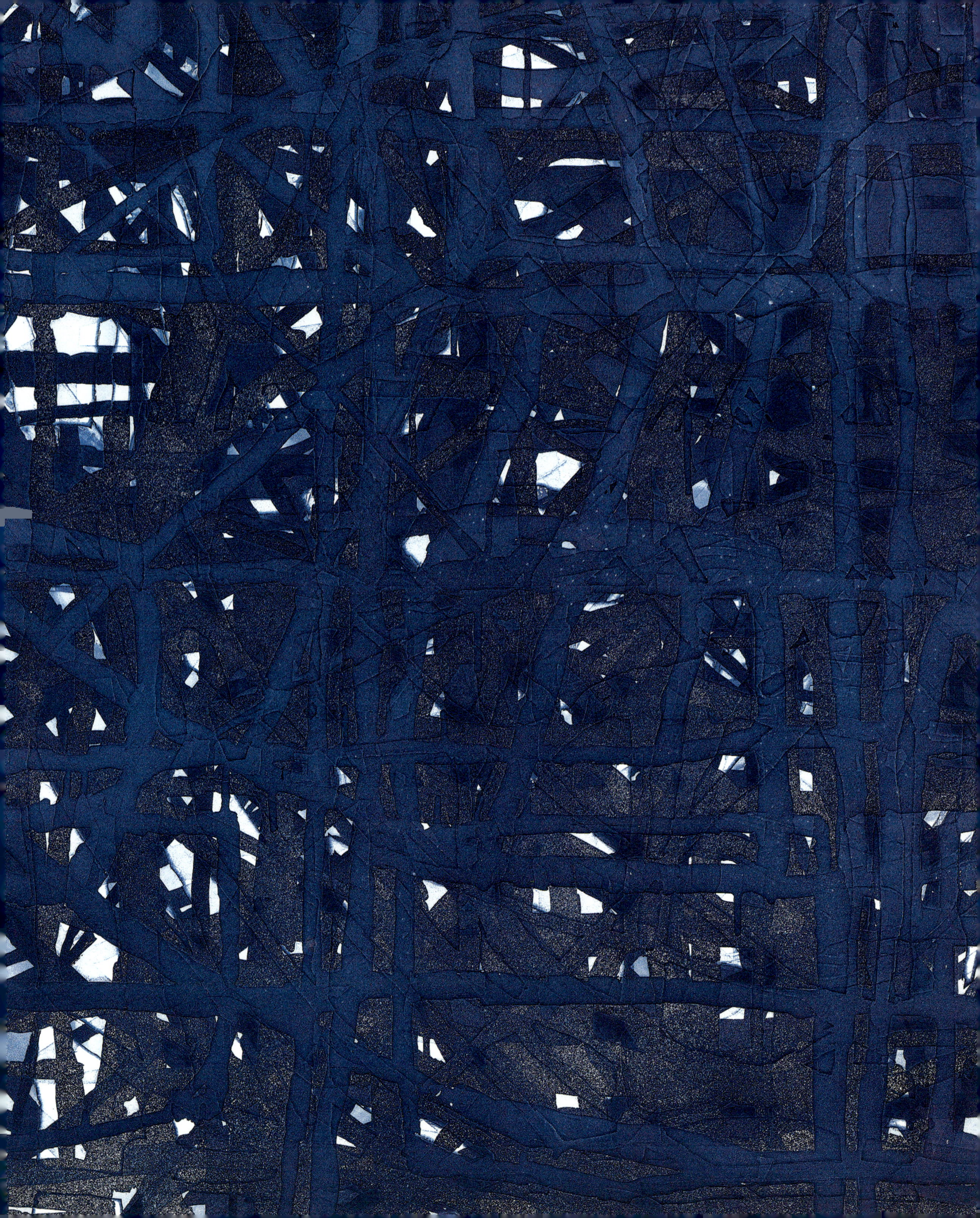

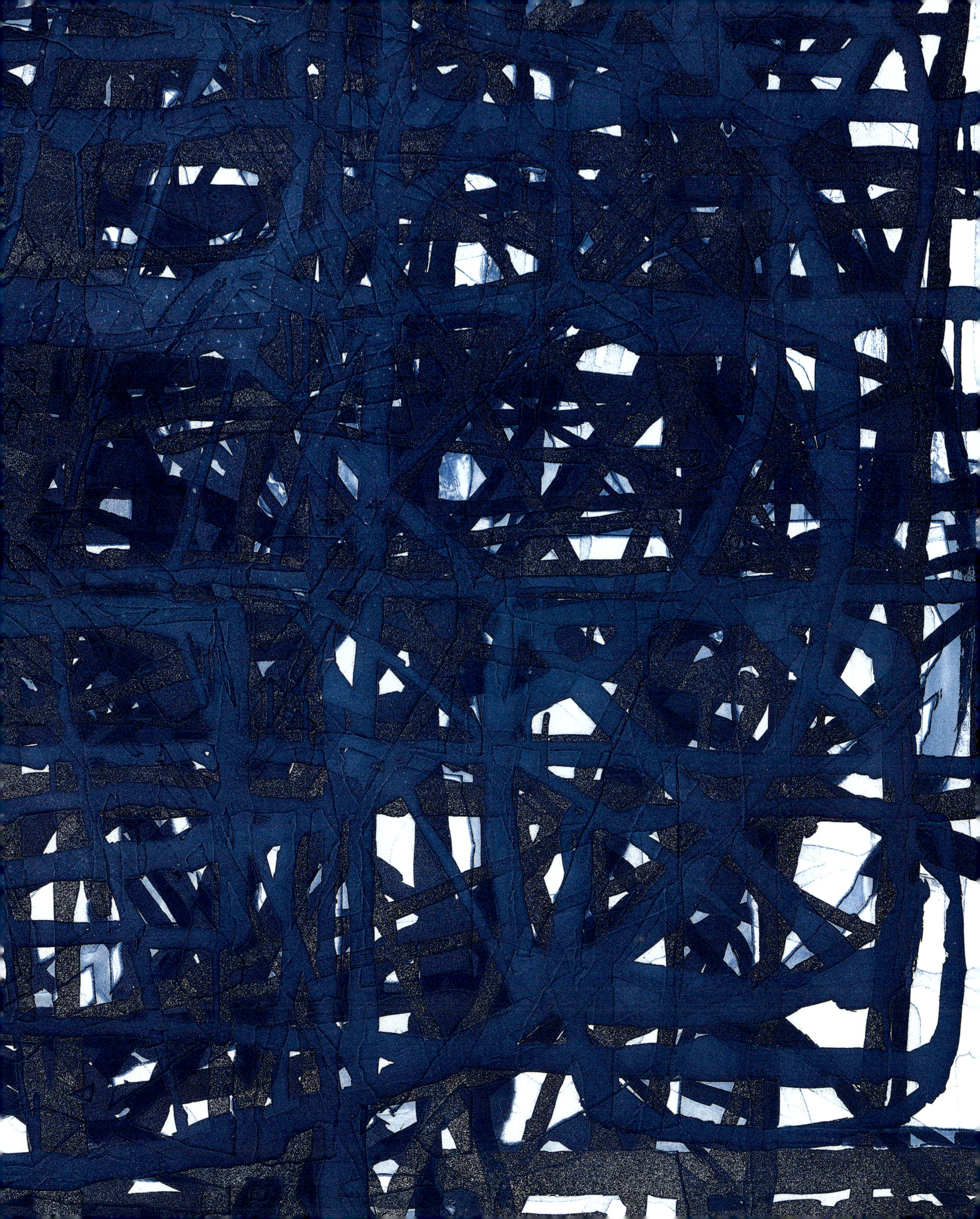

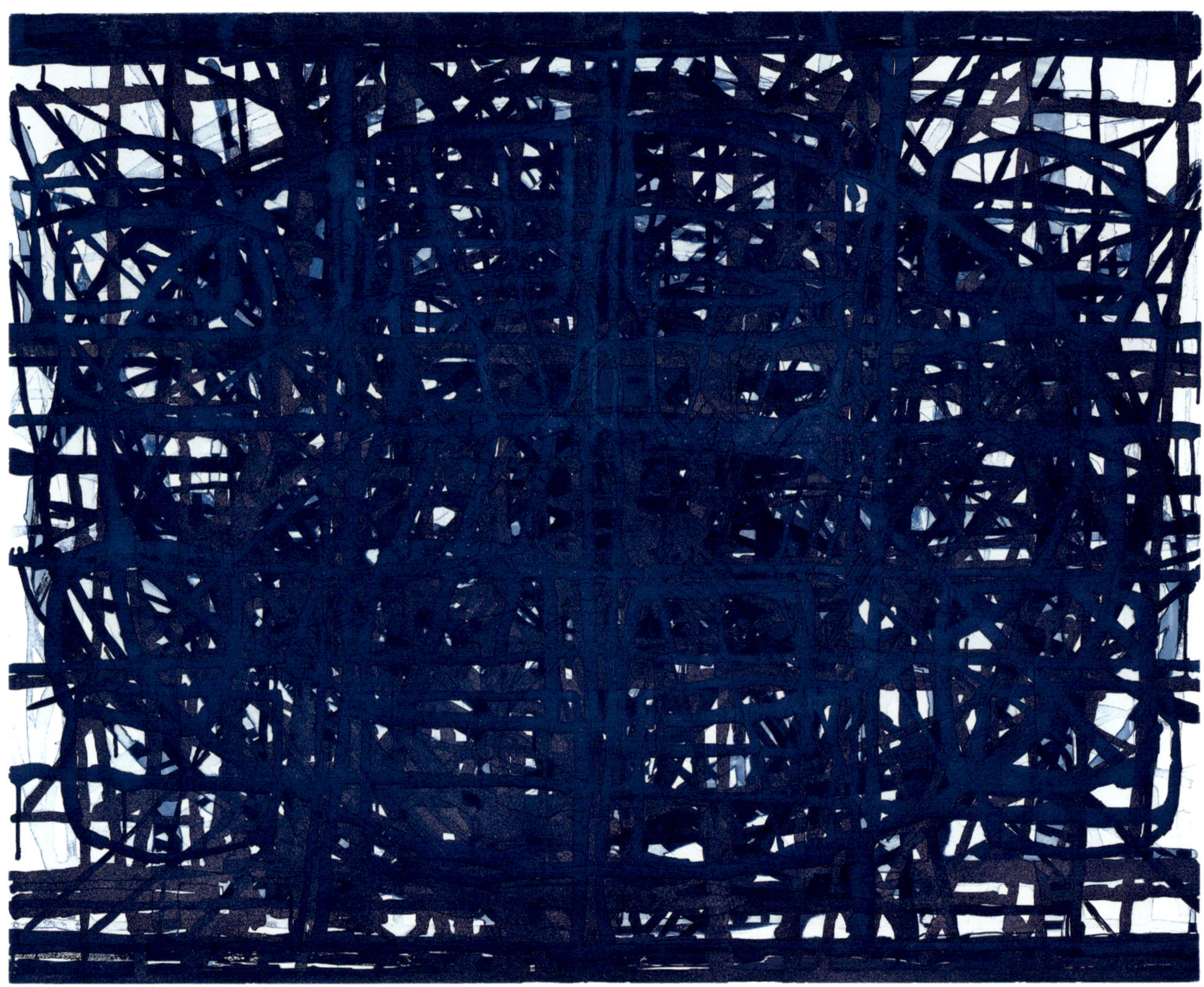

Terry Winters's more than quarter-century involvement with printmaking has been a passionate and steady one, which the artist acknowledges has broadened the scope and expression of his art. Unlike many painters working in print, he has not exploited the medium merely as a means to reproduce canvases in multiple, but rather has embraced printmaking as a mode of expression with a unique vocabulary and syntax. Winters paraphrases Barnett Newman, echoing Newman's belief that "every medium is its own instrument,"[1] and notes that prints "open up a kind of aperture . . . that has a very singular vision . . . [that] I couldn't access in another way."

Many times in the conversation recorded in this chapter, Winters remarks on his ongoing pursuit of ways "to work as directly as possible." Certainly this is true of *Internal and External Values* (fig. 1), the focus of the discussion, which was printed from a single copper plate, in a single color, and in a single pass through the press—an economy of materials that belies the extravagance of time and work that went into it. As this chapter will describe, the print marked two "firsts" for Craig Zammiello, as once again the inadequacies of available equipment in the print shop inspired innovation. First, the large size of the plates in the suite of prints to which *Internal and External Values* relates (all about 42 × 50 inches) required an unwieldy, makeshift method of aquatinting with a traditional rosin-dusting method, leading Zammiello to perfect a technique by which the aquatint ground could be applied via airbrush.[2] Second, Prussian blue ink's unique qualities—its transparency and its ability to mimic more than one color—were exploited.

Of his close involvement with a handful of master printers throughout his career, Winters has commented that "the printer is another component, a 'resist' and an 'assist,'" punning on the intaglio process.[3] Printmaking, Winters remarks, presents a uniquely counterintuitive situation in which the artist is dependent on the skill and knowledge of the printer and yet the finished product still looks and feels like the artist's own work.

FIG. 1. Terry Winters, *Internal and External Values,* 1998. Sugarlift aquatint and openbite etching printed in one color on Arches En-Tout-Cas paper torn to size, 42 × 49¾ in. (106.7 × 126.4 cm). Edition of 35. Published by Universal Limited Art Editions

ELISABETH HODERMARSKY: I've read that you started making prints in 1982, following your first solo exhibition at Sonnabend [Gallery], when Bill Goldston invited you to make prints at ULAE [Universal Limited Art Editions]. But I've also read that you were attracted to printmaking long before that time.

TERRY WINTERS: Attracted to it . . . principally through my concerns with process, in how things get made. And, certainly with prints, process is foremost in the way images are built or constructed. So I had an interest in it, but I hadn't actually made any prints before 1982.

EH: And you concentrated on lithography for the first few years?

TW: Yes, that was Bill's idea of how to introduce me to the studio—what he thought would be the smoothest transition, given the kinds of drawings I was working on at the time. I was making drawings with litho crayon. Litho crayon as well as charcoal and graphite sticks.

EH: And you began to work in intaglio—make etchings—about six years into your involvement with printmaking, working both with [Aldo] Crommelynck in Paris and at ULAE. I believe the first etching you made at ULAE was *Station* [1988; *fig. 2*] with John Lund?

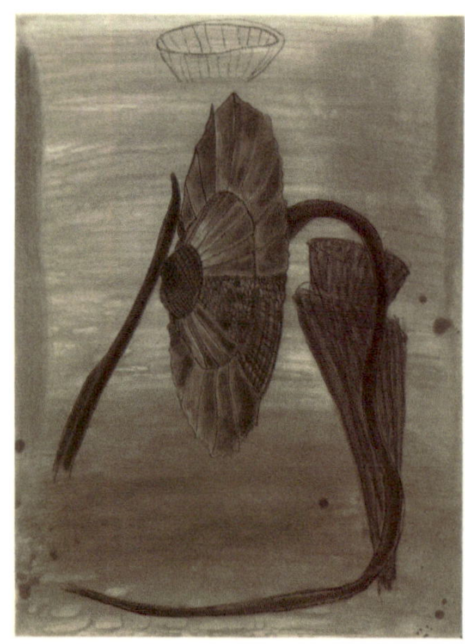

FIG. 2. Terry Winters, *Station*, 1988. Softground etching and spitbite aquatint printed in one color on Sekishu Torinoko Gampi paper laid down on J. Whatman 1952 paper, 24¼ × 19½ in. (61.6 × 49.5 cm). Edition of 55. Published by Universal Limited Art Editions

TW: Right. But, Craig, did you also work on that?

CRAIG ZAMMIELLO: No, that was you and John. And for John, that was a major moment—a real challenge for him in terms of aquatint control, because you had been working with Crommelynck, and John had to live up to Aldo's standards.

TW: Right. Because the difference between the studios—Crommelynck and ULAE—really, for me, had to do with their approaches. Aldo's strength was his adherence to, and strict use of, traditional techniques. ULAE is more improvisational.

CZ: And after the success of that first etching, *Station*, I think it gave John confidence—it proved that he could do it. John was my mentor, and I remember looking at that print and thinking, "Wow, I wish I could make an aquatint like that!"

TW: Yes, it was very beautiful.

CZ: So I was in the studio when you were working with John and others, but I think the first project that you and I actually worked on together from start to finish were these gravure-based *Fourteen Etchings* [1989; *figs. 3–4*].

FIGS. 3–4. Terry Winters, *Fourteen Etchings 2* and *Fourteen Etchings 11*, 1989. From a portfolio of fourteen hand-drawn direct gravures with various intaglio additions and photogravures printed in one color on Torinoko Gampi paper laid down on Amalfi paper, each 18⅝ × 14⅛ in. (47.3 × 35.9 cm). Edition of 65. Published by Universal Limited Art Editions

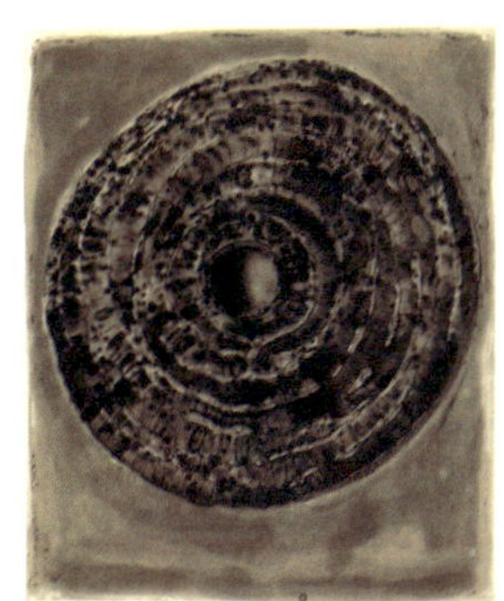
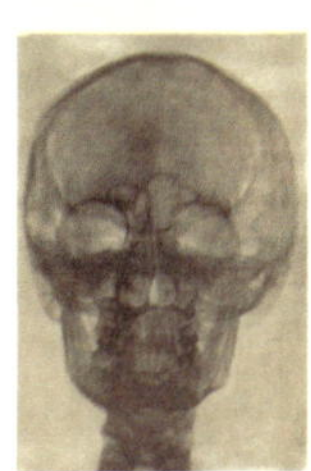
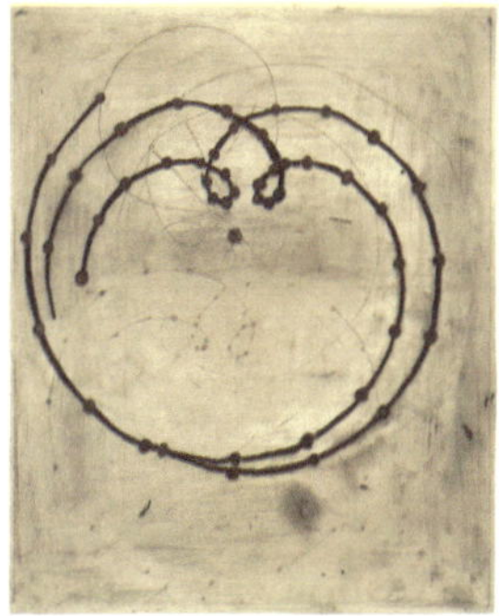
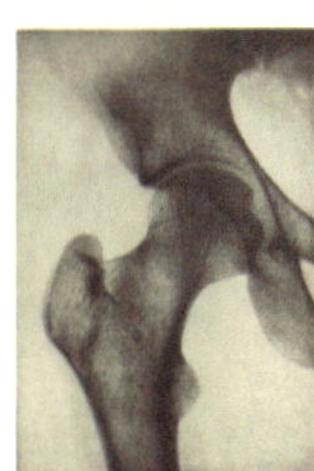

TW: Yes. *Fourteen Etchings* was a way for us to try to jump-start the process of establishing an image and also for me to take advantage of Craig's knowledge of photogravure, to see how I might eliminate a lot of the cumbersome process that goes into making a print.[4] That's always been my interest—how to work as directly as possible.

CZ: And, with these, Terry really had me cut my teeth on direct gravure. This was the first time I had worked with direct gravure. There's no real film in the main images, the film came in on the Röntgens, the X-rays at the lower right of each of these. So here I was developing that technique to give Terry a tool that he could use.

EH: So the central drawings for these weren't initially made on Mylar?

CZ: Oh yes, they were, but then Terry and John took them to another stage.

TW: Yes, we then took those plates and I worked on them in a more traditional way. Because as I had been working with lithography, I had also been working on how to avoid the indirect nature of all of these reversals and tracings—all of these intermediate stages before you actually got an image. I wasn't interested in that part of the process. Whether it was transferring drawings directly onto stones or however we were trying to get an image quickly, this seemed also to be a very immediate way of getting an image onto a plate and establishing the marks more intently.

EH: Each one of these is so different.

TW: That was another aspect of how to build a portfolio of images in which there was a singularity to each image but also a uniformity in terms of size and approach to making the plates. And to push each one to where it needed to go. Every image then had its own set of demands.

EH: And, Craig, you were working on Long Island, and, Terry, you and John were working here in Manhattan?

TW: At the Watts Street studio.[5]

CZ: Right. So we would be coming and going, sending things back and forth. And the X-rays were another issue, because they didn't behave like traditional gravures. So I had to develop a way to etch them that was not written in the books—to try to mimic the look of this Victorian X-ray to make the films. So that was fun too. And when the project was finished, we sat down and looked at them, John and I, and both said, "Wow, very interesting. A step forward." And Terry was a catalyst for this.

EH: And this is the first time you had used this technique of direct gravure?

CZ: Yes, I think so. Just fooling around, I knew it could be done. But this was the first time we had worked it out. In fact, I might have told you this, Terry, but at the time I didn't even realize it was called "direct gravure." We were calling it "Mylar gravure." We thought we had coined this new process but later found out that Deli Sacilotto had used it a few years before.[6] And from there we went to . . . was it *Systems Diagram* [1996] we made first? You know, from that group of five?

TW: Yes, that was probably the first one of those five big prints.

EH: That was in 1996, and it was followed in 1997 by *Picture Cell* [*fig. 5*], *Developmental Surface Model*, and *Face Boundary* [*fig. 6*], and finally, in 1998, by *Internal and External Values* [*see fig. 1*].

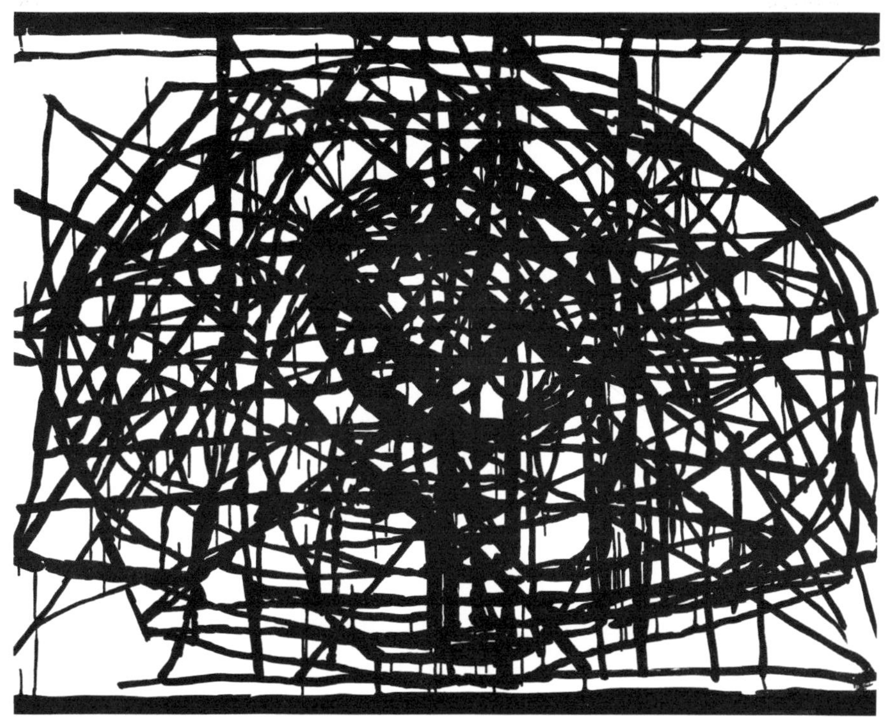

FIG. 5. Terry Winters, *Picture Cell*, 1997. Etching and sugarlift aquatint printed in one color on Arches En-Tout-Cas paper torn to size, 42 × 50 in. (106.7 × 127 cm). Edition of 18. Published by Universal Limited Art Editions

TW: That's right.

CZ: What happened with these plates, Terry, was that they had reached the maximum size—they were *over* the maximum size—for our aquatint box. So I don't believe that you knew this, but John and I had developed a way to put aquatint on them by the two of us holding one half of the plate inside the box and the other outside the box and then standing there with feathers and fanning the rosin back onto the plate as it seeped out into the room.

TW: And you must have been thinking, "Okay, we're not doing this anymore."

[*laughter*]

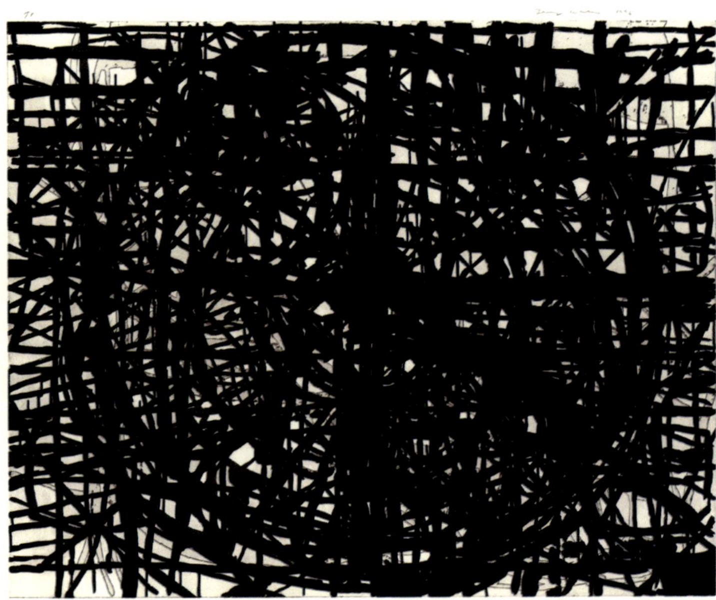

FIG 6. Terry Winters, *Face Boundary*, 1997. Etching and sugarlift aquatint printed in one color on Arches En-Tout-Cas paper torn to size, 42 × 50 in. (106.7 × 127 cm). Edition of 18. Published by Universal Limited Art Editions

CZ: That's kind of what happened. It was kind of a "necessity is the mother of invention" type of situation. It became necessary to bring in the airbrush.[7]

TW: In a way, that's how each of these projects—maybe not so consciously, but somewhat consciously—was determined. With *Fourteen Etchings* it was about developing a series of prints through which we could explore different gravure techniques. We were developing parameters within which we could experiment. And once we had made the fourteen etchings it seemed the next challenge would be to try to maximize the size, and to push another limit. After working with a group of very small plates, I wanted to get as large as we could and to see what would happen—to explore the pressures that develop from working at that other extreme.

EH: But you didn't envision these five large etchings as a suite or a portfolio in the same way?

TW: No, I saw them as individual prints, and that was another break. A group of large individual prints that also in some way mapped out different aspects of these techniques that we had initially discovered or invented in the fourteen etchings.

CZ: Right.

EH: They're extraordinary. And they seem to be a sort of culmination of several years of working in etching. They really are tours de force.

TW: At this point there was a fluidity based on that quality of directness I was describing earlier, of something that felt similar to making a painting or a drawing. It was just another medium to work in that had the same immediacy. Obviously, there's an intermediate step in printmaking, but the way that I was approaching the plates was very direct.

EH: What's so extraordinary for me about these five large prints is that there's this inherent economy of materials—because they're all printed from a single plate, right? And in a single color, a single pass through the press. So on the one hand, in terms of materials, they're so economical, and yet there is so much labor involved in terms of the layers upon layers of information, the number of etches. And this, for me, is the direct antithesis to something like your earlier portfolio of lithographs, *Folio* [*figs. 7 and 8*], in which there's a lot of labor but also such an *extravagance* of materials—of plates and colors and passes through the press—involved.

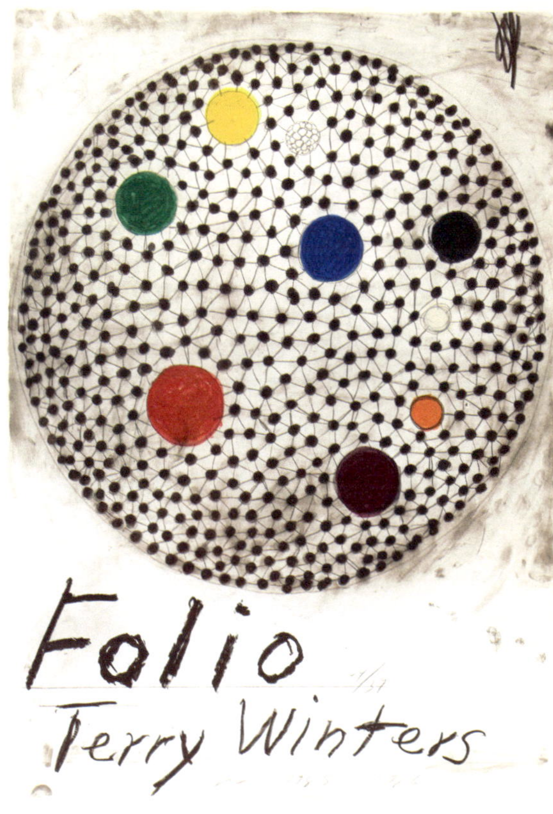
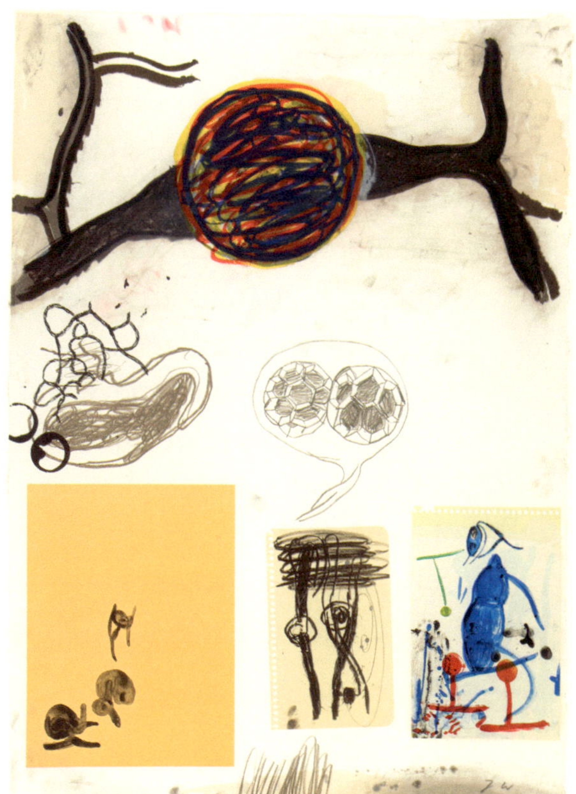

FIGS. 7–8. Terry Winters, *Title Page* and *Folio Nine* from *Folio*, 1985–86. From a portfolio of eleven lithographs printed in color on J. Whatman and John Koller handmade paper, each 32 × 23 in. (81.3 × 58.4 cm). Edition of 39. Published by Universal Limited Art Editions. Yale University Art Gallery, Gift of Arthur Fleischer, Jr., B.A. 1953, LL.B. 1958, 1991.118.1.1–.11

Terry Winters

TW: *Folio* was the complete opposite. In a way, that illustrated, for me, the two extremes between lithography and etching. That lithography could be a compendium of multiple drawings which could be combined as a single image and layered, like a painting. With etching, the plate has the ability to register marks over time and reveal the history of the image. That was also one of the limits, or the degrees of difficulty, that I was interested in ascribing to these prints—that they would only be printed in one go, one pass through the press.

EH: Something like setting a challenge for yourself?

TW: Yes, or just a limit within which invention takes place. As soon as conditions are set, there's an improvisational response that develops alongside those limits and takes you to places that you wouldn't have gone. And this group of prints—*Systems Diagram* through to *Internal and External Values*—pushed that aspect or challenge.

CZ: And with *Internal and External Values* there was a culmination—there was so much work that went into etching that one plate. Terry would draw that entire image, and then sometimes he'd erase the entire image that he had drawn the week before, but it would leave trace memories, or a history, in the metal. And when you look at that final print you see that, you see those faint marks—the outlines of open biting, or erasing. You see where marks used to be, where they cross over others and block things out. And that's something that I think is unique to etching. And for me, Terry was the pioneer artist in that respect in my history of working in etching.

The second thing—tell me if you remember this, Terry—is that at this point we were using the airbrush constantly. Though we had been gradually introducing it, using it intermittently in the course of these five prints, this was the first one that utilized the airbrush exclusively to lay down the aquatints. But what happened I believe was this: you had been painting in sugar, and we had processed the plate and I went to airbrush it, and the airbrush misfired, creating a large amount of speckled paint, not unlike a Goya aquatint. And I was horrified. And I remember that I approached you and said, "I can clean this whole thing off and repaint it right now." And you said, "Let's just etch it and see what we get." And that brought out these textures of tone [*fig. 9*].

TW: Yes, it did remind me of those very early, primitive, grainy aquatints.

CZ: Hand-dusted aquatint, right? So, by the time we were getting back in here, maybe there were two more aquatints applied that way in tones, and by the end

I had kind of mastered this airbrush technique—how to use the correct amount of pressure and the way to make it spit in a repetitive manner. And we used that in the multicolored print that we made later—*Multiple Visualization Technique* [1998; *fig. 10*].

TW: That was the move we made after this print. To use multiple plates, full color, and use some of the techniques we had learned on this print.

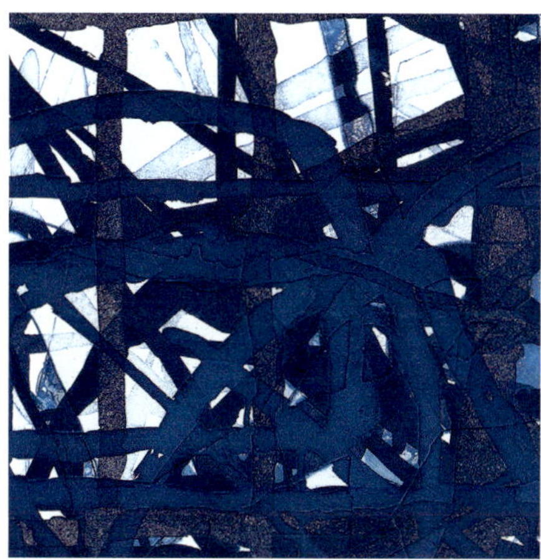

FIG. 9. Detail of *Internal and External Values*

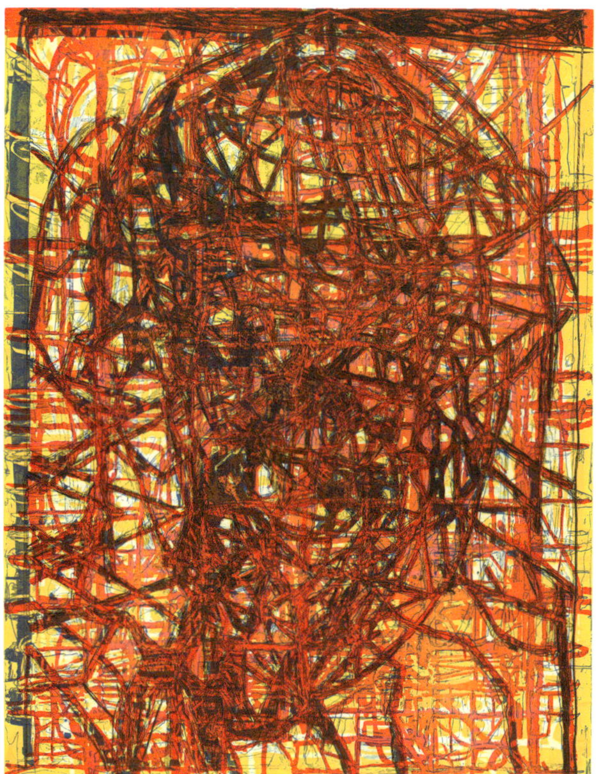

FIG. 10. Terry Winters, *Multiple Visualization Technique*, 1998. Sugarlift aquatint and openbite etching printed in four colors on Arches En-Tout-Cas paper torn to size, 53 × 43 in. (134.6 × 109.2 cm). Edition of 41. Published by Universal Limited Art Editions

Terry Winters

The other thing you'll notice about *Internal and External Values* is that it's the only one of the first four that's in color. And that was the result of the intensity of work that went into that plate—that when we pulled the first proof in black it was like . . . there was nothing there.

[*laughter*]

TW: It was strange. That we had worked so hard to make something so rich, and then when we printed it, it went completely black. There was a thought to open up the image by using a more transparent color, and then, when printed in Prussian blue, it revealed everything that we had done to the plate.

EH: Did you know at the time that it was this "magic color"?

TW: I've been very much involved in using a variety of lake colors,[8] and I have a special fascination with Prussian blue. It's the first artificial coal-tar color that was developed and has an enormous capacity for transparency. It's a pigment I use in my paintings a lot.

EH: Would a Prussian blue ink react the same as a Prussian blue paint?

TW: Yes, because it's the quality of the pigment which is transparent— whichever binder is used.

CZ: When people see the print for the first time, they always think it's printed from two to three plates. Cool black, where it's solid, and then ultramarine. And it was me, John Lund, and Jihong Shi who pulled the first proof of it in Prussian blue. Were you there, Terry? Oh yes, of course you were there. And Bill Goldston was there. We were all speechless. We all just stood around for a long time without saying anything.

TW: Because the difference between this and the proof in black is like night and day.

EH: Does the black proof still exist?

CZ: It must. [*fig. 11*]

EH: And there's open biting on this as well?

CZ: Yes, at least twice.

EH: So how many etches did this go through? How many layers?

CZ: I believe about six—right, Terry?

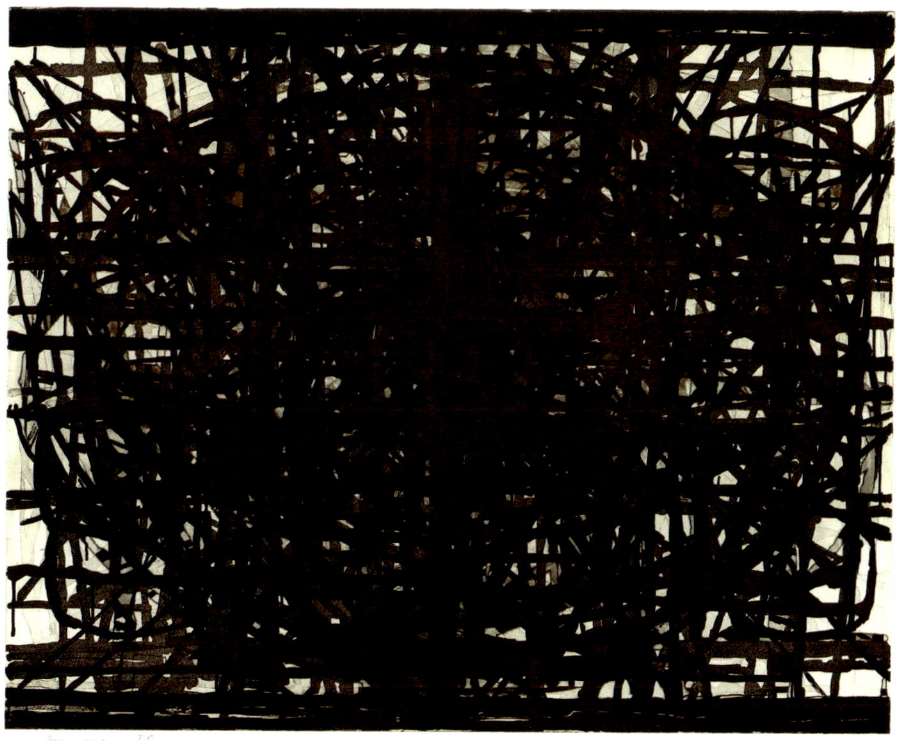

TW: That sounds about right.

CZ: But I'm not sure how many states exist because we really did a lot of work on the fly. Terry had painted this image positively and negatively six times. Sometimes he would sit in a chair and paint the negative space between each of the lines. You're talking about a lot of work; the artist working intensely.[9]

TW: It was before I had a real life.

[*laughter*]

TW: I was just having an immediate response to whatever was there on the plate. It really wasn't a lot of fill-in, of busy work. It was an accumulation of all of these integrated responses, and building an image that one couldn't predict. It never felt like traditional printmaking, with all of its precise plate registrations, et cetera. My involvement with printmaking has been how to *avoid* all of those tedious things that seemed to be a crucial part of printmaking—making the tracing, getting all of the registrations correct, figuring out what happens with the reversals. I wanted to figure out how *not* to do those things.

Terry Winters

CZ: Right. And may I add that *we printers love that.*

[laughter]

TW: You see, I always try to take it away from the labor-intensive *artist* part and put the work on the labor-intensive *printer's* part.

[laughter]

CZ: And again, I have to go back to it. Every time I look at this print I remember thinking that I was going to fall on my sword with that airbrushing malfunction.

EH: Because you thought you had ruined the print?

CZ: Yes, that I had destroyed his work and that I was going to have to recreate it. I was going to have to clean everything out in there and recreate it by hand. But instead Terry said, "Let's do it, let's use it."

TW: That's another part of the directness I was talking about, working with someone like Craig, who's so knowledgeable about these different techniques and has such an enthusiasm about the process and the procedures. And to use that as a very direct input into how this image gets built rather than to have him spend all of this time on what is just busy work to me. How to translate all of that curiosity and knowledge into establishing a unique kind of image.

EH: That's pretty generous of you, really.

CZ: Oh yeah, believe me . . .

TW: It comes back to the fact that I wasn't really interested in *re*producing anything, I was interested in *pro*ducing something, so the production in my own painting allows for accident and coincidence to contribute to the creation of the image.

EH: But a lot of artists do approach printmaking as a way to reproduce their paintings.

TW: Right.

EH: Which is something you seem to have never done. You also seem to hold a separate and equal esteem for printmaking. You give printmaking its own place—and not a lesser place—in your work. I'm a print curator, so I'm always thinking about this . . . I see how some artists and collectors and dealers consider prints less seriously, as a sort of "lesser" art medium.

TW: I always liked Barnett Newman's observation that every medium is its own instrument [*see note 1*]. So for me, the prints describe a specific pictorial territory—one that is unique to the procedures and materials of the medium. I couldn't make these pictures in another way, and the prints help inform my drawing and painting.

EH: It appears that you have never stopped making prints, once you started.

TW: You know, at certain times I'd just like to stop! But it's very much shaped the way I've been working and thinking.

EH: And you've worked mainly at ULAE and Two Palms, but you've also worked at some other presses—Grenfell [Press], Simca [Print Artists]?

TW: Actually, I've made many prints with a number of publishers, each of whom affords me a different set of opportunities. It's the variety of mediums, studios, and collaborators that interest me. I've also worked on projects with Peter Blum in Switzerland, Kido Press in Tokyo, and Mixografia in Los Angeles, as well as a couple of book projects here in New York—one with Columbia University and another just recently with the painter Josh Smith at 38th Street Publishers.

CZ: Yes, you have this healthy attitude towards printmaking, and understand its inherent quality of a certain amount of chance.

EH: There are a couple of wonderful quotes in the catalogue raisonné of your printed work that I'd like to bring into our discussion.

TW: Sure.

EH: You've said in regard to your printmaking—referring to a combination of factors: the print studio in which you are working, the printer with whom you are working, and the particular technique and materials that you happen to be engaging at that moment—that "work is driven by collaborating with circumstance."[10] Which I think is a beautiful quote.

TW: It's about allowing the medium and the set of conditions to play a part in determining how an image develops.

EH: And then, one other quote, about working with printers: that the printer is both a "resist" and an "assist."[11]

CZ: That's nice.

TW: Yes, because it's a very paradoxical situation. I mean, I could not have made any of this work without the printers. Left to my own devices, I would not have made this print [*Internal and External Values*]. Craig allowed these things to happen, but, at the same time, I always end up with something that feels like my work. And that's a very odd situation. Because anyone else that Craig's working with—even though they might be using the same tools or techniques—it feels like *their* work, it doesn't feel like my work.

CZ: Well, it's a symbiotic process too, because without *him* I wouldn't be doing *that* [*pointing to* Internal and External Values]. And when the print is done, it's Terry's. And I step back and say, "Wow, look what he did." But the joy I get—and Lisa has heard this many times—is that basically all of the artists whom I've worked with . . . I just find it to be such a great opportunity to be able to enter into the creative process and be part of this final beautiful thing. It's such an honor.

TW: It's like a band. I just want to be in a band!

[*laughter*]

CZ: [*shaking his head*] "It's like a band" . . . Terry Winters's All Stars.

TW: Well, there is a social component to printmaking.

EH: Does that bother you sometimes, that there are so many people around?

TW: No, not now. But it did initially, when Bill first invited me out to ULAE. I never paint with people around, and so that was a very big hump for me to get over. I think that's part of why I develop these long-term relationships with printers, because I start to feel comfortable. Once I feel I am able to do that with certain groups of people, that adds a social component and another quality of circumstance or coincidence that has come into the mix of making the work. Which is a nice shift from working so much on one's own. Which is basically what I do. From the first time that Bill invited me out to ULAE, I think I continued to go out there every week for a couple of years. Bill made it very clear that I was welcome. I think it really became an extension of my studio. I was always working on something, and very much outside of whatever commercial considerations there were; I felt I could work independently of that end, despite the nature of publishing. I've been fortunate to work in studios where there are never those kinds of considerations. Not that those aren't real-world determining factors—one doesn't want to be wasteful. The idea is to find the most economical and elegant solution to realize the finished print. At least that's been important for me. My struggle is focused on realizing the initial image within a framework where that prototype can be reproduced exactly. I'm interested in the fact that there can be more than one of them—those are the rules of the game for me. At least at this point.

EH: Is that what has led you to making the monotypes more recently?

TW: Yes, I suppose that's true. The monotypes I made at Two Palms in 2004 and 2005 [*fig. 12*] were an attempt at producing unique images that combined aspects of both printing and painting. In terms of the editioned work, while I'm always interested in that first image, the multiple aspect of the medium is essential and also an important component. In a way, if we had just made one of these [*pointing to* Internal and External Values] it would have been fine. But it's a part of the process for the plate to be printed more than once. Because that's what prints are about. Otherwise, that could have been a painting.

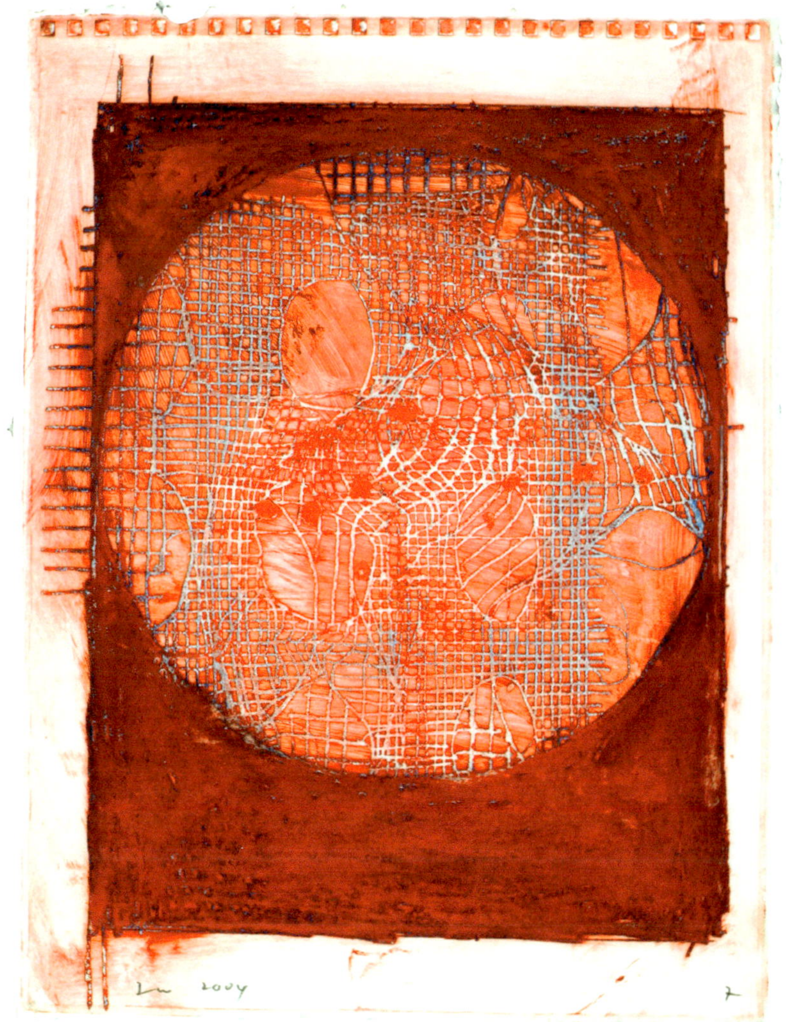

FIG. 12. Terry Winters, *Monoprint/7*, 2004. Monoprint in multiple colors on Twinrocker handmade paper, 17 × 13 in. (43.2 × 33 cm). Published by Two Palms

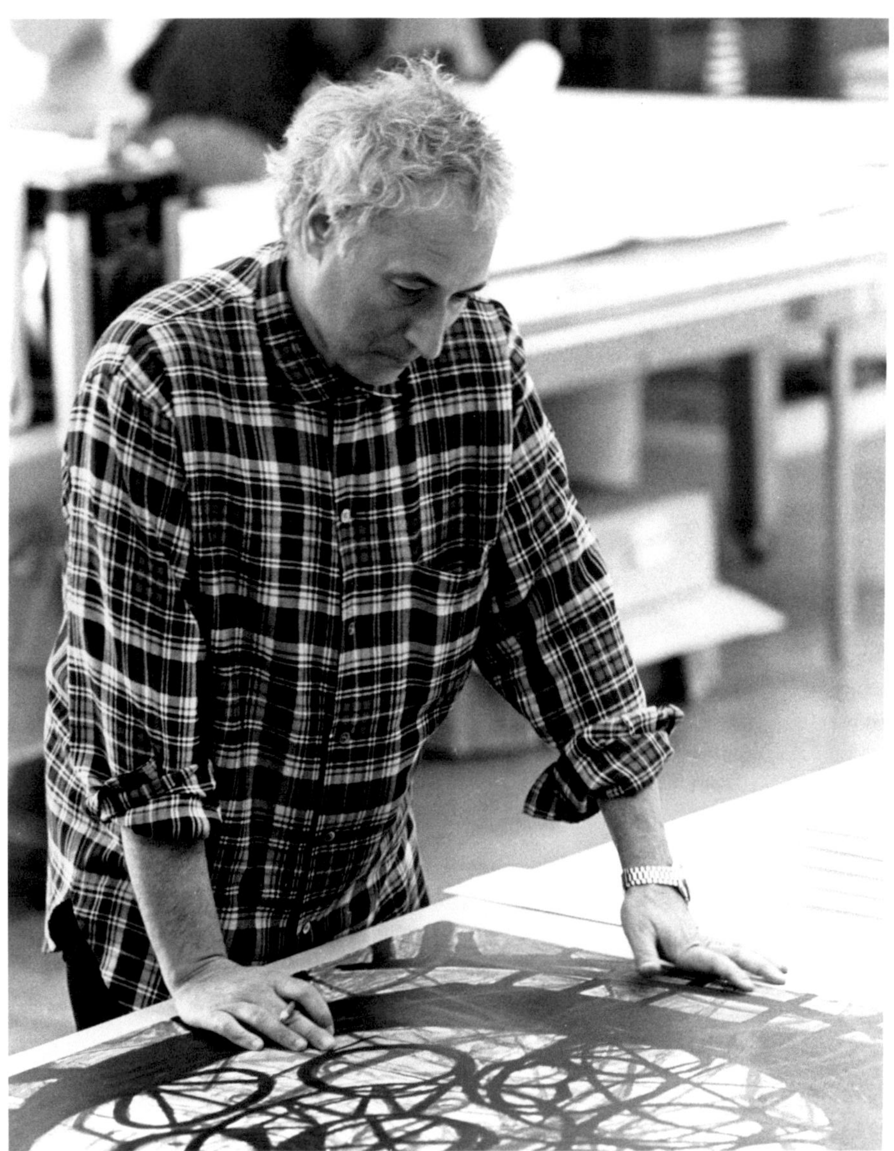

CZ: That's one of the ways in which printmaking is so special—the fact that more than one person can own it and it can be viewed in more than one place or institution. It opens up that possibility.

EH: And for university museums, which tend not to have a lot of money, it's a wonderful way to have a piece of Terry Winters's work, a piece that a modest-size institution can actually afford. So, for smaller museums or collections, and certainly for universities, it's a godsend.

TW: Well, that's a bonus. It's a bonus.

CZ: Thank you, Terry.

Notes

The preceding conversation was held on September 10, 2008, at Winters's studio, in New York.

1. "To me that is what lithography is," Newman writes. "It is an instrument. It is not a 'medium'; it is not a poor man's substitute for painting or for drawing. Nor do I consider it to be a kind of translation of something from one medium into another. For me, it is an instrument that one plays. It is like a piano or an orchestra, and as with an instrument, it *interprets*. And as in all the interpretive arts, so in lithography, creation is joined with the 'playing'; in this case not of bow and string, but of stone and press. . . . I have been captivated by the things that happen in playing this litho instrument; the choices that develop when changing a color or the paper-size." Barnett Newman, preface to *Eighteen Cantos*, a portfolio of eighteen lithographs published by Universal Limited Art Editions in 1964.

2. The traditional aquatinting box used at ULAE was too small to hold the approximately forty-two-by-fifty-inch plate, requiring the printers to coat the plate in sections—a difficult and unwieldy process.

3. *Resist* refers to the ground laid down on an intaglio plate, which protects it from the etching acid. The quotation appears in Richard H. Axsom, "The Philosophers' Stone: The Prints of Terry Winters," in *Terry Winters Prints, 1982–1998: A Catalogue Raisonné*, by Nancy Sojka (Detroit: Detroit Institute of Arts, 1999), 20. This remains the most comprehensive study of the artist's work to date. Two other invaluable volumes are Nan Rosenthal, *Terry Winters: Printed Works* (New York: Metropolitan Museum of Art, 2001), and Adam D. Weinberg, ed., *Terry Winters: Paintings, Drawings, Prints, 1994–2004* (Andover, Mass.: Addison Gallery of American Art in association with Yale University Press, 2004).

4. For *Fourteen Etchings*, Winters drew fourteen images on Mylar from which Zammiello made direct-gravure plates. Winters then worked further on the plates with John Lund, using traditional intaglio techniques such as sugar lift, spit bite, and crayon resist. Meanwhile, Zammiello made photogravure plates from a book of nineteenth-century X-rays taken by Wilhelm Conrad Röntgen for inclusion in the final prints. Röntgen (1845–1923) discovered the X-ray in 1895.

5. The Watts Street studio was a space that ULAE maintained in Manhattan from 1985 to 1995.

6. Deli Sacilotto is a master printer and the author of *Printmaking: History and Process* (with Donald Saff; 1978) and *Photographic Printmaking Techniques* (1982). He has taught at numerous schools and was the master printer at Graphicstudio, at the University of South Florida, in Tampa.

7. The cumbersome process of applying a traditional rosin aquatint via the aquatint box led Zammiello to develop and perfect the airbrush method of applying an aquatint ground, which yielded its own set of challenges and interesting effects. Quite by accident, the brush would start to spit, either from becoming plugged up with drying varnish, or from the air pressure being too low. Winters was receptive to the different patterns and varying degrees of coarseness achieved, so Zammiello began to develop patterns that were repeatable based on the size of the needle and nozzle in the airbrush and the amount of air pressure powering the brush. Another technique was to spray a very fine pattern, etch it for a certain time, and then respray over it to create a contrasting pattern. This could be repeated as many times as one wanted. By utilizing the airbrush more and more throughout the making of these five prints, Zammiello quickly developed a catalogue of different effects that could be achieved with this tool. Many of these effects are not possible with a single, traditional application of rosin aquatint.

8. Lake colors are the most commonly used coloring agents, known for their versatility and adaptability.

9. There are many different layers of aquatint as well as open bite in this print. Winters would also use sugar lift for erasing parts of the image by open biting. This would leave a faint trace, or history, of the past drawing, that would eventually, layer upon layer, add to the dimensional depth of the print. With a certain amount of randomness, because of the processes and style of drawing, sections would come to the foreground, recede to the background, or disappear almost completely, all in one step. And the more sugarlift applications that Winters applied over the previously etched areas, the more this random layering took place.

10. Quoted in Axsom, "The Philosophers' Stone," 20.

11. Ibid.

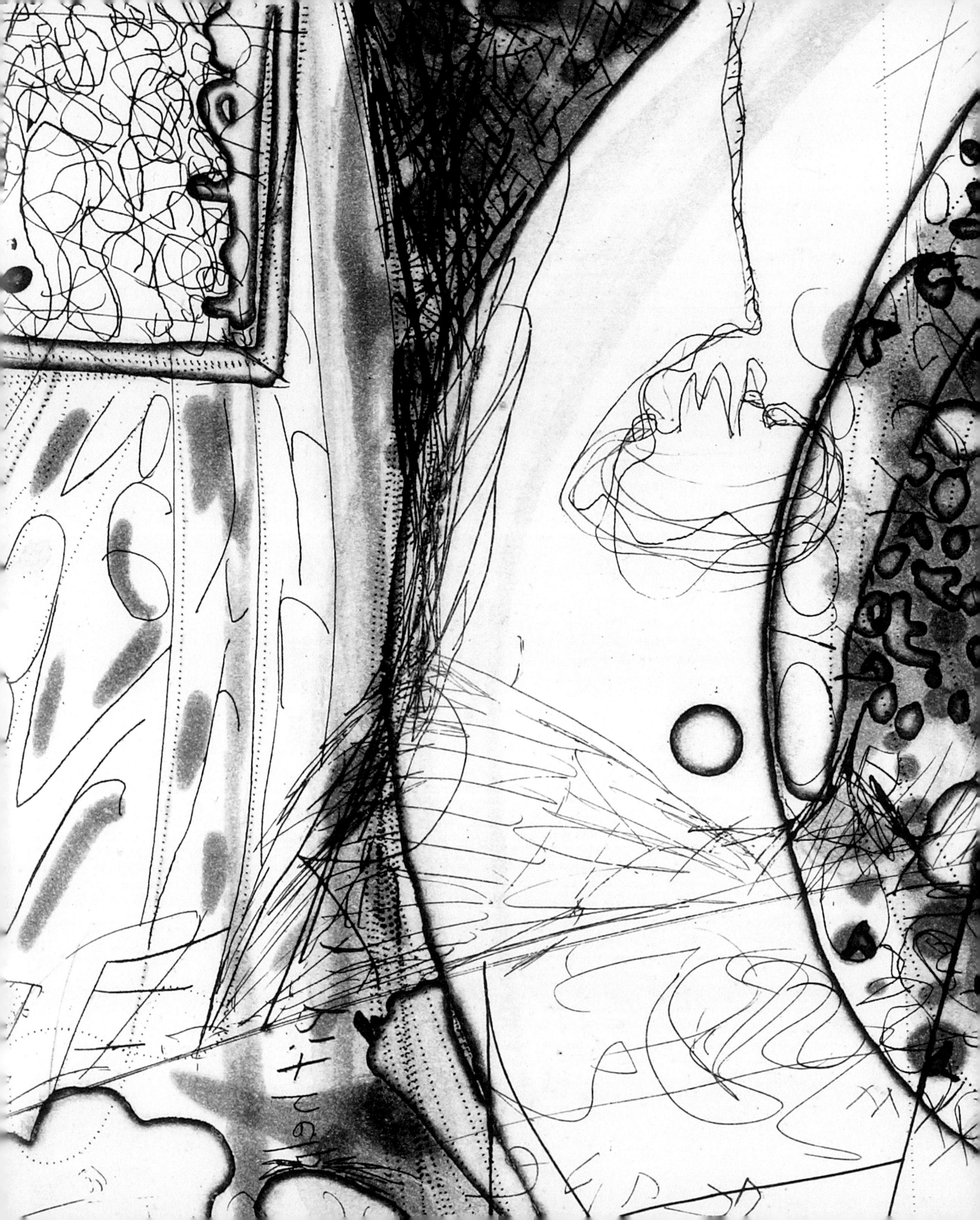

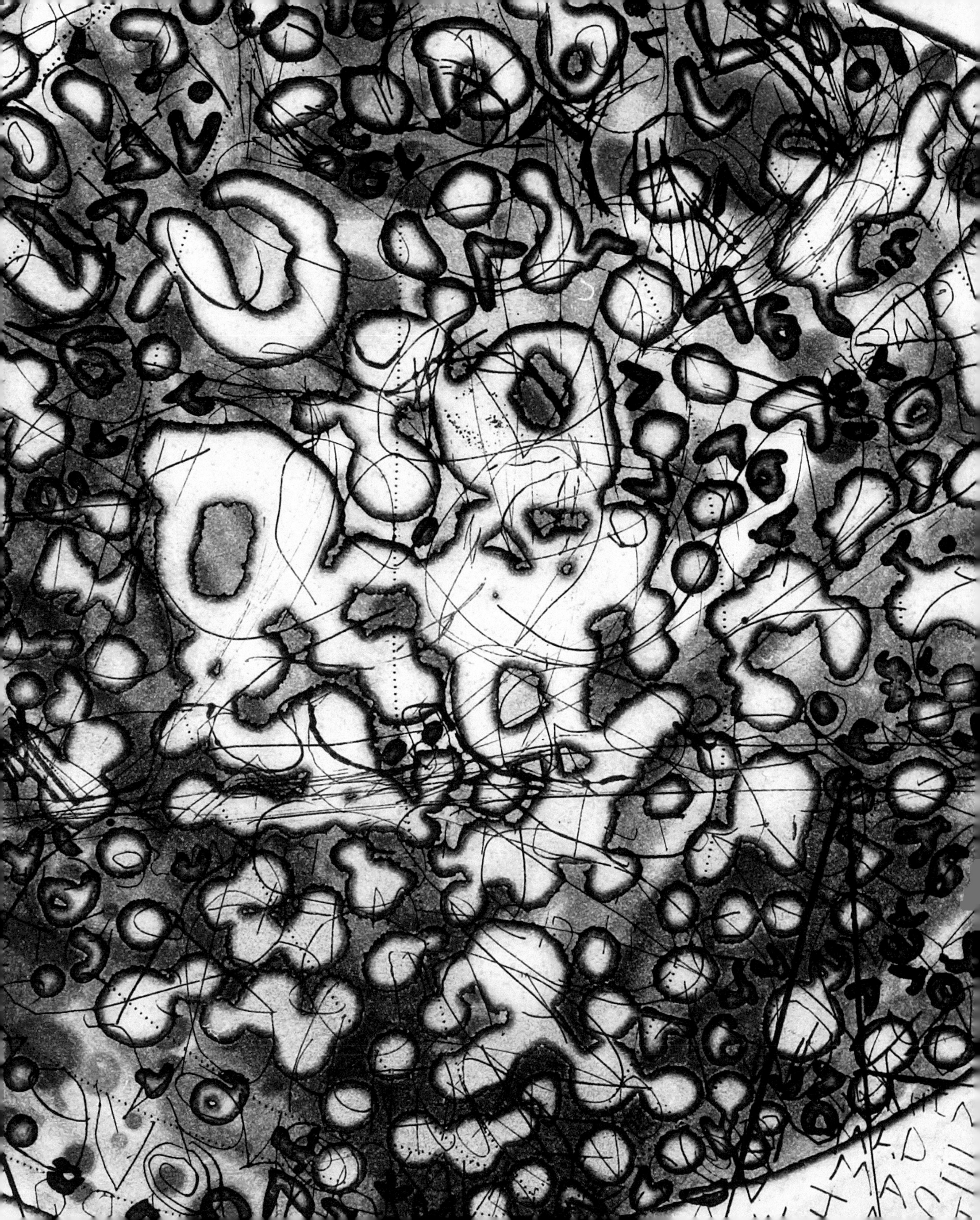

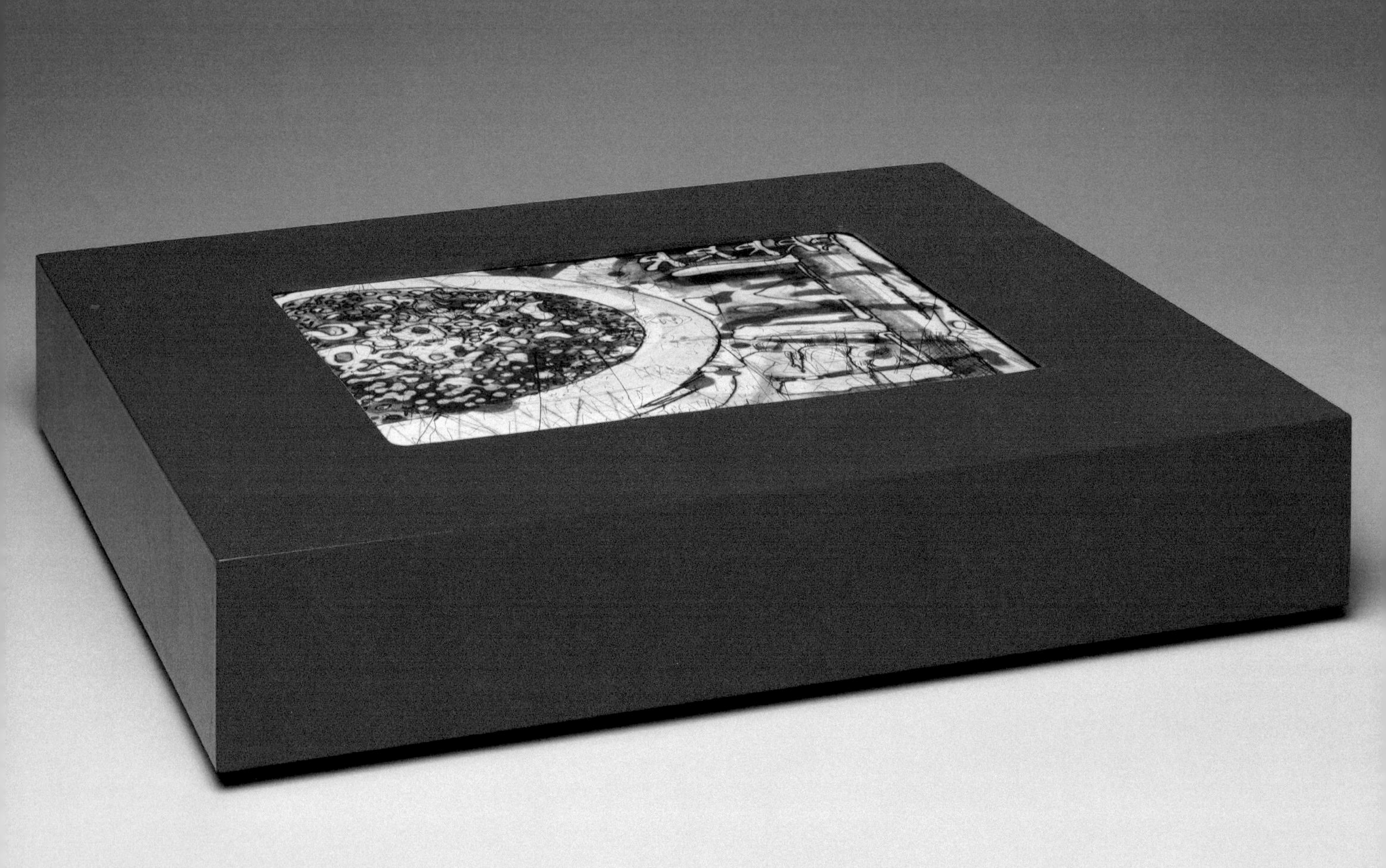

Momentum (Red Rover) (fig. 1) glides across a tabletop like a child's pull toy, or an inexhaustible, creeping Etch A Sketch. Though it slinks mutely, it shouts its written message—"help help help" and "over over over over"—from a seemingly endless etched paper scroll that spools across its top. These snippets of language are embedded in the flowing abstract lines of Suzanne McClelland's imagery. The seemingly random words might echo from a playground and, as the title suggests, recall the childhood game of Red Rover, in which players pass back and forth from team to team, attempting to lunge through the opponents' line when the rhyme is chanted: "Red Rover, Red Rover, send so-and-so over . . ."

In the following conversation, McClelland explains how initially this print was to be a hanging scroll, echoing a series of drawings that McClelland made in 1997 and 1998 on unfurled rolls of sandpaper. As work on the plates progressed, however, what was originally meant to be a vertically hanging print—intended for the more formal, public forum of a gallery wall—developed into a far more intimate, private object, more akin to an Asian handscroll.

McClelland explains that, for her, this form of the hanging scroll or handscroll was influenced by her lifelong interest in Chinese painting and recalls the concept of "meandering, wandering through landscape," east to west, north to south, and back again. She also discusses her fascination with the nonlinear nature of spoken or written language and how this resonates with the language of printmaking, which "isn't linear" either.

Momentum (Red Rover) also recalls McClelland's beginnings as a photographer and the artist's early absorption in the concept of the picture frame—the framing of an image to create a still "snapshot" within a moving landscape. That interest is literally manifested in this work as is McClelland's signature style, which incorporates random words or phrases (often inverted or backward) into her work in painting, print, and collage.

FIG. 1. Suzanne McClelland, *Momentum (Red Rover)* (exterior), 2000. Etching in black ink on intaglio scroll of Japanese Masa paper, encased in a red lacquer box, 13¾ × 16 × 3 in. (34.9 × 40.6 × 7.6 cm). Edition of 29. Published by Universal Limited Art Editions. Yale University Art Gallery, Gift of Craig and Elizabeth Zammiello, 2009.34.2

 Do you know the game Red Rover, Red Rover?

ELISABETH HODERMARSKY: I do. And now, seeing this piece in person, it becomes completely clear why you chose that title.

SM: Well—and in preparation for this conversation—I looked up on the Internet a description of the game. Because when I was making this piece, I was just working off memory. And my memory of it was that it was all about breaking through the linked arms, and that if you broke through the opponents' line, you not only got to return to your team, but you got to take somebody else back with you. And if you don't break through, you join the opponents' line. So in a way I think it's a nice game because it's really not about hitting something, it's more about breaking through a wall of resistance or becoming part of something. Perhaps that's an overly sweet way of describing it, because I suppose it can get rather rough when kids on the playground are actually playing it.

EH: What's so great about finally seeing this print—this *object* really—is that it really does have that sense of the back and forth. So that as one side of the "team"—or, in this case, the scroll—swells, the other depletes.

SM: Yes. And I remember when Craig and I were working, we had single plates and we were adding them and thinking more about the piece in relation to traveling. You know, breaking down the frame of a continuous image in the landscape. And that word over that is repeated again and again across the scroll—over and over and over again. That's the word that it started with, *over*. And then it turned into "Red Rover, Red Rover."

EH: Do you remember when it turned into "Red Rover"?

SM: Late in the process, probably near the end—right, Craig?

CRAIG ZAMMIELLO: Yes, near the end. But we probably have two different memories about the making of this print . . . which is what happens.

SM: I want to hear your memories, Craig.

CZ: Well, I remember that initially this was to be a scroll. It was going to hang as a scroll on a wall. And, as is typical of Suzanne's work, it was word-based. Then Suzanne started to frame it—right, Suzanne?—into certain distinct areas, because of the way Suzanne works off of the chosen word. At some point the scroll was going to be encased in a sort of frame on the wall with knobs that you could turn.

EH: Horizontally or vertically?

CZ: Horizontally, with the knobs on the bottom. And you could scroll through, watch the moving "film" or—my take on it was—that every few days you could turn it to a new section, a new area to look at, in this endless print. And I believe I made the first prototype out of Fome-Cor?

SM: Yes. You made it out of Fome-Cor . . . and we were hell-bent on it being a continuous loop, without beginning or end.

CZ: That's right! I forgot that.

EH: Kind of like . . . what were those nineteenth-century circular rooms called, with the dioramas? Cycloramas?

SM: Yes! And we wanted the enclosure to be a still object but to have the print on a loop. So that, as Craig describes, you could dial it to a certain section one day and then to a new section the next day.

CZ: So we made a Fome-Cor box.

SM: Do you think ULAE [Universal Limited Art Editions] still has that?

CZ: I'm not sure. I doubt it. I think that they have a wooden prototype of it with the knobs outside. But at some point—I don't know if it was you, or Larissa Goldston, maybe?[1] At some point, the box was on a table, and somebody moved it . . . and everything fell into place.

SM: It became a pull toy; we talked about it as a pull toy.

CZ: Yes! With a string on it. And we were thinking you could just pull it around with you and the print would be on a continuous loop.

EH: Well, and with this red enamel coating, it's like an Etch A Sketch too?

SM: Yes. And a drawing made on an Etch A Sketch is something that is constantly disappearing. And that was the other thing. I wanted something that wasn't fixed in time. And that's the concept that the "over and over and over" plays on.

EH: Even your style of drawing in this etching seems to play off of the Etch A Sketch idea.

SM: Yes. And it has a lot of lines through it that have to do with horizon lines appearing and disappearing.

EH: It is just so much fun to play with, such an adventure.

CZ: It's flashy, isn't it? It's a really sharp idea, right? But after you get over the initial fun of it, there's this whole underbelly. Because it's this really incredible work of art. It's a remarkable etching. When we started working together, I had no idea what to do with Suzanne. I had no idea, and you had no idea—right, Suzanne? But we hit it off immediately. And we started with some photographs that Suzanne had taken. We were going to make some photogravures . . .

EH: *Studio Pictures* [1999; *figs. 2–3*], right?

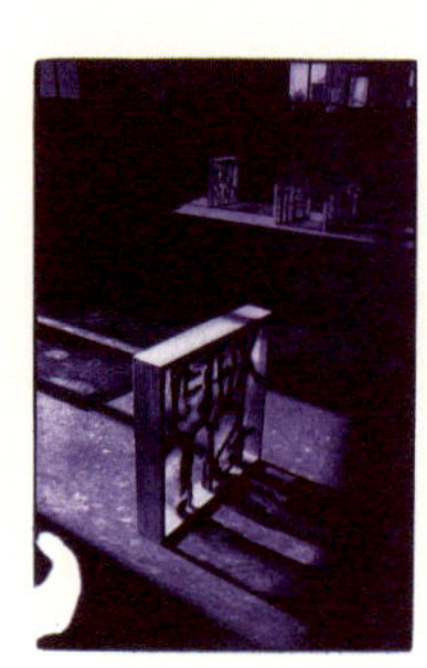 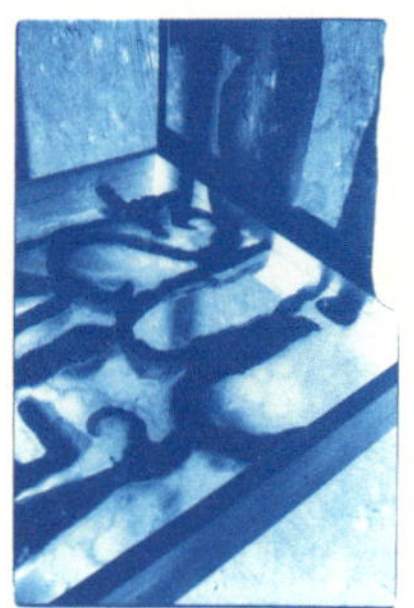

CZ: Yes. Those were photogravures of photographs Suzanne had taken of sculpture in her studio.

SM: Yes. And that was a really simple project. Here's a proof of one. It's not one of the color ones, but I just happen to have this black-and-white proof here.

EH: Oh, my. The ULAE website doesn't do these justice.[2]

SM: They were photographs that I took of sculptures that I was making in my studio, clay sculptures of phrases such as "just relax" and "never mind." They are words carved out of clay rather than drawn on paper. The clay slows down the writing—similar to the etching process, which is much slower than drawing. We made a suite of eight of these, and that was a very quick project—right, Craig?

CZ: Very quick.

SM: The nice thing is that Craig and I sort of established a rhythm. We'd have these very complex projects, like *Red Rover*, and then very quick projects, like *Studio Pictures*, that we did—where it was just about deciding on color, basically, and leaving something alone that was working.

CZ: So this project was like Suzanne putting her toe into the water . . . and then we went from there. Suzanne's a natural, really. Anything I'd give her, she'd try it, immediately get a handle on it, and incorporate it into the work. And she's the type of artist who . . . if something's not working, if she's not enjoying a tool or technique, or if she's not communicating with it, she doesn't use it. She doesn't get frustrated, she just moves on. But if a tool or technique does work, you only have to show her once. And she uses it again and again, and in these really unique, inventive ways.

SM: Wow, that's really nice of you, Craig.

CZ: No, no. I'm not buttering your bread. Just look at this etching.

EH: It is so rich. So in this one print alone [*Red Rover*], there's hard ground, aquatint, roulette work, drypoint?

CZ: Yes. And open bite, spit bite. In fact, Suzanne was one of the people who I feel really employs open bite properly. Look at the letters here. That's all open bite [*fig. 4*].[3]

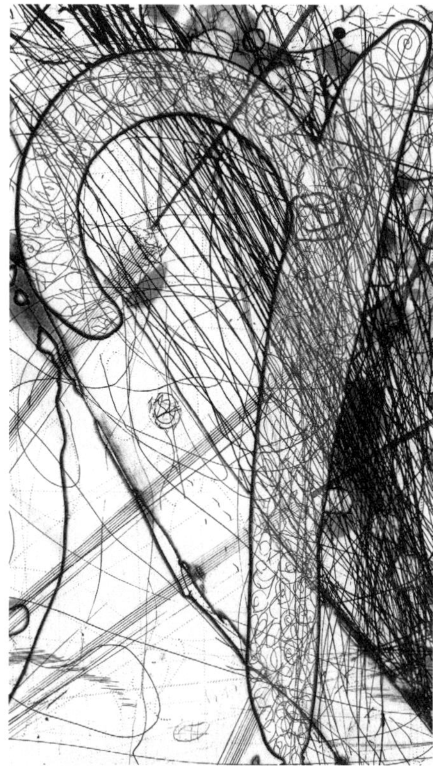

FIG. 4. Detail from *Momentum (Red Rover)* of section of open bite

Suzanne McClelland

SM: I was really into open bite with this print. But I don't think I've used it since you and I worked together. Because you have to know . . . the printer has to know, has to be flexible enough to accept different approaches in one piece. And that's something that Craig loved, but that I've actually subsequently found is a rare thing among printers.

CZ: Look at these particular lines [*fig. 5*]. That's done with an engraving tool, a multiliner. That's a burin that's used to engrave. So Suzanne picks this up, no problem, and uses it to draw right through the ground with it. And she also did that with roulettes.[4] Which, again, people would take roulettes and be very nervous with them. But for Suzanne, they were just another tool. And again, she'd just pick up a roulette and draw right through a hard ground with it and I'd etch it. And that's not a usual application of a roulette, it's usually used as a drypoint tool on an ungrounded plate. And in Suzanne's hands it just becomes part of her arsenal, another way to make a mark.

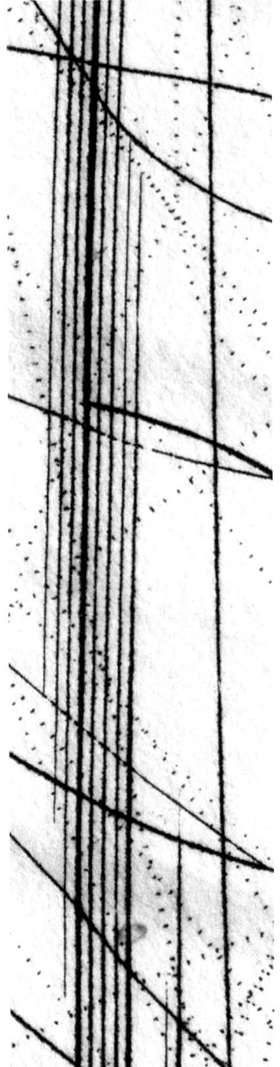

FIG. 5. Detail from *Momentum (Red Rover)* of marks made by a multiliner engraving tool

EH: Is the line of a roulette more subtle when it's etched?

CZ: No, actually it's harsher, more in-your-face. Because roulettes are used to make marks that are meant to look soft, pencil-like. But by doing it this way, through a hard ground, you're actually sharpening the dots [*fig. 6*]. Suzanne would take tools and push and pull them; they would go forwards and backwards. She'd take something and fold it into the work, and then erase it by open biting. But the history would be there.

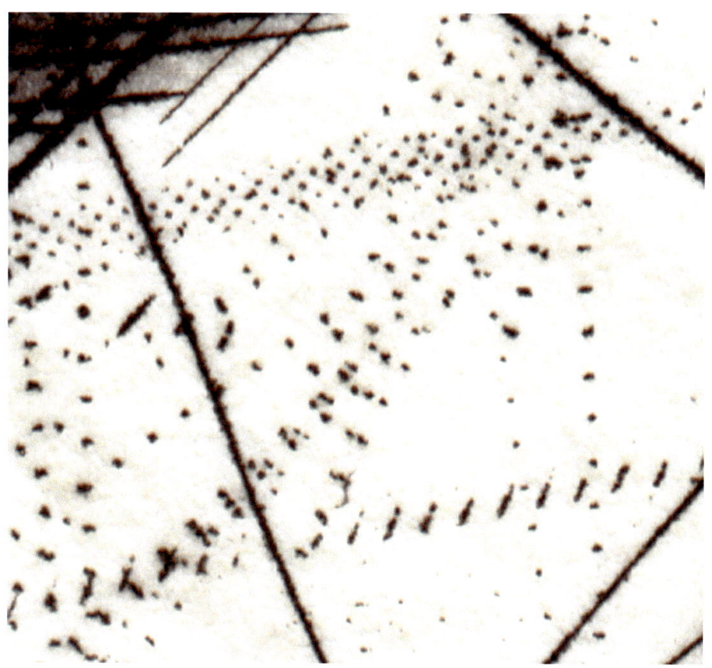

FIG. 6. Detail from *Momentum (Red Rover)* of roulette work

EH: Was this whole scroll printed from one plate?

CZ: From two plates, actually.

SM: Yes, two plates. And then did we cut one to make *Or* [*fig. 7*]?

CZ: Yes, we cut that section out of the larger of the two plates. There was one long plate and then an extension, not two plates of the same size. When the print is laid out flat, you can just barely see where the plates lined up there's a bit of a line. In fact, if we looked, we could find *Or* in this someplace. And then the whole, long print—which was on a Japanese Masa paper—was sewn to silk? Or did they glue it?

SM: I think they glued it.

CZ: So that we could treat it like a scroll.

EH: Like a Chinese handscroll?

SM and CZ: Exactly.

Suzanne McClelland

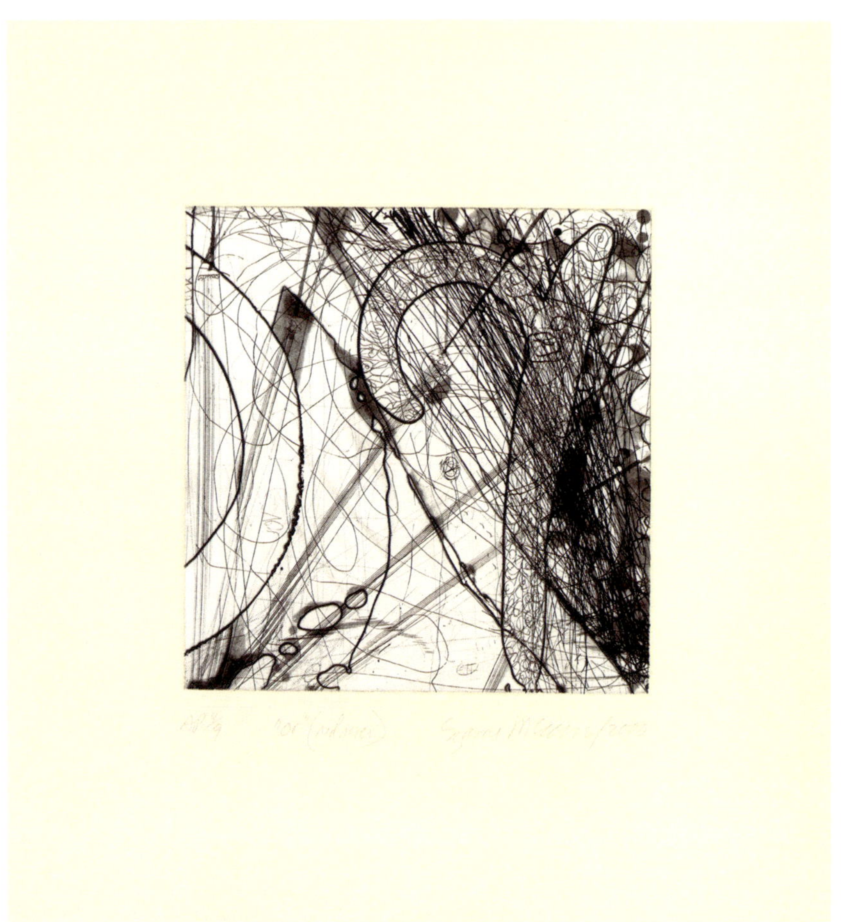

EH: Was that connection also in your mind when you made this?

SM: Well, yes. One of the first things I did as a freshman in college was take a class on the history of Chinese brush painting. And that had a huge effect on how I thought about the relationship between image and language. And also the notion of reading top to bottom versus left to right, and how in a picture, in an abstraction, you can redirect habitual ways of reading. And also the quality of meandering. Meandering, wandering through landscape: it was very related to what I had learned about Chinese painting.

EH: Absolutely. And the continuous meditation on "over over over over" across the print.

SM: And "help help help help" also throughout. I really love the fact that printmaking isn't linear, that you can really play with the backwards and forwards of things because you're working backwards. And the disorientation of that.

This piece was also a way to talk about north-south-east-west, and to allow oneself to explore language, to enjoy the way that language looks as well as what it means. It frustrates direct definition because you think you can find what something is saying, and then it kind of takes itself apart.

EH: But are you supposed to view this strictly from left to right and right to left?

SM: My feeling is that you can view it any direction you want—north to south, east to west, and the reverse—and it has a different effect. And that's why I think the final solution of having it on the table and able to roll in all of these directions was brilliant. And the objectness of it. It was really becoming an object.

EH: And since there are no marks on the box, there is no way to orient oneself. And the image itself is relatively abstract . . .

SM: Yes. It keeps it really in the realm of abstraction. Craig, you were the one to take it to the table, because we couldn't get the loop going on the wall, right?

CZ: I don't know! To tell you the truth, I don't know.

SM: And we titled it *Momentum* at the very beginning of the print, and *Red Rover* on the other end. Because it was still, you know, that idea of gathering energy. Of relating movement. And to do that by alluding to the way in which we read back and forth, the speed with which we perceive language and images in one direction or another. This print [*Momentum (Red Rover)*] actually took a long time to make—right, Craig?

CZ: Yes. It was published in 2000, but we were working on it in 1998.

SM: I think we might have even been working on it in 1997, simultaneously with other projects. I think we might have started *Mr. Man* [2001] in the middle of working on this, and that was a relatively quick print.[5]

CZ: Yes. Artist-intensive, but rather quick. Suzanne is the sort of artist who works so passionately, and sometimes she will just go with a project, and other times with, like, *Mammamay i* [2003], it takes a long time; it is work.

SM: Yeah, we really went through some hell with that one.

CZ: It was one of those things you didn't want to let go of, Suzanne, and at the same time I knew that you *really wanted* to let go of it. It was so close. And I don't know what happened, but at some point you came in and put a bow on it or something, and whoa!

SM: Well, there was a stuckness about that print. Sometimes, when working with such simple symmetries, a work just gets stuck. There was a heaviness to that print. I started with the phrase "wow mom" mirrored, and there was just a heaviness, a stuckness to it. It had energy to it, but it just wasn't . . . light enough or something.

Suzanne McClelland

CZ: Whatever it was, it ended up being one of those situations in which an artist puts something down for a while, and then revisits it, and then bang, some little thing just makes it click. And I remember you cut some paper into a ribbon, put it on the print, and it was just this immediate revelation. Boom, done.

SM: Well, I turned it into a game again, which is a strategy that I use a lot in my work. This time it was Pin the Tail on the Donkey. It was a surface that asked for attachments.

[*pause*]

EH: So, *Momentum (Red Rover)* was the second etching project you did, the first being *Studio Pictures*?

SM: Well, and there was an etching called *Zig Zag* [1998; *fig. 8*] that I had made the year before that.

FIG. 8. Suzanne McClelland, *Zig Zag*, 1998. Etching in five colors on Arches En-Tout-Cas paper, 28 5/16 × 31 3/4 in. (71.9 × 80.7 cm). Edition of 25. Published by Universal Limited Art Editions

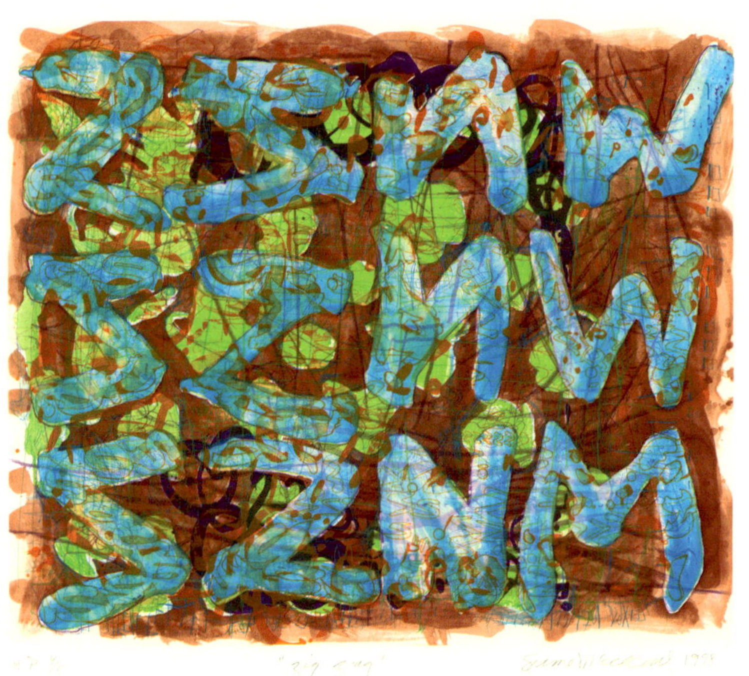

CZ: *Zig Zag*! That was monumental. It's one of my favorite prints. And *Zig Zag* was multicolored. When you see *Zig Zag*, you have to see it in person. It's so extraordinary the way Suzanne immediately grasped the language of open biting, of bringing things backward and forward with open bites, and with color.

Generally what happens with printmaking is that artists tend to block things up, and they get loaded down. Suzanne was able to open things up and create spatial relationships between the colors, which was so advanced for an artist's first major etching. It was crazy. Suzanne was so committed to her marks and erasures. I don't know, I miss your etchings so much, Suzanne. I could ramble on and on for hours about them.

> SM: I miss them too. Because I don't make etchings anymore!

EH: You started at ULAE by making lithographs, correct?

> SM: I made one lithograph, *Then*, in 1993, from a newspaper article. And then *Tea Leaves* [1996] was lithography and silkscreen.

CZ: Oh, I remember *Tea Leaves*. It's gigantic!

> SM: Seven by nine feet.

CZ: Yes! This is so big, you have no idea, Lisa.

> SM: It's from a *New York Times* article. The reason I chose the piece is that there were a couple of articles about categorizing people according to whether they were "now" people or "then" people. So it had to do with time. And then I did a whole exhibition of paintings based on that print. Because I often got my ideas for painting out of the process of making prints.

EH: You did?

> SM: Yes. I still do.

CZ: That's interesting. We're finding as we go along how people relate their work in paint to their work in print.

> SM: For me, I find that the prints are a very important source. Because you have to open up—or *I* have to open up my process—in terms of working with materials that are unfamiliar. And people who are unfamiliar. And I have to expose certain things. I find that it can be a little bit embarrassing at times . . .

EH: Were you uncomfortable working around other people? Were you used to it?

> SM: It depends on the person. And no, I wasn't used to it. I had been painting on my own for years, and anything I did with or around other people were collaborative projects—socially driven projects through people I knew at the Storefront for Art and Architecture. But I had started as a photographer. And as a photographer you're often—not always, but often—interacting with other people more than abstract painters do.

Suzanne McClelland

So, with painting, I have tended to snag language from the world. I take that back to my private studio and work to reconfigure it. But with prints, I just felt that I could move faster, and in a more open way, by changing form. Not relying on habit, on habitual ways of moving physically. I just thought it was an adventure in materials. And making my first lithograph was painful because—just as Craig was describing—people new to lithography just tend to pile things on. I just wanted to pile things onto the stone. And I didn't know when to stop, because I didn't know what the result of each layer would be. I wanted to pull proofs constantly just to see what was happening.

CZ: Well, sure, that's normal.

SM: And I think, actually, *Then*, which was my first print, is the densest print I've ever made. But once I moved to etching . . . I felt that I had a much closer relationship to the materials of etching than I did to the materials of lithography.

EH: Is that why you decided to experiment with etching?

SM: I think, when I was there at ULAE, I just wanted to start working with the acid, the incising tools . . . and then, I also wanted to work with Craig! Because he was adventurous and seemed to understand "the absurd." I found his energy at those traditional ULAE lunches to be relaxing.

CZ: Well, Bill Goldston always had a good gut response to artists' work. And he saw Suzanne's work, and invited her to ULAE.[6] Then, after working with Suzanne for a while, Bill said to me, "I think it would be great if Suzanne worked on some etchings." And I said, "Great," because I liked Suzanne's work from when I first saw it at the Whitney Biennial.

EH: Which was 1993?

SM: Yes, 1993. And that was when I first started to work at ULAE.

[*pause*]

EH: Why did you decide to pluck this one piece, *Or*, off?

SM: Because I really like the idea of a frozen frame. Ultimately, I love the resistance inherent to a still object, a still thing. And *Red Rover* was about as far as I could go without making a film—going as far as I could with it being an object—and have it move and shift and have possibilities, and then bring it back to having one freeze-frame.

EH: And that brings me back to thinking about the issues of delay, of real time, in your work. Because your work is very much based on language and that sort of delay from when a word or phrase begins to be spoken, or read, and when it ends.

SM: Yes. There are some theories about the origins of written language and its relationship to animal tracks in the earth . . . the notion of leaving behind a trail. Often thought moves faster through speech than through writing. And in human development we learn how to speak before we learn how to write; in fact, we often learn how to draw before we learn how to write. So there's this strange gap between speech and writing. And in many of the Chinese cultures, there's a much tighter acknowledgment of that gap, and words are images in the Chinese language. I found that lack of separation to be helpful. I am not a scholar of history, but Chinese painting was an eye-opener to me when I first saw the collection in the Cleveland Museum of Art as a child. And so I think that part of this exposure is present, in fact, in *Red Rover*.

EH: And what's so interesting is how printmaking plays into that whole idea, because there is, yet again, that inherent delay between the making of the mark on a plate and the printing of the image.

SM: Yes. And I often start many paintings with an impression from another canvas—to get further away from the direct image and to step back from it in a way. So I just feel like the impression or imprint is a basic part of my picture making . . . maybe it comes from spending so much time in the darkroom.

I continue to make prints. But the work that I did with Craig was, I think, particularly exciting because we had an understanding about what each one of us was doing in the process, which was great. And I've had many great experiences making prints, but this one was truly adventurous, because we had the sustained time to develop a dialogue. I never knew *what* Craig would offer, but I knew it would be engaging.

CZ: [*laughs*] Yes it was.

EH: And this work is incredibly unique and fun . . . and an interesting extension of your work.

CZ: And it was a real evolution. We can't leave Frank out of this, the person who made these boxes: Frank D'Agostino, who's so pissed at me right now.

SM: Why?

CZ: Because he has to make another one![7]

EH: He made these boxes? *Hand-made* these boxes?

CZ: Oh, yes. Not only did he make these, he designed the whole system to permit it to work. The main thing that had to be addressed was the problem of keeping the print from rubbing against the inner edge of the box as it rolls, and yet keeping it in a relatively tight spool. And Frank designed and made the entire thing by hand . . . the box, the rubber wheels, the dowels . . .

EH: No wonder he's mad at you!

CZ: But it was a real progression, how this came to be. It's a separate cover that goes onto a frame . . .

SM: And it was really hard to get the color right, remember? He would bring the boxes in whenever I was at the shop, and we would test the wheels and springs in our attempts to design a complete loop . . . beautiful engineering. He is a perfectionist even when he is mad!

CZ: Really difficult. That's a red lacquer with a clear coat. Very durable.

EH: It looks like plastic. I thought it was plastic.

CZ: Yeah, it looks like plastic but it's not. And you can get your fingers all over it but wipe it right down, because of the clear coat.

SM: It took a long time for Frank to make each one of these boxes.

CZ: Right. The scrolls were printed fairly quickly, but the boxes took a while to produce. And there still exist some copies of these that remain unrolled, flat [*fig. 9*]. And that reminds me of what we did with Kiki [Smith] with the periphery camera at the British Museum (see chapter 1), where you take something like this that's on a cylinder and flatten it out so that you can see the design, to see your writing.

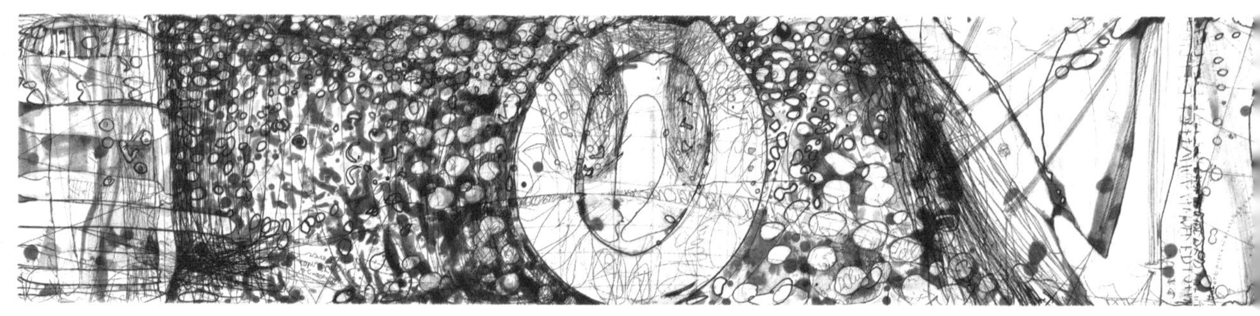

FIG. 9. Suzanne McClelland, *Momentum (Red Rover)* (full scroll), 2000. Intaglio scroll on Japanese Masa paper housed in a red lacquer box, paper 8¾ × 90 in. (22.2 × 228.6 cm). Edition of 29. Published by Universal Limited Art Editions

SM: When I was making this piece, I considered the impossibility of clearly seeing things that one knows too well. We may have an entire image stored in our brain. What we are actually looking at may only be a small piece of it. The eye completes the image. It's rare to really see what is actually *there* in front of you. There is often the *name* of the thing you see, which informs "seeing."

EH: You mean, seeing is so subjective?

SM: Yes, and also so interlaced with what you are imagining is beyond it, or what you *want* to see. I'm especially pleased with the handmade-ness of this piece, and the fact that it requires your hands to move it around. And sometimes it gets stuck, so you have to coax it, play with it, like a pull toy. Didn't we at one point actually put a rope on it, Craig?

CZ: Oh yes, we put a rope on it and pulled it, like a little wagon, on the ground.

SM: But we couldn't figure out the continuous loop, how to make that work.

CZ: That was the hang-up.

SM: And Frank was not happy, not happy with us at all.

[laughter]

SM: He didn't know how to deal with us and all our antics surrounding this project. But that didn't stop him from coming up with solutions—and pretty solutions.

CZ: Well, it was kind of a sport for us at ULAE: how to push Frank's buttons, which were many and varied. And he is a goodhearted, wonderful person and an incredible craftsman. A cabinetmaker by trade, in the old-school sense, thrust into the art world . . .

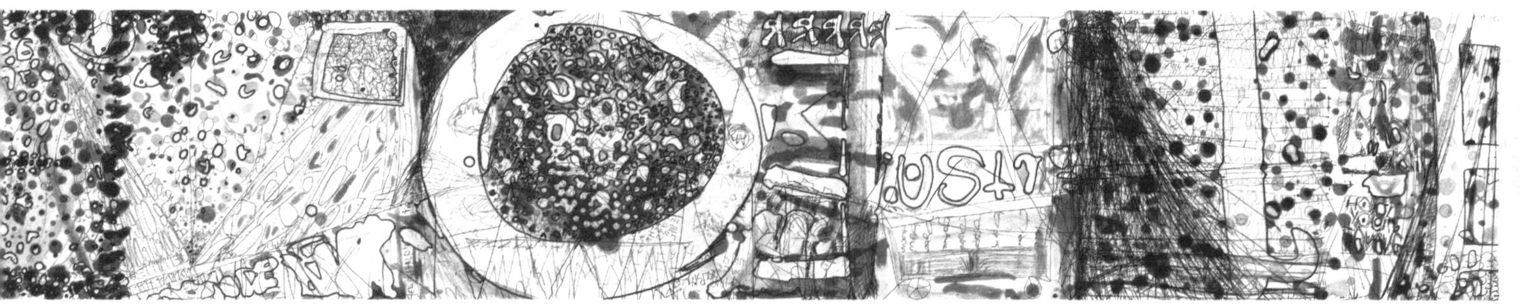

Suzanne McClelland

SM: . . . to do ridiculous things.

EH: And probably wondering what happened to his life . . .

[laughter]

CZ: But it's the ultimate collaboration, when you think about it. And he's still at ULAE and still making amazing things like this box.

SM: At ULAE you could really make things happen because there were all kinds of very capable people with specialized areas of expertise, solving problems.

EH: I've heard this from a lot of artists. The extraordinary sense of freedom that so many artists have felt working there.

CZ: The impetus was always to enable the artist to fulfill an idea . . . whatever road that idea took them down.

SM: Now I'm primarily concentrating on my painting, but I feel so lucky to have had all those years there with Bill [Goldston] and Craig and Doug Volle, and Lorena [Salcedo-Watson], and later Phil [Saunders] and Vanessa [Viola]. That's where I met Elizabeth Murray, you know. I met her at a picnic . . . it might have been the twenty-fifth-anniversary picnic in the early nineties. She is an important artist to me in so many ways.

EH: Elizabeth Murray made an enormous amount of prints at ULAE throughout the nineties. She must have been there all the time.

CZ: We so much wanted to include Elizabeth in this book, but she passed before we could meet with her.

SM: This book, this is kind of the story of your professional life, right, Craig?

CZ: It's not my story . . . it's *our* story, it's the story of collaborations, of interactions with many artists.

EH: Yes, it's more of a dialogue than a monologue, really.

SM: You see, that's what you do so well, Craig. You understand the evolution of things, and you guide the artist through the process. And that's why I say that it was an adventure to make this with you. And each print I made with you was a series of experiments . . . we observed the results and sometimes they took us closer to a "goal," but just as often the experiments opened up new territory. It's funny, because you wouldn't directly advise. It wasn't even as if you were making suggestions. It was more as if you had ideas in response to what you were looking at. So it was really fascinating, because you had your own eye, an artist's eye, and you had solutions that came from your expertise in your medium.

So, it was a very interesting thing. I would come in, and there were times that I would have a very clear idea of what I was going to do. And I would say, "This is what I've got to do to get this down." And we'd do that. And we'd look together. You would give it time, I would give it time, and then we would try some alternative procedures. And there would some-times be a radical shift in the way a print progressed based on looking at it for a couple of hours. Taking something out, putting certain plates away, recognizing what was not contributing to this image.

And that was what was interesting about the *Or* print. There was a way that having the *O*, the *V*, and the *E* of *Rover* completely disappear, and then having the other *O* function as a double form . . . It was only in this one spot that it actually worked. And it took a while, that process. It wasn't as though you were rushing me to do anything. We would take a break, and I would go to work on another print, and then let that sit.

CZ: And the prints would always find their way into being. And now Lisa's learned, through all these conversations, that when the printer and artist have worked together for some time, they sometimes get to the point where it's almost a telepathic thing, as if they may be in two separate cars but are both driving down the same road.

SM: And there is nothing like that . . . except, perhaps, playing music.

CZ: That's right.

SM: Because in the music studio, you get in this zone where you're playing together. You're not performing; you're just playing with the other person. You know each other that well. I'm not a musician, but my sister is, and my oldest friend, and my husband. And I can see that that is what happens when they play with another person or people. Even when the music is off, you know? When one person is stuck, or can't do something, the other per-son compensates for a time. In the end, everyone gets what they want.

CZ: Success. Yes. That's a very good analogy.

SM: And Drew [Vogelman, McClelland's husband] and I have talked about this. Running a print shop is very much like running a recording studio.

And because Craig plays music, I think he understands this comparison. You have a line, a bass line running through and alongside the drums, and they can come out in front of the melody sometimes, even though the guitar and voice are often expected to be running the show in rock and roll.

Maybe printmaking is more like jazz jamming in my thinking because my painting studio was separate from my home in the ULAE days. The prints that I made at ULAE were the one and only thing that I would bring home. I lived in a tiny little apartment, and I'd bring proofs home and tack them up in my bedroom, and when I woke up Drew and I would look at them and talk. Printmaking was a huge part of my private life during those years. And that's why I still have a room—this room that we're sitting in—devoted to just my prints and works on paper.

CZ: And much like music, just as there are certain musicians I just can't communicate with musically, there are artists with whom I've worked that I just can't click with. That happens. It's rare, but it happens.

EH: And you must feel that too, Suzanne, conversely. That there are certain printers with whom you have had difficulty working.

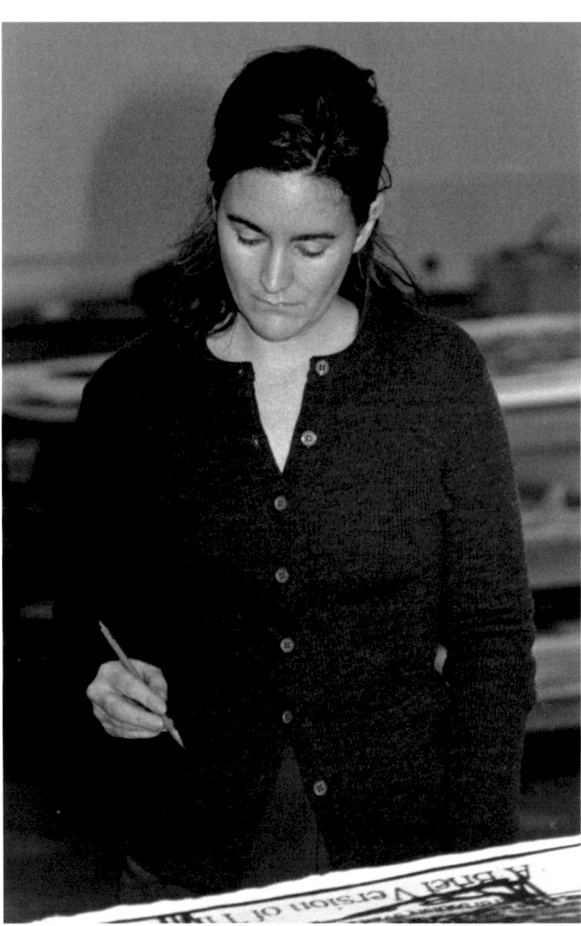

FIG. 10. McClelland signing the edition of *Tea Leaves*, 1996

SM: Well, yes, and it's a wildly different situation each time, working with a printer. And it's really like playing with somebody. You have to be able to be very open. But, you know, some people make images of their paintings.

EH: Which is completely not what you do.

SM: No. I just love the way that a final print is just not what you initially thought it was going to be.

CZ: And to me, that's what making a print is all about. That's the collaboration.

EH: And for me, this piece [*Momentum (Red Rover)*] is such a surprise—every time you move it, every direction you move it in.

SM: It's a funny object, isn't it?

EH: It's a creature. It's like an animal.

CZ: And I'm so thrilled that it's going to be in the Yale [University Art Gallery] collection, that incredible collection.

SM: Me too!

EH: Well, and me three! Yale is so honored; it's such a great gift that Craig is giving us. I just love the side to side, and the connection back to the Red Rover game. Red Rover, Red Rover.

Notes

The preceding conversation was held on October 27, 2008, at McClelland's studio, in Brooklyn, New York.

1. Larissa Goldston is the daughter of Bill Goldston, with whom she serves as co-director of ULAE. She is also the director and owner of the Larissa Goldston Gallery, in New York.

2. Images of all of the Studio Pictures prints, as well as all other prints discussed but not illustrated in this chapter, are available on the ULAE website, http://www.ulae.com/ (accessed September 26, 2011).

3. Zammiello has commented that McClelland "always showed a willingness and curiosity to make nonconformist marks on plates," and that she was "eager to try different tools and methods, not always in the way that they were intended to be used." He feels her signature method of mark-making in her etchings was her "use of free-flowing open bites." (Zammiello, unpublished description of *Momentum (Red Rover)*, 2008; copy on file with Hodermarsky.) Sugar lift applied by brush was McClelland's preferred method for achieving these open bites. Sometimes she would also use solvent-lift ground to open an area of hard ground that had already been applied to the plate.

4. Traditionally, roulettes are used in a drypoint method, in which they are applied directly on the raw metal plate surface and not through a ground. They leave behind a "burr" by actually pushing the metal aside, yielding a soft, pencil-like shading. By using them through a hard ground and etching them, McClelland wound up with a much more focused pattern that is sharp and clear. Because the plate is being incised with acid, no burr is formed, as would have been the case had she used a drypoint needle.

5. The title of *Mr. Man* was inspired by the film version of Stephen King's *Misery* (1990), in which Kathy Bates's character angrily calls James Caan's character by this name.

6. In addition to her work at ULAE, McClelland has made a suite of three etchings (*Could*, *Would*, and *Should*) with Jennifer Melby, which were published by Diane Villani in 2001. More recently, in 2006 she made a series of monotypes with Kathy Caraccio in Caraccio's Manhattan printmaking studio, K. Caraccio Printing Studio.

7. Zammiello is referring to the new box for his printer's proof, which he gifted to the Yale University Art Gallery in 2009 (inv. no. 2009.34.2).

Suzanne McClelland

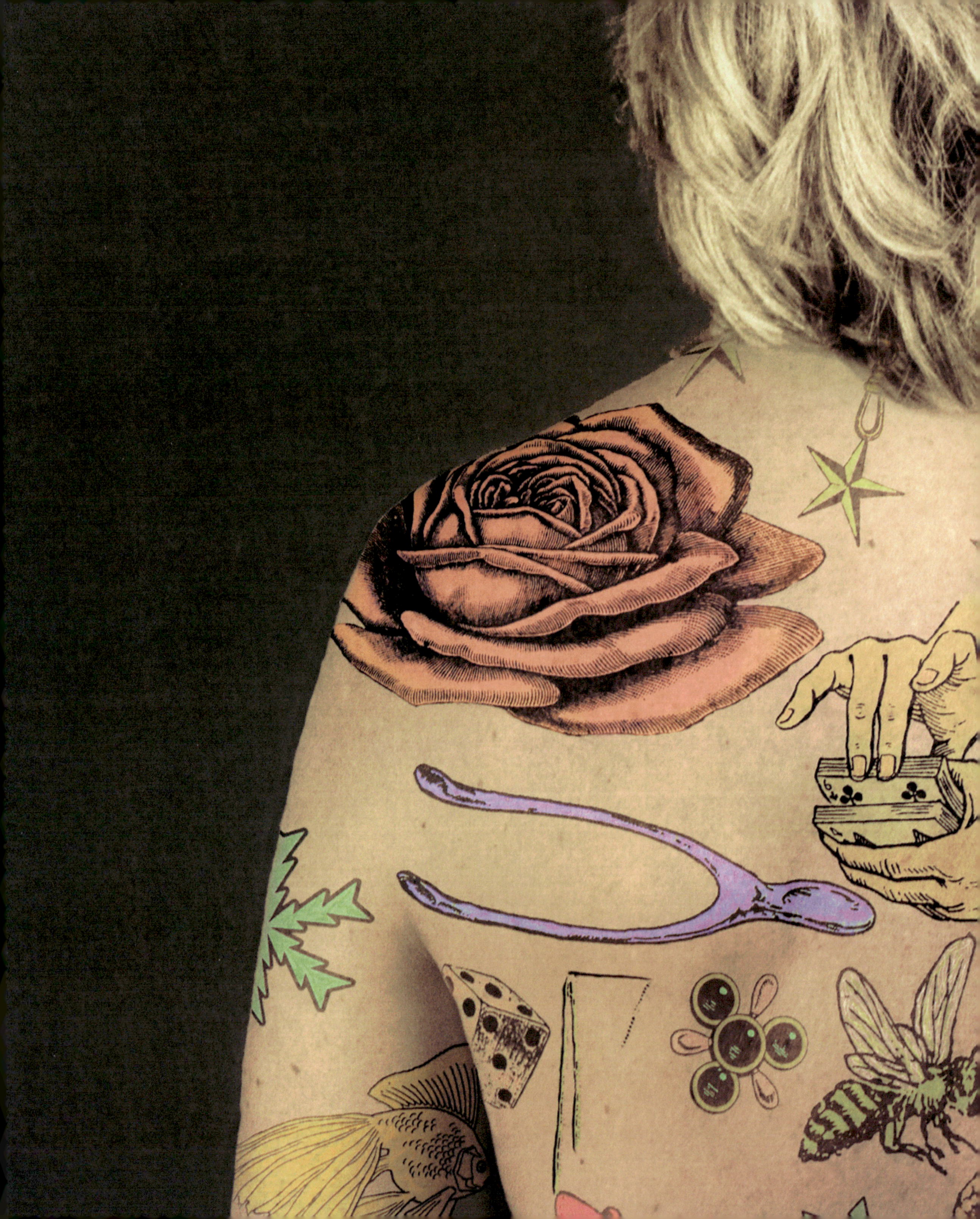

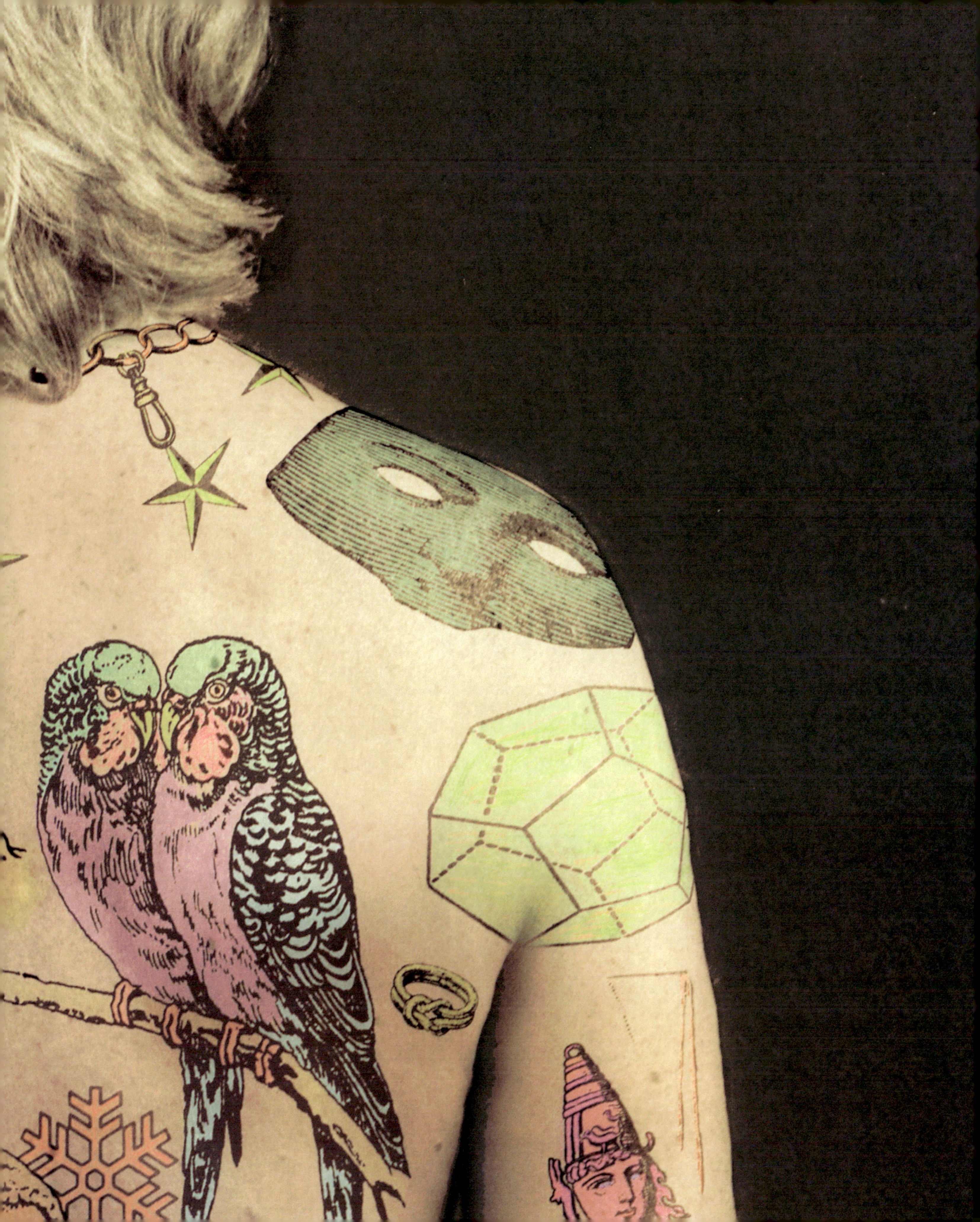

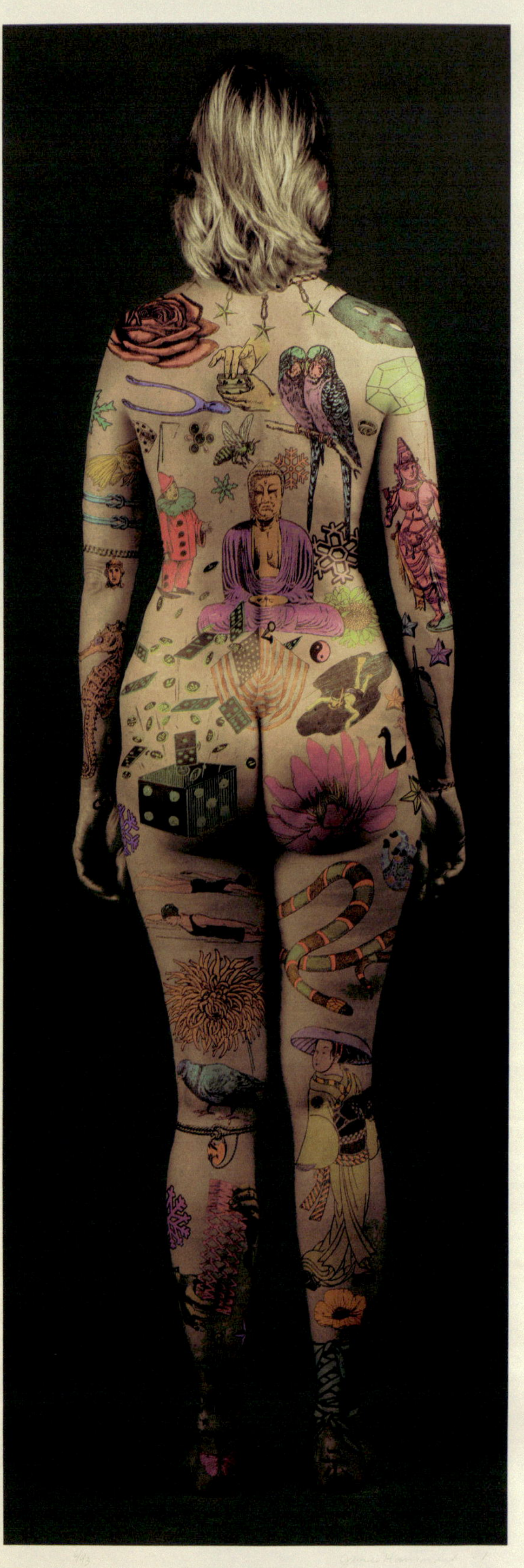

Jane Hammond
Tabula Rosa, 2001

Measuring 74 by 29 ½ inches, Jane Hammond's *Tabula Rosa* (fig. 1)—an imposing life-sized[1] self-portrait in print—is at once shockingly public and startlingly intimate. Though the artist sometimes inserts her likeness into her work, this piece was groundbreaking in its ambitious, and unvarnished, nude image of her (now middle-aged) self.[2] Hammond has credited her sound working relationship with Craig Zammiello—which encouraged mutual trust and respect—with helping her to overcome her initial trepidation about the project.[3]

For Hammond, *Tabula Rosa* was also unusual because it wasn't "physically collaged," as are many of her prints. As she has described it, it was a "collage in cyberspace." This presented a challenge for the artist, given her signature aesthetic, which she has described as a "more is more" sensibility that does not typically embrace the uniform surface.[4]

Though Zammiello had worked tangentially on other prints Hammond produced at Universal Limited Art Editions (ULAE) throughout the 1990s, this is the first true collaboration, from inception to completion, between printer and artist. *Tabula Rosa* is also the first all-digital print either had produced—and, indeed, the first all-digital print to be created and editioned at ULAE.[5] The print was a labor of love for Zammiello and Hammond, as well as the other printers involved in its making.[6] It was one of the most time-consuming prints either Hammond or Zammiello had yet worked on—a project that ultimately took a year and a half and was completed just in time for inclusion in the groundbreaking exhibition mounted at the Brooklyn Museum in the summer of 2001, *Digital: Printmaking Now.*[7]

Tabula Rosa began with the idea of creating an X-ray image of Hammond that was life-sized, covered with tattoos from Hammond's lexicon of imagery, and had a look and feel similar to Victorian Röntgen X-rays.[8] Yet, as the following conversation reveals, what began as a plan to produce a life-sized X-ray eventually morphed into an external self-portrait, as Hammond decided—quite far into the production—to abandon the X-ray idea. Skin/substance (Jane's flesh) eventually won out over translucence (bone), topography over archaeology.

FIG. 1. Jane Hammond, *Tabula Rosa*, 2001. Pigmented digital inkjet print on handmade Japanese paper, 75 × 32 in. (190.5 × 81.3 cm). Edition of 43. Published by Universal Limited Art Editions. Yale University Art Gallery, Gift of Craig and Elizabeth Zammiello, 2008.26.1

Looking closely at this print today, one may glimpse slight imperfections in its trompe l'oeil-ness—and yet, in 2001, it was a remarkably ambitious printmaking venture, and thus marks a crucial moment in time, at the cusp of the twenty-first century, when artists and printers were engaging new technologies in the fledgling years of the digital printmaking age.

———

JANE HAMMOND: I began to make prints quite by accident in the late eighties when I was given a grant to make a print at the Maryland Institute, where I taught. I had thought prior to that that I was not interested in printmaking because what I knew about printmaking was that it was this kind of process of faux drawing, a "how can I make this drawing into a print?" And that never really seemed interesting to me. However, in those years I was really formulating the way that I work, which is with found information—and I was constantly in the library collecting information. And all the information that I was collecting, albeit from a great variety of sources, was *printed* information. So, on another level, one day it kind of clicked in my mind that I actually really like printed things. I actually really like processes of reproduction. I see this as marrying very well with the world as it is now.

And then my interest in printmaking just kind of exploded, and somehow through a series of friends I got hooked up to Bill Goldston, who—I've told this story many times—came to my studio and saw all these prints I was making at Maryland. (I had kind of fallen in love with printmaking and I had learned that I could borrow Maryland's print shop between regular school and summer school for three weeks.) So when Bill invited me to come to make a print at ULAE, I told him I didn't need him because I had this print shop in Baltimore, Maryland, that I could use! So it was sort of a funny moment, because I had no idea what I would have been missing.

But anyhow, I met Bill and started making prints at ULAE—and made prints only at ULAE for quite a number of years. And they were almost always combinations of processes, because I like a kind of mix-y surface. So they were often, for example, silkscreen with some litho, or litho with some etching—you know, a mix. This [*pointing to* Tabula Rosa] is not only the first digital print but the first print done all in one medium.

ELISABETH HODERMARSKY: And Craig, when did you meet Jane?

CRAIG ZAMMIELLO: When she first came to ULAE. We actually worked the first time on *Full House* [1993].[9]

JH: *Full House* was a combo print. It was silkscreen, etching, and offset [lithography]. And it had collage in it. *Tabula Rosa* is an unusual print for me in the sense that it's not physically collaged. Because many of them are, you know, in the same way that those three necklaces are cut out [*pointing to her print* Spells and Incantations *(2007)*].[10] They're separate three-dimensional objects that sit on that neck. But what this is [*pointing again to* Tabula Rosa], is a collage in cyberspace.

CZ: And that's what we had to figure out, how to do that.

JH: One thing you should know as background is that I lived in my other loft for many years, and I was poor and working all these jobs. And at one point I had so many jobs I thought, "Well, what's the point of having this loft if I don't have time to make art in it?" So I cooked up this scam of how I was going to make more money but not work any more jobs, so I rented my loft out to a tattoo artist, and she was tattooing people while I was teaching in Baltimore. She kind of moved into my life, so the long and short of it is that I have seen lots of tattooing, and some people were even getting full-body tattoos on my kitchen counter. So, of course, this experience is part of the genesis of the idea for *Tabula Rosa*.

And at some point in time somebody showed me Adobe Photoshop. I do not actually remember who it was or when it was. But I remember saying, "Can you bend that?" And I was thinking of how you can blow up a balloon that has a rose printed on it, and then the rose becomes spherical as the balloon becomes inflated. That's what I had in my mind as I was asking the person the question, and they were basically saying, "Yes, you can contour it in a number of different ways." And then this idea came into my mind, pretty much full-blown. No pun intended.

EH: But from its inception, did you know that *Tabula Rosa* was going to be fully digital, or how it was going to be produced?

JH: I thought, in the beginning—this is my recollection—that it was going to be a series of black drawings, sort of like a coloring book, and then I was going to hand-color them, or color them in a traditional printmaking medium. I didn't think I was going to make the whole print in the computer, but I did understand that the black drawings would be contoured in Photoshop.

CZ: My recollection is that you also were going to start with an image that would kind of mimic a skeleton on a full scale . . .

JH: Yes, that's right. That's exactly right.

CZ: And I remember you saying you wanted this whole Röntgen look to it, like the Victorian X-rays, which have the sort of look of a dry cleaner's bag—you know, inflated, with this skeleton inside . . .

JH: And to make the skin almost invisible.

CZ: Exactly. And then to have the tattoos on it.

JH: Yes. That's right.

CZ: And at that time we didn't know which way we were going to do it. Originally I had thought to use traditional, silver-based film to make the portrait and then have the negative scanned to obtain a digital file. But there was a piece of equipment—a Phase One FX digital-scanning back—at ULAE that we had been using for a year or so to photograph our prints for archiving and reproductive purposes.[11] The Phase One FX replaced the film back on a standard-view camera with a scanning CCD [charge-coupled device] that was tethered directly to a G4 Macintosh computer to power and operate it. When the capture icon is clicked from the dedicated software, the CCD slowly moves across the film plane, recording the image transmitted by the lens. So the photography of Jane was actually done on this scanning camera, which meant that she had to hold still . . .

JH: I had to take my clothes off in front of all these people . . .

CZ: She had to take her clothes off in front of *two professionals*. But she had to stand still for three minutes while this thing scanned—since any movement or shock to the equipment, such as slamming a door in the studio, would get recorded in the photo as an artifact in the image, a sort of wiggle—and Jane did great. We took, I think, four shots with the scanning back. And then a minimal amount of work had to be done to the digital file, because just the act of breathing would give you these vibrations and things like that. So this [*gesturing to an image on his laptop*] actually is the actual photo of your body in three separate pieces.

JH: I know about the problem we had with the head. But I didn't realize that about the body.

CZ: Yes. That's a separate head shot. But then we also collaged in—from your shoulders down to about right around the beginning of your hips—a Photoshopped version of your torso. Because that was the main problem, the breathing. It wasn't as evident on the surface of your skin as it was along the edges of your body, such as the sides of the torso. And then your moving hair— that just couldn't be fixed digitally [*fig. 2*]. Do you remember our attempts . . . ?

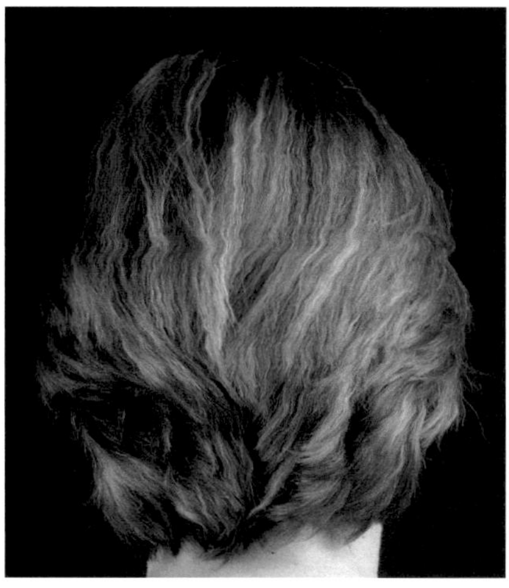

JH: Oh, yes. At one point Bill and I ran around to these beauty shops, and we bought a wig that you photographed me in, and it looked totally stupid. And eventually I think what happened was we took a still photograph of my head and collaged it on there.

CZ: And the next thing we did—

JH: Then you procured a real skeleton.

CZ: I procured a skeleton. I borrowed an articulated full-size replica from the natural science dealer Maxilla and Mandible in New York City. In the studio we positioned the skeleton to relate as closely as possible to the scan of Jane. Photographing the skeleton was much simpler because it was static. And in order to mimic the look of a Victorian-era X-ray, we shot the skeleton from the front and back [*fig. 3*] and then in Photoshop changed them from positive to negative images. This was so that, when digitally layered with reduced opacity, we could simulate the impression of looking through different bone densities [*fig. 4*]. You see the front, the eyes, the teeth, and everything. The ribs.

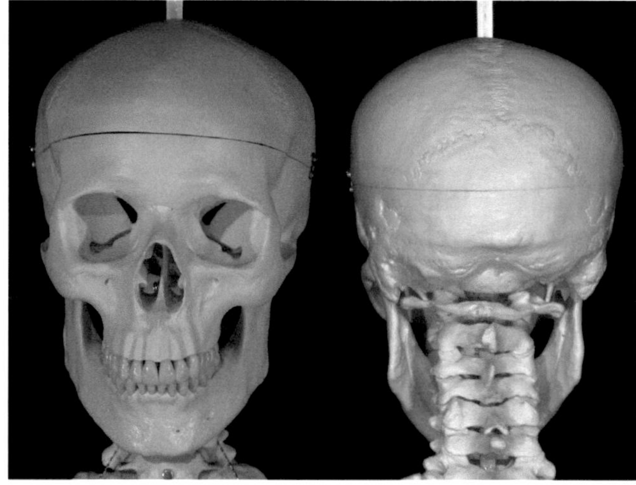

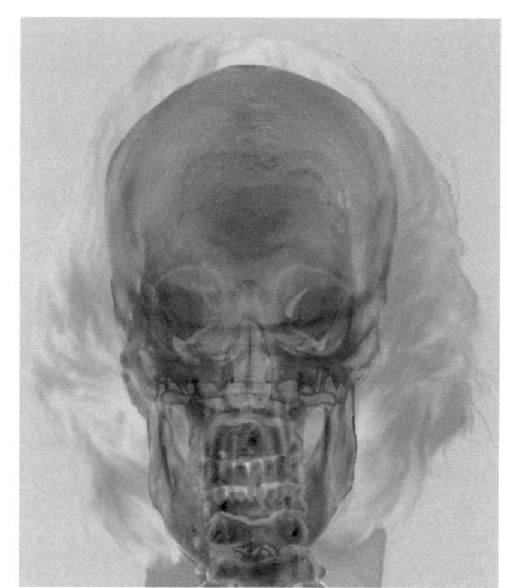

FIG. 3. Photographs of the front and back of the skull of the articulated skeleton

FIG. 4. Photographs of the front and back of the skull (fig. 3) digitally layered over the image of Hammond's hair (fig. 2)

Jane Hammond

JH: And, so it could plausibly be the skeleton inside that body, it required that you completely deconstruct it and reassemble it in Photoshop.

CZ: Exactly. Bone by bone we had to take it apart in Photoshop—me and another printer, Brian Berry. Brian did almost all of the skeletal work, especially the hard parts, which were the hands, that have, you know, so many bones [*fig. 5*].[12] I did the easy things.

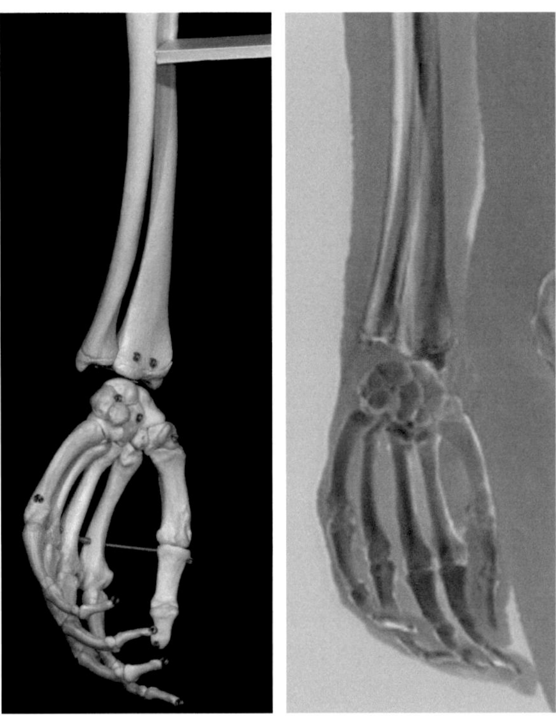

FIG. 5. *Left:* photograph of the skeleton hand; *right:* digital manipulation of the skeleton hand to conform to the scan of Hammond's hand

JH: There is one proof somewhere.

CZ: We have a proof of it and I also have the digital files. You can see it being built.
Now the other thing, Jane, that I remember was in using Photoshop—the Photoshop engine for bending things wasn't powerful enough for us to do the application of the tattoos.

JH: Yes, we got this Andromeda thing—

CZ: Yes, we bought a separate plug-in filter, a third-party filter for Photoshop called Andromeda, that was made just for wrapping things around forms. It was wonderful because you built a matrix first—which was, you know, a cylinder for her legs, a ball for her shoulder—then you would size it, and then digitally apply the tattoo image on top of it.[13]

JH: You would have to conceptualize the individual contouring problem; like let's say on the calf, you would say, "Okay, this is almost like a cylinder." On the shoulder you might say, "Oh, this is a little bit like a sphere, or it's a cylinder over here and a plane over here." And then you'd kind of have this shape, similar to a wire frame, that you would fit your image to and bend it around.

CZ: And any matter of distortion and positioning was possible, and the results were quite amazing. The one I particularly remember was how seamless a tattoo was able to be applied on Jane's elbow after we perfected the basic techniques [*fig. 6*]. A layer consisting of a tattoo image would be placed over the original photo of Jane, which had become the "background," so to speak. We would then manipulate the particular tattoo-image layer with the Andromeda filter to fit for shape and contour. The key to making the tattoo look real was adjusting the "fill" mode of the layer to about 60 percent and leaving the actual "opacity" mode at 100 percent.[14] Then, by using a layer-blending mode known as "color burn," we were able to increase the contrast just in the shadows of the layer.

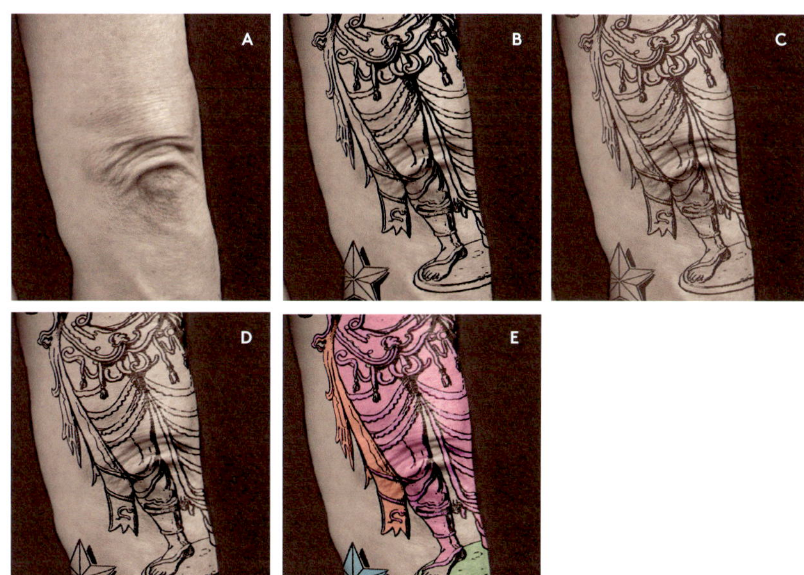

FIG. 6. A: Photograph of Hammond's elbow. B: Tattoo applied as a separate digital layer and contoured with the Andromeda plug-in, wrapping around the arm and conforming to the elbow wrinkles. C: Tattoo layer fill reduced from 100 percent to 60 percent. D: Tattoo layer manipulated by the "blending" mode of Photoshop's "color burn," which increases the contrast in the shadows. E: Final color fills are added in two separate layers

JH: And there are a lot of things—it's not just the contouring, it's the—you'd pick the shadows up and put them back down again on top of the images. As Craig says, you work with the wrinkles. All kinds of things.

EH: Oh, absolutely, I see. And each of the images that you picked, did you know exactly where you wanted to put them?

JH: Sometimes yes, sometimes no. Sometimes we would bend the water-lily scan to go up on the shoulder, and then I would say, "Ah—I don't really like it there!" and then in order to move it to another place we'd have to go back to the original water lily and then rebend it, because once it's bent to fit one place it doesn't work in another place.

Jane Hammond

EH: The American flag in your buttocks is really a tour de force.

JH: Yes, I'm really proud of it. And there are little fun parts—like, you see how the hand on the upper right thigh is right next to my hand, or the swimmers are swimming around my legs?

EH: So how long did it take?

JH: Two years or something—a year and a half? A long time. It was many, many, many visits out there [to ULAE]. And Vanessa [Viola] and I or Brian and I sat next to each other on two chairs, side by side, in front of the computer all day long. It was very slow.

CZ: Actually, for the scope and scale of this . . . we were really pushing the limits of what we could do with this automatic contouring. Because today—it's nothing. But this was pushing the limits with the technology of the time.

JH: Yes. It's funny because people think, when you tell them it's digital, people think, "Wait—no!"

CZ: It's very good.

EH: It's really amazing.

JH: And then . . . at a certain point it was just too much [*fig. 7*].

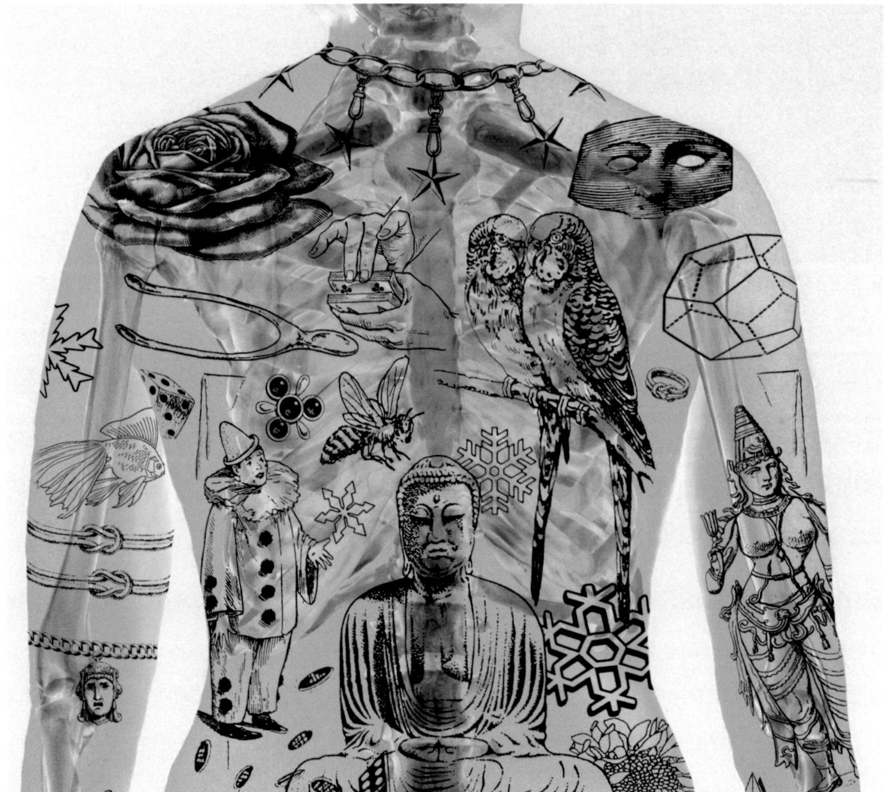

FIG. 7. The ultimate point to which the "Röntgen skeleton-with-tattoo" concept was taken. With seventy-seven layers of digital information superimposing scans of Hammond's body with scans of the front and back of the skeleton and with all of the layers of tattoos

CZ: Yeah, it got so busy, I think. And I think when you were actually laying the tattoos on, we would always go back to this—this is my recollection—and say, "Gosh, this looks so good." It looks—how do you say it?—"carny." It looks like this turn-of-the-century type of photo. And so, at some point, Jane says, "You know what? We're not married to this skeleton." [15]

JH: [*looking at the abandoned proof, fig. 7*] Seeing it now in black and white, you can think, "Oh, why did she ever abandon the skeleton?" Because in black and white I think the skeleton looks kind of cool in there. Somehow in the colored thing it just seemed too—if I think it's too much it's too much. So I decided to abandon the skeleton idea, to remove the skeleton layers.

EH: Did you do any proofs in black and white?

JH: We made this one—what do you call it, a TP [trial proof], right? And I hand-colored it and gave it to Bill for his birthday [*fig. 8*]. Looking at this now makes me feel like I should do another print that's the body with the skeleton . . .

EH: It's fabulous! You really should do it.

CZ: Let's do it, Jane . . . Okay. This is it. This is the one with all the layers [*sifting backward through the digital archive of layers in his computer files*]. So now if you were to start to take these away, you would start to see what's going on there.

EH: The incredible invisible woman.

CZ: There are, I forget how many layers, Jane.

JH: Oh, it's like a hundred or eighty or—it's a very high number. [16]

EH: I can't believe you have all these digital records. It's fantastic.

CZ: Well, that's the nice thing about the digital too—is you can—it doesn't take up much storage to have the archives, if you know what I mean.

JH: Also the final piece has sixty-five tattoo images. But you don't just make sixty-five—you make ninety to get sixty-five.

EH: You know, I think Craig's right—that the final print has a bit of a nineteenth-century look, not only in the tone . . . but everything about it.

JH: Yeah. It has that feeling. Also, see this indication of how we put a cloth down [*gesturing at the backdrop of* Tabula Rosa]? You can see a kind of horizon line right there. This kind of paper is cloth-like. And I always felt there was

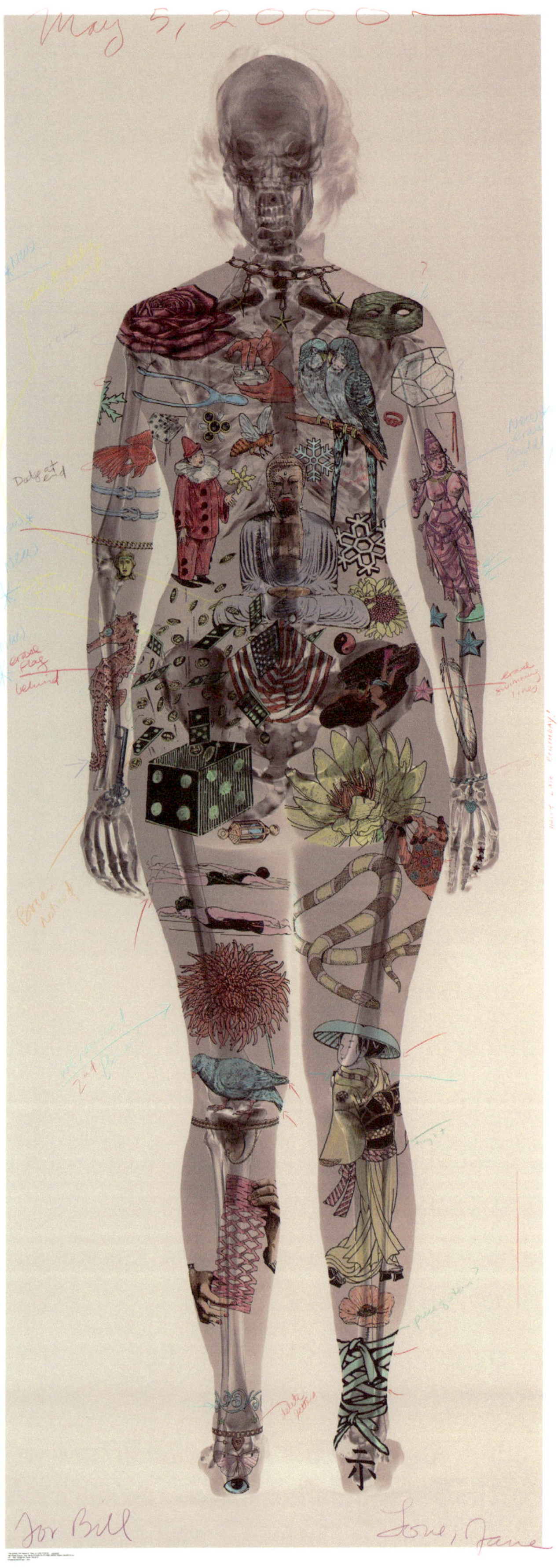

FIG. 8. Trial proof for *Tabula Rosa*, 2001. Hand-colored pigmented inkjet print with notations by the artist in colored pencil, 75 ½ × 30 ¼ in. (191.8 × 76.8 cm). Given by Hammond to Bill Goldston as a birthday gift

Jane Hammond

sort of a marriage between the final support the print is on, and the cloth I was standing on for the photograph.[17]

EH: And had you picked the paper early on?

JH: Actually, no.

CZ: Bill Goldston had it made.

JH: Bill Goldston had it made in Japan. But I knew generally what I wanted. I'm a big fan of rice paper.

EH: It's a substantial rice paper, though.

JH: Yes. It's a *gampi* paper, actually. And I knew I wanted a paper that would soften the image.

EH: But it's coated?

CZ: Well, it had to be coated to accept the inkjet sharply.

JH: This is probably one of the very first custom-made digital papers.

CZ: Yes, I would say so.

JH: And then, God, remember there was some kind of strike and there was the show that the Brooklyn Museum was doing on digital printmaking looming [*Digital: Printmaking Now*], and we had finished the print and then couldn't get the paper out of airport customs because of the strike. The clock was ticking. My triumphant moment at the opening of that show was when Dick Solomon [president of Pace Prints], who had seven prints in that show, came up to me and said, "You have the best print in the show."

CZ: Oh, that's wonderful.

EH: That is wonderful . . . [*pause*] Well, and there are shadows you can see—so you must have simulated that.

CZ: Oh, yes. There's a lot of simulation here.

JH: And then at a certain point we started fooling around with coloring it, and I decided I liked coloring it.

EH: They're colored by hand? What a lot of work!

JH: They're colored by hand with the stylus, in the computer.

CZ: On a Wacom tablet, with a stylus that is manipulated much like a pen or pencil. The tablet provides the user a more natural way to draw on the computer, since it is pressure-sensitive and thus responsive to nuances of drawing.[18]

JH: Often we would fill in with a base color, and then I would color over
that with another color using the stylus [*fig. 9*]. So it is colored by hand
in that sense. When you do it, it feels like you are doing it "by hand."

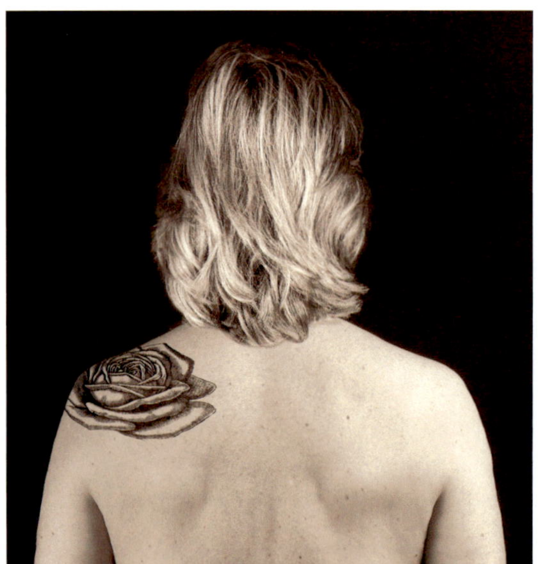
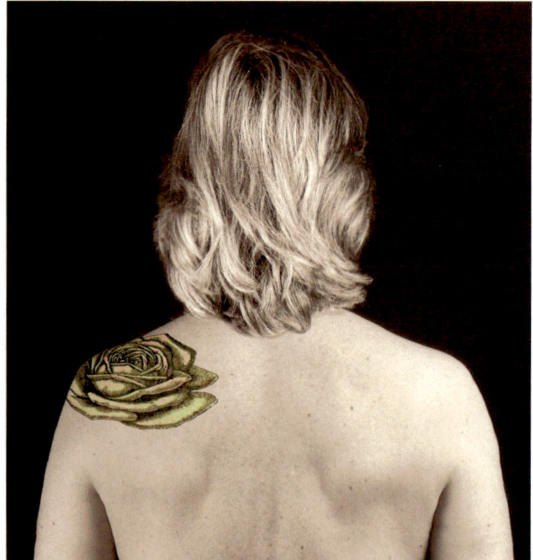

FIG. 9. *Left*: Rose image applied to Hammond's shoulder. *Right*: Color layers added underneath rose

EH: I see, and the color responds to the contours of the body.

JH: Yep.

EH: It gets lighter and darker, which is really wonderful.

CZ: And to me it's like, well, this is how a print evolves. You start with an idea
and someone like Jane, an artist like Jane, who has a very particular strong idea
of the outcome, you know . . .

JH: Is usually wrong!

CZ: No, it's—it's a pleasure to work that way, because there's a goal in sight . . .

JH: . . . that I can articulate to you, so therefore you can help me. Whereas if
I'm just exploring, you don't know what to do, right?

CZ: But at least you have a goal. And that's one thing in my work with Jane that
I look back on and think, "Sheez, I wish we would have been working together a
lot longer." Because there were a lot of times when, you know, I worked for years
floundering with stuff. And it was so refreshing that we knew where we were
going on this project. Not that we knew how to get there, but we knew how we
were going to wind up. So that was nice.

EH: Can I ask a few other questions?

JH: Yeah, ask anything you want.

EH: So what strikes me—or one of the things that strike me about this print—is that tattooing really implies permanence. Like a permanent stain upon the skin, an image that's literally fused with the physical body so that they become one. But since this print doesn't really reference that sort of incising—because it's not, let's say, an etching or an engraving—it doesn't have that sort of . . . point of reference. Does the digital embedding, the sort of the trompe l'oeil-ness of this, render the tattoos somehow erasable?

JH: Mutable? Yeah. I'm going to answer that question obliquely. When I first started making paintings out of this lexicon of found information, one of the things that I wanted to achieve was to have these things come together in the painting—and this would be a real painting and it would have a meaning, you know? Maybe not sayable in a didactic sense, but it would have a meaning. But over time you could see these things dissolve and go back to the locker room and others of them come together to create another meaning that was at odds with the first meaning, or counter to the first meaning, or unrelated to the first meaning . . . as opposed to the work of an artist who has a thematic sense and concerns, and every painting develops that theme. So I'm into this idea of a mutable, conditional, dissolving state of truths.

EH: So the digital is perfect.

JH: So it is perfect for me and it does have that implication that you could output seventeen tattoo prints and you could use the same body—read the body as like the canvas in a painting, for example—and it could have different tattoos in number two, then number three, then number five. In fact, having just made a mummy print [*Spells and Incantations*], I'm now making a unique mummy. And somehow I've done this a number of times—follow a print with a unique variant. I've recently made unique scrapbooks. It's partially my own need to say, "But it could also be this way." You know?

EH: Yes, I see. Now this is a personal question. You don't have to answer it. And as I ask this, I'm thinking about Craig's ongoing tattoo project on his own body . . .

CZ: [*sheepishly*] Oh.

JH: Do I have any tattoos?

EH: Yes. Are any of the tattoos in this print real?

JH: No. I don't have any tattoos and in some ways the reason I don't have any tattoos is related to what I just said about painting. There is no image

                                                                 Jane Hammond

that I would unendingly be happy with. If you could have something between temporary tattoos and real tattoos that would last for a month or two, I would have had seventy. But if they were permanent, I would think, "Wow! When I'm seventy am I still going to think this is really smart and interesting?" You know?

CZ: Well, Lisa, the thing is that Jane, with this print, got me so excited. I mean, I've always wanted tattoos . . .

EH: But did it begin with this?

CZ: Yes.

EH: It did? Jane, did you know this?

CZ: She knew I had no tattoos while we were working on this print, and then when she started the *Scrapbook* [*fig. 10*], I had my first tattoos because it kind of spurred me on. It was like Jane kept bringing me more source material for tattoos. And it was like, "Oh my God! This is just what I want! No, no, no . . . *this* is just what I want!"

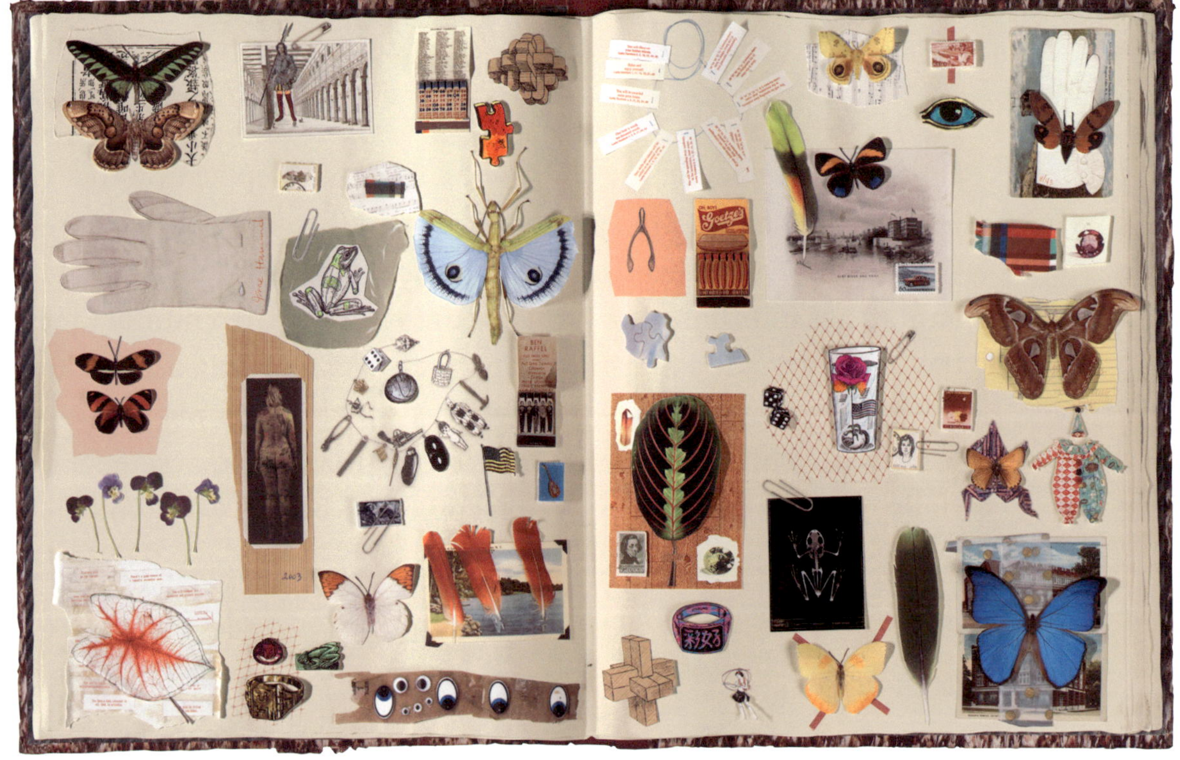

FIG. 10. Jane Hammond, *Scrapbook*, 2003. Pigmented inkjet print with inkjet, woodblock, and watercolored, hand-cut, and collaged elements, 33 × 48½ × 1⅜ in. (83.8 × 123.2 × 3.5 cm). Edition of 43. Published by Universal Limited Art Editions. Yale University Art Gallery, Janet and Simeon Braguin Fund, 2006.22.3

JH: I really like tattoos. I have all these books on tattooing and have for years.

EH: Me too. I love tattoos. I think they're incredibly sensuous.

CZ: So that was the beginning. That pushed me over the edge. It was like, "Okay. I'm doing this."

JH: I did not know that.

EH: Can the two of you comment a bit more about your thoughts on digital printmaking? Because there really is quite a dramatic range—from something as technically involved and conceptually smart as this print to what actually amounts to a glorified Xerox.

JH: You know, a lot of people are doing something where basically the digital print is a copy of a watercolor they made. That is, to me, very uninteresting. I can't think of a single example where I would contradict myself on that. Maybe you could copy the watercolor and make something else on top of it. But then it has that really "neither fish nor fowl" kind of quality.

CZ: It's a reproduction, that's what it is in that case. To me.

JH: I'm not down on reproduction. I think we're just beginning to explore how interesting reproduction is. So it's not that it's reproductive, it's just that it's not interestingly reproductive. I like prints that look . . . that look *printed*. I'm not a person whose high praise for a print is that it could pass for a drawing.

EH: You once referred to the printer as a magician. Can you comment a little bit on that?

JH: Well, there is something very magical and transformative about printmaking.

CZ: There's a lot of smoke and mirrors that we employ.

JH: Yeah. I'm sure that's true.

EH: Obviously you're both proud of this [*Tabula Rosa*].

JH: Oh, yes. I'm really proud of this print.

CZ: I think—I'm not sure . . . I'm 99 percent sure this was the first published digital print of ULAE.

JH: I think it was.

CZ: I think it was, which is another landmark . . . I must say Jane never asked for any, you know, William Shatner Photoshop stuff.[19] Nobody was even thinking along those lines . . . but when you look back now you realize, "Hey, Jane could have done that." But that's what makes this special.

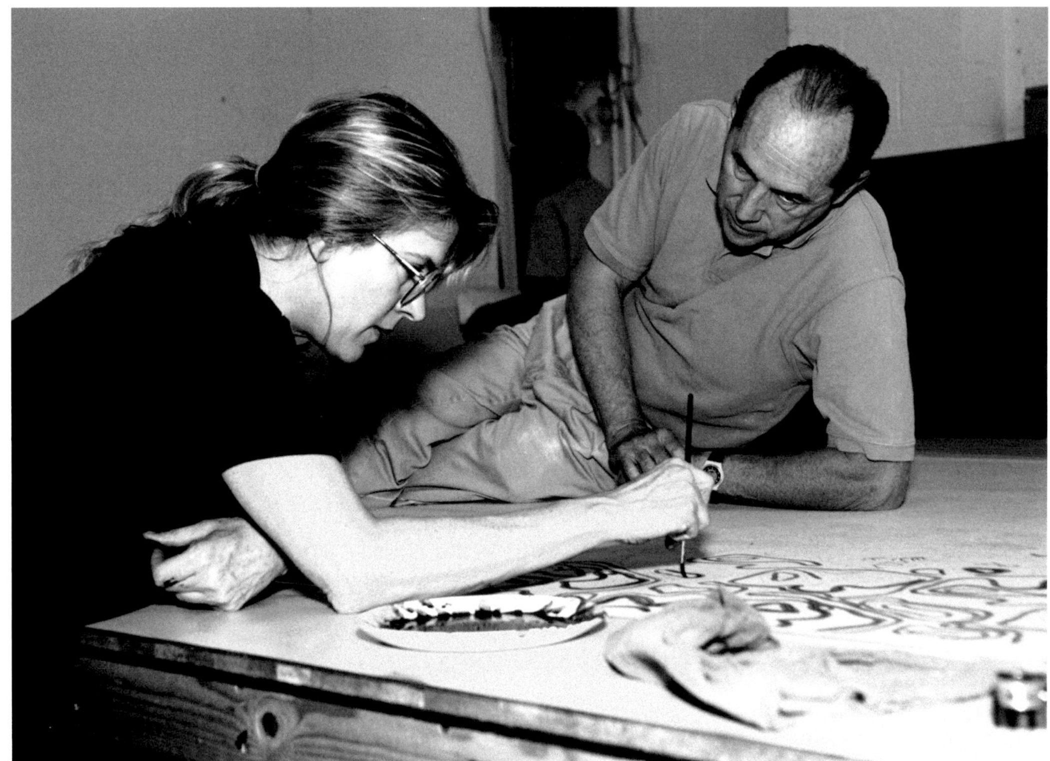

EH: It does. That you allowed yourself to just be out there the way you are.

JH: I had to get through it, you know, if I wanted to make that print. There were about ten minutes where I considered trying to talk Larissa [Goldston] into it. Because Larissa—have you met Larissa? She's got this fabulous body, and I was thinking, "Oh! I can do it with Larissa!" But then I thought . . .

EH: Well, it really is an amazing print.

JH: Yeah, I'm happy with it.

CZ: Me too.

Notes

The preceding conversation was held on November 15, 2007, in Hammond's studio, in New York.

1. The image of Hammond in *Tabula Rosa* is actually one inch taller than the artist. Hammond admits that she has always longed to be taller—and so Bill Goldston and Craig Zammiello made it happen in this print. Hammond shared this information during a portion of the Nov. 15, 2007, conversation not included in this chapter.

2. The best resource on Hammond's printmaking is *Jane Hammond: Paper Work*, ed. Marianne Doezema (South Hadley, Mass.: Mount Holyoke College Art Museum, 2007). Note in particular Faye Hirsch's essay, "In the Forest of Signs: Jane Hammond's Prints and Photographs," 13–21, which has an excellent description of *Tabula Rosa*.

3. Hammond shared this information during a portion of the Nov. 15, 2007, conversation not included in this chapter.

4. Ibid. Hammond remarked that this was an ambitious print project in another sense, in that it is not commercially marketable: "You know . . . you can't sell this print to a corporation. Period. End of story. They will not buy somebody's naked butt."

5. This is the first editioned ULAE print that was digital from start to finish. Other projects had included digitally produced components, but all of the imagery for *Tabula Rosa* was photographed, modeled, and rendered digitally.

6. Bill Goldston, the president of ULAE, and the printers Vanessa Viola and Brian Berry were all integral to the successful completion of this print.

7. *Digital: Printmaking Now* was organized by Marilyn Kushner, curator of prints at the Brooklyn Museum, where the exhibition was on view from June 22 through September 2, 2001.

8. Wilhelm Conrad Röntgen (1845–1923) discovered the X-ray in 1895.

9. Jane Hammond, *Full House*, 1993. Intaglio, screenprint, and lithography in twelve colors with collage on handmade Torinoko paper, 78 ½ × 51 in. (199.4 × 129.5 cm). Published by ULAE. For an image of *Full House*, see Marianne Doezema, ed., *Jane Hammond's Paper Work* (South Hadley, Mass.: Mount Holyoke College Art Museum, 2007), 103, fig. 32; or the ULAE website, http://www.ulae.com/ (accessed September 26, 2011).

10. Jane Hammond, *Spells and Incantations*, 2009, seven-color, three-dimensional lithograph and screenprint on White Rives BFK paper with gold leaf, 60 ½ × 18 ¾ × 7 ½ in. (153.7 × 47.6 × 19.1 cm). Published by Sharks Ink, Lyons, Colorado. For an image of the work, see the Shark's Ink website, http://www.sharksink.com/ (accessed September 26, 2011). See also Cydney Payton, ed., *The Legend of Bud Shark at His Indelible Ink* (San Francisco: Hardy Marks Publications, 2009), 116–17.

11. *Tabula Rosa* would be the first time Zammiello and ULAE would exploit the Phase One FX digital-scanning back to create art instead of just recording it. At the time, the Phase One was an extremely powerful digital imaging system. The Phase One FX travels at different speeds according to the file size selected. (A small file will expose more quickly than a large one.) The photo is transferred to a computer via a FireWire link between them. (At the time, this was the fastest method of transferring large amounts of digital information.) It is processed by the computer's software and then displayed on the monitor. It is quickly apparent if the shot was successful or if adjustments need to be made with regard to exposure, lens aperture, light balance, and other factors. The Phase One uses static studio lighting that has to be controlled for voltage fluctuation. (A probe mounted at the front of the camera, which takes continuous readings of reflected RGB (red-green-blue) levels on the subject being photographed, aids this process by adjusting for any abnormal fluctuations in the color temperature while the image is scanned.) As a backup, Zammiello shot a roll of 35 mm black-and-white film before making the Phase One exposures for *Tabula Rosa*, since at the time he did not trust that the digital back would produce a usable image.

12. Brian Berry, a printer and photographer at ULAE, was instrumental in the production of *Tabula Rosa*. He was responsible for most of the work of resizing and positioning the skeleton, as well as the application of the tattoos. Vanessa Viola, a graphic designer who was also working at ULAE, took over part of the way through the process. She sat at the computer with Hammond, applying more of the tattoos and their numerous color layers. Vanessa was also in charge of printing the final edition.

13. With the Andromeda plug-in, one is able to create an object—cylindrical, rectangular, or circular (to mimic the particular contour of a certain part of the body)—size it, and then digitally apply the tattoo image on top of it. Once the image was shaped to the proper distortion, it was saved and applied to the main image as a separate layer. This was repeated approximately ninety-seven times as each individual tattoo and its elements were applied to the image of Hammond's body. In addition, it was necessary to manipulate the tone of each tattoo to make it appear natural and match the lighting—otherwise it would look like a decal pasted on top of the photo.

14. In Adobe Photoshop, fill only affects the opacity of the pixels in a layer without altering the opacity of any other layer effects that have or will be applied.

15. Zammiello believes that one of the reasons that Hammond dropped the idea of the X-ray—besides feeling it was visually too busy—is that, as she sat in front of her naked image day after day, she became more and more comfortable with the concept of baring herself to the world.

16. There are seventy-seven digital layers in *Tabula Rosa*.

17. The sepia tone, achieved through a particular mix of six pigmented inks, was created in the computer. But the inkjet printer, a Roland forty-eight-inch with Epson head, determined the correct mix of the six colors (cyan, light cyan, magenta, light magenta, yellow, and black).

18. Many times during the creation of *Tabula Rosa*, multiple colors were applied on top of one another in separate digital layers within the parameters of the tattoo outlines. Hammond did this work herself over many long weeks, with Vanessa Viola sitting beside her to aid with the complicated control of the layers and other aspects of compiling the digital file.

19. A popular rumor has it that William Shatner's posterior was retouched in every scene of the last of the "classic" Star Trek films. It is more likely that he wore a corset or girdle, though Shatner denies it.

Jane Hammond

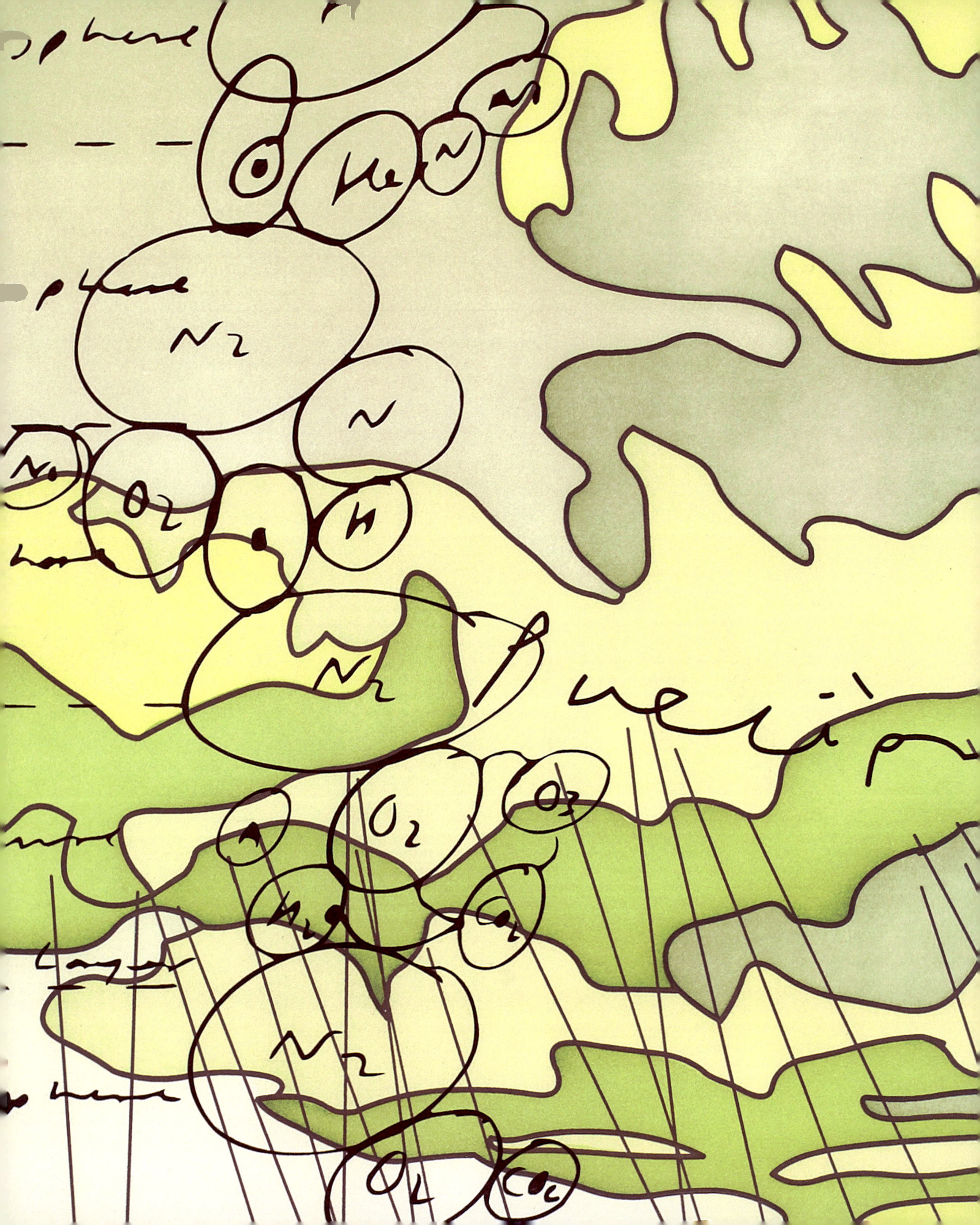

He
N2
N2
N
O2
H
N2
O2
O2
N2
O2
CO2

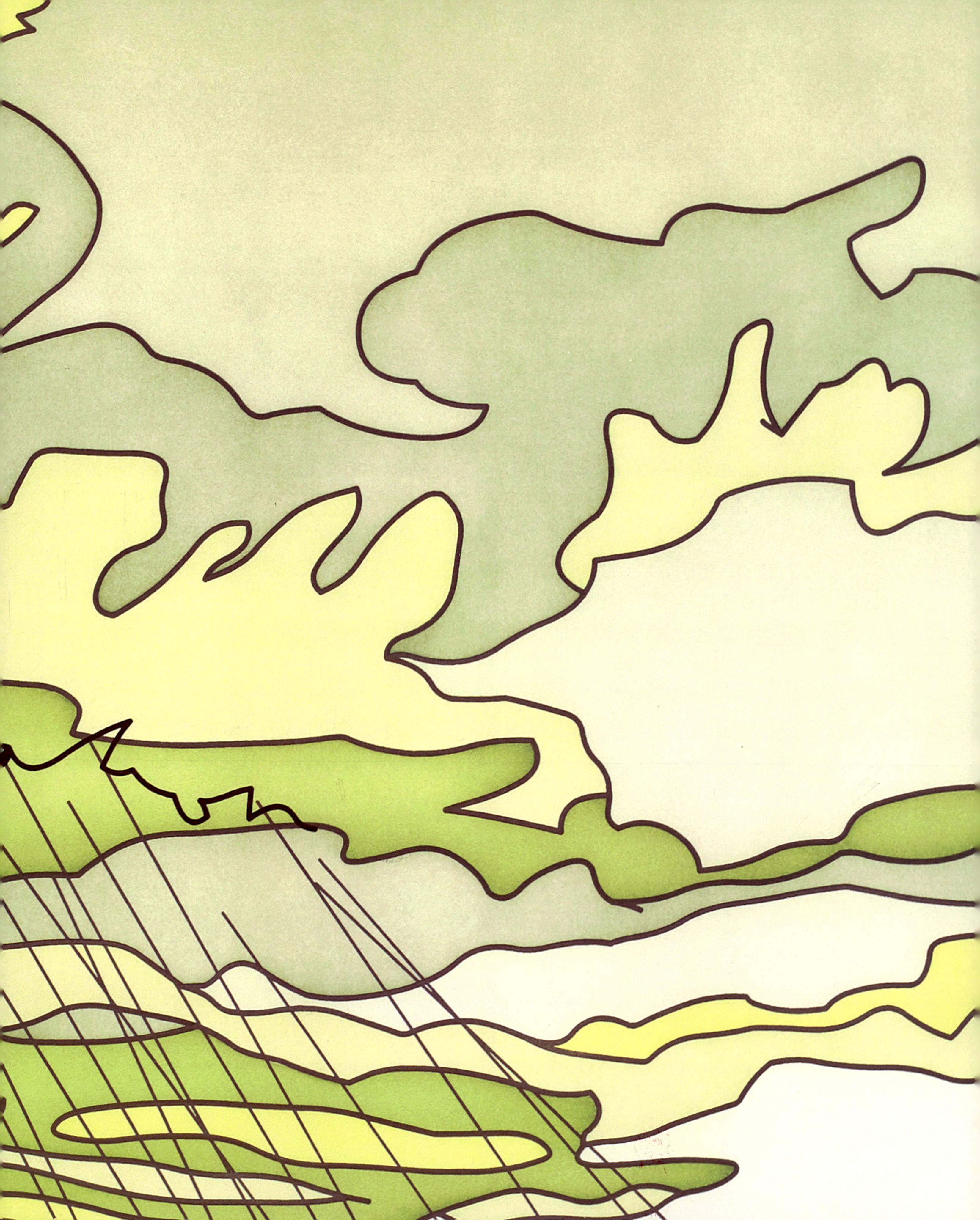

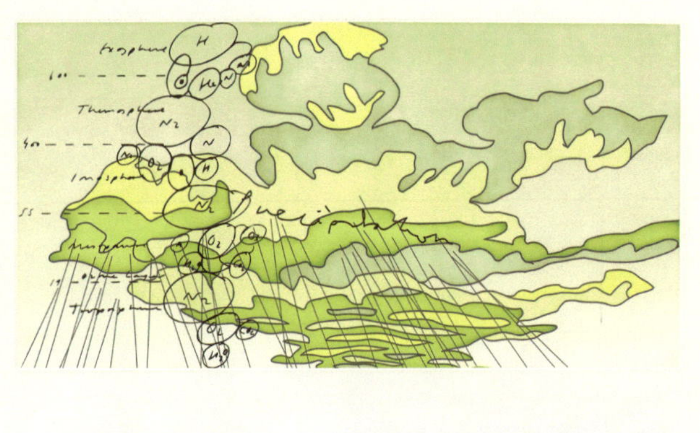

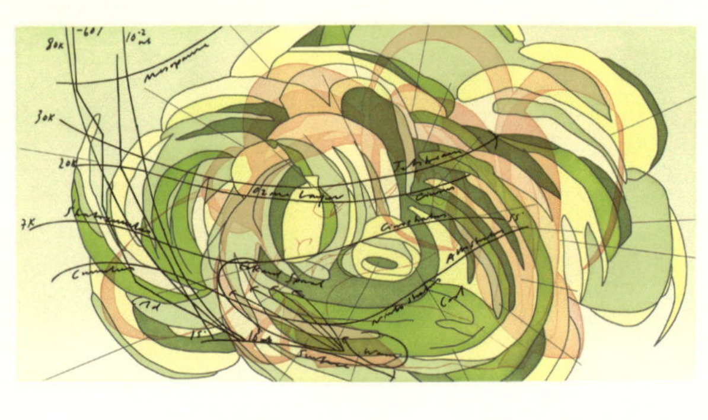

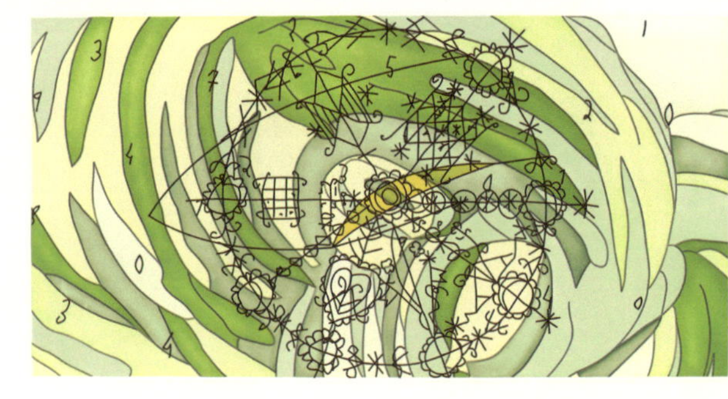

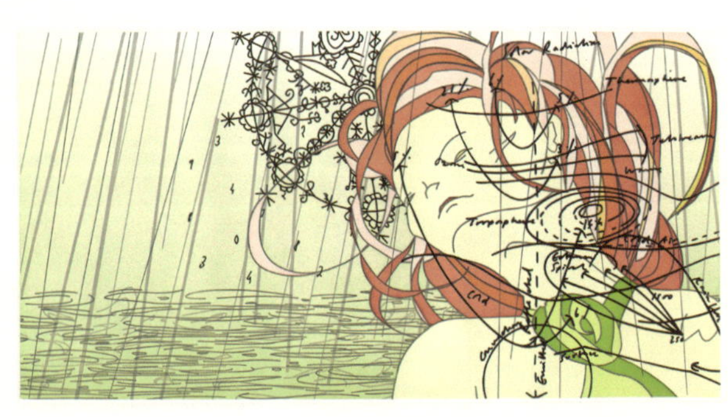

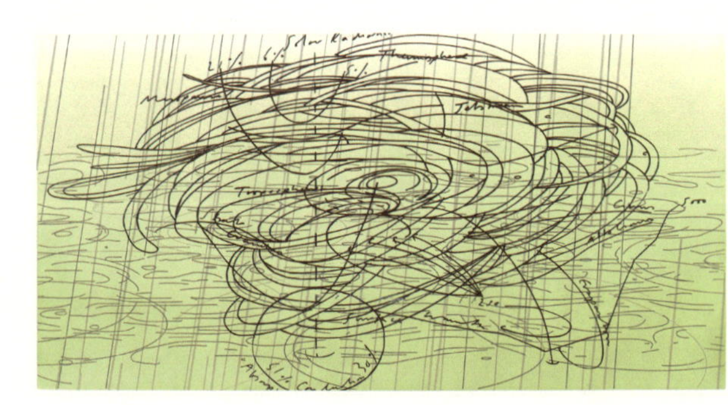

Throughout history, cultures have created mythologies—or religions—to explain complex scientific phenomena. As Matthew Ritchie explains in this conversation, "The great mythological narratives were originally formulated to describe problems with the ontological structure of the world and the epistemological structure of the world—where does it come from and where is it going?" In *Sea State Five*, Ritchie, an artist deeply engaged in exploring scientific theories, creates his own twenty-first-century visual mythology to explain the oceanographic measurements of the free surface of water known as "sea states" (figs. 1–5).

The five prints that constitute *Sea State Five* were derived from an Adobe Flash animation Ritchie made in 2001, which itself was composed from hundreds of the artist's drawings scanned into a computer and manipulated. In making this suite, Ritchie was essentially "reverse engineering"—recapturing into the realm of the physical something that was once digital, or, in his words, "in the vaporware of the visual world."

Working with Ritchie on this suite of prints provided the catalyst for Craig Zammiello to develop a practical means for using the CO_2 laser in the process of etching copper plates. Previously used at Two Palms to create acrylic relief plates, the laser clearly harbored untapped possibilities, and with Zammiello's arrival at Two Palms, founder David Lasry knew he had a master intaglio printer with enough ingenuity and energy to exploit them. In addition, the creation of *Sea State Five* was the first time that Zammiello—or Two Palms—had worked so exclusively with high-tech digital technologies, and so the project became one in which all involved were learning by doing. Both challenges are addressed by Zammiello and Ritchie in the following conversation.

Top to bottom, left to right: **FIGS. 1–5.** Matthew Ritchie, *Sea State One, Sea State Two, Sea State Three, Sea State Four,* and *Sea State Five*, from the suite *Sea State Five*, 2003. Five color etchings with aquatint, each 24½ × 39 in. (62.2 × 99.1 cm). Edition of 28. Published by Two Palms

MATTHEW RITCHIE: The only real print project I ever worked on before I went to Two Palms was the cover of a student magazine for the University of East Anglia when I was in art school. I had the brilliant idea that every cover should be an individual silkscreen monoprint. And I think I made one thousand monoprints, so that every single cover of the magazine would be completely different. We built a silkscreen press in an abandoned house and did the whole thing over the course of a very hot, muggy British summer. I was scribbling with an oil stick on the screen and then pulling the print through. Finally we laid them all out on the floor like a beautiful carpet. But that was all just silkscreen monoprinting. Later I did a little etching. A friend of mine had a little etching press here in SoHo, down in his basement. So I tried to make some monoprints there.

ELISABETH HODERMARSKY: And then David Lasry invited you to Two Palms?

MR: I had been talking with David Lasry for a while, and he showed me some experiments he had made with the CO_2 laser cutter. He had tried this experiment of cutting into paper, and it had charred all around the cut edges of the paper, and I thought that was a very interesting kind of side effect. He had just bought the laser and was experimenting with ways to use it.

CRAIG ZAMMIELLO: He purchased it to incise acrylic plates to make relief prints.

MR: That's right, thinking of it as a printmaker would. And I began to cut things out of black museum board in a way that resembled my wall drawings. I had this idea that you would be able to cut a linear print through the paper and reveal the black line. The very first thing we made was a combined lithograph-laser piece for Artists Space [*fig. 6*]. It was an etching prototype. And we printed it in this woodblock method and then cut through the paper to reveal a black drawing underneath. It was absolutely beautiful. It was completely charred around the edges. It looked great, but it took an insanely long time. It was totally unsuitable as an edition. So we made the piece for them which was called . . . let me see . . . *Sea State One*?

CZ: Yes. That was right before I came to Two Palms.

EH: So this is where *Sea State Five* actually began, then? And this earlier piece is based on the same Flash movie as the suite of five *Sea State* prints?

MR: Yes. These were actually frames from the same Flash movie. And we chose one of those frames for this print, which was the print for Artists Space [*fig. 7*]. A couple of years earlier I had made this series of Flash

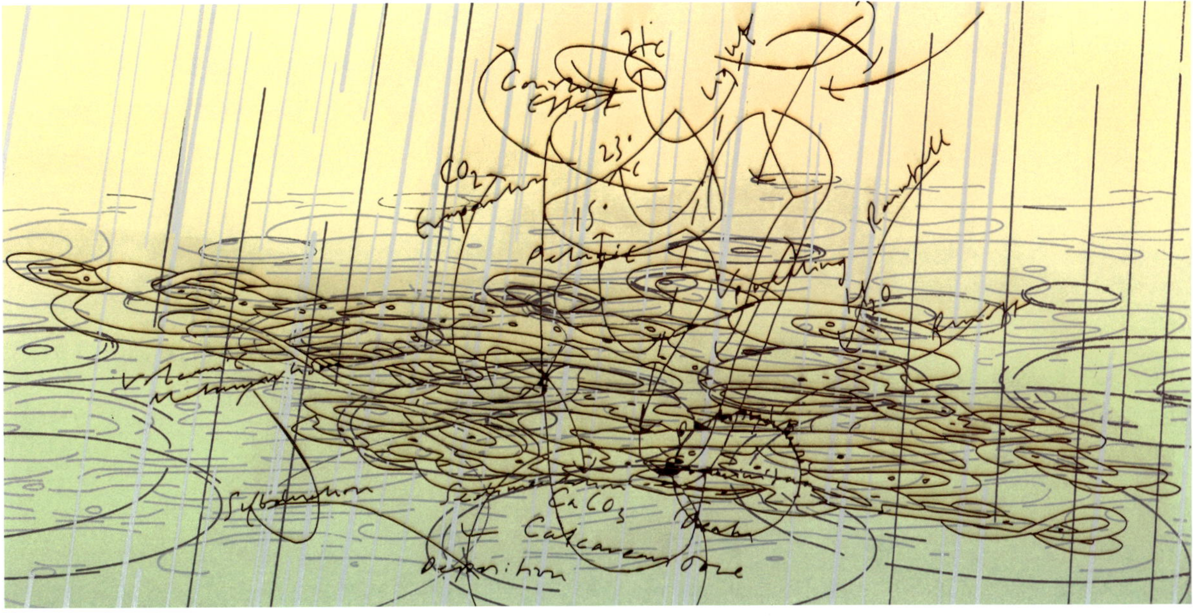

FIG. 6. Untitled, uneditioned Artists Space print, 2002. Relief print with laser engraving on black Sintra plastic sheet, 16 × 32 in. (40.6 × 81.3 cm)

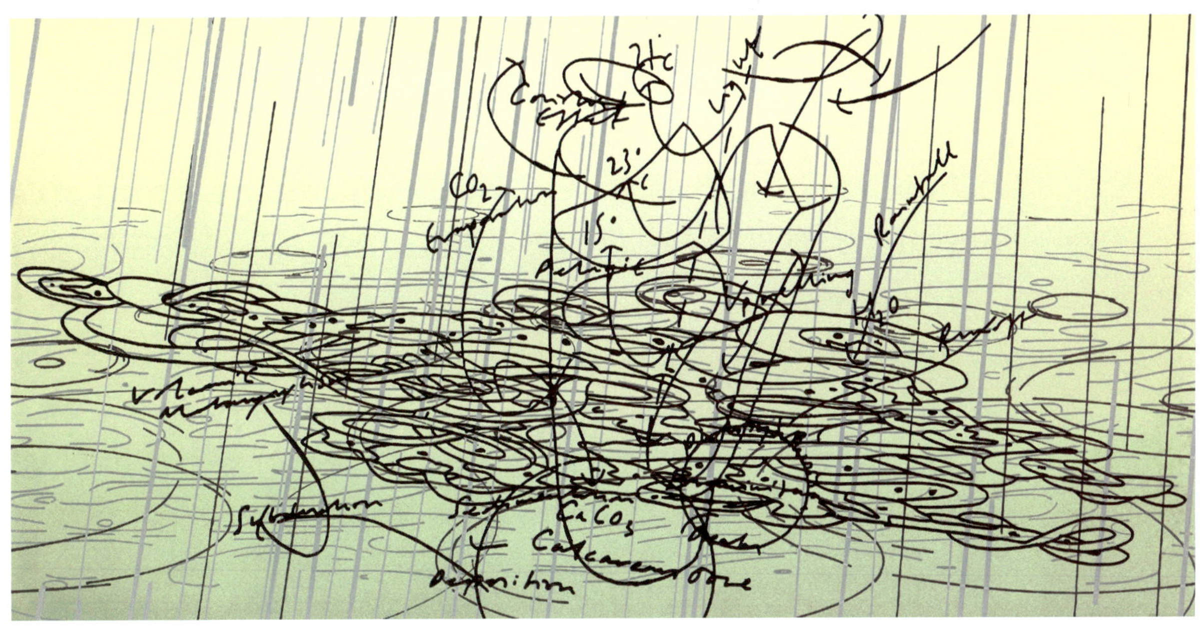

FIG. 7. *Sea State* One, editioned Artists Space print, 2002. Relief print from laser-cut acrylic plates, surface-rolled with colored inks, 16 × 32 in. (40.6 × 81.3 cm)

animations for a commission by San Francisco MoMA for a show called *010101: Art in Technological Times*.[1] It was at the very end of the dot-com boom, when people thought it was all going in the direction of digital art. And we can see how *that* worked out . . .

[*laughter*]

MR: But everyone was experimenting with digital then. So I made these Flash movies, which seemed very advanced at the time, with a programmer called Brian Clyne. I know the basics of computer programming, but I have to work with an expert. What I do appreciate about it is the idea of an

Matthew Ritchie

infinite sequence, recursive sequencing. So that you don't have to be iterative; you can move things in and out of the sequence. Like a layering system that creates this huge database. So after we made this piece, I had this enormous database of drawings that I had made and that had been scanned and manipulated for the Flash animation . . . this collection of imagery that theoretically did things in infinitely variable sequences, which seemed initially to be such a great way to start making physical objects, because instead of the traditional idea of a collage, which is just one thing on top of another on top of another—what Harold Rosenberg called the "workbench"—this was proposing a kind of infinitely deep information space.

What I missed when thinking it through, though, was that each time you do that you have to actually materialize each of those layers into independent physical objects. So that instead of just having one large, infinitely scalable suite of ideas, you now have to have thousands of individual objects, all of which have to perfectly fit with all of the other objects. Which is why this project took a couple of years. Literally, we sat down and said, "Okay, we've got all these Flash movies." And I had done the drawings. And so we thought we'd have twenty or thirty of these prints within a couple of months! Just pop them out . . . but then, of course . . .

EH: Reality sets in.

MR: It became a kind of reverse engineering, collapsing infinity into specific objects—which is a kind of metaphor for the modern print, the relationship between digital technologies and printmaking. It actually doesn't work quite the way you would think. It's not a one-to-one ratio at all.

EH: Could you discuss the theme of *Sea State*?

MR: Sure. The film tells the story of these seven interrelated characters who collectively embody the forces of thermodynamics. It's all documented in this little book [*showing a copy of* Matthew Ritchie: Incomplete Projects 01-07].[2] It's a noir narrative, set in the 1960s in Florida.[3] There's a kind of picture story, which is showing you what it might look like if you saw it happening in front of you, and there's a kind of abstract story, which is about what it's like on a scientific level. It's really the story of the relationship between system energy (represented by a character called the "actress"), free energy (represented by a character called the "astronaut"), enthalpy (the totality of all these things, represented by their child), and then entropy (represented by a mass of entangled snakes) and work (represented by a character called the "Golum," a weird hotel operator living underground).

Florida is made of limestone—a sort of coral reef. Which is why people who live in Florida are so concerned about global warming. It's a giant limestone sponge, like a giant tunnel system, a highly entropic environment. You can actually swim underground through huge parts of Florida. Which is why it's a favorite spot for divers. It's also the place that [Juan] Ponce de León arrived at looking for the fountain of youth, and thought he'd found it. As the first law of thermodynamics is conservation of energy, the fountain is used in the story as the symbol of enthalpy, the opposite of entropy, unceasing renewal.

These characters are all in play with each other. And they're all represented by colors. So in that way it's related to the idea of being an artist, which involves dealing with substances that are always tilting one way or the other. You are either introducing entropy or fighting against entropy, making some kind of exchange—taking free energy and turning it into system energy—in order to work. It's all about this kind of system of engagement of storytelling and color. The characters in this part of the story on which the *Sea State* prints are based are represented by colors: the color green represents the actress (energy); the color yellow represents enthalpy, which is the child of the actress; free energy is represented by black (the astronaut); and then in other parts of this story there's this character called "the swimmer" that represents the infinite space in which these relations take place.

EH: And what color is he?

MR: He's blue. But this particular part is the story of the actress, who's also physically based on my wife, who has red hair. And the red hair becomes the symbol of entropy, the sort of iconic spiral. So it's about how energy—this green energy—is materializing out of a storm, which is a natural chaotic system. And it gradually takes form.

Now, form is actually an increase of entropy. Through what we perceive as the increase of order in the universe—like building, and things like that—we're actually adding entropy to the system. So, the more you do, the more entropy is added to the system. So this is what's going on in the story. And ultimately the character, the actress, dissolves back into the system—comes out of a cloud system but just dissolves into pure information in the end.

"Sea states" are these states of increased activity in oceanic systems. A "sea state one" is a light storm, a "sea state five" is a hurricane. There's this gradual escalation. So across here [*indicating an area of* Sea State One; *fig. 8*] there are these various notations—these are the layers of the atmosphere, as you go up through the sky. This is how wind moves through the atmosphere. And solar radiation penetrates at these percentage marks—these are the heights, the kilometer heights.

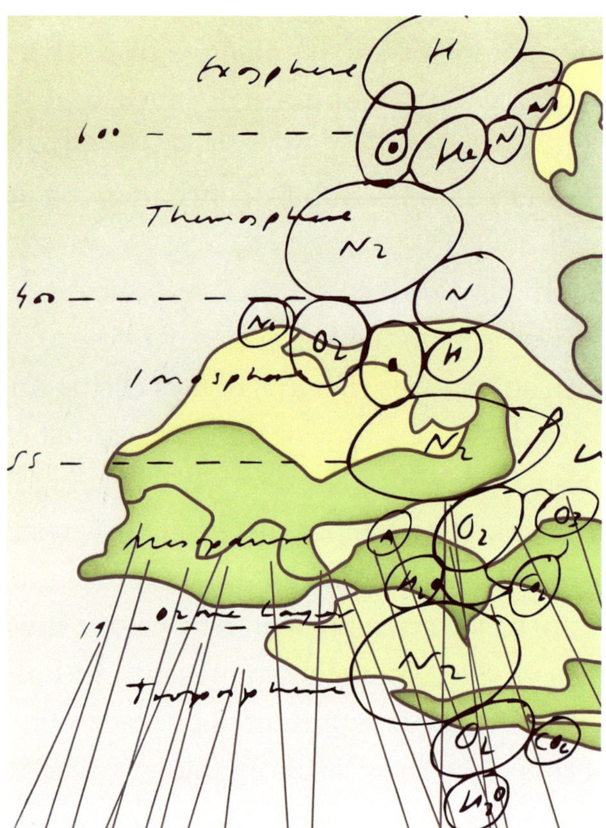

FIG. 8. Detail of the left side of *Sea State One* (fig. 1) showing atmospheric notations

CZ: Is the movie still accessible?

MR: Yes, it's on my website.[4] But in fact, of course, none of the information in this suite of prints, or almost none of it, was actually in the film. The film had some things happen, but as we tried to rebuild it, only fragments of it were useable. So we had to reconstruct this whole sequence in the making of these prints. And as we did that, it changed. So you would see the film now and you would think, "Oh, this is sort of like the prints." But that's a sort of reverse-engineered connection.

CZ: Well, I remember when we set out to make this suite, Matthew handed me a screen capture in which you could see the actress just starting to appear through the atmosphere—it was one of those fade-through things—and I looked at David and said, "David, please, how am I going to do that?!"

[laughter]

EH: In fact, I just noticed that this morning. That red hair just faintly appearing here in the second print [*see fig. 2*].

CZ: It's beautiful.

MR: But that's what you see in the Flash, where you get a better sense of the actress. I made a drawing of the actress and a drawing of the cloud. But in reality, you take a film still and that information is no longer useful. So what you have to do in printmaking is make two plates with two levels of information . . . to simulate that look.

CZ: So what you got for the actress was actually Craig in Adobe Photoshop just selecting tones.

EH: So now we're talking about the fourth print, *Sea State Four* [*see fig. 4*]?

MR: And presumably the second, where we were able to reuse that particular plate holding the information of the actress's hair.

EH: So you didn't create this suite sequentially then, did you?

MR: No, not at all. And this is what happens with digital information. Which just proves that it's really just "stuff." And, for me, this is what becomes especially interesting, because you're not committed to a linear narrative. When you choose something from an earlier project for a print, you're bringing that element of the story back. Or foreshadowing what's to come. To the extent that you consider a color or a number to be an indicator, it's a sort of déjà vu, but the printmaking process offers that as a condition anyway— that's its basic premise. So adding the layer of a digital ecology to it really makes it about this sort of endless recuperation.

EH: So, just focusing on *Sea State Four*, how many plates were used for this one print? Do these ten files, or separations, represent the number of plates used?

CZ: No, I believe there were only five plates used, but I needed these ten files. Which goes to Matthew's technical point: how do we transpose something from a digital file into a physical print? Which is where the laser came in. We needed to work out the process. Matthew was the catalyst for my figuring out how to use the laser to create the copper plates.

EH: Could you walk me through that?

CZ: Sure. When I arrived at Two Palms in 2002, the most notable element of the work being done there were these incredible acrylic relief plates that were used in making their characteristic prints [*fig. 9*]. The plates were being cut by a

Universal fifty-watt CO_2 laser that Two Palms owned. David was always curious about applying it to produce etching plates and set me to work on the problem. I found out quite quickly that traditional liquid hard ground would be of no use, because the laser would not burn it away cleanly. It would basically just melt it, it being too oily. The ground would heat up, a percentage being burnt away, but then flow back at the edges, resulting in a sloppy area. If you were trying to burn a vector hairline, it would just fill itself back in as soon as the laser passed. You could see the line in the ground where the laser had burned the vector, but the metal was not exposed for later etching.

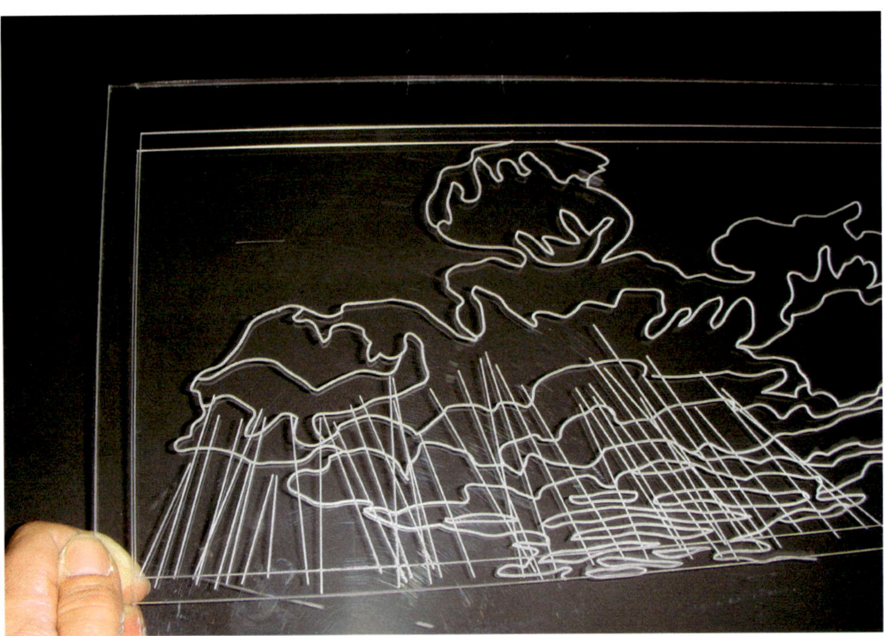

FIG. 9. Detail of one of Ritchie's acrylic plates, engraved by laser

In a conversation with John Lund[5] I mentioned this problem, and luckily he had done some work on his own, experimenting with a local signmaker who had a CO_2 laser. What he found is that you needed a ground that would not necessarily be good as a traditional hard ground to draw through, but one that was brittle and more likely to chip, and that could withstand high heat in proximity to tight areas. Ultimately, the best results were obtained by using high-heat enamel spray-paint meant for coating barbecue grills. It burned clean with no melting and produced the best detail from the digital file assigned to the laser.[6]

> MR: What we had wanted to do initially—before Craig worked out how to create etching plates with the laser—was to make a traditional Japanese woodblock print. Because the look is so beautiful. And we even talked with a traditional woodblock maker . . .

CZ: That's right, Keiji Shinohara.

MR: Who basically took six months to say, "Nooooo!"

CZ: Well, that's some hard stuff to do. I think he printed some ukiyo-e fades for the backgrounds. But, like Matthew said, months and months and months went by, and we didn't hear anything.

EH: Well, but here, just looking here at this background plate of *Sea State Four*, you have that wonderful ukiyo-e fade in this suite [*fig. 10*].

FIG. 10. Airbrush aquatint plate from *Sea State Four*

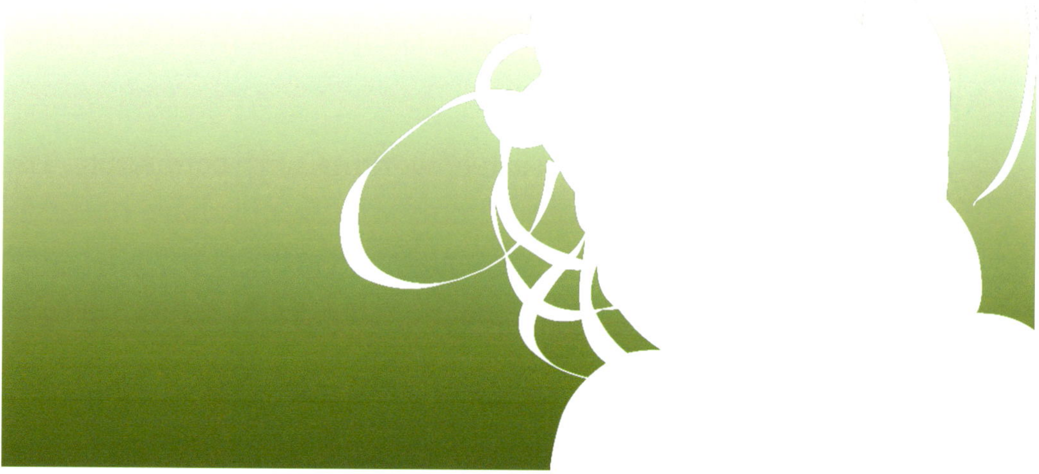

CZ: David asked, "How are we going to do a fade?" Well, that's one thing I *can* do, with an airbrush. We can kind of imitate—in a slick Western way—a ukiyo-e look.

MR: And the irony of that is that ultimately we were trying to imitate what is done in film, which has all these fades, which in film you just do [*pushing an imaginary button*]—you make a fade.

[*laughter*]

MR: So, again, there's the technology, and of course there's the traditional equivalent to this, but neither of them are going to deliver you a physical object in a time that is viable.

CZ: And all the fades in these *Sea State* prints are done by hand. Because, like on this one in *Sea State Four*, the laser would take away the black [*fig. 11*], so I'd have an open background and I would just airbrush this fade into it [*see fig. 10*]. The laser's not capable of giving us any tonal direction; it's either there or not. So the laser gives us the capability to stop-out—or protect from an etch—but any tonal fades are done via airbrush aquatint. And what I had to do with these in order to keep a consistent flavor, or feel, was to execute all of the aquatints on all five of these prints with the airbrush, right down to the basic black lines.

This outline would be drawn, so that you have the outside drawing, and then you have the inside colors. So the laser would take the drawing [*see fig. 11*] and burn the ground off the plate. I would take the resulting plate, airbrush it, and etch it. And that is how plate one and the other six plates [*figs. 12–17*] were all realized.

EH: But this is all Matthew's drawing—drawn information, correct?

CZ: That's Matthew drawing in the computer, right?

MR: I have a suspicion that in the end I redrew a lot of these. But it makes no difference, because all of the drawings for the film were hand-drawn anyway. There's essentially nothing computer-generated in any of this.

EH: Which is the irony.

MR: Yes. But that's also the truth of working with computers. There's nothing computer-generated ever. It's only what people have made the computer do. And what has been a consistent feature of my relationship with digital art is that I've basically had to redo it all by hand. There's no piece that I've made that hasn't been hand-rendered. You're just using a different kind of pen. I can show the two of you a couple of films that I made that appear to be entirely hand-drawn, and that's because they essentially are.

[*laughter*]

MR: But they are also hour-long animated films. So there's a point—almost a breaking point—at which the computer allows you to suddenly do something digitally that you could never do otherwise, because you wouldn't have the time. Because the computer can do it again and again and again. It becomes a sort of "super hand." But up to that breaking point everything still has to be done essentially by hand. Unless it's using photography.

And that seems to be the big difference between how I work with digital media, and with Craig and David, and other artists who work with digital media but in other contexts. What we're doing here is turning digital fabrication media back into real things, instead of just pressing "Print." There is this course in which you can just take a screen grab and print it. But everything that comes out of Two Palms seems to be fairly involved: "No, that isn't what we do here. We wouldn't do anything so easy."

[*laughter*]

EH: So you might begin with a screen grab, but . . .

MR: It's really about taking that, dismantling it back down to a kind of atomic level, and then reconstituting it.

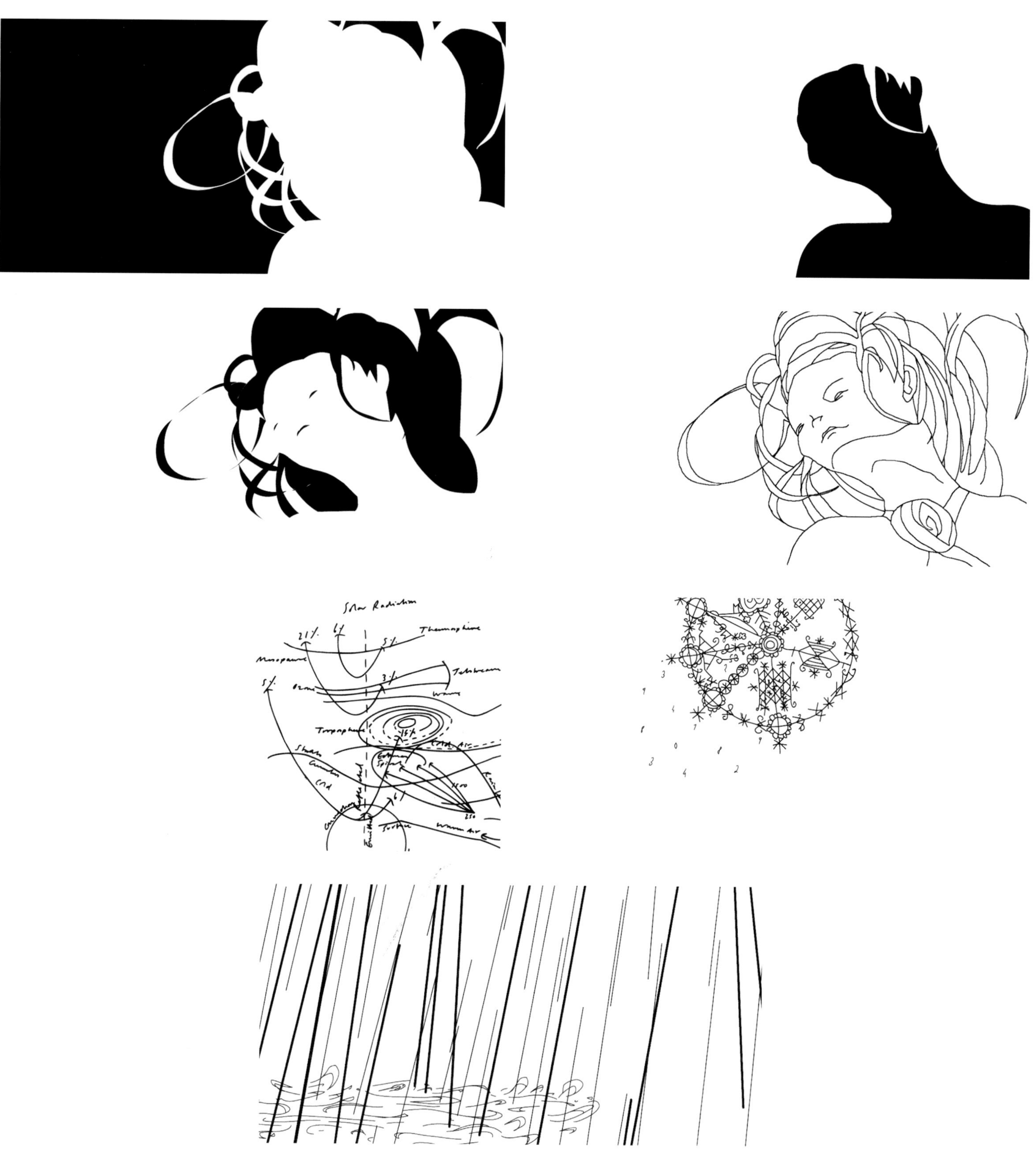

Matthew Ritchie

EH: And that's why you work at Two Palms.

MR: Yes, that's why I work at Two Palms instead of anywhere else. Because a quick screen grab—I could do that myself. But then it's kind of a straight version of photography, really. And there's nothing wrong with that, but it's a very different angle on handling material.

EH: Well, and etching in particular is such a tactile, hands-on medium.

MR: Yes, although I manage quite successfully to never touch an etching plate.

[laughter]

CZ: He tries not to, he really does, but he has indeed touched them. And he's so darn good at it! Not the avoiding, but the actual working on the plate.

EH: Well, and this reminds me of a particular discussion in an interview with you that I read, Matthew, in which you talk about your use of Mylars. That you have these drawings on Mylar which you overlay, one atop the other—a process you refer to as a tunneling of information.[7]

MR: The thing about these layering techniques is that they allow you to exist in a state of grace. You haven't committed, but you have this layer. And because it's a layer, it's there forever, held in this kind of magical suspension. Which allows you to bring it into being or remove it from being at different times. It's not that sort of progression through the plate like Picasso would do, starting with the lights and working progressively toward the darks.

EH: But working with these Mylars—it is a language or a technique that lent itself so well to working in printmaking, with all of these layers of information carried by a succession of plates.

MR: Absolutely. But I think what was especially appealing to me was its reversibility as well. It also allows you to go backwards and forwards in time and space without being limited to that one-way street.

CZ: Well, the whole thing about the use of Mylars is the transparency but also the reversibility. With a painting, you're laying one mark on top of another and essentially locking it in. And this Mylar technique opens up another universe. And I see that myself with the direct-gravure process which we use often. It allows us to make these plates and then possibly later decide to lose one or to add another.

EH: And also the possibilities that it opens up with color. The bringing forward or the muting of a particular color.

MR: Yes, absolutely. And because my work is so wrapped up in narrative, and because each of the colors represents a particular application of an idea, I'm particularly interested in working in this way. So, essentially, every time you're changing an idea, you're changing how the story unfolds.

I work with several scientists and I've found that they're amazingly sensitive to color. They have strong likes and dislikes. They'll look at a scene and say, "Oh, that's horrible!" And then you'll show them the same scene, just changing the color values, and they'll say, "Oh, that's beautiful!" We read certain colors as happy or sad, and we can't help ourselves. And although we'd like to think that we somehow evaluate art differently, we don't.

Here are some etching proofs. And you start with these and then you can tint them, so of course this could be the red one or the green one . . . in which case you would read it entirely differently as a mineral or a vegetable or a flesh-based organism, depending on the color. So you would see this and say, "Oh, that's really a plant, or that's really an animal." And in a scientific sense, there's no inherent color in the universe. Nothing has color. But our perception of color is also conditioned by our physical beings. A dog or a monkey would see a completely different set of colors—not because the object is different, but because their eyes see it differently. And women have an extra range of reds, which I suspect is why they like pornography less.

EH: Well, that actually touches on another interesting section of an interview with you I read. You've been quoted as saying that, according to legendary canard, the three big no-nos at MoMA [the Museum of Modern Art, New York] are sex, science, and spirituality.[8] And what's ironic for me about this in relation to your work is that I think you engage all three simultaneously, and somehow the combination cancels out the no-no factor.

MR: Well, MoMA has recently shown Marlene Dumas and Joseph Beuys—so perhaps there's hope for me yet. But there is a complicated dialogue in our culture around the various competing, heated, and sincere ideas of science, sex, and spirituality, all of which rely on competing and divergent ideas about originality and propagation. This discussion obviously relates to the evolution of the idea of the copy or multiple, which was originally intended to recapitulate the authentic aura of the original, as I'm sure you know.

Matthew Ritchie

But in the postmodern period, that primary model became maybe a little embarrassing, a little too "authentic." A cooler, more distanced point of view emerged and engendered another side of the art world, more interested in secondary reactions—which has had the intriguing side effect of invalidating the first idea of the copy. Today, the copy not only validates itself but, in some cases, has even been described as invalidating or replacing the original. And in my time in the art world, which hasn't really been that long, you can see new schools that are interested in yet more involuted modes of self-referentiality. There is a whole group of artists now who only make reproductions of existing things in the world, revalidating the copy as a copy of a copy. Something that used to be a relative novelty with someone like Charles Ray—you take a manikin and bring it into a gallery. Now there are hundreds of manikin artists. It's like a school. "I'll make a red tractor." "And I'll make a blue tractor." "And I'll make a pink one!" And then there's another group that is interested in excavating how the art world responded to new media—or didn't.

An alternative approach seems to characterize the artists working at Two Palms, who are interested in addressing the world though explored objects—that are then recreated rather than reproduced—through a collective process of manifestation with the team. They draw on history without being overwhelmed by it. To my mind, they belong to a larger, unaffiliated group of artists, who remain interested in the manifestation of all of the aspects of the real world through art, without either necessarily validating a putative "eternal original" or invalidating it. And of course, the real world—as opposed to the world of mediated constructs—is mostly composed of sex, science, and spirituality. Which is why it's so embarrassing and vexing, and so difficult to grapple with. Because it keeps turning into real problems. It's not black and white. It's a full-color world filled with full-color emotions, and it's messy, like the objects we make. Of course we must all acknowledge the tendency of large-scale systems to cool down and accept the entropic drift toward homogeneity, but we must also celebrate the constant emergence of new and interesting exceptions to that. It's this difference between a world view based on doubt and one based on possibility that defines the spectrum of movements like Cubism, Surrealism, Abstract Expressionism—which were all about sex, science, and spirituality as well.

EH: But a lot of the artists involved in those movements are dead.

MR: Yes, they've cooled off.

[laughter]

MR: So I think it's kind of a courageous but maybe just an intuitive approach that attracts artists to Two Palms who want to make "real things."

EH: I never saw that link, until you mentioned it today, among the artists working at Two Palms, but it's true.

MR: And the most mediated artist there is Richard Prince. But he's also the most explicit about dealing with sex. Like, I may have cooled myself down, but I still get pretty hot under the collar.

[*laughter*]

EH: Chris Ofili deals a lot with sex too.

MR: Yes. Ofili, Cecily Brown.

CZ: Even Carroll Dunham.

MR: So, when you think about it, Two Palms is just a porno factory . . .

[*laughter*]

CZ: I've never realized that!

EH: Well, if worse comes to worse in this terrible economy, David can always push that angle.

MR: It's not a bad idea for a rather interesting little plain-covered book.

[*laughter*]

CZ: The other thing I wanted to show Matthew, because he probably never saw this [*pulling out some 8 × 10 printouts with hand notations; see fig. 18*] . . . this is the stuff I had to do. I had to match tonal ranges on the aquatints. In this sheet I added the orange and yellow to tell me how dark to make the tones in the hair.

EH: Now why are those so jagged-looking?

MR: They're bitmap prints.

CZ: Yes, they're bitmaps. They're actually from what we call a raster [graphics] file, as opposed to a vector file.

EH: Can you explain that to me?

MR: Well, a raster file is made of dots, like hundreds or thousands of little dots, depending on the resolution at which you set your file—so many dots per inch. If you had a million dots per inch, it would appear to be completely smooth. A vector file is a computer file that shows you literally a line between two points with a degree of curvature. So there are only two dots, which is why a vector file is so tiny. It's nothing, really. A vector file simply says, "There's a point here, and there's a point here, and there's a curve that connects them, and that curve has this particular angle of curvature to it."

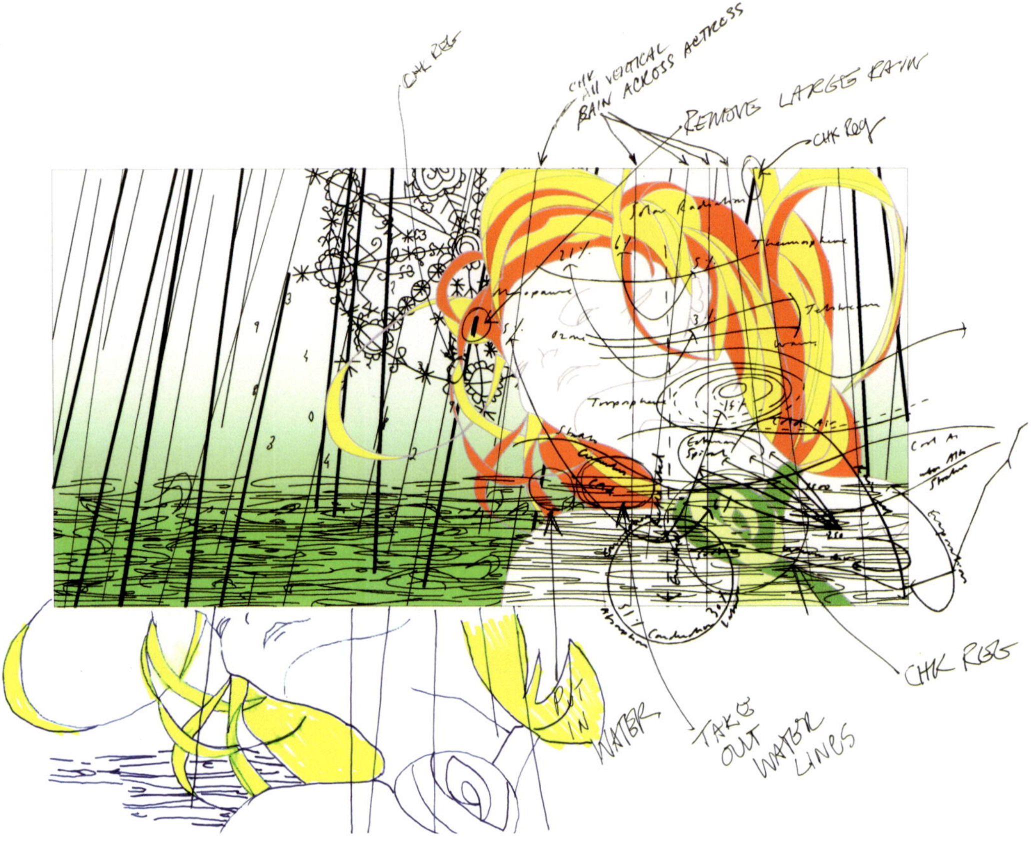

FIG. 18. Zammiello's color notations on a printout of a screen shot from Ritchie's *Sea State Two*

EH: So the *Sea State* prints are a combination of those two types of files?

CZ: Well, towards the end of this *Sea State* series David was starting to trace Matthew's drawings in vector, so you get that type of look. But the first few prints were pure bitmap raster files. There are programs such as Adobe Streamline that one can use, but they tend to assign too many nodal points to be of use.

EH: Too much?

CZ: Yes. Too much information. The laser wouldn't be able to draw it. So that's why you see this jagged line. We were able to clean it up, though. But the outline in the analog world of printing, the physical printing of the etchings . . . as Matthew was saying, all of these little pixels . . . you're able to take that sawtoothed look and trap it with the outline drawing that's around everything.

And that covers up that jagged look. So there's very little of that evident if at all in the final prints.

MR: I think that was the appeal. Every year that went by there would be a new iteration of these programs. They would turn some features off and then turn them on again. Some things would get better, some things would get worse. So the vector tracing—this feature by which you can turn a line into two points—is a technology that came and went and then came back again during this whole process. We started with this very cheap program called Adobe Streamline that I had a copy of. It was a program that started as Aldus, and then the technology was bought by Adobe, which was ultimately bought by Apple. But during this time it would come and go without forewarning, and suddenly we'd realize, "Oh my God, it's not working!" And then, "Now it's working again." Or, "Now it will do this but not that."

EH: Oh, how frustrating.

MR: But I think that's the appeal of working with digital technologies and tools. Because the moment it becomes a totally stable platform, we would probably all lose interest in it immediately. As, in fact, we all have. So we haven't made any more of these since.

[*pause*]

CZ: The actress was the first print we did [*see fig. 4*], because, in effect, it's the most literal, the most figurative. But this gave me a way to relate the rest of the four prints, to let them have at least a certain consistency with each other. And here [*indicating fig. 10*], this is showing you how the airbrush makes that fade, so that I could reproduce that fade to the best of my ability in an analog way on each of the prints in order that they would have a similar feel. So I looked back at these notes that I have, Matthew, and they're all notes on the etching times, and at some points I'd actually be working on the commuter train to or from work, doing separations on my laptop. And I think by the time we got to the end, I wasn't taking many notes. I knew how to do it by rote.

EH: Here, in this [*fig. 19*], you're breaking out the color scheme.

MR: Yes, we made all the colors in Flash for the original movie, which I believe this is a still from.

CZ: It is. That's a direct screen capture.

MR: And, of course, they're all Flash colors, changed constantly. They're not Pantone colors, so they have to be matched and rematched. And if you go off cue with one little bit of yellow, then all the other colors are off, so you have to refind all the colors, basically. That's what was going on here. And we had to proof the colors constantly.

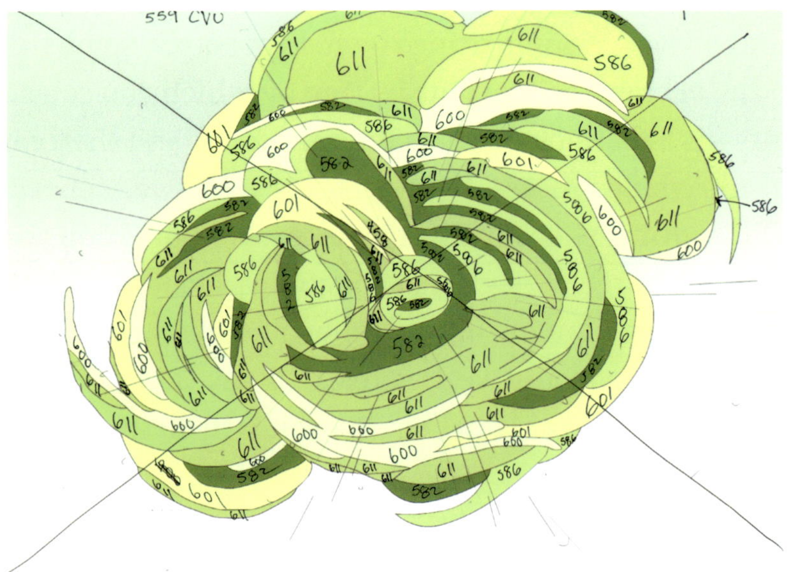

FIG. 19. Screen capture from Flash movie with color notes

CZ: Yes. When it got to the point that we were actually printing the colors, one on top of the other, then Matthew would come in and he was able to visualize when a color needed to be adjusted. And he was able to see two or three colors down in any given proof [*fig. 20*].

MR: Again, all of this kind of perverse turning of something that was entirely mechanical back into something that is entirely handmade. Handmixing all of these actual ink colors to match a color that had never really existed in any concrete form. Because when you pick from the spectrum, there are something like 250 million colors. There are actually more colors than can be chemically made.

CZ: So it's an approximation . . .

MR: Two hundred and fifty-six million colors, or something like that. That's the gamut. I understand that there's now an application for your iPhone that will allow you to take a picture of anything and it will then give you the corresponding Benjamin Moore color of paint. But, of course, it's not really the color that you saw, it's the color that your iPhone has captured.

[*pause*]

 I love this one quote from an interview with you, and was wondering if you'd expand on it?

MR: Go ahead.

EH: You say, "Some people who are trying to put a popular spin on science end up simplifying it into either the Frankenstein argument—it's going to be bad for you—or the utopian argument—it's going to be amazing and there'll be a flying car and a robot in your kitchen. So you get these two poles, neither of which is remotely true."[9]

MR: I have to take that back, slightly, because there is a flying car. There's been one since the seventies. But they're just awful, you want nothing to do with them. And there is a robot in your kitchen—it's called a microwave—and there is a man with a face transplant.

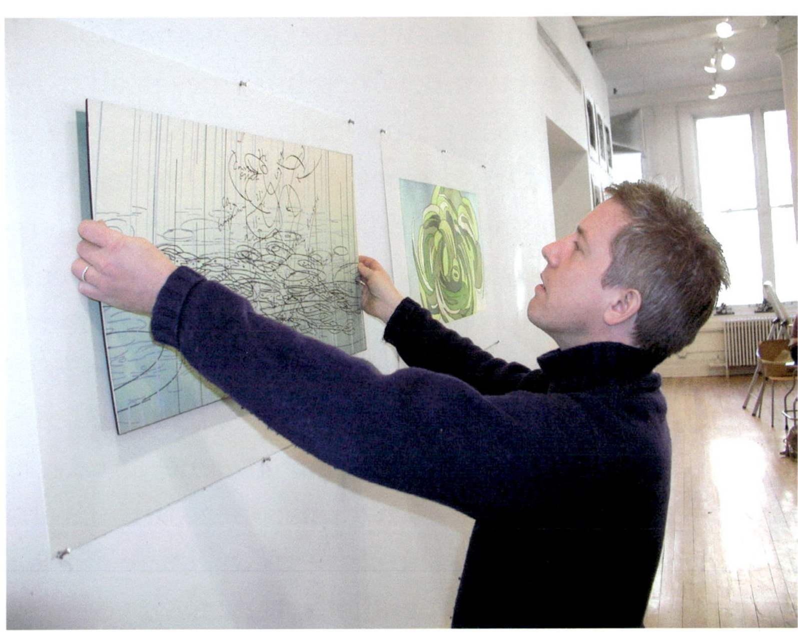

FIG. 20. Ritchie examining proofs at Two Palms

EH: Right. But you've also said that "the appearance of science has nothing really to do with what it actually is."[10] And I'm wondering if you could speak about that in relation to this suite of prints.

MR: Well, the great mythological narratives were originally formulated to describe problems with the ontological structure of the world and the epistemological structure of the world—where does it come from and where is it going? We debate these concepts over and over and over again, and one response is just to say, "I don't care." But it was not the original mythos of the people who came to America. They cared a lot. Successive waves of peoples who came to America cared a great deal. So I think "I don't care" is actually an expression of exhaustion, and also of failure. Some people might say, "I don't care where the world came from," but they also apparently believe in UFOs and angels and all sorts of things—various strands of millennial or mystical Christianity. So these same people might say, on the one hand, they don't care, but on the other hand, they very much do care. And what they care about is a narrative that describes the underlying predicament of being. And this is where I think science has failed to explain itself adequately through what already exists and was specifically being developed throughout the twentieth century—which was a visual vocabulary of immense richness and complexity that was specifically being evolved to address existential questions of being and of the conscious life in the twentieth century. And for various complex reasons that project was abandoned and replaced with a secondary thought process—this exhaustion, the "I don't care" mode—which extends absolutely through the very highest reaches of the art world, which imagines itself to be extremely cultured in many respects. This is a cross-cultural problem at every level.

So one of the impetuses of my project overall was to begin to reestablish what I saw as preexisting connections between these different vocabularies which were created over thousands and thousands of years of effort to describe and work on these problems. And the last major iteration was during the pre–Second World War period. It's not like it's really the distant past, it's relatively recent, and I thought it could be recuperated fairly easily. This notion of narrative is directly related to science. And science has to be understood simultaneously in two terms: one is that it's an enterprise whose project is the questioning of the physical structure of the universe, a very difficult, inductive process; its parallel enterprise is the analysis of the data that it gets back from that questioning—a deductive, analytic process which is, of course, even more difficult.

It's easy to reopen the large-scale questions of the arts, or relatively easy. It's much harder to reintroduce the idea of analysis in terms of reflecting on the new data that's come in since—say, the Alain Aspect experiments that began in 1974, which redefined the physical nature of reality through experiment rather than through hypothesis. So, in other words, in the 1920s you have Einstein's general theory of relativity. You have the establishment of quantum mechanics and the beginning of a revolution in physics that completely rearranges the physical consciousness of the universe. Then you have the war. And the war provides a tremendous experimental effort towards proving some of the theories of quantum mechanics, but it doesn't provide any theoretical background for that. Theory is put to one side. So much so that right through the 1960s the logical conclusions of quantum mechanics are largely put aside in favor of large-scale experimentation in military weapons systems and civilian power systems. In other words, it's too difficult to go into what's wrong with quantum mechanics when it's creating these spectacular results.

EH: Like nuclear energy.

MR: Like nuclear energy and nuclear weapons. So [Edward] Teller and his gang take over, and Los Alamos becomes dedicated to the production of munitions and energy. And these are significant questions, but the culture sets aside the fact that this is all based on a series of hypotheses about the nature of the universe which are really quite disturbing.

In the 1950s, [John Archibald] Wheeler puts forward the Everett–Wheeler theory of the multiverse. Hugh Everett is the guy who invents the theory of parallel universes, who discovers this. It's inherent in quantum mechanics, in what's called the Copenhagen interpretation: how does the universe materialize itself? In other words, how does the universe make itself real? There has to be a machine that does it. But the machine has to be as big as the universe to make itself real. So, is it something outside the universe, which is called the "observer effect," or is it inside the universe? Which comes to why I'm so interested in all of this, because it's just like being an artist—does somebody make you do this or do you make yourself do it? Especially on Monday mornings. Who is making you do this, and why?[11]

[laughter]

MR: So we all face this dilemma every day. Science, at the early part of the twentieth century, proposed the central question of human consciousness, but it reproposed it in a way that was entirely different than ever before, although it's the same question: is there a God? (which in quantum mechanics is called the "observer effect"). Or is there no God? In which case, who decides? Do you decide yourself? And if so, how does that happen on a quantum-mechanical level? Are *you* authoring the universe? And if you are authoring the universe, then everyone is able to author the universe. Which means that it's inevitable that there are multiple universes, which was Everett's observation about the multiverse. And he took that theory to

Matthew Ritchie

the establishment in 1954 and was just laughed out of town. And he was so frustrated that he went in the weapons design business and became enormously wealthy . . .

[laughter]

MR: And so twenty years after that, it's the 1970s and the Cold War is no longer fun, and that question is brought back up again. And this time they do some experiments—called the Aspect experiments—and they find out that, well, Everett might be right. There might be multiverses. The experiments aren't conclusive in either way, but from that point forward the scientific investigation of alternate states of matter and alternate states of being has gone from strength to strength—to the physical manifestation of new states of matter, the Bose-Einstein condensate, which is where all quantum states exist simultaneously. They made that in 1995. Teleportation—where they teleported two atoms—took place in 2001, I believe. So they've moved from a hypothetical statement—"Well, science has discovered these very strange things"—in 1905 [with the publication of Einstein's special theory of relativity] to, by the end of Einstein's century, proving they're real. The universe really does have these strange physical phenomena at its most basic level.

So, to my way of thinking, this allows a reopening of what that narrative was that was being proposed through these visual metaphors. What are the arts doing with this information? For most of that period they're not doing much at all—legitimately, because culture didn't want to deal with it. So it's no surprise that the arts didn't want to deal with it either. You don't see lots of artists dealing with quantum mechanics after, say, 1960. There were a few, but it's really just a subset. Then you see it picking up again in the 1970s hand-in-hand with the Aspect experiments. But only in the past ten years, really, has there been any real movement. And it's no surprise that not a lot of artists deal with it, but I think it's a huge opportunity.

One of the reasons people don't care about science is because there are no narratives that tell them about it. Except in the movies, which are of course the largest pop cultural form and which deal constantly with science. So many blockbuster movies are about alternate realities and parallel universes and the near future and time travel, and it goes on and on. So there is this idea that culture is, on the one hand, totally disconnected from science—that is what people will say—when in fact the culture is producing dozens of stories in the form of movies that are *only* about science. Which shows you how disconnected large parts of the art world are. The "fine art" world, the world of visual artists, may claim that it's about the community, or pop culture, or the media. But I would counter that: "Well, but you're not about *Terminator.*" And [*The*] *Terminator* is a movie based solely on time travel, and on a fairly sophisticated series of things called the "grandfather paradox," which is actually a rather complex, quantum-mechanically based proposition. So this notion that we're not telling ourselves stories about science is incorrect. We are, in fact, but just haven't acknowledged that that [sort of science-fictional storytelling] is what science looks like in one of its manifestations.

So the *Sea State Five* prints and the story from which they came is a way to say that science is like the movies. And it goes back to this kind of curious avoidance of these things that are massively central. And maybe because the way science manifests itself as story is so central, it's too overwhelming for the more fragile elements of the art world to deal with and they find it vulgar.

[pause]

MR: It's an interesting thing working with Craig on these print projects because it's a way to bring these things into focus or alignment. Discovering, "Oh, I see, this fits on top of that on top of that." And if it doesn't, you just throw it away. And then redraw it.

[laughter]

EH: And redraw it again.

MR: And again and again and again. And then the final thing that I think is particularly interesting about this way of working is that these files are very, very small to begin with. There's nothing to them. It's not a one-to-one mapping. And there's an idea underlying the universal structure that's called gauge symmetry—which is how very small things become very big things, how they have to scale. Gravity has to scale. You still are subjected to gravity whether you're an ant or a planet, but it has to scale, and it has to scale flawlessly. There's never a place where gravity stops. But the differences between the forces that hold things together are immense. Nonetheless, they're all perfectly scaled to each other at all levels, at all times, and under all circumstances. Whether it's a trillion degrees Fahrenheit at the beginning of the universe or it's now three degrees above zero. Everything always works perfectly in all directions. So the idea of creating a continuum is what's very beautiful about all of these processes. Because hopefully you're not creating a series of arbitrary stops and starts, but gradually introducing ideas into practice. Like Craig was saying earlier, "Oh, I can do *that*," and "I can do that." Now you can constantly recuperate fixed points—not just techniques, but actual relationships. "Oh, let's do that again this time over here, and this time let's make it twenty feet long," or "This time let's make it really tiny." And I don't think you get it just out of working digitally, because digital technology is itself riddled with these arbitrary gates—it's not a symmetrically stable system. But if you figure out how to translate it back into the physical world, that's when you have a scalable, infinitely manipulatable space, a mental space that you can theoretically make anything in that you've already made, in relationship with anything else you've already made. So, in other words, we could put this fade in the background . . . [*placing one Mylar drawing over another*]

EH: That's beautiful.

MR: That's what started us on this whole thing.

CZ: Also, when I work with you, Matthew, I don't think that "I'm going to make a print with Matthew" and then out comes the print. And sometime later, "Okay, it's time to make another print with Matthew" and out it comes. I know that any work I do with Matthew is an ongoing process.

MR: But I think this is a much more traditional idea about artmaking than what happened in the twentieth century, which was much more this guilded, craft-based, successive, linear thinking. Old Master artists used to routinely take things back, rework them. You think of all of the pioneers of etching . . . the idea of the piece was much more the idea of the multiple states, the many years of further consideration. Nobody works in that way anymore—they say they do, but they don't really. So I don't want to present this as though we've discovered the idea of the artistic continuum. It certainly preexisted, but I think oftentimes now it gets lost. But I do believe that thinking about it digitally actually helps, because it forces a reconsideration of the continuum. Because it exists simultaneously as a continuum and as a continuum that's failing—because the software goes out of date, the data gets lost. So, on the one hand, data is preserved for further consideration and, on the other hand, it is stored in a media that you can no longer access, unlike a copper plate, which you really can pull out again in twenty years.

So I think that's what's so compelling for me about working in the print medium, because now something is physical; it's not just in the vaporware of the visual world. Now it's a real thing. It's the idea of a continuum that actually exists physically.

Whenever I give a lecture, I'm asked, "Why do you make paintings?" And I'm thinking, "No, the question is, 'why do I make all this other stuff?'" I'm constantly trying to take the things that are in the paintings into the digital world and then turn around and make them real again, not just leave them in that digital space. That interim state is a very desirable state, but, nonetheless, it doesn't leave you with anything. Twenty years from now you have nothing. Maybe that's why the digital artists vanished. They got tired of updating.

Notes

The preceding conversation was held on June 8, 2009, in Ritchie's studio, in New York.

1. The exhibition *010101: Art in Technological Times* was held at the San Francisco Museum of Modern Art from March 3 to July 8, 2001.

2. Matthew Ritchie et al., *Matthew Ritchie: Incomplete Projects 01–07* (n.p.: Wild Card Crew 2000–2006, 2006).

3. For a more comprehensive description of the narrative, see Matthew Ritchie, "The Fast Set," in *Matthew Ritchie: Incomplete Projects 01–07*, 8–17.

4. *The New Place: A Matthew Ritchie Project* can be viewed at http://www.matthewritchie.com/src/sfmoma/index.html (accessed September 26, 2011).

5. John Lund is a master printer who works directly with the artist Jasper Johns at Johns's home studio. He and Zammiello worked together throughout the 1980s and 1990s at Universal Limited Art Editions (ULAE).

6. Initially Zammiello ran tests with various thin, brittle grounds, such as Cronite Janes' Ground, but none yielded the results that he found were easily achieved by spraying the plates with Krylon High Heat BBQ and Stove black aerosol paint. The one drawback was, no matter how high the power output or speed of the laser pass, there always remained a thin, semi-transparent film of paint on the surface of the plate where the laser had removed nearly all of the ground. This film was strong enough to block out the etching of the copper with ferric chloride. Zammiello's best explanation for this artifact is that when the light beam got close enough to the metal, it was deflected by the copper's mirror finish. When viewing this film left on the surface after the burnt soot of the paint has been cleared away, one can clearly make out the scanning passes of a raster file on the metal's surface. Luckily, the film is removed quite easily by scrubbing the exposed copper with Twinkle Copper Cleaner and water. This is also another testament to the durability of the enamel paint's strength as a ground.

7. Matthew Ritchie, "Information, Cells, and Evil," undated interview with Art21, PBS website, http://www.pbs.org/ (accessed September 26, 2011).

8. Matthew Ritchie, "Proposition Player," undated interview with Art21, PBS website, http://www.pbs.org/ (accessed September 26, 2011).

9. Ibid.

10. Ibid.

11. This conversation was conducted on a Monday morning.

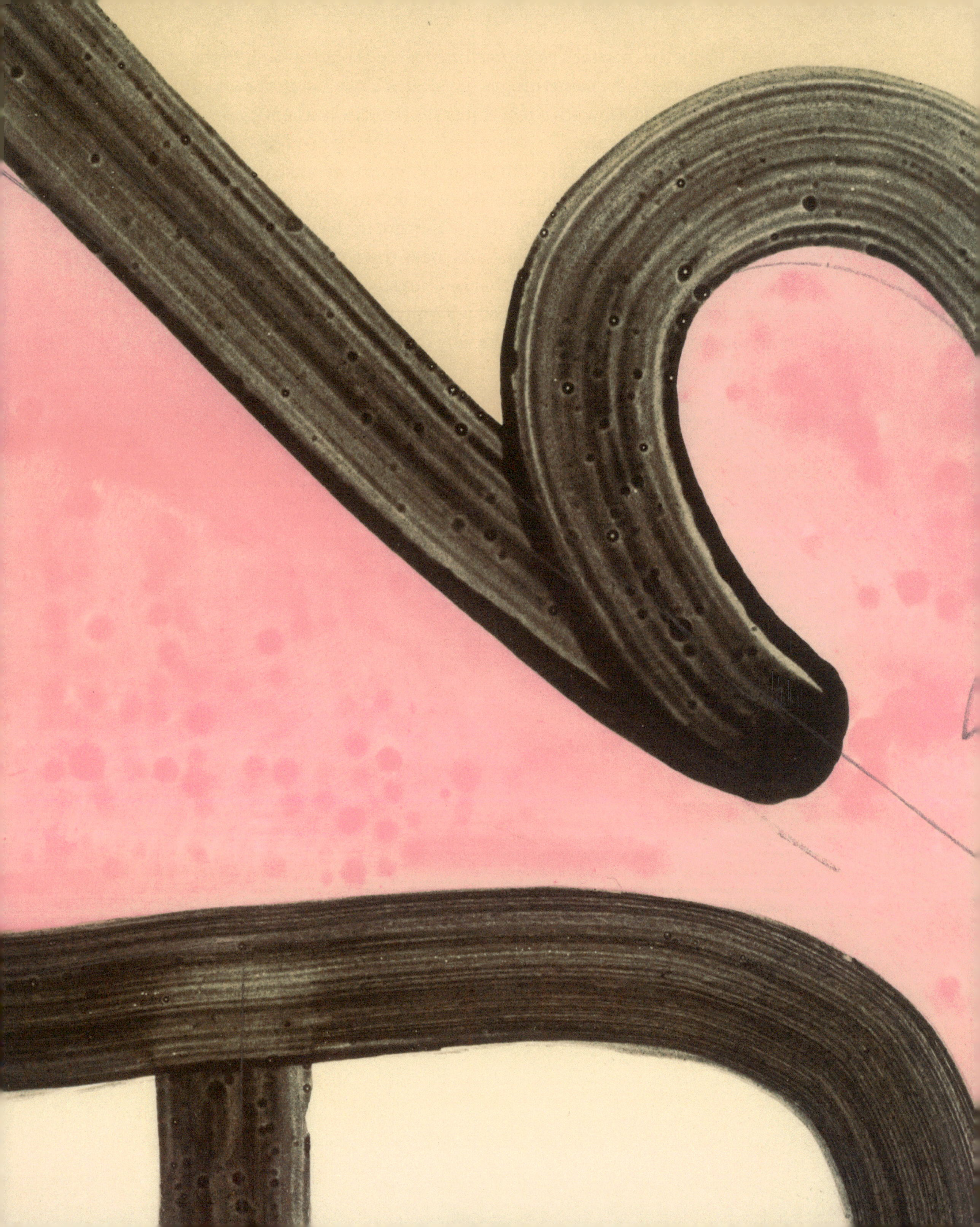

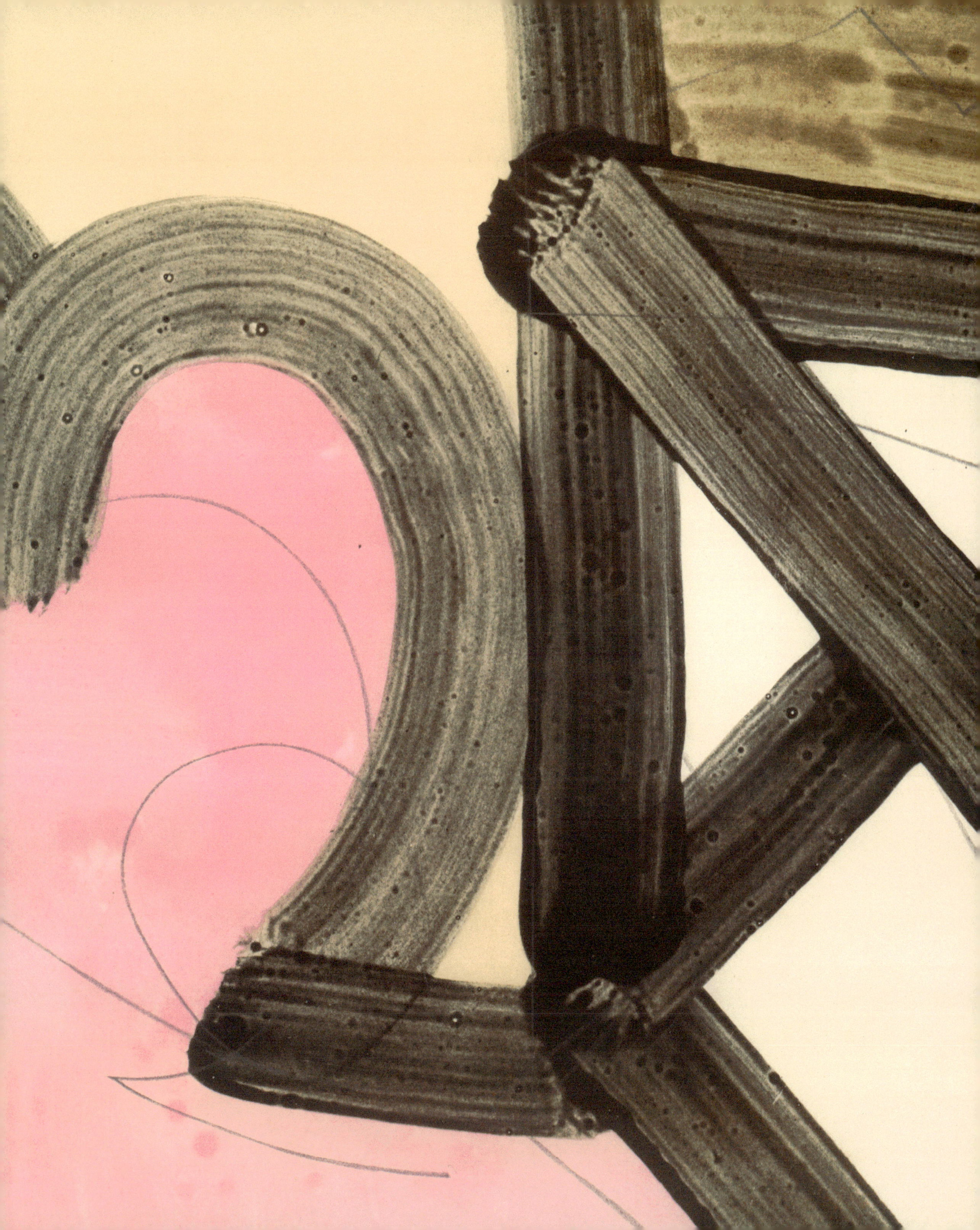

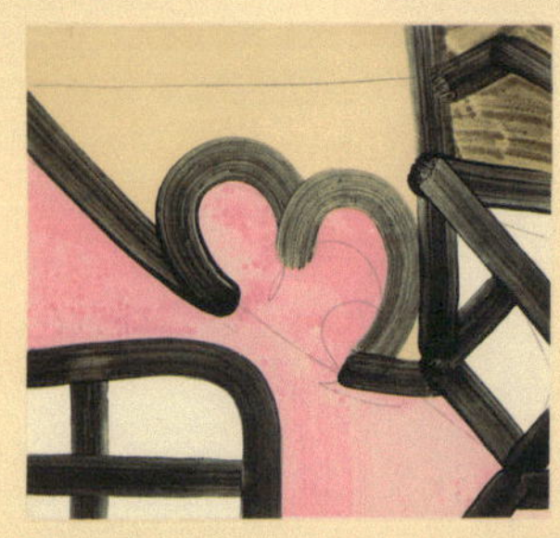
C.D.   2003-2004   4/21   1

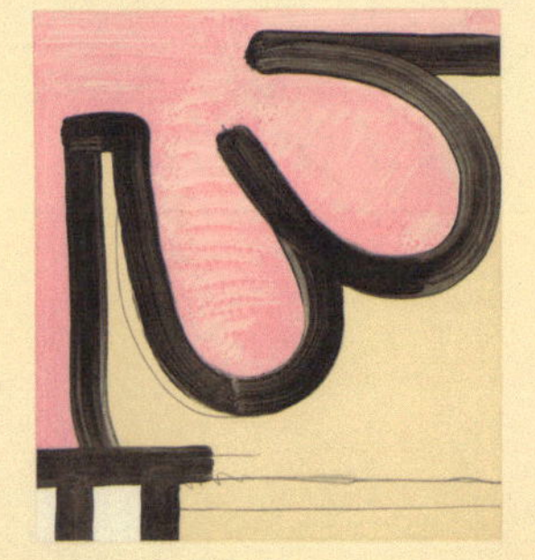
C.D.   2003-2004   4/21   2

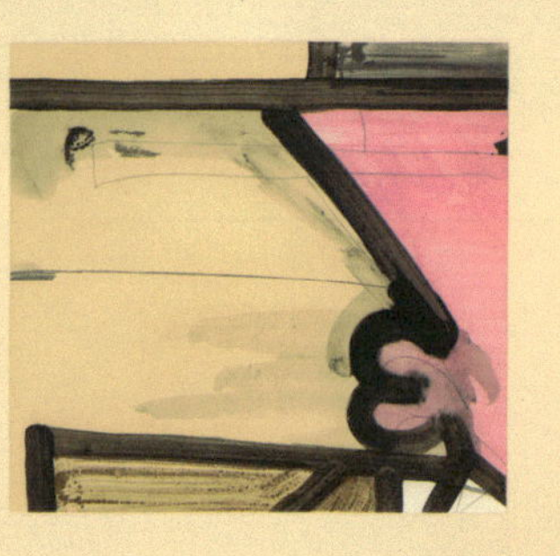
C.D.   2003-2004   4/21   3

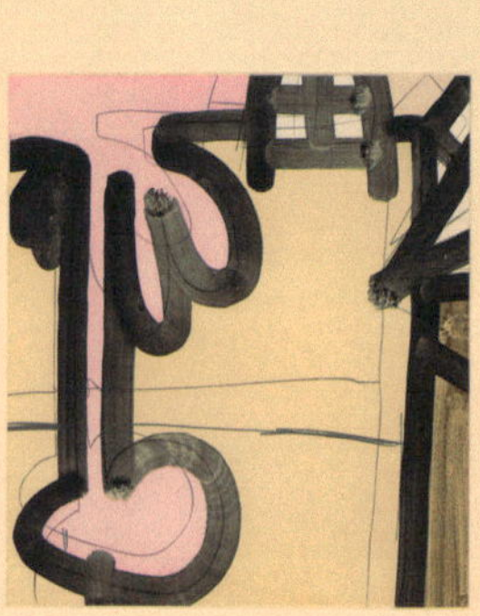
C.D.   2003-2004   4/21   4

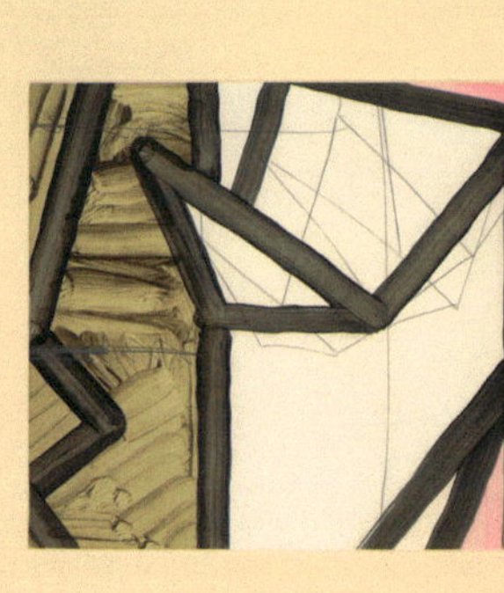
C.D.   2003-2004   4/21   5

Carroll Dunham has been making prints for more than twenty-five years, working regularly at Universal Limited Art Editions (ULAE) and Two Palms and occasionally at other presses. Each year during that period the artist has been actively involved in at least one print project. In the following conversation, Dunham speaks about his immersion in printmaking and how years of experience—and maturity—have expanded and freed his art. Early conceptions about maintaining a separation or "purity" between the media in which he works (painting, drawing, and print) have given way in recent years to a more fluid approach, as Dunham has gradually become less concerned with such lines of division. More and more, his drawings inform his paintings, which in turn inform his prints and back again, and he has become increasingly fascinated by this cross-fertilization.

Dunham touches on his experiences of working in print shops in which "the meter's running," or in situations in which he does not like the printer with whom he is working —situations that have in the past triggered in him a "total system shutdown." While time pressures can sometimes be a catalyst for creativity, Dunham has always felt most inspired in situations in which he has built intellectual and personal relationships with the printers involved. Of his two-and-a-half-decade relationship with Craig Zammiello, he states: "I don't want to put words in his mouth, but I've always felt that Craig was always more responsive to the direct aspect of my work. And we work together a lot, in the same studio, at the same time." Dunham draws the distinction between this sort of direct collaboration, which involves intimacy and trust between artist and printer, and the very different experience of working in a situation that is more akin to "a chess game where you write your move down and mail it to a person and then they mail back their move."

The focus of this conversation is Dunham's *Closing In* (figs. 1–5), a portfolio of five direct gravures with etching and aquatint created in 2003 and 2004. The suite was conceptually "leveraged" from a series of drawings Dunham was working on at the time, which David Lasry and Zammiello had seen at the Armory Show in 2002, and marks Dunham's first experience with direct gravure.

Left to right, top to bottom: **FIGS. 1-5.** Carroll Dunham, *Closing In*, 2003–4. Five five-color direct gravures with etching and aquatint on Fawn Stonehenge paper, 24 ¾ × 20 in. (62.9 × 50.8 cm). Edition of 21. Yale University Art Gallery, Janet and Simeon Braguin Fund, 2006.39.1–.5

CARROLL DUNHAM: I started making prints in 1984—lithographs, at ULAE—and basically just kept doing it after that. I didn't know when I started to make prints that I would enjoy it as much as I did. Printmaking has been a fairly continuous part of my work since then—with some periods of recess, but I'm always thinking about it. So, at this point, I think I've made prints in many different media, most in the obvious ways you would think of and some less obvious.

ELISABETH HODERMARSKY: Yes, it would seem that you've worked in almost every print medium I can think of, except for maybe mezzotint?

CRAIG ZAMMIELLO: There's an idea.

CD: I haven't made anything that's called mezzotint, although I think I've used some mezzotint techniques in other etchings . . . little bits and pieces. The first etchings I made were a project I did in 1987 at Studio 2 RC, in Rome, published by Editions Ilene Kurtz.[1] That's when I realized how different it was to work in another studio. It was also my first experience of having a publisher and a printer be two different entities, which I found interesting but not as rewarding as having it all be in an integrated situation. It got me interested in working on etchings out at Universal [Limited Art Editions], because I knew that I would be comfortable there, and I could just kind of play around and not have this feeling that "the meter's running," which is an aspect of working with printers when there's a schedule. At ULAE we never worked with any sort of schedule. For a long time I worked there almost exclusively, and that's where Craig and I became friendly. There was a guy there named Keith Brintzenhoff, who I was mostly working with, and Craig was there as one of the other printers. And at one point Craig got involved with helping on a project, and from then on we started working together.

EH: And that was one of your first etchings?

CD: No, actually it was a lithograph that involved screenprinting elements, and Craig was asked to come over to the studio we were working in to do the screenprinting part of the print. So I think that's when we started to work together.

CZ: Yes.

CD: I later realized when we were working on this book [*Carroll Dunham Prints*[2]] that there was a very compressed couple of years during which I made a lot of different kinds of etchings. And then we began those four really large ones [*Untitled*, 1988-89; *Wave*, 1988-90; *Point of Origin*, 1988-92; and *Another Dimension*, 1988-95, *fig. 6*], which ended up taking a long time.[3] We started those all at about the same time, while we were working on some drypoints and on other normal gravure-type things . . . we made a lot of intaglio prints in a rather short period of time.

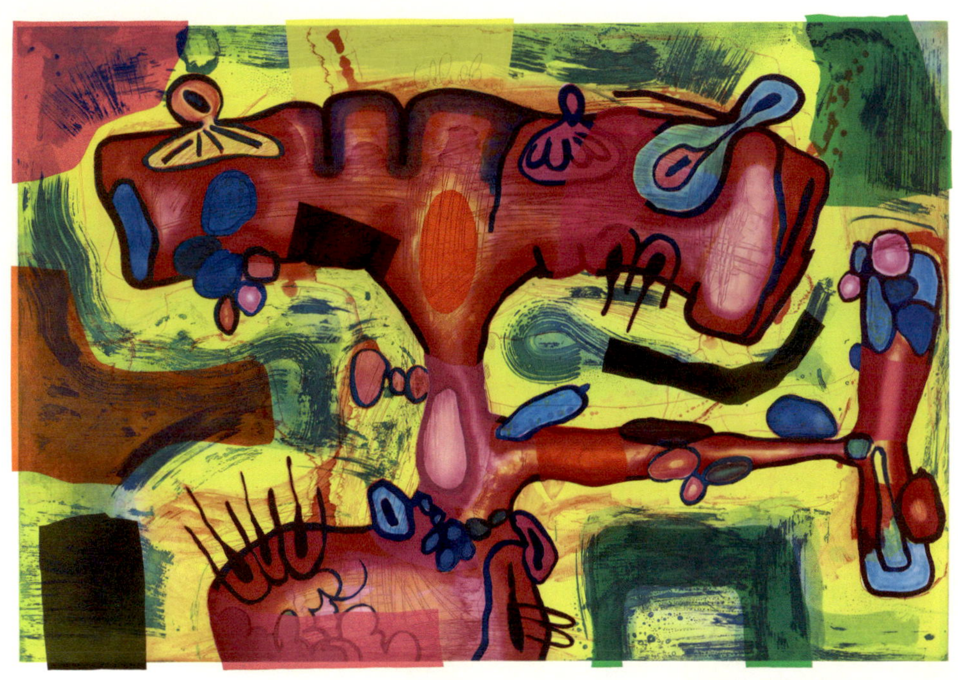

FIG. 6. Carroll Dunham, *Another Dimension*, 1988–95. Six-color etching, spit bite, sugar lift, and aquatint with collage on Arches En-Tout-Cas paper, 47 ¾ × 67 ⅝ in. (121.3 × 171.8 cm). Edition of 23. Published by Universal Limited Art Editions. Yale University Art Gallery, The Heinz Family Fund, 2009.59.1

EH: And what attracted you to etching, since you had been working almost exclusively in lithography?

CD: Lithography has such a specific look. It's so immaterial. And—like a lot of things—the thing that's so great about it is also the thing that annoys you about it. And so you try something different, and then *that* starts to annoy you, and the other thing seems great again, and . . . it wasn't anything more than that. I knew by that point that I was serious about printmaking, as they say, and I knew that if I was really going to figure it out in a broader way, that I needed to throw myself into etching. And I was up for something different.

EH: And those four large etchings were the first prints the two of you made together?

CD: Well, this was the first time that Craig was the principal printer on one of my projects.

    Carroll Dunham

CZ: I had known Carroll for years—got to know him while he worked on his lithographs at ULAE. We talked a lot.

CD: Yes, we had a lot of fun socially together, at lunch and other times. Then Craig became part of the "brain trust." There was a group—Craig and John Lund and Keith, and other people that aren't there anymore either—in the studio, and depending upon what we were doing, certain people would be more or less in the foreground. I made a few prints with John Lund. Just John and I working together. And Keith was kind of the coordinator of all of it; he was directing traffic. And then at a certain point Keith left, and it started to be more direct, just me working one-on-one with the different printers. But I think, Craig, when you and I started to work more directly with one another was with those big etchings.

CZ: Yes. And like you said, we worked on all four at about the same time, as well as the portfolio *Shadows* [1989], which was a series of ten pure drypoints.[4] The thing about *Shadows* that's so interesting is that it was just Carroll, working alone. Basically, we would just bring him these pewter plates, and that's it. The only thing he would need us for was the proofing. It's a gorgeous portfolio.

CD: That project demonstrates one of the things about open-ended exposure to a print studio that's very different from just doing "print projects," because I wasn't even thinking about drypoints. I was working on other things, and I saw this pewter lying around and I asked Bill Goldston about it. And they got me some drypoint tools and I started messing around. And then it was so interesting and it felt so good, that I said, "I'd just like to keep doing this while you guys are doing other stuff." And so then Craig got me more tools, and it ended up becoming this portfolio, *Shadows*.

EH: Pewter is really soft, isn't it?

CD: Yes, it's really soft. That's why the editions are so small. We tried to steel face one, and it just burned a hole in the plate. The electroplating thing didn't really work right.

CZ: Well, it had to have two different metals put on top of it before you could even put the steel on.

CD: But we melted a hole in one.

CZ: Well, yes. That was done out of house. It wasn't us. I get a call one day and the guy says, "There's a problem with the piece you gave us." And I said, "What problem?" And he said, "There's a hole in it." And I said, "There's not supposed to be."

[laughter]

CD: But that was good, ultimately, because that clarified what it was. That clarified that this would be a very small edition, that there would be a certain amount of "image fatigue" built into the printing. It was kind of lovely, really, to have something like that made so clear.

CZ: It makes them kind of precious too.

CD: And the images really change, one to the next.

CZ: They do. And then *Seven Places* [1990–94; *fig. 7*] was another jump, where we used photogravure.[5]

FIG. 7. Carroll Dunham, *Seven Places: Eta*, 1994, one from an album of seven intaglios with hand-separated photogravure on *gampi* paper laid down on J. Whatman 1952 handmade paper, 19¾ × 24¾ in. (50.2 × 62.9 cm). Edition of 25. Published by Universal Limited Art Editions

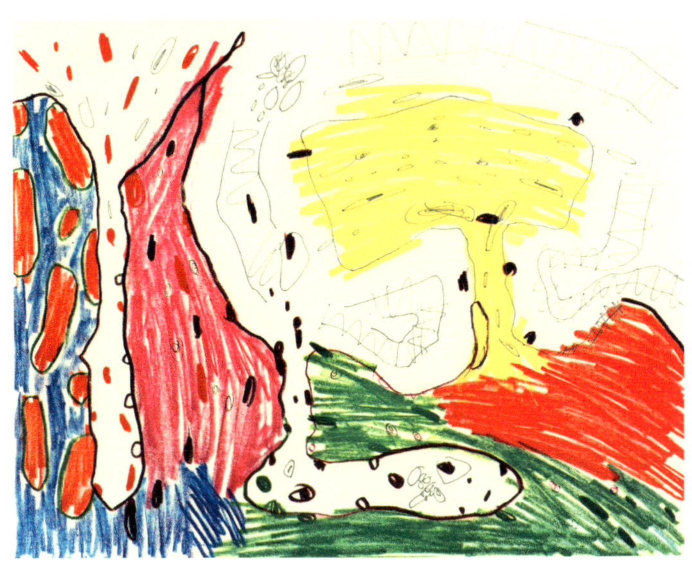

CD: Yes. That started because Craig knew a lot about photogravure.

You know, in the beginning it seemed very important to demonstrate that my prints could exist as a separate thing. And then at some point it was suggested to me that it might be interesting to use a drawing from a sheet of paper as a point of departure for making a print. Which is an idea that would have been doable when I first started to work at ULAE, but it wouldn't have made sense to me then. It would have been premature. It would have felt cheesy somehow. But when it came up in about 1989/90, it made sense.

So I made a lithograph like that. And then we decided to do a bigger project. And I had this group of little drawings that I liked a lot, colored-pencil drawings. And I liked the idea that they would be lithographs. So we

   Carroll Dunham

started out thinking that it was going to be a portfolio of lithographs. And we proceeded with that idea for a while, but they just never really looked right. So Bill got the idea that they should be remade as photogravures— that we should redo the whole thing as etching. So Craig, who was the photogravure guy, started redoing every single plate as photogravure, right?

CZ: Well, yes, this was actually an interesting moment, because it was at the same time that I was working out the four-color photogravure process for Bob [Robert] Rauschenberg. So, Carroll, you actually beat him to the punch on it. I got to cut my teeth on *Seven Places*.

CD: But I'm right that we did all seven in lithography and then switched, right?

CZ: Oh, yes. Hopefully there are still proofs. Absolutely, that project started as lithography. But, as you said, it just didn't feel right. It didn't do justice to the drawings.

CD: It needed to be something else. So then we got into this whole thing of turning them into four-color-separated photogravures. And then it just kept going and going. It was basically two years of finding the right embodiment of this thing. And then we ended up adding one level of soft ground that I drew, that kind of fit in with the rest of what I had done in the photogravures. We ended up taking out the black printer so that the color has this weird look . . . the blacks aren't really black, so there's this lurid edge to it all.

CZ: So they resemble the drawings, but they're not reproductions.

CD: Yes, they are similar but really don't look like the drawings. We also changed the size. That was the other thing. The drawings were on a sheet of typewriter paper, so we blew them up. So the mark is much fatter. It's like a colored-pencil line that's been blown up. They're completely strange. It's really one of my favorite print projects.

For a long time I didn't really see the point of working with other publishers or printers, because I was having such a good time and it was so wide open at ULAE. But during this time I had also been trying to find some analogous process in printmaking to some things that I was doing in my paintings—with what I guess you would call "relief elements" on the surface of my paintings, for lack of a better word. And nothing really was coming out of it. My friend Mel Bochner knew David Lasry and was making some prints at Two Palms. He told me about the overhead [hydraulic] press David had, and it seemed like that would be a way to explore this idea of relief, which it didn't really turn out to be, exactly. But it was a reason to meet and try something new.

CZ: I remember when you were trying to do that, and we were experimenting. Cutting holes in different matrices and . . .

CD: We were tearing a lot of press blankets. I was trying to make etchings by either putting solder on the plates or cutting holes in the plates . . . something that would deform the paper. And it wasn't really right. It was really interesting, but it wasn't really right.

So David and I met, and we liked each other, and I made a few prints with him in the mid-nineties. And then I started diversifying. I made some other things with other publishers—one-off projects. And then at some point I was really interested in working at Two Palms again. And then Craig went to work for Two Palms so we began to pick up aspects of our past print collaborations in that new context, and it went from there. I still work in these different places, but because I've gotten so involved in making monotypes recently, I've done more at Two Palms than I had before.

EH: And has that tended to be the case in your recent printmaking? That you go to certain presses for certain techniques?

CD: Well, not exactly, because I'm only really interested in working with people that I'm friendly with, so there are only those two presses where I do things regularly. I've been working on lithographs out at ULAE—there's no lithography at Two Palms, so that's actually kind of a logical split—and then working on monotypes and etchings at Two Palms. I did do a screenprint project a couple of years ago. That was something I had been wanting to do, and I knew that if a situation came up where I could do that, that I would do it. But again, it was one of these one-off things with a publisher that I don't have an ongoing relationship with.

ELIZABETH C. DEROSE: I'd actually like to ask you about those screenprints [*Interior A*, *Interior B*, and *Interior C*, 2006⁶], which to me have such a different look [*fig. 8*]. And the idea of you working with different techniques and imagining, for instance, what this drawing might look like as a print. Screenprinting of late has such a different look than it used to.

CD: Those screenprints weren't what I imagined I was going to do with screenprinting either. But the more I understood what the printers were capable of, the more I kept going in that direction . . . it is a strange way of making a facsimile of a mark, which is one thing that prints can be. Which,

   Carroll Dunham

again, is something that earlier on I would have mistrusted, but now I find the idea that it's a facsimile of something kind of fascinating. But that's not your question.

ED: Well, it kind of is, in that it has a completely different quality to it. So even if it started as a drawing . . .

CD: Yes. I made some drawings. I made them almost as a perverse gesture towards screenprinting. I just thought . . . what a counterintuitive idea about screenprinting. And the more I thought about it, the more I just loved the idea that they'd be making eighteen separations to create this effect, which is in one way a facsimile of an instantaneous mark. It's a strange notion. And it's not a way that Craig and I have ever worked.

CZ: No, it's not.

CD: With all that Craig knows about photogravure, there would be a way with photogravure that we could certainly push in directions that would not be unlike that. Maybe we should.

CZ: It's always a possibility.

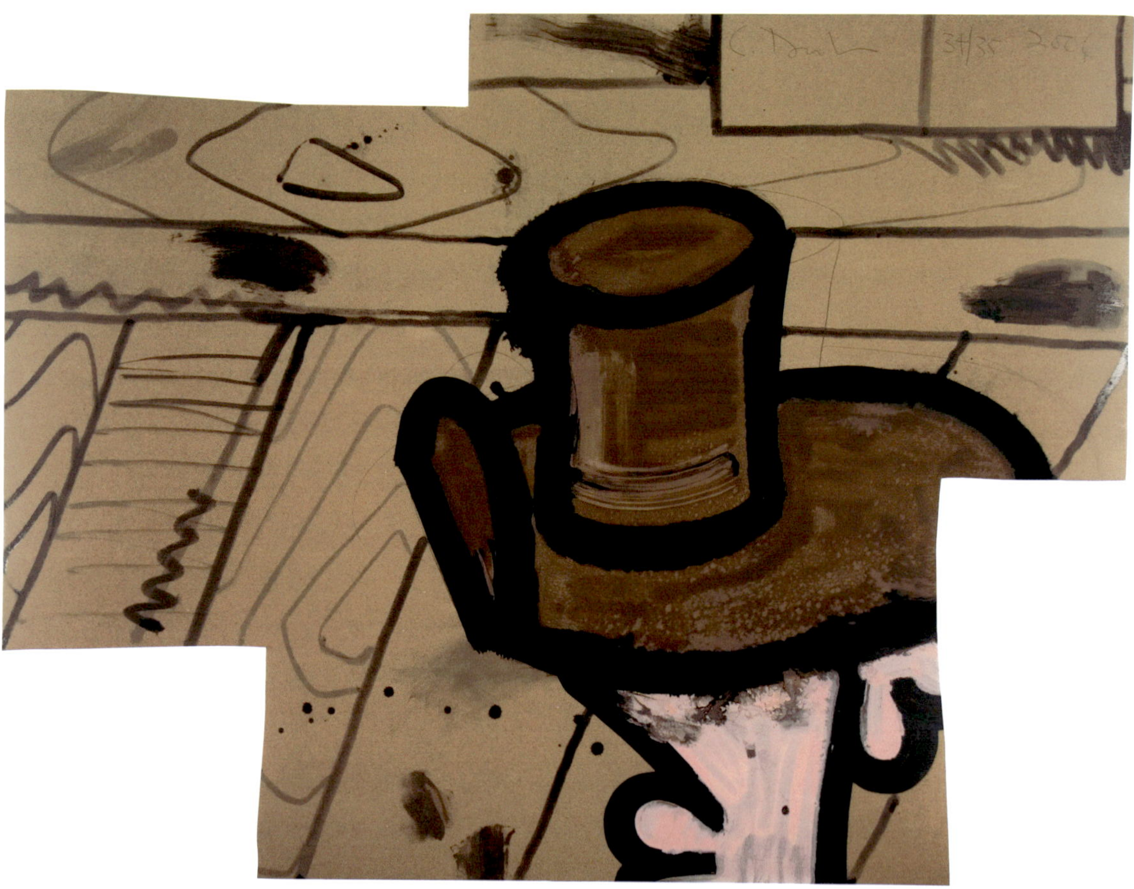

FIG. 8. Carroll Dunham, *Interior C*, 2006. Screenprint on laminated archival book board, 32¾ × 43¾ in. (83.2 × 111.1 cm). Edition of 35. Published by Pace Prints

CD: But we haven't. Craig has always been more responsive . . . I don't want to put words in his mouth, but I've always felt that Craig was always more responsive to the direct aspect of my work. And we work together a lot, in the same studio, at the same time. Something like those screenprints comes about in a completely different way, and the premise is much less intimate. The premise is more like a chess game where you write your move down and mail it to a person and then they mail back their move. You know? That's really very much how those things happened.

ED: And then, when you look at something like this [*gesturing to a photograph of one of CD's drawings and then to one of the* Closing In *prints*] . . . this black line in the drawing versus this black line in the print. The quality is completely different. This isn't a reproduction of that. Even though based on drawings, these prints really have their own material qualities.

CD: Well, we changed the scale slightly, and we changed the color of the paper. I can't make reproductions. The idea is that these things are sort of leveraged from the drawings—it's that kind of relationship. It's different from *Closing In*, which in a sense is leveraged from drawings but, you know, that would be like if we took that drawing, scanned it, separated it into its bazillion little components, and then printed them back together again. And that's completely different from the way Craig proposed that we think, and that I responded to.

[*pause*]

EH: And that's really a nice segue into a discussion of these prints, the *Closing In* portfolio [*see figs. 1–5*]. Like those screenprints, the prints that comprise *Closing In* were "leveraged" from drawings you had done, right?

CD: According to Craig.

CZ: According to me and David Lasry.

EH: In 2002 you exhibited some work at the Armory Show?

CD: Well, Craig had seen some drawings in a booth at the Armory Show. Which, in my mind . . . I don't think the thought ever entered my mind once that these things had anything to do with making prints. [*looking at a snapshot of the drawings hanging at the Armory Show; fig. 9*] Wow, look at that. That's the wall, right? That's amazing.

CZ: That's the wall. Yes, so David brings me to the show, saying: "You have to see these drawings, you have to see these." And, you know, I had seen a lot of

Carroll's work, at the studio and other places, being one of his "enablers" or "collaborators," or whatever you want to call it. And when I saw these with David, I immediately visualized the image in my mind of what could be done. David was not sure how we would do it, so I produced kind of a mock-up, what I like to call a "teaser," to show to both David and to Carroll [*fig. 10*]. And it was based on the direct-gravure method, which is essentially photogravure but without the "photo" part. The artist makes the plates by painting or drawing on Mylar, a very thin sheet of plastic. The gravure plates are made from the Mylar sheets and consist of traditional aquatint, which the artist can then work back into utilizing any conventional intaglio method.

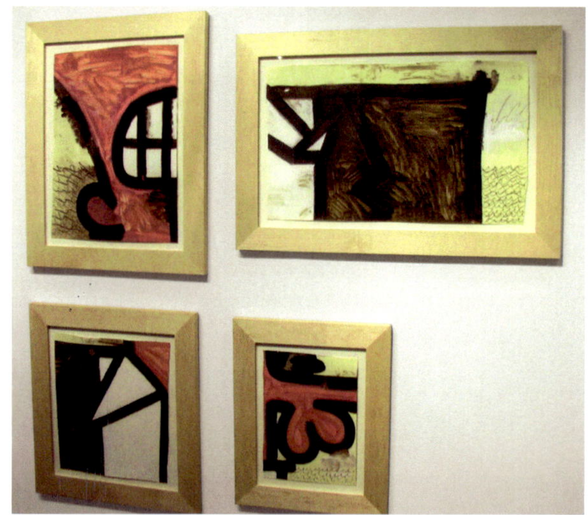

FIG. 9. Installation snapshot of Dunham's drawings at the Armory Show that inspired *Closing In*

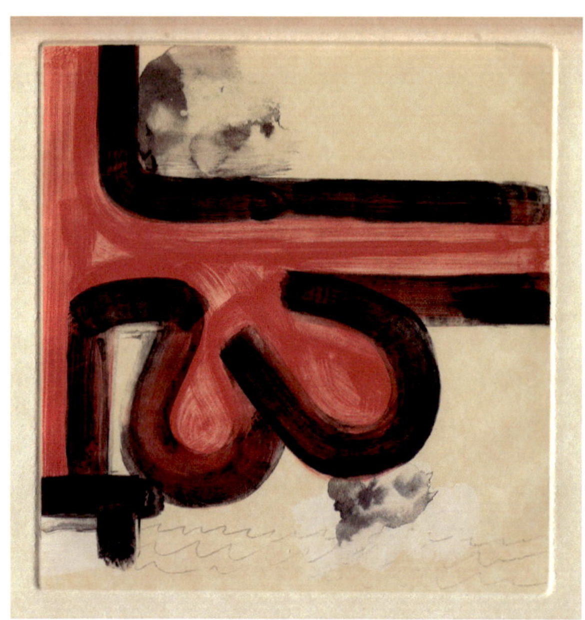

FIG. 10. Zammiello's "teaser" direct gravure

So the prospect of doing this with Carroll excited me. [*to CD:*] And I think that's when I showed you the mock-up.

CD: Yes. And I understood it immediately. Plus, I could tell that you weren't going to give this up.

CZ: That I would keep bugging you.

CD: More like I was feeling some energy from you that I liked, so I thought that I would just go with it. I was at a point in my work where I knew what the imagery should be, and I saw how it could be a portfolio. It had a really nice logic to it. It came up at just the right time too.

But, you know, this whole idea of these fragmentary images and strange orientations and croppings and all . . . I was thinking about it recently. The first time that it dawned on me that this would be something to think seriously about was when David was showing me something on the computer. We were scanning marker drawings . . . I guess what I'm try-ing to say is that there was a precedent for the idea that there could be this step to printmaking that almost could happen not in the material universe, you know? I didn't do very much for these prints to happen. I don't know how to articulate it in a way that doesn't end up sounding . . .

It's weird how little work was involved on my part to make these prints. I just sort of saw them in my mind. And I know that it came about from having been exposed to this dematerialized imagery. Obviously people are doing more with scanning and computers, and when David was showing me stuff on the computer one day, I realized that you could shift outlines and bracket different parts of the image, and that got me thinking about things to draw and paint. And so when Craig came back to me with this idea about a way to make prints, he was responding to my mark-mak-ing—but in a funny way it all came out of printmaking.

CZ: My excitement was that throughout my history with prints, something I've always been fascinated with is watching an artist like Carroll work—I just love to watch him paint. There's this incredible thing that happens from point A to point B when Carroll makes a line with a brush. And here I saw an avenue to bring that out, with the direct gravure.

CD: Yes. And when you look at these prints, you'll see that the marks are pretty surprising for etching.

EH: Different from the look of a line in sugar lift or spit bite?

CD: Yes. One sees lightness in etching, and a kind of liquidity to the marks and all of that, but that sort of continuous brushmark isn't something you really associate with etching. It's much more of a lithographic kind of mark. But lithography doesn't do to paper what etching does, so they have a totally different physical feeling.

EH: What about the choice of size? The drawings are quite a bit larger I'm assuming?

CD: Yes, I think they are. Some of those drawings are fairly big. Once Craig put the idea in my head of the approach, it was pretty clear to me how I could construct a group of prints based on what I was thinking about at the time. I didn't want them to be big, for whatever reason. They could have been; there wasn't any reason we couldn't have made much bigger things this same way. I think we're actually going to start something bigger this same way soon. But, you know, I just sort of saw it. That's the thing about printmaking collaborations. Somebody tells you one thing and then it triggers a whole bunch of clarity. And I needed Craig to sort of walk me through how we would break it all down. Like, how many different Mylars we would need to create the image I wanted to make in each print, and then how we would order it. To orient me within the method. But it was pretty straightforward, it really was.

CZ: Yeah, there's not a lot of fencing with this group . . .

CD: And that's what I suppose I mean when I say I didn't do very much work. It was just very clear.

EH: You drew them . . .

CD: Yeah, but I didn't even draw that [*gesturing to one of the* Closing In *prints*]. I mean, that's the weird thing about printmaking. I didn't draw *that*, I drew four different things that add up to that. Which is not the same as making a drawing like this.

I mean, Craig knows that *I* know how to think like that. And I know that *he* knows that I know how to think like that. And so, I don't think earlier on we would have made something like this. Because we both had to be at the right place to do it. And I had to believe that something that inconsequential could be consequential from my side. And Craig had to know, I guess, that if he came up with this genius idea of how to make something, that I'd step up.

EH: So each is three or four plates?

CZ: There are four to five plates each.

> CD: There was a plate for each color, including the white, and then there was a plate for the background. Oh, I remember—Doug Volle was helping us too.[7] I told them that I wanted the field of the plate to look like the color of the paper if it were slightly damp.

CZ: Which you had seen coming off the press.

> CD: Which I had seen coming off the press.

CZ: Because with this particular paper, in the area where the plate concentrated the pressure, it held the water, even as it was drying. It would take about an hour and a half to lose this look.

EH: The sheen?

CZ: Yes, and then the paper would be all one color. And Carroll wanted to keep that wet look, that tone. So that was an added plate, that was added onto each one.

> CD: And Doug mixed the color.

CZ: Doug was able to match that up. Actually, Doug went in and meticulously figured out where that color did not belong, such as in the pink areas, and in the white areas. So the tone was just added to the background.

> CD: Yes. So that relationship was something that I had seen in the process of proofing that I really liked. And when it dried there wasn't enough there. So I said, "Mix me a color that looks like that does when it's wet." And that's what Doug did. Because I don't think I could have done that. I mean, I probably could if you gave me a month, but I wouldn't have known how to go about it.

CZ: Yes, and thank God we have a colorist, because I'm color-blind. Doug Volle. But the making of this print was really straightforward. I agree with what Carroll's saying: right time, right place. And to me it was just another one of these jumps that happens throughout a relationship that an artist and printer have. And I was really happy to be able to get the structure of one of Carroll's brushmarks on an etching [*fig. 11*]. For a long time I considered that my personal triumph. Because when you make a sugar lift, you're painting the same way, but you're not capturing what happens with the brush [*fig. 12*]. When you're spit biting, you're also painting, but you're not capturing the skeletal structure of the bristles [*fig. 13*], which you can see in these. And as I said, that's one of the things that fascinates me with the way Carroll works: he goes from point A to point B. His way of painting has always been an inspiration for me. I use it as a Zen direction in my life.

CD: [*laughter*]

CZ: I do. I think of it at the weirdest times.

ED: And then the concept of the portfolio. Could you comment on that? The sequence and the housing . . . I know even for *Seven Places* the portfolio was very elaborate.

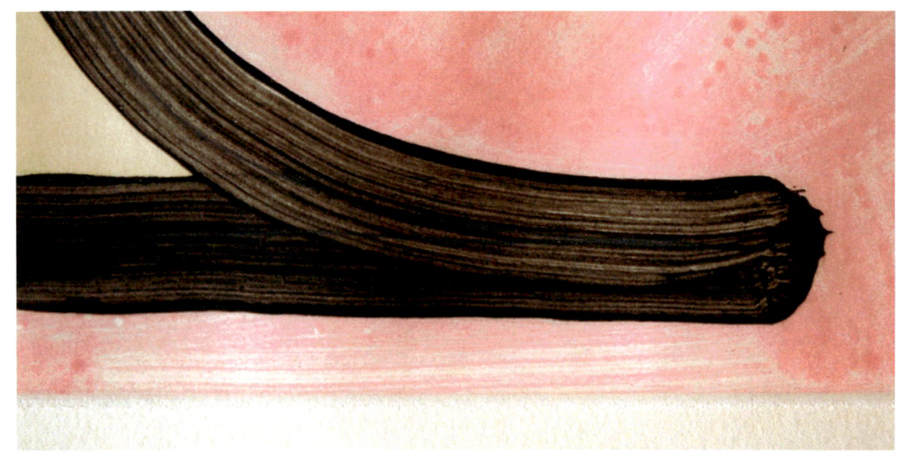

FIG. 11. Close-up of brushmarks in one of the *Closing In* prints, revealing the quality of the direct-gravure stroke

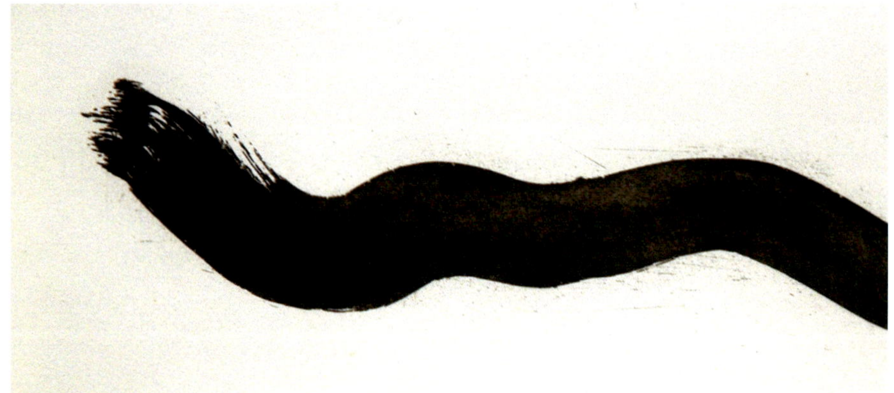

FIG. 12. Close-up of a sugarlift brushmark, illustrating the lack of interior detail that is characteristic of this technique

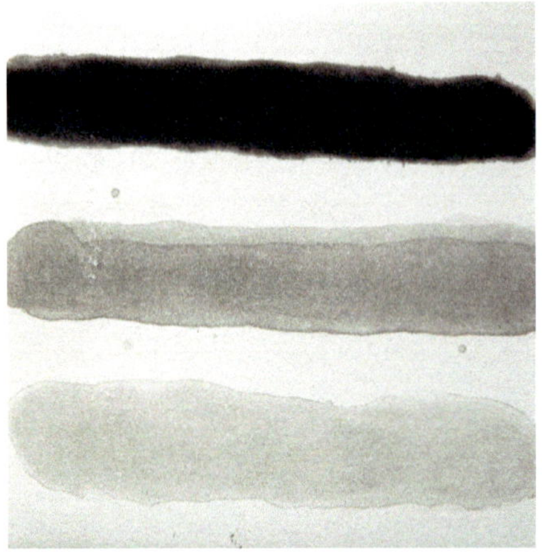

FIG. 13. Close-up of spitbite brushmarks, illustrating the soft edges that are characteristic of this technique

ED: And then even for *Atmospherics*, you had an elaborate box.[8] And then this [*Closing In*] has a very thin portfolio cover [*fig. 14*].

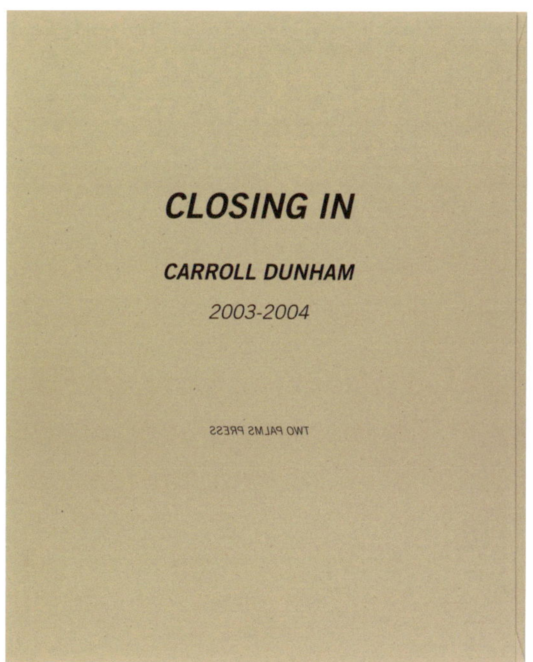

FIG. 14. Carroll Dunham, portfolio cover to *Closing In*, 2003–4. Screenprint on Fawn Stonehenge paper, 24¾ x 20 in. (62.9 x 50.8 cm)

CD: Well, I've made several portfolios that have only five sheets, and five sheets doesn't seem like enough to put in a box. You don't get much of a box when you're holding five sheets of paper. You can do it, but the portfolios that we've put in boxes tend to be upwards of ten sheets of paper. *Seven Places* is obviously seven sheets of paper, but they're extremely high-energy sheets of paper. And I wanted to make a box, even though it was only seven sheets of paper, because I felt that they contained lots of force and they needed a box. Bill Goldston had the idea—he had gotten some material from a box and album maker in Japan. And Bill threw that out at me: "Would you ever imagine that?" And I loved the idea. So we ended up making this silk-covered book, which is also the idea that I used on the *Mr. Nobody* [2001] project that consists of over fifty little engraved facsimiles of drawings.[9] I like this album idea.

So there are folders, boxes, albums; those seem like three ways for separate sheets to compose one thing, to be kept together or bracketed in a way that has a personality. I like the offhand nature of the folder for *Closing In*. It feels like a stationery-store level of material, which seemed in the spirit of the project somehow.

CZ: It also was a venue for a different sort of titling, dating.

CD: Yes. The voice of the type. I've always liked doing these things with the people I collaborate with. I've never gotten a graphic designer involved or anything like that. I know from doing books that graphic designers have very interesting ways of thinking about type, but it's fun for me to have a hand in things like this.

EH: Did you choose the typeface?

CD: Yes. With . . . I forget how this one happened. Were you involved in that, Craig?

CZ: No, that was really Doug.

CD: Yes. Doug Volle and I have worked together on a couple of these folders. There's the *Female Portraits* portfolio that I made at ULAE [in 2000]. Doug made the folder for that. It has a kind of kinky structure of paper within plastic. Doug thought of all of that.

EH: Did you have five prints in mind?

CD: No, I just like the number five. Five seems like a good number for a portfolio. It's enough things to be more than a few, and a manageable quantity to think of as one thing. I mean, I could have organized something this way with seven things or nine things, but five seemed good.

EH: And about the choice of paper? It looks like a manila folder–type paper.

CZ: It's Fawn Stonehenge. [*to CD:*] Well, you expressed a desire for a certain range of color.

CD: Yes. But I don't remember even proofing this thing on white paper.

CZ: I don't think we did. I think we immediately grabbed a few sheets from the paper monger, and this is the one you chose.

CD: Yes. Paper . . . I have rather a stronger vision of that than I did at an earlier point. It's logical to proof something on a generic sheet of white paper so that you have something to look at, and then go from there. A few times I've had very strong ideas of what a paper should be. So we find the paper and work almost as though the paper is the given rather than the plate. And on this project, I think we determined the plate size before we chose the paper, but I think we determined the paper by the look of the drawings. I had been doing the drawings on this sort of manila-colored paper, so I knew that I didn't want it to be a bright white.

EH: So, in a way, the drawings also influenced the choice of paper for the prints?

CD: Yes.

CZ: Well, I remember when I made the demonstration piece it was on a much yellower paper . . .

CD: Oh, yes! That's right. I remember now . . . I said I wanted the paper to look like faded newsprint.

CZ: That's right.

CD: And we looked at some different papers. But, you know, nothing really compares to faded newsprint, which is one of the most beautiful colors of paper you can ever see.

CZ: Unfortunately, paper manufacturers actively try *not* to get that color.

CD: I know. Someday we're going to get a paper that color.

CZ: It should be named that too.

CD: So it was that kind of idea. Something that was a bit dingy—not in a bad sense, but something that was not bright.

EH: More neutral. I remember when Elizabeth bought your *Atmospherics* portfolio for Yale [University Art Gallery]'s collection, and how jarring was the look of that very yellow paper . . .

CD: That was the most fabulous paper discovery. That was the strangest thing. I made those with the master printer Greg Burnet, and I knew from the very beginning that I wanted just one plate per print, and that we were going to go crazy on those plates. I wanted for it to be a very dense thing. We were proofing them all along on white paper, and at a certain point I remember wanting it to be duller, dingier, so we started to use gray paper. Then Greg went to . . . New York Central [Art Supply], I guess, and poked around and came back with a piece of this yellow paper, and I immediately said, "That's it!" I would have never thought of yellow paper. It's made by some guy in Spain, who's copying the pages of old bibles.

CZ: Queen Anne.

ED: Queen Anne Bible Yellow.

CD: That was a case of something just changing the look of the prints completely. And now I can't even remember what they looked like in proof form.

My feeling about where prints fit into the bigger picture is a little different now from when I was first making prints, because I was so worried—I guess I said this before—I was so worried about making clear to myself that prints could exist as something other than, you know, posters of my drawings, posters of my paintings. And something like this *Closing In* portfolio is . . . Craig has a reaction to something I'm doing, and he proposes something that in a way operates as an analog to the drawings. It's close to the drawings in one way, but in another way it's very different. I don't think I would have been comfortable doing it at an earlier point, because it would have felt like cheating. It wouldn't have felt like enough establishment of its own territory. I don't worry about that now, I suppose because I've made a lot of prints by now, and it doesn't seem like an issue. So it was nice the way it came about so easily, which I also used to mistrust. I used to be more involved with the idea that my work should reflect some sort of struggle. And with these there really was no struggle. All the struggle took place elsewhere.

EH: Have you used direct gravure since?

CD: No, we're going to do something soon.

CZ: It's time. Now there's a different format, different scale, different subject matter in your work.

CD: Yes. I have different subjects that I'm working on, and I actually think that all the liquid media that I've been working with in printmaking—these things [*indicating the* Closing In *prints*], and I think even more the monotypes that I've been making with watercolors—has had a big influence with the way that I've been working on my paintings. So now I feel that there's material in the paintings that needs to come back into the printmaking. It won't be the same, but it can inform something in the prints. So, yes, we're going to work on something soon.

CZ: And my interest gets piqued because I think to myself, "What's Dunham going to bring to the table this time?" We've established this, so we have a starting point.

CD: I have such trouble sometimes imagining what it must be like to be a master printer. And, as you know, Craig's an artist too, so he has his own interests; it's not like he's a tabula rasa that only does procedures, he has his own take on things. So for a master printer to receive what I am emitting, I always think that it must be so strange, because I'm not going to make the thing that he thinks I'm going to make.

CD: And I know that *you* know I'm not going to make the thing you think I'm going to make. This [*Closing In*] is probably as close as I've ever come to making the thing that you thought I was going to make.

[*laughter*]

CZ: That's possible.

EH: There's a wonderful statement by you in this book [*Carroll Dunham Prints*] in which you touch on that. Can I read it?

CD: Sure.

EH: "The quality of relationships necessary to productive collaboration is unique. I can't make my own prints; I don't know how. No matter how much time I spend around master printers, and how firmly I grasp the principles of what they are doing, I can't internalize any of it. There is an odd mixture of intimacy and boundary maintenance, where openness to suggestion and adherence to vision on the artist's part must coexist with the simultaneous suspension of ego and confidence to assert one's perspective on the part of the printer, a special chemistry which somewhat counter-intuitively clarifies the reach of intention and sensibility while constantly challenging and modifying it."[10]

CD: Well, that's what I meant.

EH: You two have worked together for a long time.

CD: We started with a print called *Full Spectrum,* and that was in, what, 1985 or '86?

CZ: I think 1985.

CD: So twenty-plus years ago.

CZ: And it helps when you get to know someone and you realize that you have a lot of things in common. After a while, it becomes . . . it's a relationship with somebody. And I think that's true of every artist that a printer works with. And with some artists you have a certain relationship that's more—what's the word?—more intimate. You think along the same lines.

CD: I need to be pushed a bit. I need to have my capacity to imagine something expanded, but I also need for somebody to know when to leave me alone. And there's so much chemistry involved. Like with anything, I guess.

I could not make prints with somebody I thought was a jerk, you know, I couldn't do it. There have been a very, very few times that I was in that position, and it was "total system shutdown." Because also, it's embarrassing to do this stuff in front of other people, and that's something I had forgotten about, and I remembered when I was working on this book [*Carroll Dunham Prints*]. My biggest concern when I went to a print studio was "how on earth am I going to do any of this with everyone around watching me?" I just couldn't imagine that. And I don't think about that very much now, because I only go into situations where I'm fairly unselfconscious. Like the idea that—think about it—the idea that *he's watching me.* I don't even like to think about it—that *he's* [*pointing to CZ*] watching *me* draw.

CZ: And now that's ruined . . .

CD: You've ruined it!

[*laughter*]

CZ: You think I'm just talking about movies, but . . .

CD: And the fact that I can sometimes talk. A lot of times I can talk and make jokes and be there in the room with people and be working. And I think it really affects what comes out. The drawing's a little bit freer, even.

CZ: Yeah, it's a special thing. It's happened to me in a way—not in my role as a printer, but as an artist: "What am I going to do? How will I deal with these people observing?" And so I can imagine, in your position, how that would be difficult. But, on the other hand, what kind of privilege is it to even be asked by another artist, "How do you think that looks?" I sometimes think to myself, "You're asking *me*?"

CD: Yes, it's funny, because I don't normally ask people their opinion about my work. I'm interested in people's opinion, but I don't stop in the middle of making a painting and call people up and ask them to come over and tell me if I should finish this painting, you know?

CZ: Well, I think that's what happens in a print studio, when you're comfortable. But, yes, when I was younger, when an artist asked me my opinion, I would just blubber away. Whereas with Carroll, I think I'm comfortable enough to just say, "That's great." And he knows that I mean it, I'm not just buttering him up.

EH: You've both seen printmaking change a lot too. Because it's really—in the past forty or fifty years—witnessed a lot of new technologies and techniques, or combined techniques.

CD: It's really difficult for me to talk about, because I really don't understand who looks at prints other than the four of us in this room. I have no idea who's interested in these things. I really feel that it's this weird little club of people who want to see it, and want to talk about it. It's like a parallel art world. It barely even touches the "Art World," which is one of the things I like about it. It's ghettoized in a way that I think is interesting, even though one might wish sometimes, from a business point of view, that it would be different, because it would be easier for people to make prints. And I think it's a struggle a lot of the time for publishers. But I don't even know how to compare it to an earlier time, because I came into it for such personal reasons.

And not many people know what they're looking at when they're looking at a print. Many people who are actually rather well informed about contemporary art haven't a clue what they're looking at when they look at a print.

EH: Do you think people who are comfortable with paintings don't tend to look at prints?

CD: As a generalization? Yes. As a rule, I think generalizations are a bad idea. But, yes, I think it's a different audience, which is unfortunate. Because I think it limits how people understand what artists do, and how they see paintings.

EH: It's kind of ironic, actually. Because certainly print collections, especially those in universities, are frankly where a lot of the history of art gets taught—just because the nature of the collection is so comprehensive and accessible that you can show great examples from various cultures and periods. And so, in a way, it's rather ironic that many very art-knowledgeable people find prints so foreign, so difficult to look at.

CD: Well, it's ironic on many levels. It's also true that printmaking—techniques of reproduction—have entered the world of painting as a completely acceptable way of doing things. That's been true since the sixties, at least—that techniques that are traditionally reproductive are embedded in objects that are quite clearly intended to be paintings. And, in a way, that has made it even harder for people to know what they're looking at.

As I said in that piece that I wrote for this catalogue [*Carroll Dunham Prints*], I like the "printedness" of prints. I like to think about printmaking as a tradition, but it's not something that a lot of people understand. And I

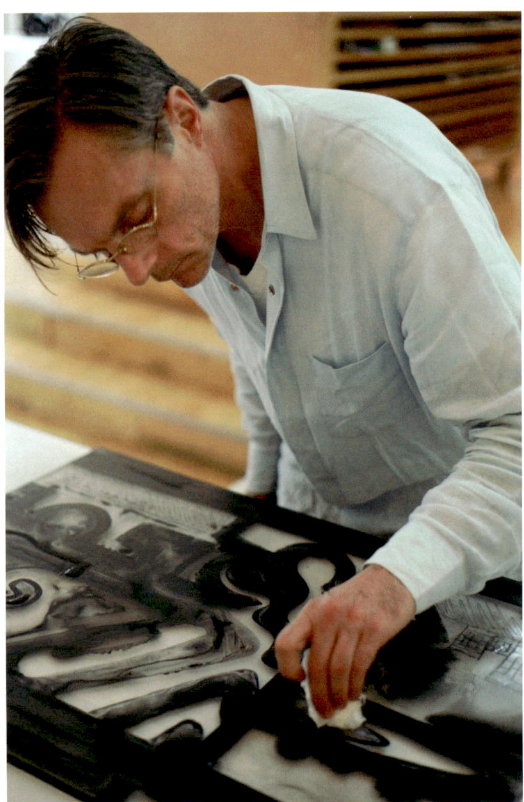

think that this "proverbial viewer of painting" that you refer to frequently thinks they're seeing something that's only a shadow of a work of art somehow if they're looking at a print. People don't know how to look at them.

EH: So you don't think that's changed at all?

CD: No, if anything I think it's gotten worse. But I like looking at prints and making prints, and I like it when I see any artist that's really into it—when it feels like an artist is getting something from making a print that they wouldn't get in any other place. I don't think that there are many people like that, but the ones who are are really doing something great. You know, it doesn't have to be popular.

CZ: Yes. It's a little club.

CD: It's all very strange and ironic, because you would think that prints would be a very widespread . . . because the interest in art has become so much broader, and there are so many people who want to get involved with it, you would think that prints would represent that sort of an option for people.

CZ: I think with that comes the charlatans too.

CD: From the supply side or the demand side?

[*laughter*]

CZ: From the supply side. There's never enough demand side. And that kind of muddies the water.

CD: I've just given up trying to understand how the art world is structured, how it works for people who aren't directly involved with making art, or people like the two of you [*indicating EH and ED*] who are working in museums. I just don't understand how any of it works anymore.

CZ: I just go home every night and think, "I'm getting paid for this." I'm having a ball. I'm doing the most enjoyable thing I can think of doing as long as that continues, as long as these people continue to let me into their worlds while they're creating things.

Notes

The preceding conversation was held on June 25, 2008, in the James E. Duffy Study Room of the Yale University Art Gallery, in New Haven, Connecticut.

1. Here Dunham is referring to his *Three Etchings* (1987), published by Editions Ilene Kurtz, New York; printed by 2 RC Edizioni d'Arte, Rome.

2. Allison N. Kemmerer, Elizabeth C. DeRose, and Carroll Dunham, *Carroll Dunham Prints: A Catalogue Raisonné, 1984–2006* (Andover, Mass.: Addison Gallery of American Art, Phillips Academy, 2008).

3. All four intaglio prints measure 47 ¾ × 67 ⅝ in. (121.3 × 171.8 cm) and were published by ULAE. Illustrations of all four works can be found in Kemmerer, DeRose, and Dunham, *Carroll Dunham Prints*, 216.

4. Carroll Dunham, *Shadows*, 1989, portfolio of 10 drypoints, each 15 ⅜ × 22 ⅞ in. (39.1 × 58.1 cm), published by ULAE. Images of the prints can be found in Kemmerer, DeRose, and Dunham, *Carroll Dunham Prints*, 217; and on the ULAE website, http://www.ulae.com/ (accessed September 26, 2011).

5. Images of the prints that constitute *Seven Places* can be found in Kemmerer, DeRose, and Dunham, *Carroll Dunham Prints*, 219; and on the ULAE website, http://www.ulae.com/ (accessed September 26, 2011).

6. Carroll Dunham, *Interior A*, *Interior B*, and *Interior C*, 2006, screenprints on laminated archival book board, *Interior A*: 32 ¾ × 43 ¾ in. (83.2 × 111.1 cm); *Interior B*: 43 ¾ × 32 ¾ in. (111.1 × 83.2 cm); *Interior C*: 32 ¾ × 43 ¾ in. (83.2 × 111.1 cm). All printed at Axelle Fine Arts, published by Pace Editions. Images of the prints can be found in Kemmerer, DeRose, and Dunham, *Carroll Dunham Prints*, 244.

7. Douglas Volle is a master printer at Two Palms. Volle and Zammiello were also colleagues at ULAE.

8. Carroll Dunham, *Atmospherics*, 2001–2, portfolio of 8 etchings with aquatint, edition of 21, each 13 × 15 in. (33 × 38.1 cm). Published by Burnet Editions, New York. The etchings are housed in a silk-covered clamshell portfolio box with a blind-stamped title ("Carroll Dunham / ATMOSPHERICS"), designed by the Grenfell Press and made by Claudia Cohen. Box dimensions: 14 × 15 ¾ × ¾ in. (35.6 × 39.9 × 1.9 cm). Images of the etchings can be found in Kemmerer, DeRose, and Dunham, *Carroll Dunham Prints*, 234; and on the Burnet Editions website, http://www.burneteditions.com/ (accessed September 26, 2011).

9. Carroll Dunham, *Mr. Nobody*, 2001, album with photoengraved facsimiles of 57 drawings, each 3 ½ × 4 ⅜ in. (8.9 × 11.1 cm) or 4 ⅜ × 3 ½ in. (11.1 x 8.9 cm). Edition of 9. Published by the Grenfell Press, New York. For images of the *Mr. Nobody* suite, see Kemmerer, DeRose, and Dunham, *Carroll Dunham Prints*, 232–33.

10. Carroll Dunham, "Third World," in Kemmerer, DeRose, and Dunham, *Carroll Dunham Prints*, 207.

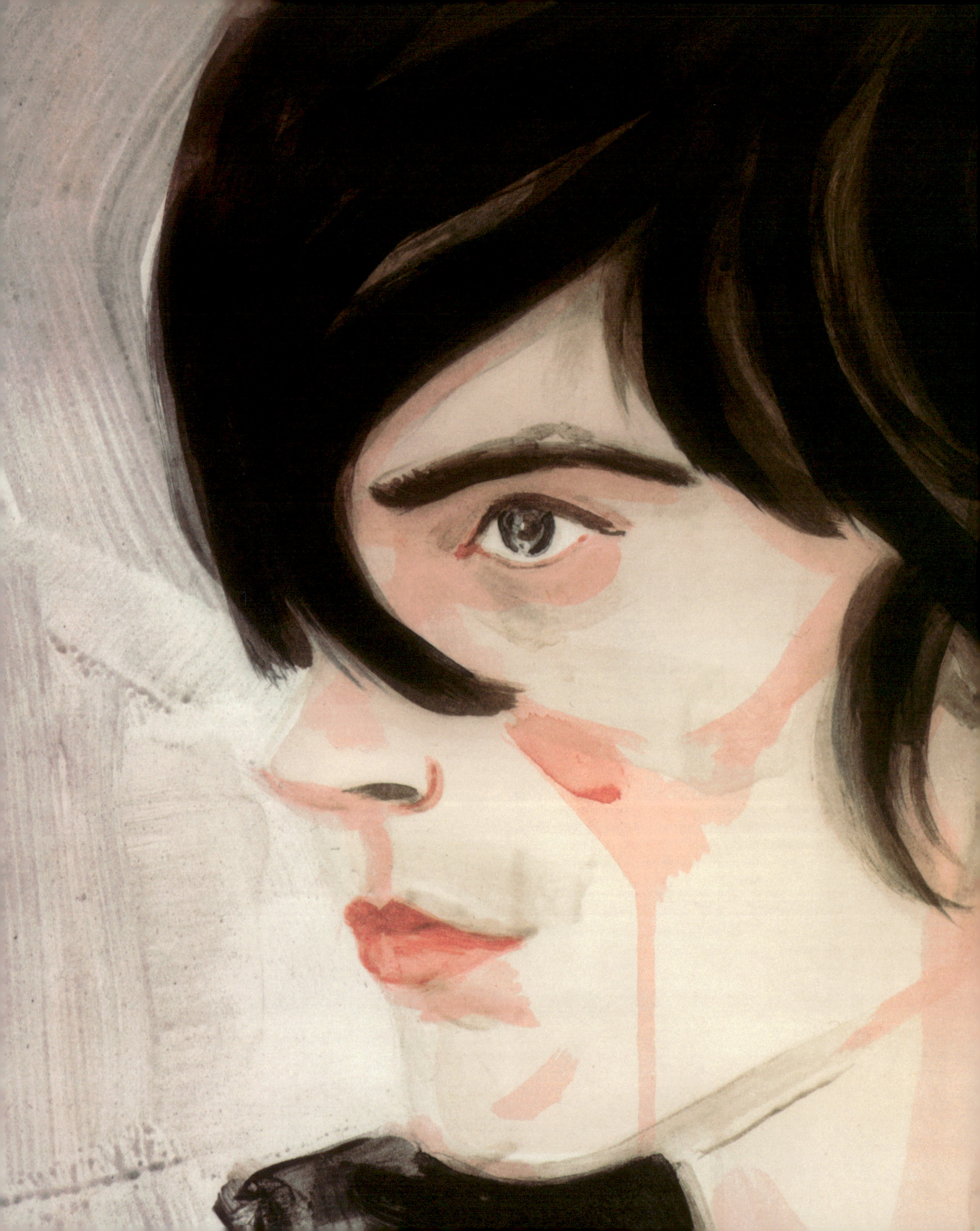

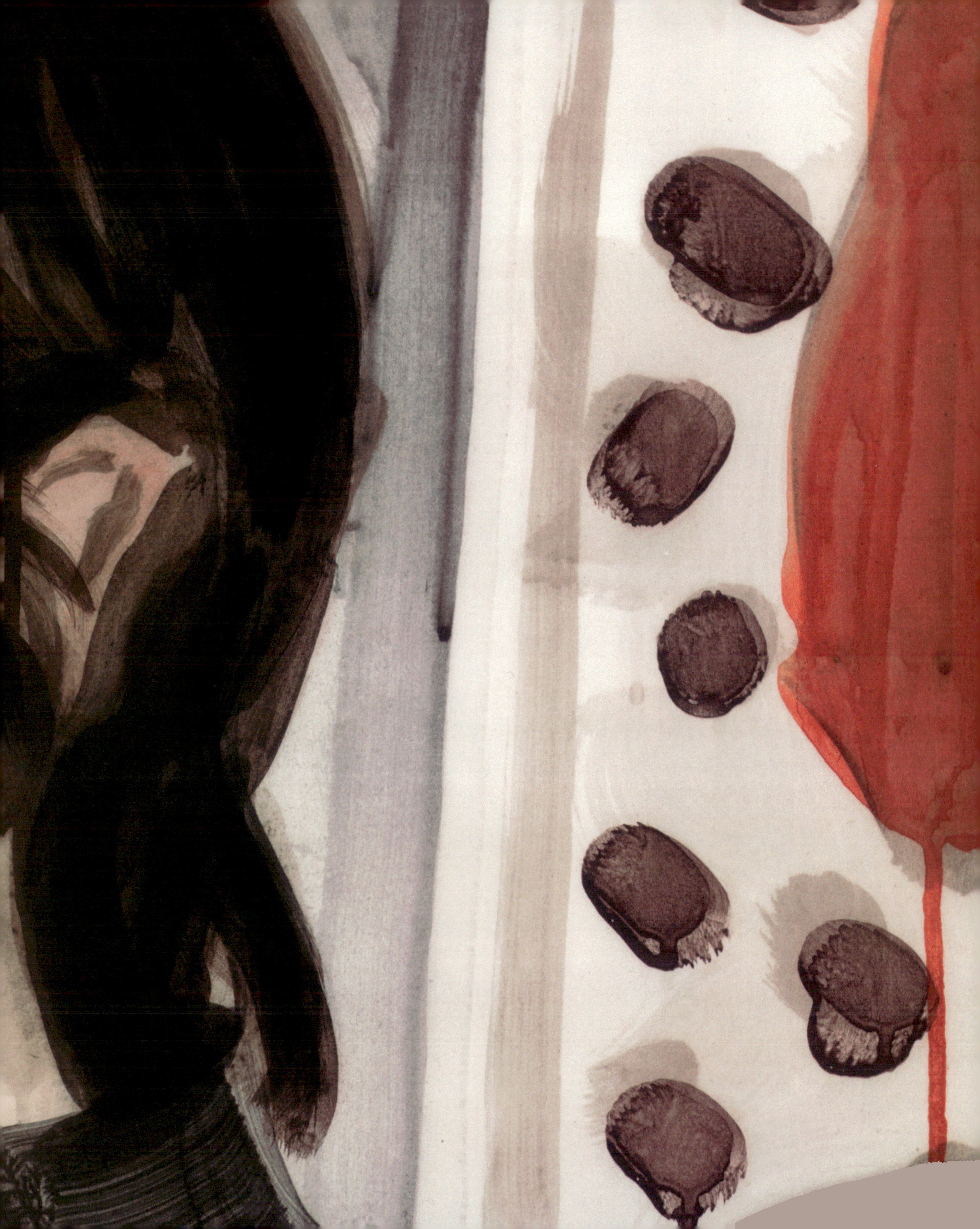

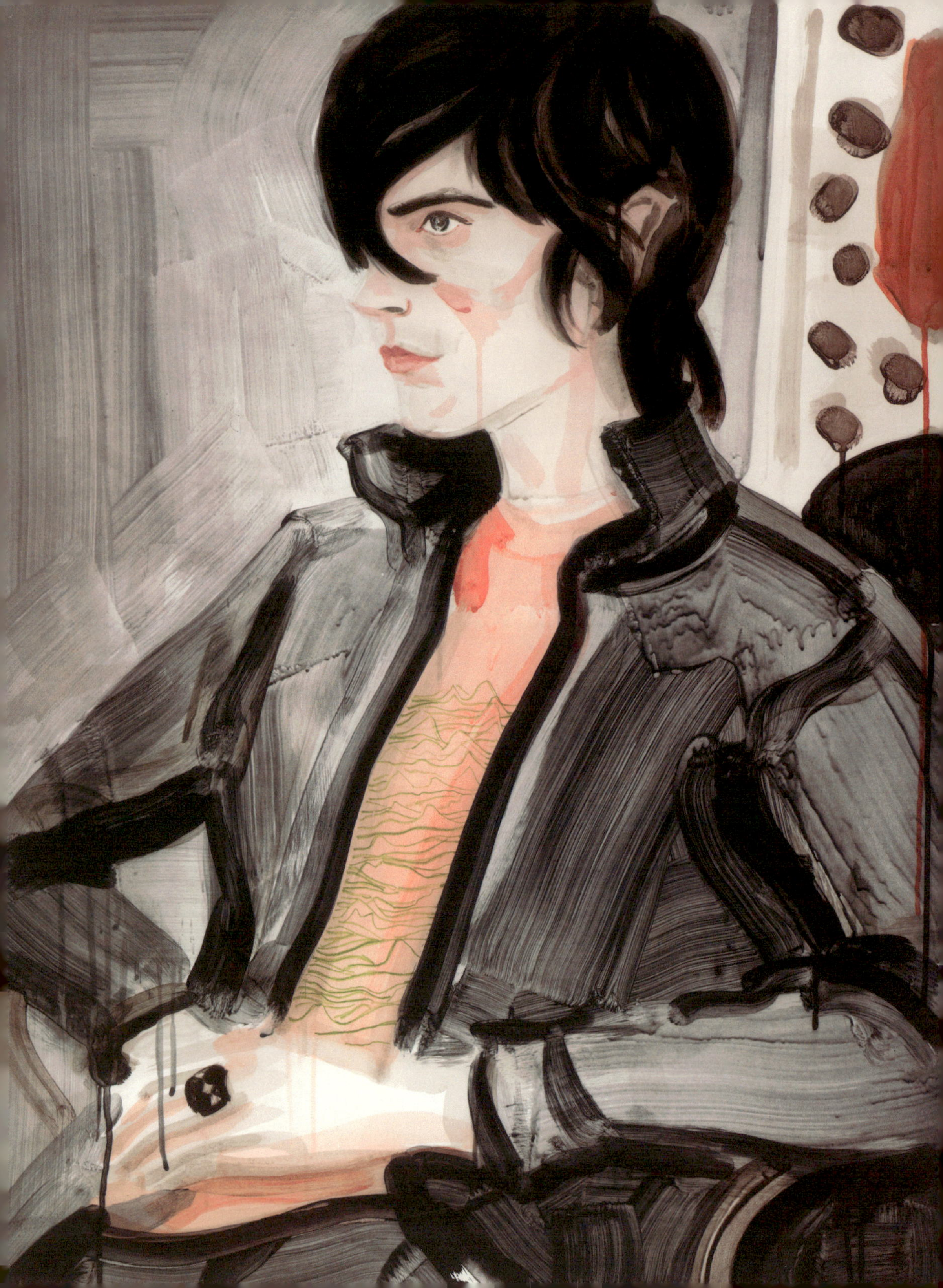

It is interesting to note that Elizabeth Peyton, while one of the youngest artists represented in this book, is also perhaps the most traditional—in both her choice of subject matter and drawing style. Peyton is first and foremost a portraitist, and her portraits are created in *real time* with sitters, using traditional techniques. Hers are not hyperreal depictions but rather suggestive, intensely personal impressions of her sitters, and one would be hard-pressed to name another living artist who is better at achieving such sensitive, evocative results.

For Peyton, printmaking is an extension of her work in painting and photography. Prints such as *Nick* (fig. 1), the focus of this chapter, are executed in a manner surprisingly similar to that of many of her paintings or photographs—with her sitter present in the studio. When working in the medium of direct gravure, Peyton paints her Mylar "canvases" vertically, on an easel (fig. 2), and watching her inevitably evokes a sense of filmic time travel to the studios of such masters of portraiture as John Singer Sargent or Mary Cassatt.

Peyton admits to being wholly conscious of the special relationship that printmaking has to portraiture, in that a likeness can be drawn on a matrix, printed in a large edition, and mass-disseminated, potentially becoming the iconic likeness of a person. This point is driven home by the fact that her subjects are often famous historical or popular figures, many of whom she has never or could never have met. And yet there is an *implied* intimacy to these rendered likenesses that is as uncannily believable as that of any of her portraits of her contemporary, real-life friends. This quality is conveyed not only in her gorgeous, painterly rendering but also in her manner of titling, which exclusively employs first names: *Em*[inem], *Georgia* [O'Keeffe], *Frida* [Kahlo]. For Peyton, this intimacy is a very real, even visceral one; whether or not she knows them personally, these are subjects for whom she has a great deal of admiration, a fact that is absolutely apparent in the finished works, which are so sensitively rendered, so luscious and gestural, so very *alive.*

As the reader will discover in the following dialogue, there is a tremendous honesty—and, frankly, an intoxicating simplicity—in Peyton's approach to printmaking, a straightforwardness and calmness that is quite rare and refreshing. As Craig Zammiello comments in this chapter, "It's just something I can relate to, the way Elizabeth works. . . . There is a lot of magic, but there's no mystery."

FIG. 1. Elizabeth Peyton, *Nick*, 2004. Seven-color etching with aquatint and direct gravure, 40 ½ × 32 in. (102.9 × 81.3 cm). Edition of 30. Published by Two Palms. Yale University Art Gallery, Janet and Simeon Braguin Fund, 2008.28.2

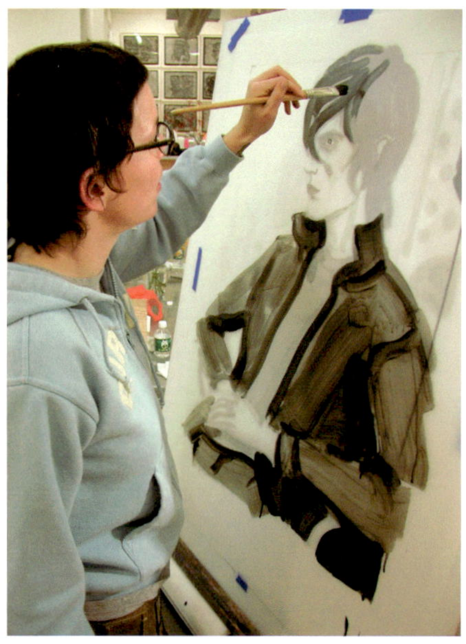

ELIZABETH PEYTON: The first print I made was a lithograph of Oscar Wilde and his boyfriend Bosie (Lord Alfred Douglas) [*Oscar and Bosie*, 1998]. It was on commission from *Parkett*. I made that with Maurice Sanchez at Derrière L'Etoile [Studios] here in New York. And then there was one series I did for the Public Art Fund, also with Maurice, that they put in the guestrooms of a hotel downtown—I think it might be the Embassy Suites. There were five portraits, I remember, five lithographs. One was called *Kiss*, it was of Tony [Just]; there was one of John and Jackie Kennedy; one of John Kennedy, Jr., when he was young; one of Prince Harry and Prince William; and one of Prince William by himself.[1]

ELISABETH HODERMARSKY: And the edition was big enough to put one in each room?

EP: Yes. It was a huge edition, I think maybe 200 or 250 of each. Some were multiple colors, some were one color. And there was one other print—one of my favorites—that I made in my studio but that Maurice printed, of Lord Alfred Douglas, maybe three or four colors, called *Silver Bosie*.

It was different to work with Maurice, because I never actually worked in his studio. Maurice is great to work with, but I was never part of the studio. Here at Two Palms you become part of the studio.

EH: And you came here to Two Palms in 2002?

EP: Yes.

EH: And since Two Palms isn't set up for lithography, you began to work in other media. Was it difficult to launch into a new print medium?

EP: Well, I like things that I don't know how to do. And David [Lasry] and Craig and Doug [Volle] kept introducing new techniques to me, which was great. Like monotype, for example. When I first came here, David described to me the monotype, and I remember thinking, "Why would someone want to do *that*?" I really thought it was so funny, I went home thinking, "Huh." But David had sent me home with books on the monotypes of Degas and others, and as I looked through them I finally understood. And then when I met you, Craig, you started introducing various new techniques to me that I had never used and I really loved that. And that's really one of my favorite things to do, to be a bit off guard.

CRAIG ZAMMIELLO: I remember seeing one of Elizabeth's pieces before I came here—it was the painting of Kurt Cobain [*Kurt Cobain*, 1995]. My favorite kind of work is figurative work, and I remember thinking, "Wow, I'd like to work with this person someday." So it was so great when I came to Two Palms and you were here.

EP: So when did you come here, Craig?

CZ: I came in 2002, right after you had finished those first etchings. But you and I started in on a small line etching, also of Nick: *Nick in L.A.* [*fig. 3*].

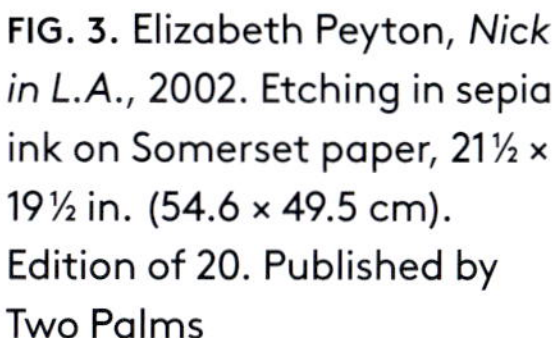

FIG. 3. Elizabeth Peyton, *Nick in L.A.*, 2002. Etching in sepia ink on Somerset paper, 21½ × 19½ in. (54.6 × 49.5 cm). Edition of 20. Published by Two Palms

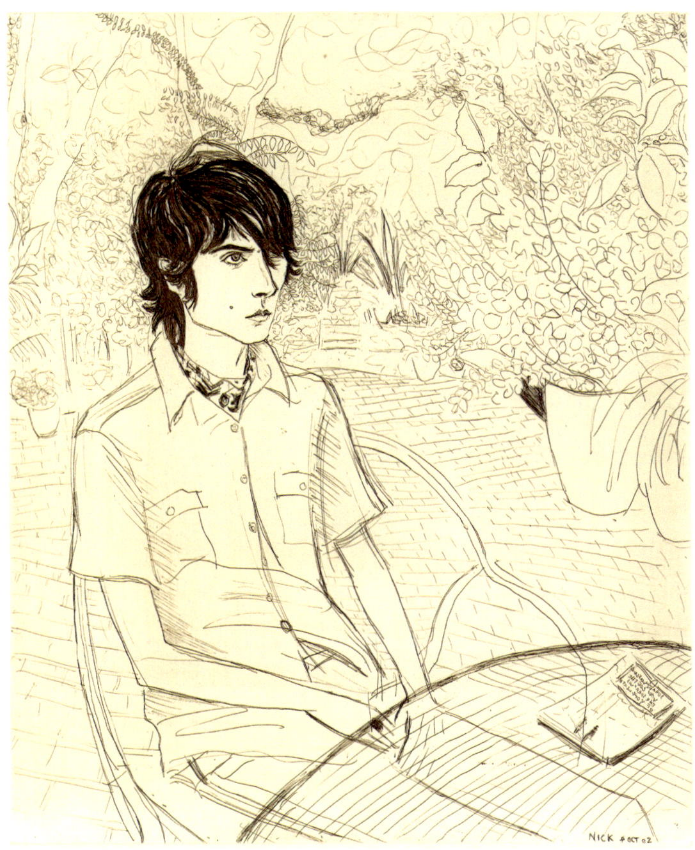

EP: Right. Which I didn't make here in the studio, I made it on the spot there in Los Angeles. Which was great.

CZ: Yes, I sent you a plate. And after that we did some more line work, traditional line-etching work. And then some soft grounds. And I love the way Elizabeth works. She works a lot with a sitter, drawing and painting from life, which you don't see much of nowadays, especially in a print studio. After a few months of working with hard and soft ground we thought it would be nice to introduce Elizabeth's incredible way of painting—her brushstrokes, her mark-making with a brush—to the print process. That's when I gave you some Mylars, Elizabeth, and you produced *Em* [*fig. 4*]. *Em* was the first direct gravure we made together.

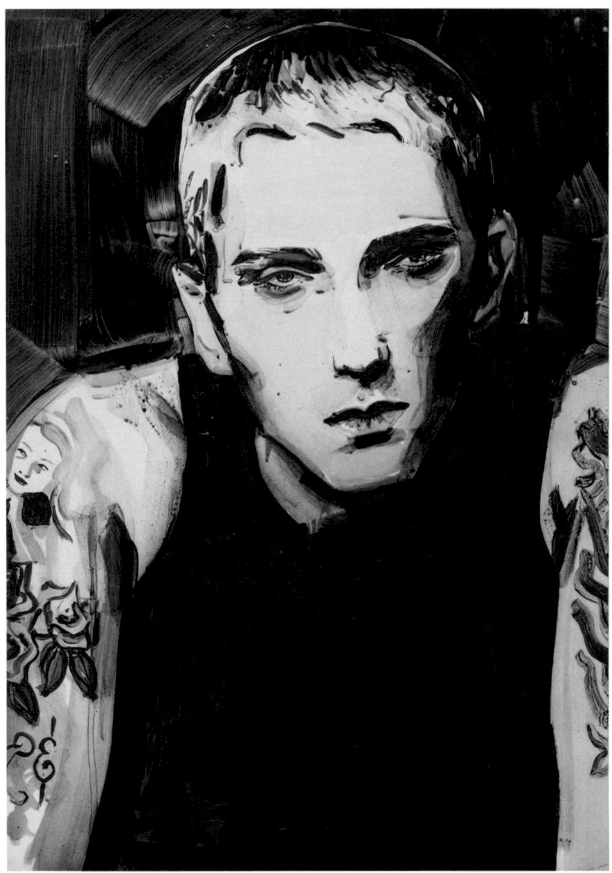

FIG. 4. Elizabeth Peyton, *Em*, 2003. Etching with aquatint and direct gravure, 26¾ × 20¼ in. (67.9 × 51.4 cm). Edition of 30. Published by Two Palms

EP: Right.

EH: But that was monochrome—black—correct?

CZ: One color.

EH: And was that done from life, with him posing?

EP: No, it was from a photo . . . [*sheepishly*] by a famous photographer.

[*laughter*]

CZ: This is a good example of the artist bringing an innovation to the studio. I gave Elizabeth some India ink, to be thinned with water. And since she works upright on an easel, she needed to add body to this to make it act like paint and not just watercolor or ink wash. And she just naturally put gesso in it.

EP: It was matte medium. But that was something I learned doing lithographs with Maurice Sanchez. We used modeling paste mixed with Xerox toner.

CZ: That makes sense. But I had never thought to give the India ink body to mimic the feel and workability of oil paint before. You brought that to the studio.

EH: Did you make *Em* here?

EP: I did it out in the country. And sent it back here to Two Palms to be printed.

CZ: I remember when it came. It was close to Christmas time, and I remember unwrapping it and thinking, "Wow!" It was our Christmas present from Elizabeth.

EP: And then there were a few other prints we made in between, but then I remember you told me I could use oil paint.

CZ: Yes. We've graduated from the time *Nick* was made in 2004 [*see fig. 1*]. *Nick* was still done using the matte medium and India ink. But I think you asked me sometime after that if you could use oil paint and I said, "Yes!" Yes. Why not? It's just going to take time to dry. So, yes, *Georgia* was done using oil paint [*fig. 5*].

EP: Yes, and maybe the small *Nick? Nick (in Berlin)* [*fig. 6*]?

CZ: No, I don't think so, I believe you were still using the India ink–matte medium mix at that point. *Georgia* was the first time we introduced oil paint on Mylar. Also, in between you broke some ground with the print *Ben* [2004].[2] I would never have thought to use charcoal as a medium, because of its fragile nature. We had to be very careful handling the original drawing during the exposure of the carbon tissue. I still have trouble handling that particular print, because it looks like a fresh charcoal drawing!

EH: So those were all made later?

CZ: Yes. This *Nick* [*see fig. 1*] was your second direct gravure, Elizabeth.

EH: I don't know if I told you, but I purchased this print for Yale [University Art Gallery], and it's much admired and shown. And I've always wondered, and wanted to ask, if those wonderful drips were intentional?

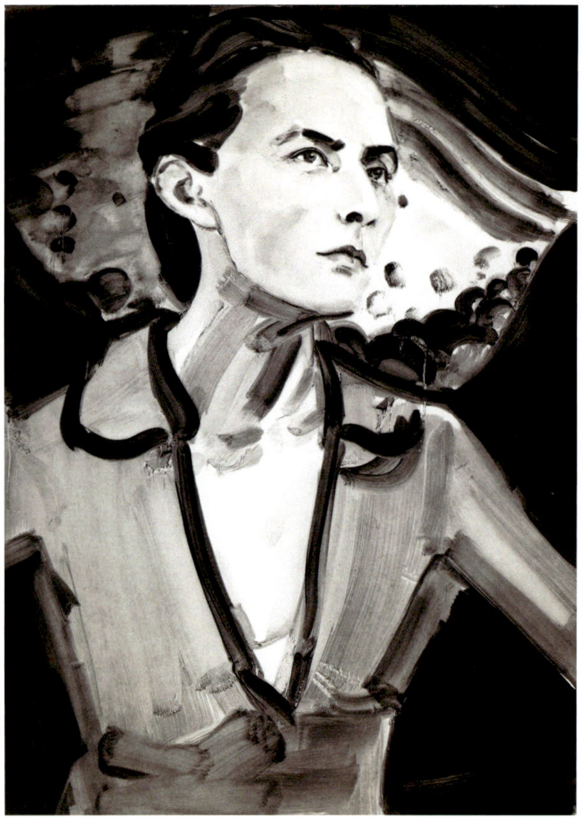

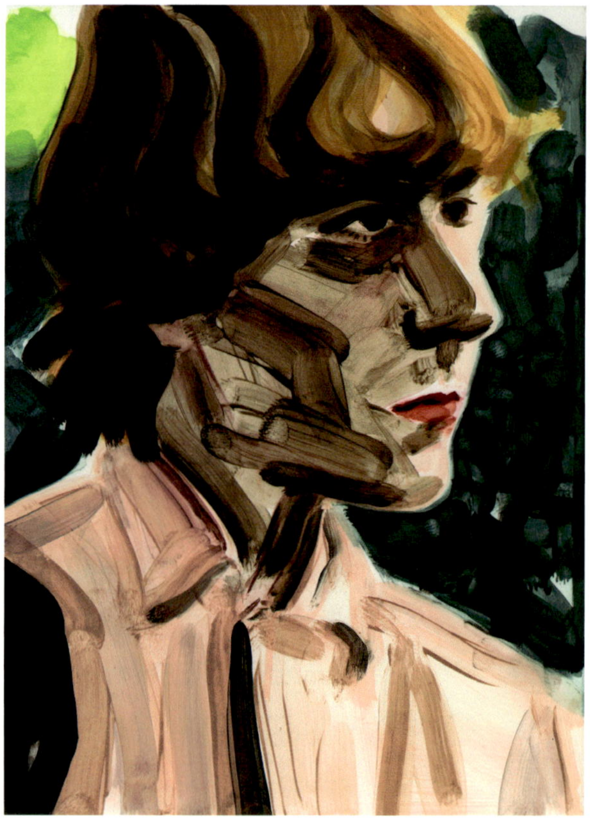

FIG. 5. Elizabeth Peyton, *Georgia (after Stieglitz 1918)*, 2006. Etching with aquatint and direct gravure, 30 × 22 in. (76.2 × 55.9 cm). Edition of 40. Published by Two Palms

FIG. 6. Elizabeth Peyton, *Nick (in Berlin)*, 2005. Eleven-color etching with aquatint and direct gravure, 15⅞ x 11⅞ in. (40.3 x 30.2 cm). Edition of 30. Published by Two Palms

EP: Well, I think it would be wrong to say they were intentional; they just happened. An accident.

EH: And is that just because of the India ink being so fluid?

EP: Yes. It's just watery. But you can make it more or less watery. And I would experiment with that, making it thinner and more drippy at first, then heavier. But I like these gravures. I like how direct they are—what you see in the print is exactly what was on the plate.

CZ: The body, the structure that the matte medium gave it was a new thing for me. I had never seen it before in an etching. Whenever I had used the direct-gravure process before, it had more of the look of an ink wash or a graphite drawing. But I had never reproduced a brush structure. And Elizabeth brought that to the process. [*to EP:*] You brought that out and now it's been channeled into other artists' work . . . [*sheepishly*] by me. I'm sorry.

[*laughter*]

EP: No, that's okay! I didn't come up with that, somebody else did.

EH: You brought it from your experience with lithography.

EP: Yes. Because I made the lithographs on Mylar too, so it was a similar process for me. A similar approach from my end.

EH: But the look of these gravures versus that of a lithograph is different. Could you talk about that?

EP: Well, this might reveal how much I don't know about prints, but I really don't think about things like that. I just see them as different prints. I mean, I suppose I can see that this is denser [*looking at* Nick], that there's a denser quality to the ink.

EH: Could the two of you walk me through the process of making *Nick*?

[*pause, then laughter*]

EH: Or don't you remember?

EP: Well, it's not very complicated.

EH: But this was the first color gravure you made. Using several Mylar separations?

CZ: Well, yes, and to me, other than being an incredibly accomplished work, the reason I feel this print stands out is that Elizabeth was able to visualize the separations in real time, from life, with a model.

EH: So he—Nick—came to the studio?

EP: Yes. We did this all from life. He came to the studio and sat for me, and I painted these Mylars vertically, on an easel. Nick's an artist. Nick Relph. At that moment he was working with another guy named Oliver Payne, making films. He's a pretty young guy. At the point I made this he was probably about twenty-two?

CZ: But, yes, Elizabeth did this from life, and was able to visualize all of the color separations on the spot.

EP: Well, I knew what I was doing. I had had a little experience separating colors.

CZ: These Mylars are numbered [*figs. 7–11*]. They reflect the order in which they were painted.

EP: Yes. I always work from light to dark.

EH: So I've read that this print used a total of seven colors and four plates . . .

CZ: So sometimes there are two to three colors on a single plate.

EP: Wow, the Mylars look nice! Maybe we should reprint this, all in grays.

CZ: That would be interesting. To revisit a print in that manner would be an interesting idea, Elizabeth. We never proofed it in black and white to see what that would look like.

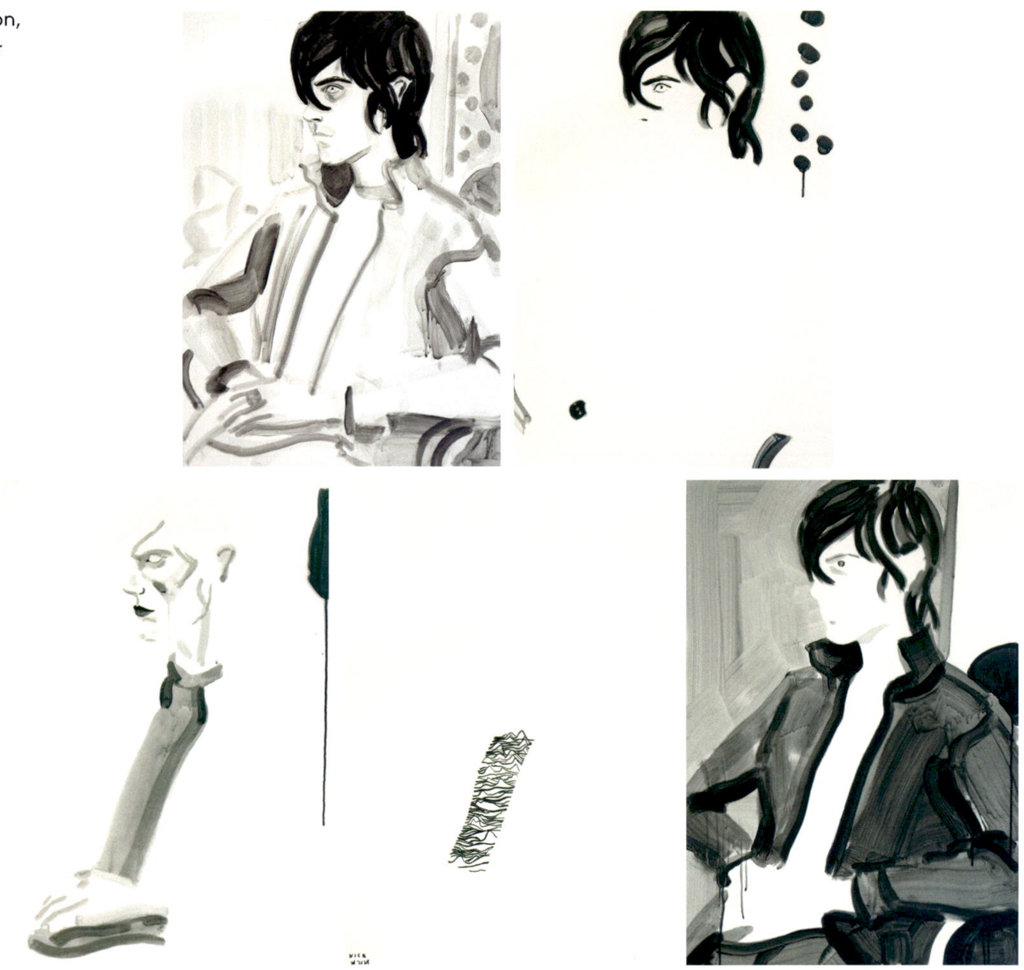

EH: And how were these marks made [*pointing to Mylar separation #4*]?

EP: With a litho crayon.

EH: It's nice. It gives it a chalky look.

EP: Craig, you pretty much told me that I could use anything to draw on these that was black.

CZ: Right, that's really how this process works. If you can block the ultraviolet light, then it's going to work. And that's what is so difficult about making these separations. You can't see the colors to see what you're doing; you have to mentally visualize them. You have to envision the colors mixing together, on top of one another in the order they are printed, creating new colors in [the] course. That is one of the difficulties of separating colors by hand.

EH: So you made these by continuously overlaying a new Mylar on the easel?

EP: Yes. And these were drying really fast, so that wasn't a problem. Maybe we also had some hair dryers? But the whole process maybe took three hours or so.

CZ: Yes. Probably.

EH: Wow.

CZ: It was so quick, Lisa.

EP: We had been working on something else earlier, and I remember it was nearing the end of the day. And perhaps this size Mylar was hanging around and I had been looking at it, I don't remember. Something made me know it was possible. But it happened late in the day.

CZ: There are photos of you working [*fig. 12*], and outside the windows it's getting darker and darker . . .

[*laughter*]

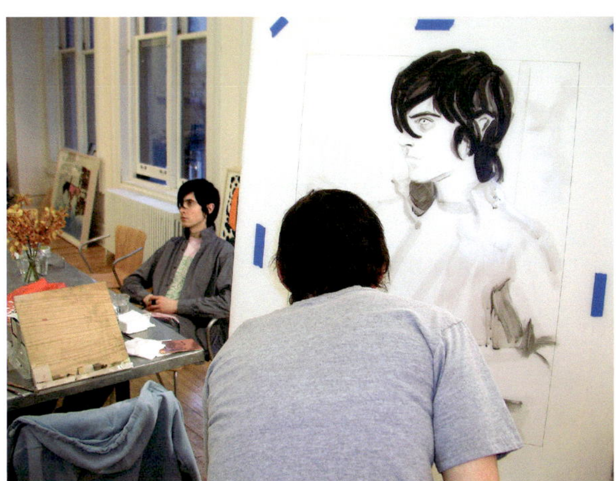

FIG. 12. Peyton, in the foreground, at work on her portrait of the sitter, Nick Relph

EH: And this is life-size.

EP: Maybe even larger than life.

EH: I think it would look marvelous in grays.

EP: Yes. I'd like to see it.

CZ: So working with Elizabeth has been so . . . direct, for me. And we've sat and talked about this before. It's just something I can relate to, the way Elizabeth works. It's so interesting. There is a lot of magic, but there's no mystery.

EH: What I find fascinating, Elizabeth, is that you make your prints in the same way you make your paintings. In real time. On an easel. With your model seated in front.

EP: Yes, but I wouldn't do it any other way. It's just another opportunity for another thing. I don't really treat the prints any different from any other part of what I do.

　　　　　　　　　　　　　　　　　　　　　　　Elizabeth Peyton

EH: And you have been making prints pretty steadily since you first came here [to Two Palms] in 2002?

> EP: Well, I haven't really made any prints in the last year or year and a half. But it's nice to be back.

CZ: Even when you haven't come here regularly, we always seem to have something being printed. There's always something in the works. Elizabeth always keeps us happy.

EH: What are you making now?

> EP: Some new things. I had a sitter here yesterday, and I've been working on some still lifes.

CZ: Beautiful still lifes.

> EP: Thank you, Craig.

EH: Can I ask you a couple of questions?

> EP: Sure.

EH: Historically speaking, the multiple has a special relationship to portraiture—the idea that a certain likeness can be mass-disseminated and that that image can become the iconic view of a person. So you think of currency, or of engraved portrait illustrations in books, and that it is those images through which we have come to "know" these people. Given that your portraits are often of historical figures and celebrities, I wonder how this concept might or might not inform your work.

> EP: It's something I'm very conscious of, actually, because it's the only opportunity I have to make more than the single object, to reproduce something. And also I'm very aware of the fact that if it's going to be reproduced, it's got to be worthy of being reproduced. Or it's got to be something that I really want to spread around. Like when I was working on pictures of Georgia O'Keeffe, I thought, "I really want to make a print of her." Because then it could be in a lot of different places. So, yes, it's something I think about a lot when I'm here at Two Palms.
>
> It's one of my criteria, really. I often use the monotypes as a medium in which to try things out—usually new material, often something I've never made a picture of before. But then, with the etchings, it's more condensed, quiet. But there has to be a good reason for making them.

EH: And the titling? You usually use just first names, which carries a sort of implied intimacy, a closeness with your subjects, living or dead.

EP: Yes. Absolutely. Total love and admiration. But also, sometimes I do that because I want to always remember. It's transformative. My interest is not about literally copying a subject line for line but about atmosphere, and magic. And there's a transformation that happens. So that's why I don't include the last names. Because then it becomes so much about biography— "Oh, Nick Relph, born 1980 . . ."—which adds another element to the picture. The print is totally about him, but there's a more intimate aspect too.

EH: So interesting. There's a quote I read from you in a 2002 interview which I would love for you to comment on—or not comment on, if you don't want to. You were talking about your influences, in particular David Hockney, and how he in a way paved the way for your work, or made it somehow permissible for you to do the sort of work you do in a time when it wasn't really vogue to do the work you do: "I love that in the '70s, in the time of high dry conceptualism, Hockney was doing portraits, and he was really rendering them."[3] And I'm just interested, has the fact that Hockney himself has been so deeply invested in printmaking throughout his career also influenced your being drawn to the medium?

EP: No, not really. But also, I'd rephrase what you said. *I gave myself permission to do what I was doing; I never needed permission from anybody.* But David Hockney was inspiring to me. And it was also interesting that no one ever talked about him in school. Or Georgia O'Keeffe. Or Frida Kahlo. No one ever brought those names up to me. Or Alice Neel, strangely. So, it's more that I think people assume they know who these artists are, and it's really just so much bigger and more unimaginable, who they are. Like when you see a Georgia O'Keeffe, it's mind-blowing! The paint is the paint! And everything else is just projection—about who and what that artist is. It doesn't have much to do with the art, actually. And that Hockney lives, and does what he believes in, and believes in what he believes—in humanity and being human and making art that is human—was a big inspiration to me.

Notes

The preceding conversation was held on July 22, 2010, at Two Palms.

1.   In 2000 Peyton was commissioned by the Public Art Fund and the developer Forest City Ratner Companies in New York to create a series of five lithographs for the newly opened Embassy Suites Hotel in Battery Park City and the Hilton Times Square: *Kiss (Tony), John and Jackie, John, Prince Harry and Prince William*, and *Prince William*, each 24 × 19 in. (61 × 48.3 cm), except *Prince William*, which is 24 × 18 in. (61 × 45.7 cm). Edition of 350. Copublished by Derrière L'Etoile Studios, in New York, and the Public Art Fund.

2.   Elizabeth Peyton, *Ben*, 2004, etching with aquatint additions, 32 × 24¼ in. (81.3 × 61.6 cm). For an image of *Ben*, see Sabine Eckmann and Beate Kemfert, eds., *Ghost: Elizabeth Peyton* (Ostfildern, Germany: Hatje Cantz Verlag, 2011), 67.

3.   Elizabeth Peyton, quoted in Alison M. Gingeras, *Vitamin P: New Perspectives in Painting* (London: Phaidon, 2002), unpaginated.

                                                                                   Elizabeth Peyton

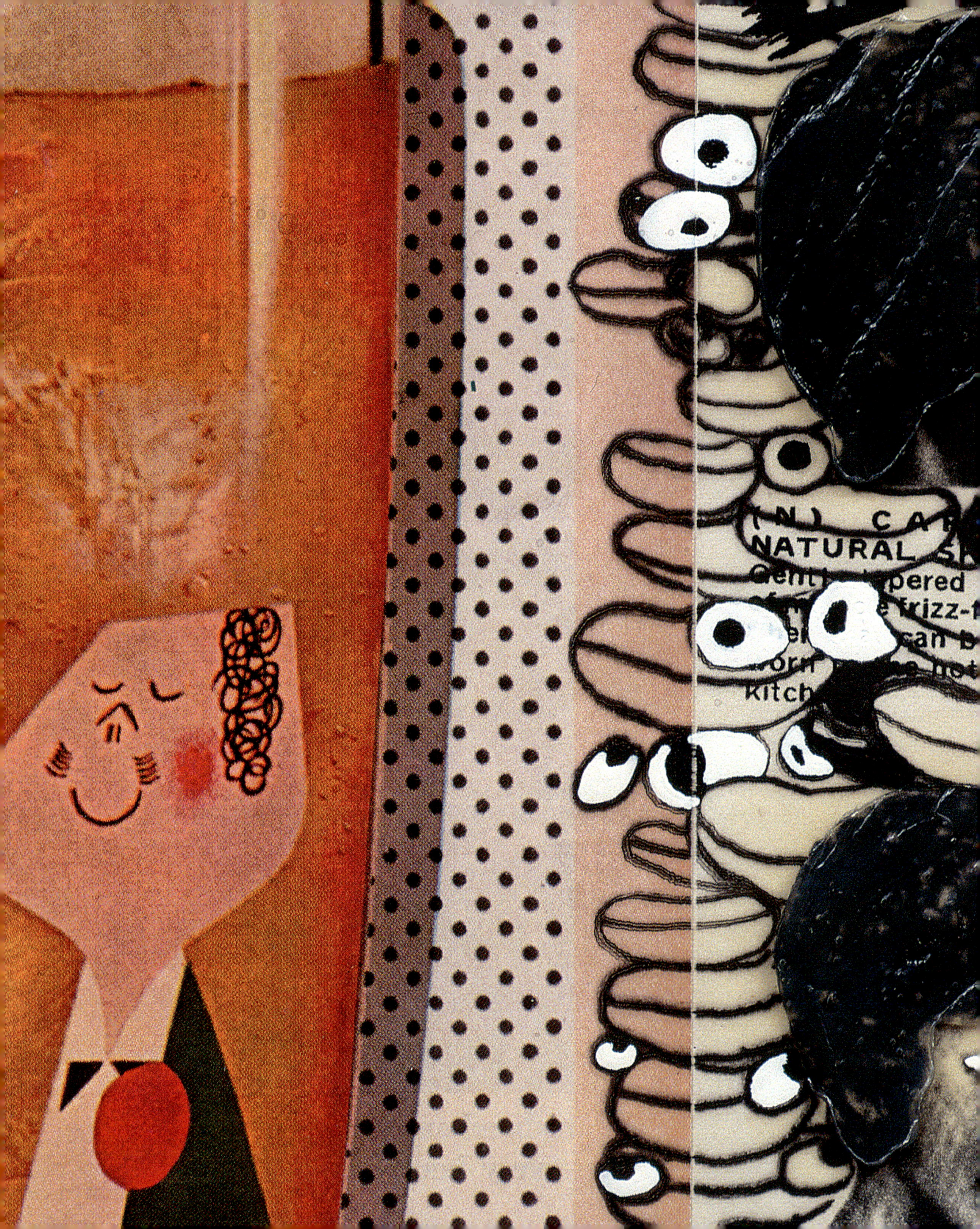
(N) CA
NATURAL S
Gentl pered
frizz-
can b
worn not
kitch

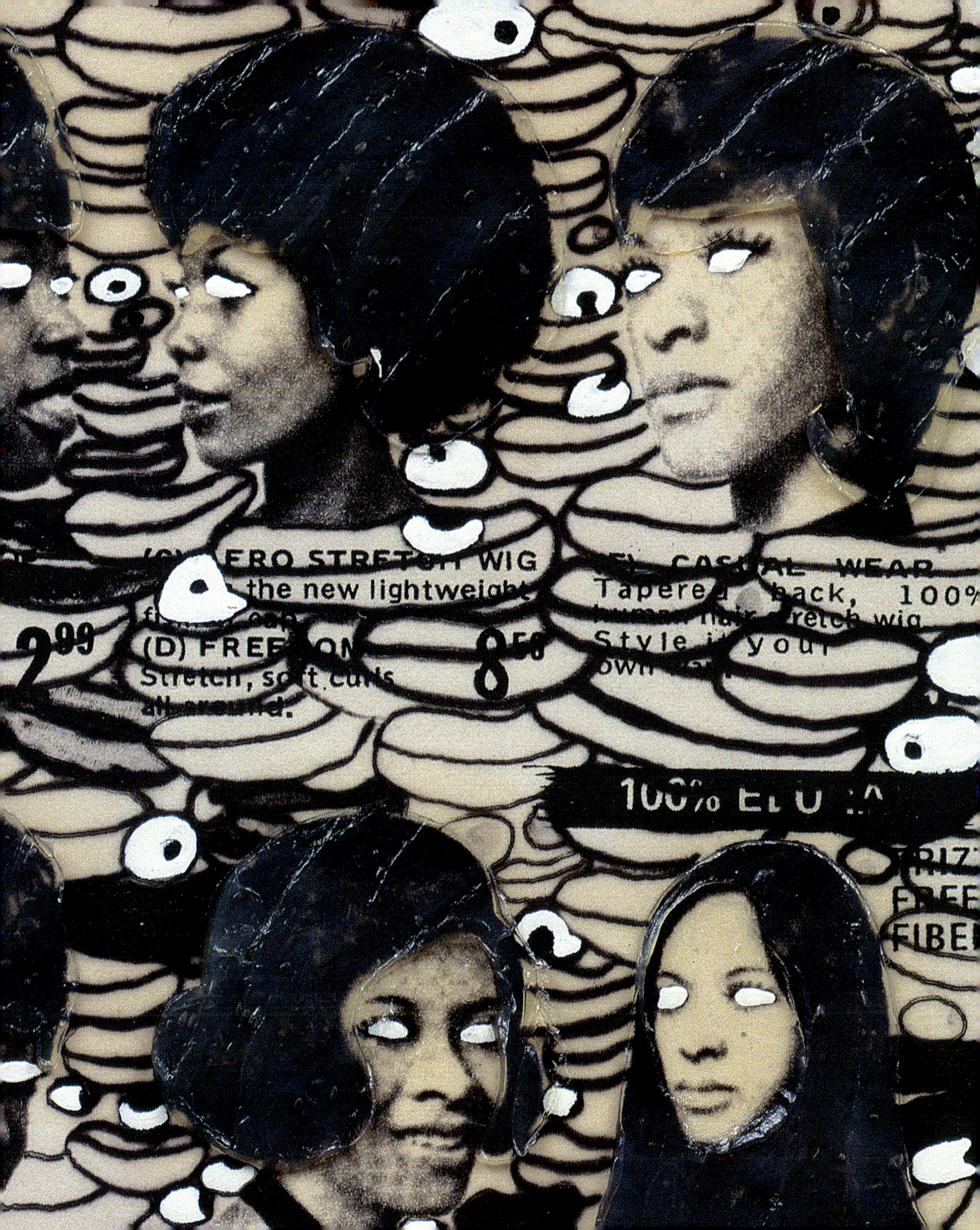
ERO STRETCH WIG
the new lightweight
(D) FREEDOM
Stretch, soft curls
all around.
2 99
8 50
CASUAL WEAR
Tapered back, 100%
human hair stretch wig.
Style it your
own way.
100% ELURA
FRIZZ
FREE
FIBER

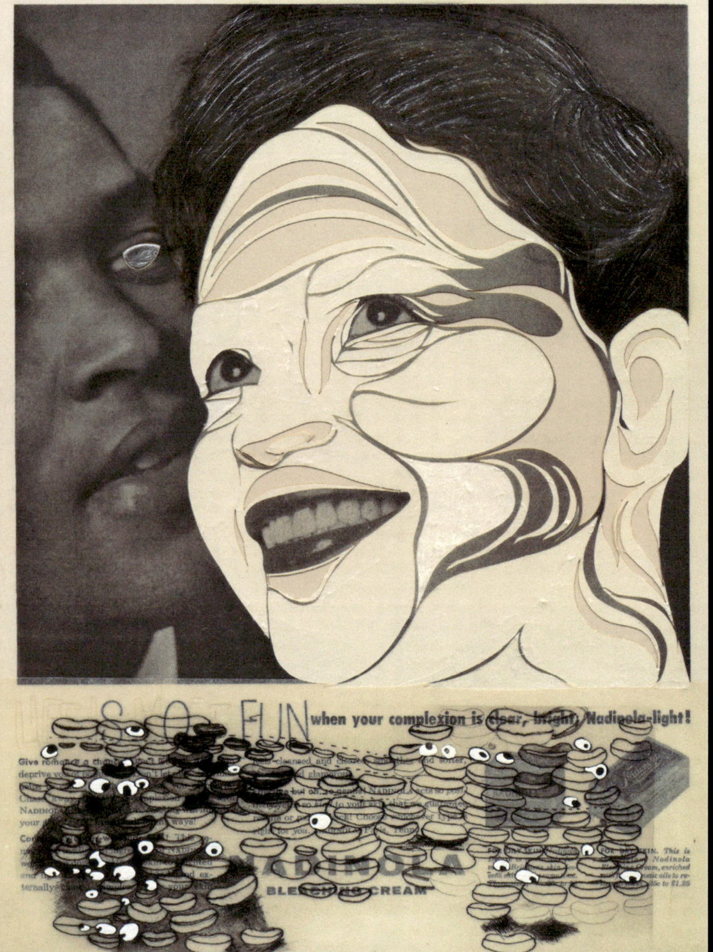

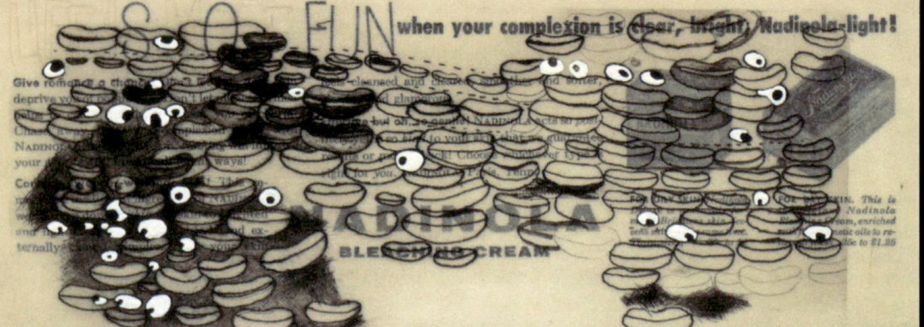

LIFE'S MORE FUN ... when your complexion is clear, bright, Nadinola-light!
NADINOLA
BLEACHING CREAM

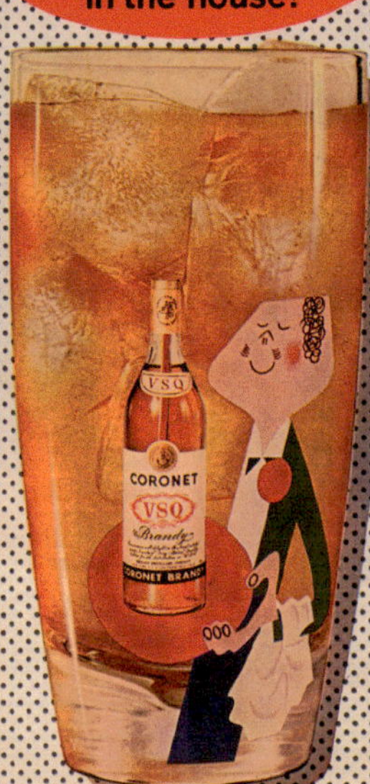

© 1963, BRANDY DISTILLERS CO., N.Y.C. 80 PROOF
CORONET
VSQ BRANDY
Smooths any drink in the house!
CORONET
VSQ
Brandy
CORONET BRANDY
Versatile Coronet VSQ makes 32 different mixed drinks and because it's especially smoothened, improves every one of them! Mix with pleasure, mix with Coronet VSQ—only the taste is costly!

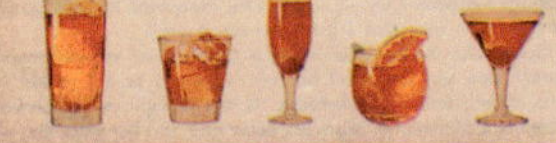

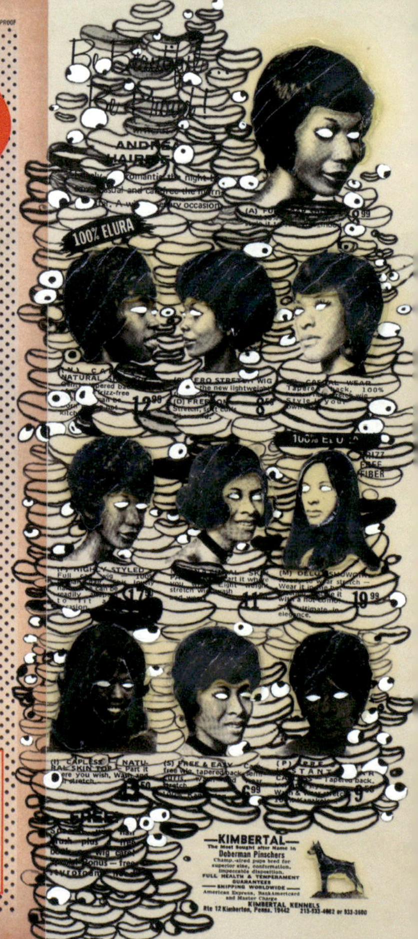

ANDREA HAIRPIECE
100% ELURA
KIMBERTAL
The Most Sought after Name in
Doberman Pinschers
Champ.-sired pups bred for superior size, conformation, impeccable disposition.
FULL HEALTH & TEMPERAMENT GUARANTEE
SHIPPING WORLDWIDE
American Express, BankAmericard and Master Charge
KIMBERTAL KENNELS
Rte 12 Kimberton, Penna. 19442   215-933-4962 or 933-3600

Ellen Gallagher's monumental, sixty-component print *DeLuxe* is one of the most ambitious and groundbreaking print productions of the last half-century, a composite object that expands our conception of the traditional print suite. In essence intaglios (photogravure, etching, aquatint, and drypoint), the prints that *DeLuxe* comprises also incorporate a veritable smorgasbord of relief and planographic techniques and collage elements: lithography, screenprint, embossing, tattoo-machine engraving, laser-cutting, and *chine collé* are joined by additions of Plasticine, cut-and-pasted paper, enamel, gouache, varnish, graphite, oil, polymer, watercolor, pomade, velvet, glitter, crystals, foil paper, gold leaf, toy eyeballs, and toy ice cubes. Thus, each of these modest-sized print components is a complex production in its own right—an extrusion and incrustation—each using as its conceptual springboard a page from one of the magazines produced for African American audiences between the 1930s and 1970s (such as *Sepia, Our World,* and *Ebony*). The pages that Gallagher has chosen are often edgy: advertisements for such products as wigs, hair pomades, and skin-bleaching creams that promise African Americans (usually women) ways in which to lighten or "improve" their appearance.

Unlike most of the prints discussed in this book, *DeLuxe* necessitated a complex production to achieve its impressive scale, one that included more than just one or two printers. Indeed, a small army was necessary for its completion, a group that Gallagher commends again and again: Craig Zammiello, Roger White, Hilary Harnischfeger, Doug Volle, Georgia Küng, Amy Pryor, David Lasry, and a host of interns.

This chapter focuses in particular on two of the sixty components of *DeLuxe—So Fun* and *Coronet* (figs. 1–2)—which together represent the physical and intellectual complexity of the larger whole. These prints are fascinating in their multidimensionality—both physically, in terms of materials, and conceptually, in their engagement of the concepts of time and place, history and memory. As Thyrza Nicholas Goodeve has commented: "Process, Layers, Materials—physicality is everything to [Gallagher]. Flesh is a texture as much as a color."[1]

FIGS. 1–2. *So Fun* and *Coronet*, from *DeLuxe*, 2004–5.
Mixed-media prints, each 13 x 10 in. (33 x 25.4 cm). Edition
of 20. Published by Two Palms. Left to right: **FIG. 1.** *So Fun*,
photogravure, tattoo engraving, laser-cutting, chine collé,
gouache, and pomade; **FIG. 2.** *Coronet*, four-color lithograph
with photogravure, tattoo engraving, gouache, and pomade

ELISABETH HODERMARSKY: The first published print you made was in 1997, at ULAE [Universal Limited Art Editions], an untitled lithograph. But had you ever made prints before that, at Skowhegan or at the School of the Museum of Fine Arts, Boston?

ELLEN GALLAGHER: I did make a few prints as a student, both at Skowhegan, and at the MFA School in Boston. Actually, my first art class was a printmaking workshop with Paul Arnold at Oberlin [College], who—I think—had studied with Stanley William Hayter. I remember we based our standard etch on the time it took to smoke a cigarette. I hadn't had any drawing or painting experience before that, so it was really overwhelming. Still, I immediately loved the feel of the drypoint needle on the plate, the way in which a plate had to be ground down—prepared—and I liked the whole layering process on one object. And that it was an object that could accept all of these layers. But, I was sixteen years old and didn't know how to draw. Arnold took my hand and drew into the plate. We spent a day where he actually sat and drew with me. I brought in magazine images and photographs to draw from. Oh, and this is so strange, I'm just remembering it . . . I was working from an image found in an *Ebony* magazine.

CRAIG ZAMMIELLO: You're kidding!

EG: I think it was a Kwanza family calendar. I remade it starring my mom, my sister, and me. Arnold held my hand and showed me how to move the needle, and how to shade. The plate came alive for me. That experience sent me on my way. After that, I stopped printmaking for a time and started drawing.

I made prints again at Skowhegan, and that was because Kiki Smith introduced us to Xerox transfers. This was in 1993. I was already a huge fan of Kiki, and she was incredibly generous. She invited us all to her studio, whoever wanted to come. Of course, everybody came. We had all been given instructions to come with Xeroxes and paper, and we printed with toluene. She went around the room and helped everyone get these great results—gooey transfers, rubbing with burnishers. When it was my turn, mine came out blank!

And Kiki doesn't remember this, but she came over and asked, "Why is yours blank?" And I said, "I don't know, I'm not getting anything." Everyone else had gotten something and was happy. She was so annoyed that one person had failed. She couldn't accept that! I was very embarrassed. Apparently, my Xeroxes were too old or something, because the ink has to be fresh. What I had Xeroxed were lips. I was already drawing lips and then copying them. I had different sizes, shrinking them and blowing them up. I had these old Xeroxes lying around, which were what I brought.

CZ: After a while, if the Xerox is too old, it doesn't want to transfer anymore. It really sets up.

EG: And so Kiki said, "Get some fresh Xeroxes and do it over." And she showed up later in my studio, at Skowhegan, with some toluene, and said, "You are going to make this print." She would not accept failure.

And, although we're talking about printmaking techniques, a few months later—when I went to the Carpenter Center [for the Visual Arts] at Harvard [University]—it was my thinking that these pages would form a painting. After that summer, I got invited to participate in a group show at ICA [the Institute of Contemporary Art] in Boston. It was in collaboration with the Carpenter Center and the Graduate School of Design at Harvard. The director very kindly said to me that it was a Bauhaus tradition that when there was an artist in town who needed to use the print shop or any facilities, they would be invited to do so. So they gave me the keys to the print shop. Since I wasn't a student, I couldn't take up much space. But there were never any students around, which was odd, because in those days, the art students were given their supplies for free—big tubes of oil paint—it was insane! And the print shop was empty. I know that these were Harvard students, who had many classes and exams to study for . . . but they would only show up in the print shop when they had a deadline to complete a project. It wasn't very lively.

Still, meeting Kiki and a year spent in an empty print shop were the catalysts for this shift in my work, the incorporation of printmaking into my painting process.

CZ: Well, just one more thing about Kiki. After your time with her at Skowhegan, Kiki came to us at ULAE and said, "There is an artist you have to look at. Her name is Ellen Gallagher."

EG: Really?

CZ: Absolutely. And Bill Goldston looked at your work, and said, "Kiki, okay."

EG: She put me in my first group show in New York (*Artists "Select,"* at Artists Space in 1993). I didn't really know Kiki at that time. I mean, I knew her in the way that one gets to know another artist, or mentor, during a studio visit. In the paintings that I made while I was at the Carpenter Center, I was basically incorporating the Xerox transfers I had begun making at Skowhegan. I carried the pages around in a briefcase, because I always had to be ready to go. So I'd go to the print shop and make more, generating a supply, and I'd lay them out and think about them. It wasn't really a print that I was making in a traditional way, with a plate. There was no plate, only a series of drawings. After building a form with the printed pages, I glued them to the canvas. This work became *Afro Mountain* [1994], which is in the Whitney [Museum of American Art] collection now. The painting was first shown in the 1995 Whitney Biennial.

EH: Which was a particularly good Biennial.

EG: I was really honored to be included. It was such a beautiful time for me in my life—these artists opening up to me, this technique opening up to me.
Kiki and I met again because of ULAE. I was hesitant because I didn't know much about printmaking.

CZ: And when Ellen came in . . .

EG: And didn't know anything . . .

CZ: Well, nobody knew that. She started working with Doug Volle right away, on offset lithography. On doing her lips and eyes, and hand-coloring them, and creating the most beautiful offset litho [*Untitled*, 1997; *fig. 3*]. I must say, to this day I look at that print and think, "Wow, what a sweet work." It's all about color and outline and drawing . . .

EG: And I remember, while I was working on that offset, Doug taught me the acid technique, where you paint directly on the plate with the acid.

EH: Did you produce an etching then?

CZ: Ellen just worked in lithography at ULAE.

EG: No, no, Craig. I think that there might be some etching in that print. Remember? I had to open up the eyes, what I wanted to do is get rid of the color—wanted to open it up.

CZ: Oh, so perhaps we were using the deletion fluid. So this is the history. It's funny how Ellen and Doug and I have traveled all together. Because what year was that?

EG: That was 1996? It was published in 1997, but that was in 1996–97.

CZ: So . . . jump ahead a few years.

EG: Yes, so to jump ahead: according to David Lasry, he was trying to get me to come and make a print at Two Palms. And I don't really remember this, but he says he had been trying to get me there for two years.

CZ: He had!

EG: But that's not my recollection. He has this memory that he was being really aggressive, but I don't remember that . . .

CZ: David's aggressiveness is nonexistent. If he says hi to you, that's being aggressive enough.

EG: Yes!

CZ: So David comes in one day and says, "You don't know Ellen Gallagher, do you?" And I said, "Sure I know Ellen, why?" And he said, "She's coming over this afternoon." And I said, "Fantastic!"

EG: And when I walked in and saw Craig . . . !

EH: Did you know Craig was at Two Palms then?

EG: I didn't know anything. I just went because David asked me to come. And I really don't like to unpack all of my stuff in a new environment. That's just how I am. But then when I do, of course, they wish I would leave.

CZ: No!

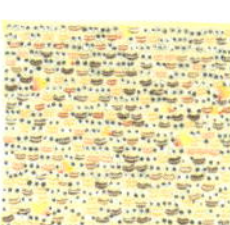

FIG. 3. Ellen Gallagher, *Untitled*, 1997. Lithograph in eighteen colors on Rives BFK paper, 53½ × 40½ in. (135.9 × 102.9 cm). Edition of 42. Published by Universal Limited Art Editions

EG: So when I walked in and saw Craig there I just thought "yes." We were going to do something.

EH: And you had been away from printmaking, working alone in your studio, for several years, right?

EG: Yes. By then [2003], I had been away from New York too. I had already been living in Rotterdam for some time—and printmaking is such a collaborative process. I don't easily open up in the studio. But when I saw Craig there, I knew I was in good hands. Craig has a way of transmitting his talents so that, as an artist, you just feel very invited. You feel that it's not this overwhelming "technical stew"—which it is, but he doesn't present it to you like that.

CZ: Well, we had this comfortable relationship. Ellen brought in a bunch of material, which encompassed all different techniques. And I remember that you had to do a print for the Venice Biennale, right? So there was a project involved. And it ended up being *Bouffant Pride* [2003].[2]

EG: That was really an incredible process.

CZ: It worked out so well.

EG: I had already done a project at the Drawing Center with Catherine de Zegher—*Preserve*—where I had drawn directly into the pages of *Ebony*, *Sepia*, and *Our World* magazines. I began that body of work while living in Provincetown [Massachusetts] in 1997. MoMA [Museum of Modern Art, New York] has a drawing from that series [*fig. 4*]. I was already thinking of the magazine drawings as a sequence of some sort. And then Artists Space also asked me to do an edition . . . perhaps in 1997. At one point I thought I might make them twenty different *Ebony* pages, but it turned out to be so labor intensive just to do one. I didn't exhibit the early magazine drawings—or, I only showed them to other artists and writers at the Provincetown Fine Arts Work Center. I wasn't sure that I wanted to bring this into my work. You know, sometimes you make things, but you don't necessarily want to make them a focus of your work, or think that you want them to be seen. So that was in 1997, my last year in Provincetown. And then I started drawing again in 1999, and completed this suite of sixteen drawings [2001], working directly into the magazine pages.

EH: Were they three-dimensional?

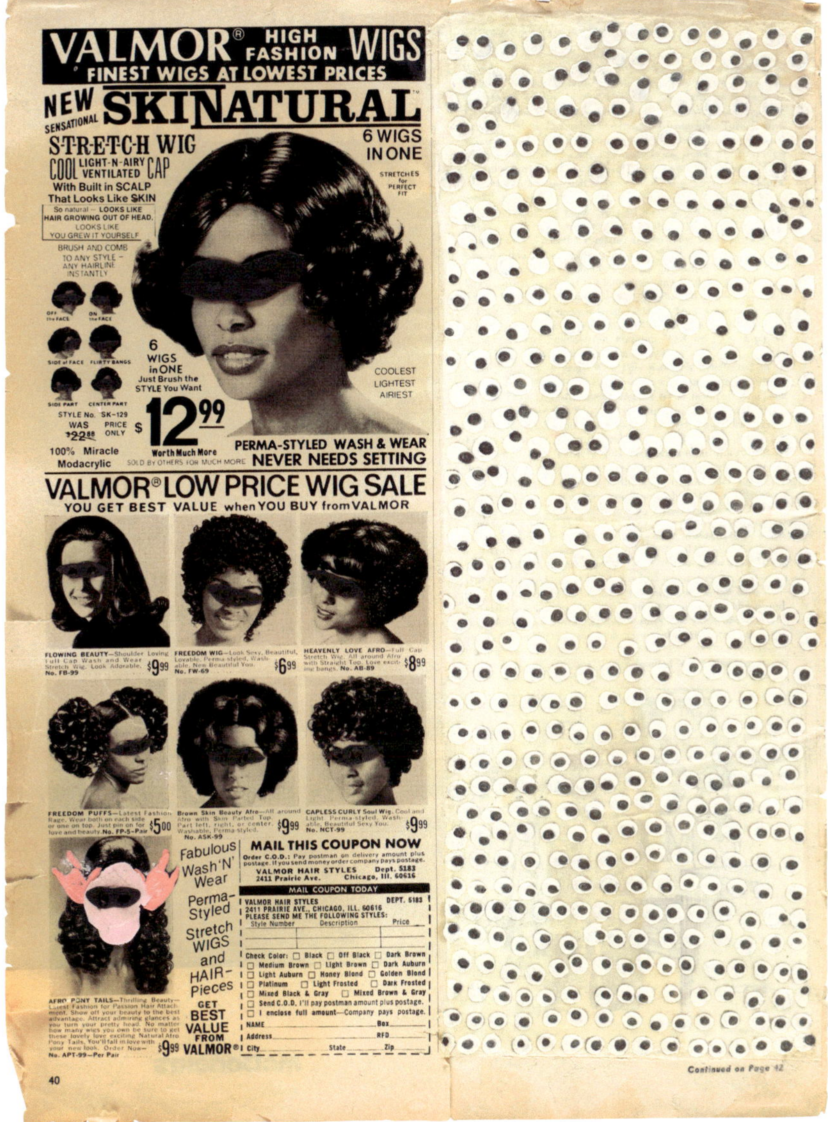

FIG. 4. Ellen Gallagher, *Skinatural*, 1997. Oil, graphite, and Plasticine on a magazine page, 13¼ × 10 in. (33.7 × 25.4 cm). Museum of Modern Art, Gift of Mr. and Mrs. James R. Hedges IV, 296.2000

EG: Not as three-dimensional, strangely enough, as *DeLuxe* [*fig. 5*]. And we should talk about that in terms of layering—because, in fact, I find that *DeLuxe* is three-dimensional in many directions. Because of the plate, but also because of Craig's ability to feed me technical information as it's needed, as a conversational process *as it's happening*. It's not like he's instructing me, "You can do this, this, this, and this." It's more like a dialogue. I'm drawing, and Craig's occasionally looking on, and at some point says, "You know what? You know what you can try?" And so it would just sort of grow like that, organically. And so I'd be layering all of these techniques without being overwhelmed by this amazing network that Craig has. This incredible network in his mind.

Because that's always the fear, as an artist coming into a print studio: that you will get overwhelmed. That the person you're working with has so

Ellen Gallagher

much more technical talent than you do, and that possibly could shut you down, shut your creativity down. But not with the way that Craig works with artists, which is far more organic.

One of the things with the drawings—and you can't really compare the drawings and the prints—because the drawings are finite in terms of material and scale, the drawings get built up beyond recognition. They're almost *boli*.[3] They get to a point, in terms of the collage, where they can't go any further—that's it.

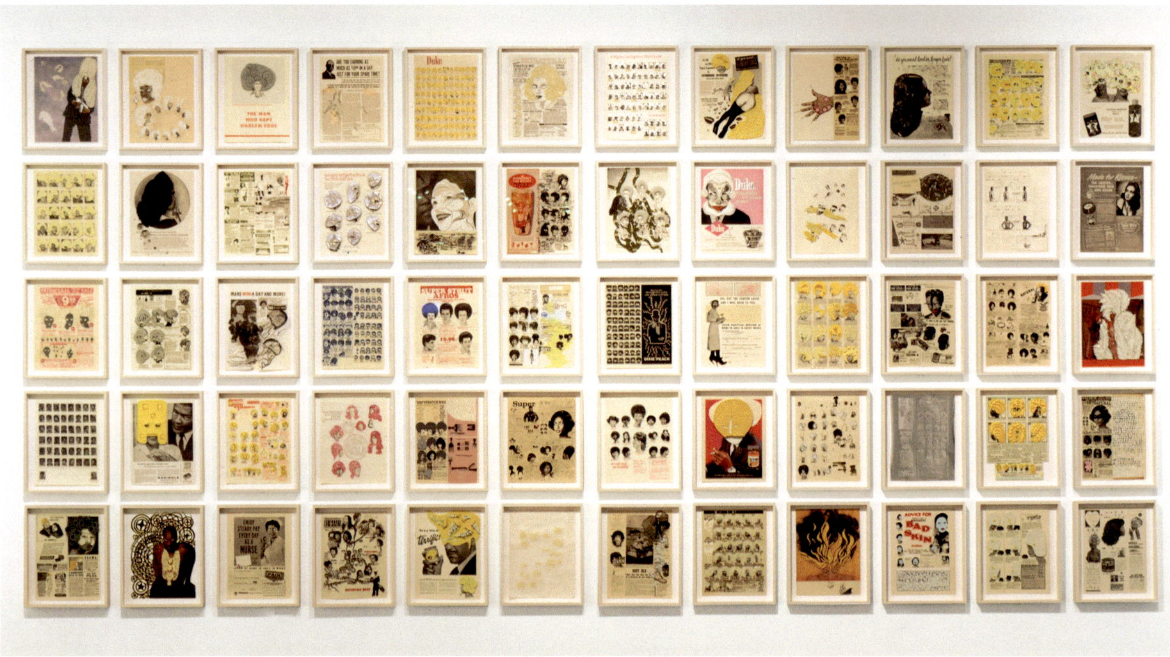

FIG. 5. Ellen Gallagher, *DeLuxe*, 2004–5. Installation view of sixty printed objects with aquatint, photogravure, spit bite, lithography, screenprint, embossing, tattoo-machine engraving, laser-cutting, chine collé, collage, crystals, cut paper, enamel, glitter, gold leaf, gouache, graphite, oil, Plasticine, polymer, pomade, toy eyeballs, toy ice cubes, watercolor, velvet, glitter, and foil paper, each component 13 × 10 in. (33 × 25.4 cm). Edition of 20. Published by Two Palms

EH: And with the prints in *DeLuxe* you're working them in both dimensions, into the plate with the etching and above, with the collaging.

EG: That's what I'm saying. It's layering in many directions. I would often start by doing a drawing directly onto the magazine page—arriving at the same point I got to with the *Preserve* drawings, where they would be just on the edge of lucidity, they're getting so stuffed. And I love that precarious moment. There's this point in my work where it verges towards the oblique. At the same time I strive for lucidity, even if it doesn't occur in a literal way. With *DeLuxe*—because of the intervention of the plate—the drawings were built up densely. And Craig would have watched how the drawings were made, because many of them were done in the studio, and then he would make a plate from that and we'd start again. So there might be several plates for a single image. The intervention of the plate makes scale infinite.

EH: But *DeLuxe* incorporates this earlier piece, *Bouffant Pride*?

EG: Well, we had made *Bouffant Pride* to see if we could all work together.

CZ: *Bouffant Pride* was our litmus test. Ellen came in and she discussed what she wanted to do with *Bouffant Pride*. And when you left, Ellen, David looked at me and said, "Can we do this?" And I said, "No problem, we've got the technology. We can do this . . . there are just a few things we'll need to work out . . ."

[*laughter*]

CZ: And we did work them out. And so *Bouffant Pride* became this structure—the backbone of *DeLuxe*.

EG: Absolutely. And what I'm trying to communicate here is this intuitive way that Craig and I work together that's really hard to put into language. For example, I knew from the start that I didn't want to print this series on printmaking paper. The body had to be indiscernible from the actual magazine page we took as our starting point. The amazing thing about *DeLuxe* is that it *is* an edition. On occasion you can find found materials in it. There are a few instances where you might find a random clipping from a magazine page, but that's a very specific moment, and it's carefully delineated— really marked as such.

And that first day that I came into Two Palms, I went to New York Central [Art Supply] and I just had this intuition about layering various papers. I spent about a hundred dollars on different sheets of paper . . . maybe I came back with fifteen sheets of paper—they weren't cheap.

CZ: Well, you bought the best, Ellen.

EG: And I remember David Lasry had to go rebuy what I had bought as samples, and the salesperson warned him about me: "She has expensive taste." But it was incredible. And to this day I don't know how that came into the mix, that we were going to laminate it.[4] Because I just felt it would work. I knew that we were going to do this.

But then the next step was for Craig. How was Craig going to print all of these heads on tissue paper? And Craig came up with this technique with the rubber mats.

CZ: Well, that was a technique that had been worked out before, with Robert Rauschenberg: how to print dry on Asian papers, on Japanese papers.[5]

EG: This project would never have happened without that.

CZ: I don't think it would have, at least not in its present form. It has a look to it. And it enabled us to do things like here, in *So Fun* [*figs. 6 and 7*]. You have three layers of paper there, maybe four, all with different levels of printed information.

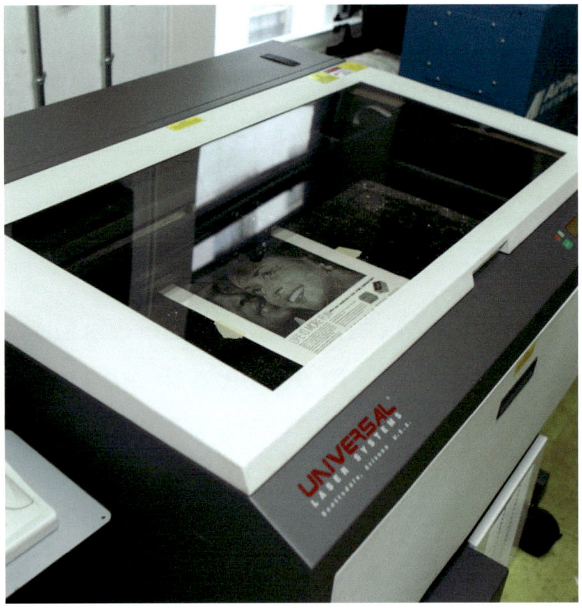

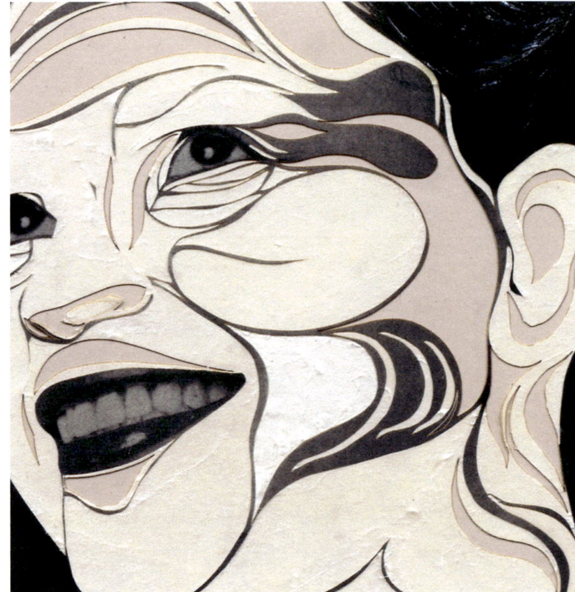

FIG. 6. Printed photogravure of the magazine page used in *So Fun* on three layers of *gampi* paper inside of the laser platform, before laser-cutting

FIG. 7. Close-up of paper layers in *So Fun*, after laser-cutting and hand-peeling

EG: And this *gampi* paper actually has clay inside it. It has a flesh-like texture and appearance.

EH: Is the gampi the top layer?

CZ: It's three layers of gampi, laminated. Then it's printed. Ellen then takes a scalpel and peels away sections and draws others. David Lasry then takes the piece, scans it, and traces her exact cuts on the computer, and with the laser we go down to the exact depths for peeling each layer of lamination [*figs. 8 and 9*].[6]

EG: They can actually stop the cutting at the exact millimeter of depth for the exact cut.

CZ: This project will go down in history.

EG: In the print [*So Fun*], this is the first time I did this to a face. That's the other thing: drawing techniques developed out of this project. I never use printmaking to make versions of my paintings or drawings. Printmaking is its own thing.

In this print, the male character's eye is picked out and I layered silver leaf behind it [*see fig. 1*]. Then that silver leaf has been burnished with a spoon from behind so that the silvered eye pops up. Down below, beneath the lips, is an advertisement for Nadinola Bleaching Cream—skin-whitening cream.

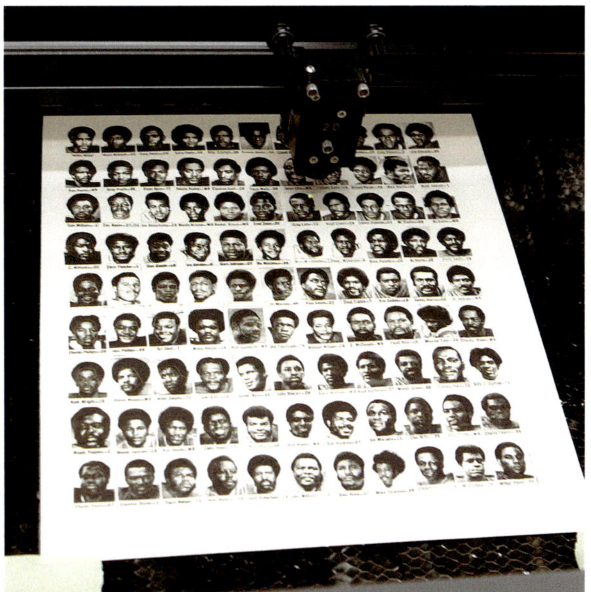
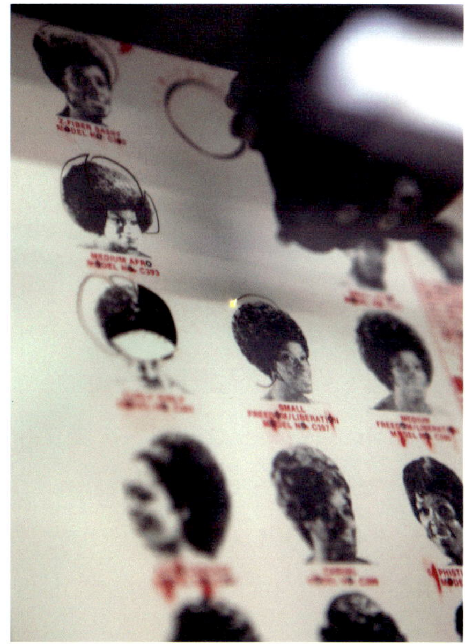

CZ: Skin-bleaching cream. People would—and in fact still do—actually burn themselves.

EG: *So Fun* became this destruction/creation image.

EH: Well, and that's obviously what one responds to, both intellectually and physically: this sort of additive and deductive work playing off of each other in these really edgy ways.

CZ: And then to top it off was the final chine collé of the tattoo drawing of the lips, over the type at the bottom of the image.

EG: Oh, right! And this chine collé is just a thin little piece of gossamer-like tissue.

CZ: You could read through it.

EG: That was intense. I wanted to give up. Because tattooing in flesh is one thing, but tattooing into a copper plate . . . ![7] [*fig. 10*]

CZ: Well, it's engraving.

EG: Your whole body is shaking. And I was really clumsy, but . . .

CZ: No, you weren't clumsy at all! It was a direct way of drawing for Ellen . . .

EG: And you can turn the plate, and engrave at different levels. It's a bit like sewing, where you use your foot to operate the machine while directing the needle with your hand. Ultimately, I loved it.

CZ: You know, I'm sure somebody has used it somewhere before, like with any other technique, but I like to think this was my personal discovery. Ellen was the first artist I know that really took to this. And I've seen many artists try it subsequently, but nobody has ever clicked with it like Ellen. She started to draw, and it just became a central part of many of these compositions.

And—just to describe what's going on here—*Coronet* is a composite image [*see fig. 2*]. On the left is a collaged offset lithograph. It was printed to mimic the look of an old, yellowed magazine ad that it was scanned from onto magazine stock. This was then laminated onto two sheets of Shikabu Gampi paper in a heat press using archival heat-set glue. Ellen drew her trademark lips and googly eyes on the right side of the image using the tattoo machine directly on the photogravure copper plate that contained the images of the women and the small ad at the bottom for Doberman pinschers. This plate was then printed in black ink onto the laminated offset lithographic reproduction of an advertisement for Coronet brandy (on the left side of the print). It was printed dry (as opposed to traditional "damp paper" printing of intaglios) by wrapping a rubber blanket around the cylinder of the etching press and doing away with the traditional felt blankets so as not to distort the thin laminated sheets of gampi.[8]

And *So Fun* is a photogravure of a magazine ad printed on four sheets of laminated Japanese papers. The face of the woman has then been "peeled" to different layers of the laminated papers, as Ellen described. On the bottom of the print is a chine collé of a tattoo drawing of lips and googly eyes that has also had the eyes hand-painted in white gouache. The print is finished off with an application of hair pomade to the woman's printed hair.

EH: Now were both of these prints [*So Fun* and *Coronet*] made about halfway through the entire *DeLuxe* project?

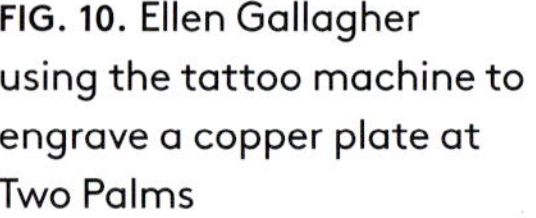

FIG. 10. Ellen Gallagher using the tattoo machine to engrave a copper plate at Two Palms

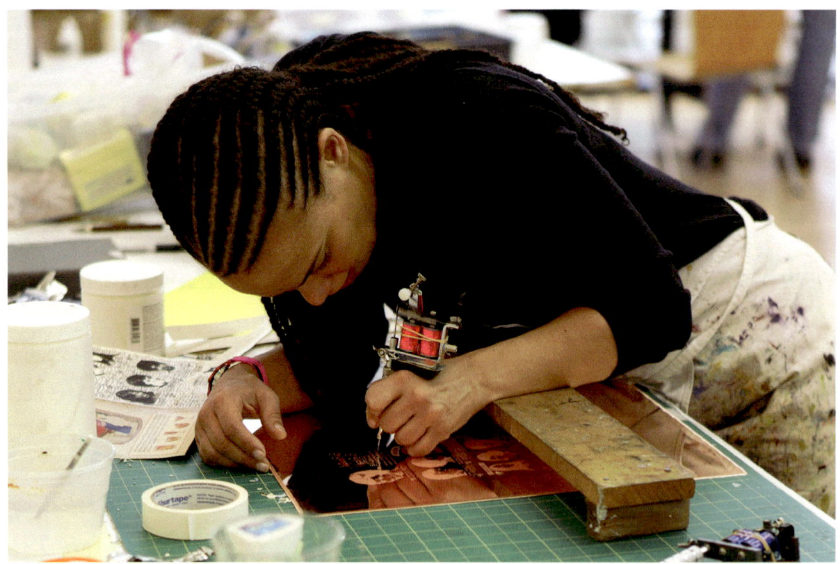

EG and CZ: Oh, God. [*looking at each other*] We don't remember.

CZ: We would really have to look back. We do have a book. We do have a lot of archival history [at Two Palms]. What would be interesting would be to see this deconstructed. And then we'd have to bring in Hilary Harnischfeger. Hilary must be mentioned.

EG: When did Hilary come in?

CZ: I think Hilary was actually there right at the beginning.

EG: No, Hilary joined the project much later. She was dating a friend of mine and I recommended her to David. Thank goodness he hired her. She pulled us together midway into the project. She very carefully organized our building systems.

We were so lucky Hilary came onboard. And I bet if we looked in her black book, where she documented the making of *DeLuxe*, we could find out at what point these two prints came in.

EH: You know, of any of the projects produced at Two Palms over the years, this one seems to be the perfect candidate for that type of documentation. Because it is so unbelievably complex.

CZ: And what Hilary, along with Georgia Küng and Amy Pryor, recorded, was a whole three-dimensional documentation: this is how you put this together; this is how you build the print.

EH: That's invaluable.

CZ: And we've kept it all. We know what archives are. Tanya Grosman taught me about archives.[9]

EH: Because inevitably, at some point, you want to go back and untangle the story.

EG: Hilary kept impeccable notes. And—I have to say this—Hilary had to fight for me sometimes, and say to David and Craig: "Ellen wants it like this." It did take some convincing to get Craig and David to agree to a sequence of sixty.

CZ: Craig thought that we were going to crash and burn.

[*laughter*]

EH: Sixty pieces. But how many sheets of paper in each? How did you know how much to order?

EG: Well, that's just the thing. We didn't know. We sort of started in the middle of this project.

CZ: This whole project had its own life. It grew organically, exponentially.

EG: Like the drawing process I was explaining. I'd be sitting there drawing and Craig would come by and say, "Oh, you could try doing this . . ." And so, it just grew. That's when I knew that Two Palms wasn't just a print shop, this was an *atelier*. This was a place where an artist would come and really grow.

CZ: Lisa, there is one plate left that we didn't use.

EG: Really?

CZ: Just one. It's just sitting there.

EH: I read that there were at least one hundred plates used in the entire project . . .

CZ: Oh, far more than that . . .

EH: Fifty cans of Murray's hair pomade, and two thousand sheets of paper.

CZ: Easily.

EG: And the thing about the papers—they were made by a woman in Japan, whose name is Hiromi.

CZ: Hiromi Katayama. Hiromi Papers. She imports the finest Japanese papers into this country.

EG: And depending on the time of year, the season, the bloom, the bees—I don't know, but the papers can change. Which is great. Except if you're making an edition. So Hilary noticed, as we were getting down to the end, that the new batch that we had ordered wasn't matching up. The tonalities weren't right. David contacted Hiromi and she made a new color just for this project. You know, we're talking about all of these really fine papers, but, for me, what's really important is that our page is believable as a specific magazine page.

EH: So that's why you were so choosy about all of these papers? Because you wanted it to have that antiqued-magazine-page look?

EG: Well, not "antiqued," per se, but yes, the look of the magazine page. And the thing that I liked about the midcentury "race" magazines we were referencing is that they used different kinds of papers within a single issue.

EH: This here [*pointing to the left side of* Coronet] looks so realistic as having the patina of a fifties magazine paper.

CZ: That was printed.

EG: That's printed! That's not even the raw paper! That's all Craig. He did this. Craig would ride home—imagine this—on the train every night, and he would do homework. So half of the work is nineteenth-century print work, but the other half of it is computer work.

The project is so much about racial instability. And the paper, the yellowing page, is such a thing with me. It's really a sign in my work, even though it's also a texture, and a feeling.

One of the characteristics of *DeLuxe* is that the work addresses a period from the 1930s until about 1976. It's a very specific time frame, from the New Negro constructions of the Harlem Renaissance to the Black Pride movement—this molten codification of race in twentieth-century America. And yet, this conversation that I'm having is, of course, with myself as an artist but also with Craig and Hilary and David and Doug and everybody at Two Palms. That the process was syncretic is, for me, really important.

Sometimes, you know, when you read criticism about your work, it out-and-out states, "And these are her issues . . ." And I think, "Well, thank you for telling me what my work is about," as if I am suddenly a race expert. Which is really perverse. When, in fact, that kind of interpretation is actually a denial of what this project was about—which was really a conversation, a shared language. And speaking with you today, Lisa, and hearing your comments—you've just added to it. And everyone who comes at this thoughtfully adds to it. And so it's really a conversation that has moved beyond the making of the print. It's something very specifically American.

And so the criticism that came out after *DeLuxe* was published—and I don't know where it comes from, perhaps it comes out of some postmodernist impulse, where you want to put people in these little boxes, as if this is not a shared language, which, of course, it is. And the fact is that we are all familiar with this history.

But it was strange for Craig, I think, sometimes, going home and working on this on the train, working on this in public.

CZ: I'm sitting on the train next to a seven-foot black man, and I'm working on a 1970s afro on my laptop, and it says something like "so white!" And I look over at him, and he's looking at me like I'm some sort of white supremacist. And I want to say something to him like, "Oh no, sir, you don't understand, this is fine art."

[*laughter*]

EG: But that collusion is actually something that I think printmaking adds to my practice. So often when you do something in the studio alone it can become a one-off gesture, whimsical. Making *Bouffant Pride* we sat across from each other. And in *Bouffant Pride* there's a kind of obliteration. Because the names and addresses of these women (in the advertisements) are actually printed underneath their heads, I wanted to obliterate that, to give them some privacy. So I conceal the names with these little squares of cut paper. And I wouldn't explain it in this way usually, if I were working alone on a drawing. I'd just do it. But because it has to be repeated twenty or thirty times, it has to be catalogued, archived. And each little tear—everything— gets repeated back to you. It becomes this language—what was a one-off gesture becomes open-ended language. You become aware of your own choices, having that kind of an elongated process enter the work.

EH: Well, each one—each of the sixty prints—has its own vocabulary.

EG: Yes. Each print is really a stage, and you can go deeper into each one. Because it is also true that each print involved a conversation with at least four other people.

CZ: You know, I want to add that, in thirty-two years—or however long I've been doing this—this was the most elaborate collaboration between people. With someone and their vision, and then people figuring out how to make that happen.

EH: But not every artist would take this on.

EG: Well, not every artist would get this lucky to be thrown together with this particular group of people. And that was the thing about Craig specifically—that whatever weird ideas I was having in my mind about yellowing paper ... the final look of the print, it had to make my skin crawl. Because I don't see it as antiquing. In fact, I did not want these papers to crumble and fall apart; they had to be archival.

CZ: I remember the day that Ellen said: "Okay, now we're going to put a Plasticine wig on this." And I said, "That's *clay*?" And so I thought, "Call in the cavalry, I'm lost."

EG: On the one hand, you're with a master printer. I mean, Craig has worked with Rauschenberg and [Jasper] Johns and I'm like, "Shit!" And at the same time, I'm going ahead and saying, "Okay, now I'm going to cut up your work and put Plasticine on it." When you think about the amount of time and care he's putting into this to make this creole filigree, you wouldn't think it's necessarily the first thing Craig would want to do.

EG: But it was! And that he would have an intimate relationship with it.

EH: Well, Craig's always up for a challenge . . .

EG: I know! I got to know Craig through this. That's the best part of it, when you don't know that somebody has the interest in making this whimsical fantasy. It is a pity the way these [the *DeLuxe* prints] sometimes are discussed as if they are the "true history," almost as reportage. When, in fact, they're so creepy, and are really specifically my reading, and my *mis*reading.

CZ: Ellen made me feel ten years younger. I got excited again about making prints. And it was really a great project. And then when it went up at the Whitney . . .

EH: Well, that's what's so incredible—the overall impact of all sixty of these. I mean, these are such perfect prints unto themselves, but then as a whole . . . it's as if you've developed this vocabulary in the individual prints, and then a whole new *language* when they are displayed all together.

EG: But that level of destruction is part of it, back to the Plasticine and the cutting—when you're dealing with this kind of fine, gorgeous, technically rich printmaking, with all the layering and fine detail . . . and then to go back into it, so that it doesn't get precious. And that's the bravura, the machismo, if you will, that it has all of that. That's the wild thing about it. And you would think Craig would have backed off, or gotten fed up—"Oh, fuck, she's cutting up that exquisitely printed head." And that's so crazy that he didn't, it just rocks me. No matter what I did to it, he would take that and run with it.

CZ: Well, when Ellen went back and took something one step further, it always made the piece better. Always made it better. I would show Ellen a new technique—spit bite for instance—and she would become a master of spit bite.

EG: But if you say that, it becomes overwhelming. You have to know how we worked. It was really starting in the middle, this conversation. And I thought, "Oh, this guy can do *everything*," but he's saying, "Okay, now you're going to make it." And so he's watching me and knows just when it's the right time to introduce a new technique—at a point when it wasn't going to flip me out. Because he could also just stand there and give me the lecture, and that would have been the end. This never would have happened.

CZ: No. Some printmakers do that, though. For want of a better term, some printmakers are not "user friendly," just as some artists can be not willing to open up. But we made a good pair.

EH: Well, and especially with intaglio printmaking—there can be a kind of preciosity about it. It's a medium that can be intimidating in its fineness. But these prints push intaglio to the other extreme. For instance, these eyes [*pointing to the women in the right side of* Coronet], these creepy, pupil-less eyes … how unprecious are *those*?

EG: And, by the way, that's also Craig.

CZ: No … is it?

EG: Yes, it is! Because I had been looking my whole life for a flat white eye. How do you get a flat white eye? That's why I use Plasticine so often, because it gives that flat, white, nonhuman effect. And I'm always looking for that. And I must have said that out loud, because Craig suddenly suggested, "Oh, do you know what will give you that? Flat white gouache." So a lot of the washiness, the painterly aspects of these, were also suggestions from Craig.

EH: When did the pomade come in?

EG: Well, the pomade is something that I don't generally use in paintings, because of their large scale, but I had used it in the *Preserve* drawings. So this project really has a relationship to those drawings. The drawings are allowed to be what they are, to fall apart. But these prints [from *DeLuxe*] I really wanted to be archival, to last. These are layered in a different way. It's hard to recreate the making of these, despite the black book.

I've been thinking about that a lot, archiving. Cultural heritage, and historical content, and how we pass information from one person to the next. And I think secrecy is such an important part of that, in a strange way—such an important part of transmission. And I know that's true with Craig. He's a real fetish/secrecy-type of person. And that's something that's weirdly important to this project. It's also an aspect of the realm of printmaking—certainly Craig's realm of printmaking. There's so much privacy and layering and magic to it. It's almost voodoo. It really is.

EH: And then the foil additions?

EG: The foil additions happened at the same time as the cuttings.

EH: And the googly eyes—the ones that are actually toys?

EG: I first came across the toy eyeballs when I was in Mexico City for a group exhibition.[10] Francis Alÿs brought me to a miniature toy shop—it was incredible: eyeballs, hair, little suits. It was an anatomy lesson; the anatomy of my paintings laid out before us on shelves. I bought several different sizes of eyeballs but couldn't figure out how to use them in the work for a couple of years. Finally, I embedded some deep into the black Plasticine of a drawing [*Power Falls*, 2001] from the *Preserve* series. I didn't work with the toy eyeballs again until I was constructing *Bouffant Pride* in 2003.

It's interesting to think about, that during the same time and even before we were making the prints, I was making animations, with Edgar Cleijne. There's a shared process: literally working frame by frame, then ending up with a projected image. I finally started to understand printmaking while scratching directly into 35 mm film and seeing the color stocks underneath. I was working with Jan Scholten, a master film printer in Rotterdam, who could wet gate it and smooth it out or not smooth it out.[11] There are only a few optical benches left in Europe, and one happened to be in Rotterdam. It's a very old-school way of working.[12] I started making animations in 2001–2, but by 2003 this starts to really take form, which is when I went in and made *Bouffant Pride*. And, just to clarify, *Duke* [2004; *fig. 11*] was meant to be, conceivably, the next work that was to start *DeLuxe*, except that we got carried away and never could fit it in.

CZ: That's right. It's a larger print.

EG: It just grew much too big. So the reason it's not in *DeLuxe* is that it just didn't fit into our process.

CZ: There's a different *Duke* in *DeLuxe*, but a smaller one. With the puffing of the hair . . .

EG: Oh my God, the puffing is such a Craig and David thing. There is so much collaboration in this whole thing.

CZ: There are no rules . . . actually Doug Volle came up with the idea to screenprint puff ink, which is a type of ink that is normally used in textile printing.

EG: I remember we had to spend a whole day in the ovens. They wanted to cook this thing so it would puff up. And I was like, "Why are we doing this?"

EH: It sounds like little boys making mud pies.

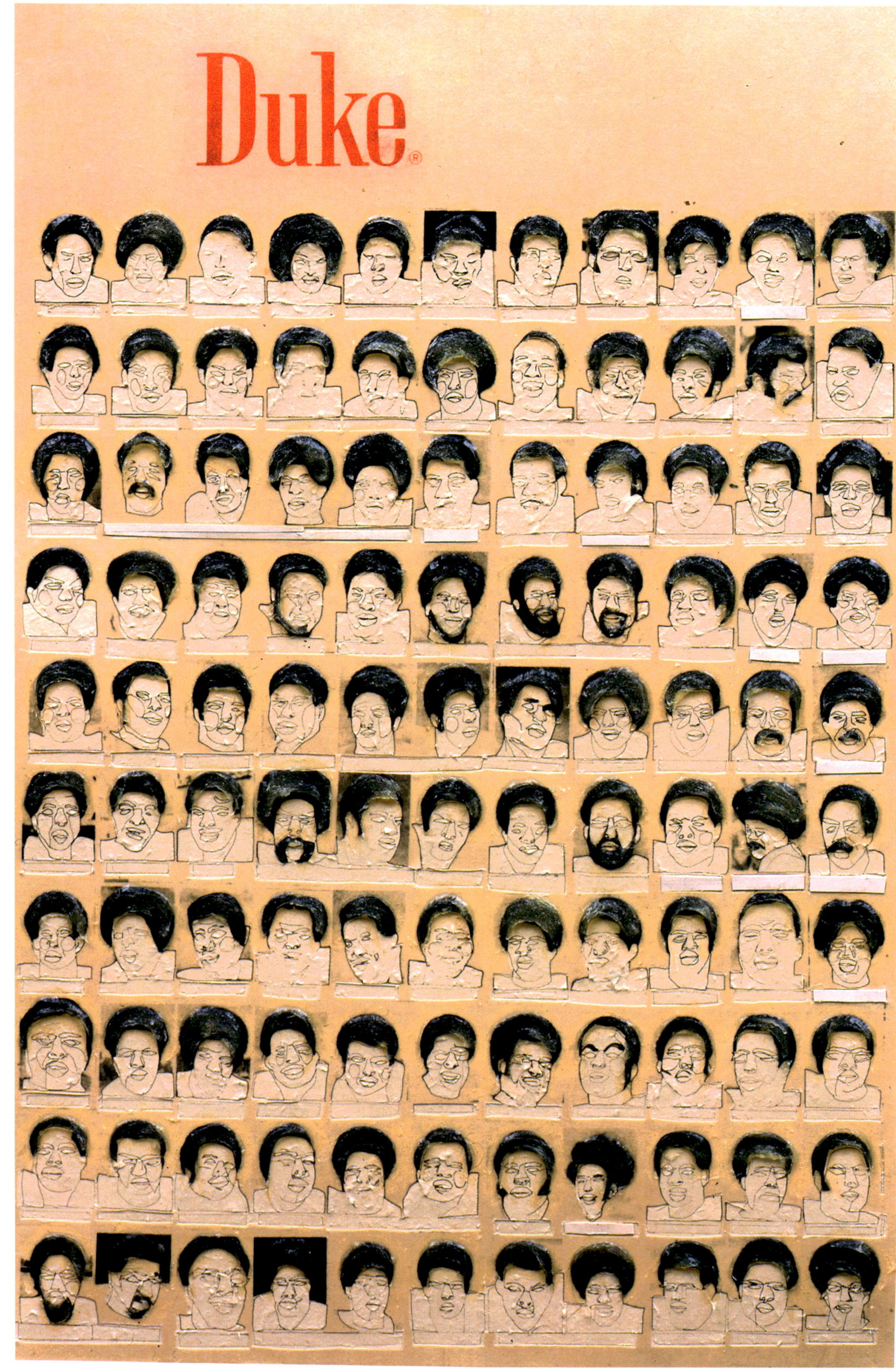

FIG. 11. Ellen Gallagher, *Duke*, 2004. Photogravure with laser-incised peeled paper, collage, and hair pomade, 14 × 10½ in. (35.6 × 26.7 cm). Edition of 20. Published by Two Palms

EG: Little boys, totally. And I remember I kept telling them, "Look, we have work to do," and meanwhile they are baking my afros!

[*laughter*]

EG: Remember those little plastic ovens we had as little girls, the Easy-Bake Ovens? They were doing that with my afros! But a friend visiting the studio at the time was right when she said, "You know, back off, Ellen. They need to have their fun."

CZ: And you know? This never would have happened at another studio. Only at Two Palms. Because other studios have these *rules*. And I'm a pirate. I don't want rules! I want googly eyes that move. *Why not?*

EG and EH: Yes!

CZ: Why can't we cook this thing to see if it will puff up?

EG: And, by the way, that was a failure.

[*laughter*]

EG: *By the way . . .*

EH: Did it burn?

EG: Yes! They did a giant one . . .

CZ: And it was like a soufflé.

EG: It was fabulous! It puffed way up . . .

CZ: And then it collapsed [*fig. 12*].

[*laughter*]

CZ: It worked out in the end, as these things eventually do.

EG: Yeah, yeah. I covered them in pomade. I put my own stamp on it. I thought to myself, "You know, I'm going to let them have their little bake-off, and then I'm just rubbing pomade on that shit when they're done." It was really a wild process.

EH: I'm going to quit my job and come bake afros at Two Palms . . .

[*laughter*]

EH: Did you apply the pomade with your fingers?

EG: No, with spatulas.

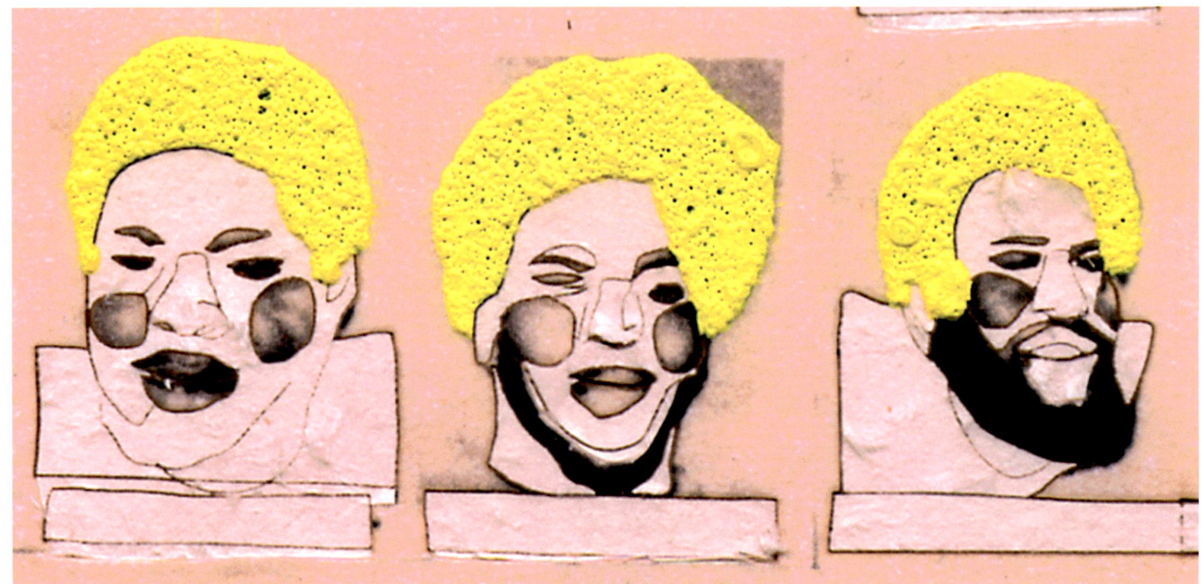

CZ: But the most amazing thing about *DeLuxe* is that there are amazing stories like this about each one of the prints. There are sixty stories here.

EG: Yes, and the stories sometimes come out of the historical material and cultural material, but the stories also come out of all of our childhoods . . . like when we were kids playing make believe with our friends, we made it up as we went along. You improvise as you go. And so a lot of that story-telling is really so collaborative in that way. I remember *American Beauty* [*fig. 13*]—that one, I really think we made that up together as we went along. We decided, "Oh, yes, she's been lied to and hurt, and these are just sorry suckers . . ." And you helped me, Craig, with the guys, to make them sorry with the spit biting, because they just had to look really pathetic.

CZ: Right!

EH: It sounds like a soap opera.

EG: Oh, it was such a soap opera, or we turned it into one. But the technique went with it. Craig would say, "Yeah, he's a real sorry sucker, he needs to be *spit bit* . . ."

[*laughter*]

EH: So with the entire group of sixty, do you have a specific way in which you want them to be hung?

EG: Absolutely . . . and that was the beauty, that David let that growing body of work be tacked up on the studio walls for—what?—a year or two? It was always up, always up.

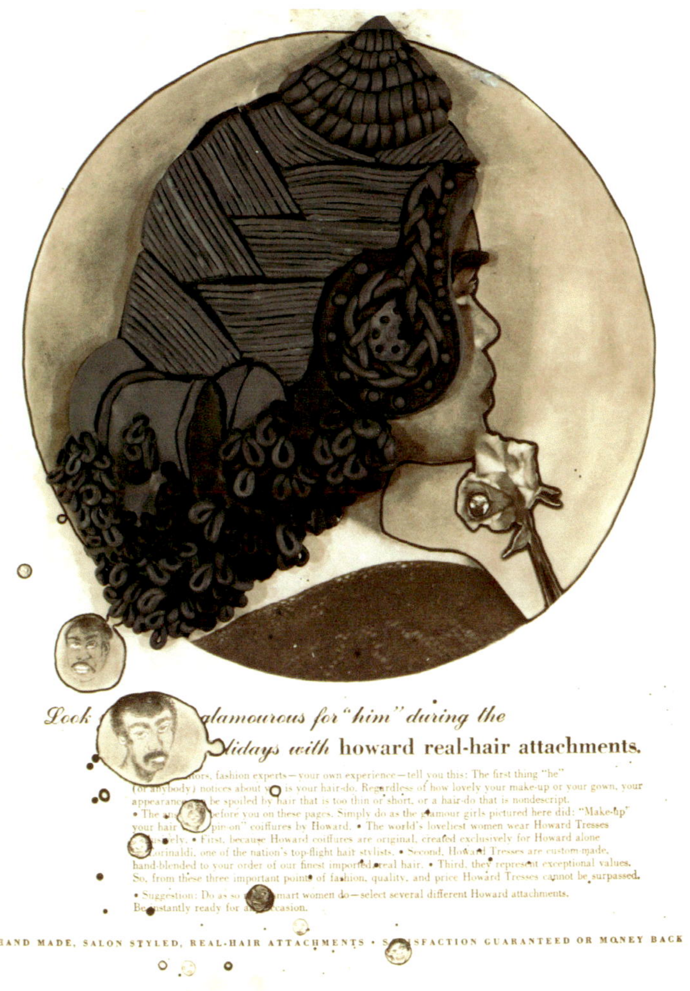

FIG. 13. Ellen Gallagher, *American Beauty*, from *DeLuxe*, 2004–5. Photogravure, aquatint, spit bite, and Plasticine, 13 × 10 in. (33 × 25.4 cm). Edition of 20. Published by Two Palms

CZ: Do you remember that, Lisa?

EH: Oh, of course! And I miss it now.

CZ: Well, it was the War Room. And that's another thing about David. He understood that it was necessary to keep that up, absolutely necessary.

> EG: And now, of course, in hindsight, that was a hugely generous part of the project on David's end. So the way it came together was quite natural. It wasn't as if I never saw them all amassed, and then one day I had to arrange them. I saw them constantly. We all saw them constantly.

EH: Well, David of course realized how huge this was, how groundbreaking.

CZ: He did. He did.

EH: And it must have been a huge investment for a smallish print shop.

> EG: We were all so wrapped up in it. It was like a film set.

EH: When did you decide on sixty? I've read it was originally supposed to be fifty?

EG: It was more like, "Well, how many does it take to make it feel complete? Is it ten? Is it twenty? Is it fifty?" It was more like that. And no, it was sixty.

CZ: That's exactly what it was.

EG: And there is something that happens on the scale shifts between those numbers that is really hugely important. When you have sixty, you have an historical ruin that you can look at from an aerial view. And into that we brought four-color lithography. It had to be machined color, a four-color process.

CZ: Right.

EG: What I realized going through the pages of these midcentury "race" magazines is that there wasn't much full-page advertising. There were not a whole lot of pages that made up the magazine—maybe only 120 or so pages in an early *Ebony* magazine from 1945. And maybe only 8, or maybe 16, are in color, early on. You move through all of the black-and-whites and then some color bursts, now and then. I wanted to reinscribe that machine imprint—the way the color pops, as it did in the actual body of the magazine. *DeLuxe* recreates that body as an aerial view. At that scale, the body becomes something that you can never quite grasp, only approach.

EH: And the fact that these pages from the magazines you selected span the civil rights movement must be quite intentional.

EG: It was intentional by the time I got to *DeLuxe*. And the thing that's most interesting, to me, is that it is not all my experience. I was born at the end of the sixties. I don't have direct access to 1930. Of course, we all have access to this material. But some of the content remains hidden. I think this is an important element in the work: that I don't have access to all the histories and secrets. I have my own level of secrets. And Craig has his own level of secrets that I don't have access to. There's so much that's in here being transmitted from Craig to me, and from Craig to the world of printmaking. There's an urgency of transmission and secrecy at the same time. So it's something that is inherent in the raw material—in terms of our access to it—and inherent in the way we approach the material.

CZ: Well, I remember when you had the show at Gagosian [Gallery] in 2004— those large paintings?[13]

EG: Those were the paintings that inspired *Bouffant Pride.*

CZ: And I remember walking in. And it was the first time I had seen these things—these full-scale paintings with the wigs. And it was like putting a key in a lock, for me. So this thing really cascaded at that point.

EG: And that's probably the first time I used Plasticine in my paintings— particularly at that large scale, where it was threatening, where it becomes a threatening force. Literally threatening in terms of the imagery but also—back to the idea of the yellowing page, the fragility, and the ruins. That's really inherent in Plasticine, that it's fragile. It's kind of like encaustic. Someone can stick their finger in it and it's ruined. It does harden more in time, but it's fragile.

I got those paintings back from Venice and they were pockmarked with the impressions of kids' fingers. Children see Plasticine and they think, "mine"—they don't have some logic to know that this isn't to be touched. It's *their* material. So I had a lot of work to do when we got all of those paintings back for that Gagosian show. I was there two nights before with a spatula and olive oil, rubbing those wigs.

CZ: I didn't know that.

EH: You've been talking today about the inclusiveness, not just of the materials themselves—the materiality of these prints—but also of the whole team of people at Two Palms whom you allowed not only to work on this but to very much have a say, even a sway, in how it came out. And there is something about this recent election [of Barack Obama as U.S. president]—there is something that these share.

EG: I think that there's an interest in syncretic form. This ambivalence creates a space in time, however transient, when we can actually recognize loss. And in that instant there is a shared language that can make the ingredients and the histories less opaque. The specificities become part of a common language, including secrecies, and irretrievable losses, and some understanding of mortality that is a part of living—that some things ain't coming back, they're gone. There was such a radical bridge of affinities in this project. Something about loss and recovery and the futility of that, you know? Erasure and layering—it has to do with making something that is imbued with a kind of "precise nonsense," which is both elastic and very precise, specific to a time frame. We're talking about 1930 to 1976. It's about an American publication, specifically a black American publication—and it's been reimagined through the prism of this collaborative process.

I do think that this process is about a cultural moment in time. And, certainly, a lot of people worked for it too, but it's really a gift. And you really never know when these openings will happen. They seem to have their own life. And for some people this political moment didn't happen in time; it's much too late. And for some people, who are eighteen now, this is their world; it's a given. So it's a moment that we all can share in, but there are varying levels of that.

EH: Are you planning to do more prints at Two Palms?

EG: Oh, definitely.

CZ: When you develop an intimate working connection with an artist, you tend to continue to explore and grow together.

EG: Well, I feel that I still have a relationship with Craig in the work I'm doing now—I learned so much.

CZ: Well, Bob Rauschenberg had that freedom of exploration, that fearlessness in his approach to both art and life. And, Ellen, you're the only other person I've ever met that's like that.

EH: Frankly, I think you both are fearless. And David [Lasry] too. To throw yourself into this open-ended project wholeheartedly.

EG: That was the environment. It was the time that this happened; the place and the people. You know, going back to what we were talking about, Lisa, these openings—when historical strictures loosen and certain areas of culture can be shared—are fragile. Nobody gets to be in control of that. Something happens in nature, some patch that grows strangely in the forest.

Notes

The preceding conversation was held on November 18, 2008, at Markt Restaurant, in New York.

1. Thyrza Nicholas Goodeve, "The History Lesson: Flesh Is a Texture as Much as a Color," in *Parkett*, no. 73 (2005): 43.

2. The evolution of *Bouffant Pride* took on a quick momentum as Zammiello and Gallagher explored different avenues of reproducing the artist's particular style and methods. The first obstacle to overcome was the absence of a darkroom at Two Palms for creating films for photogravure. David Lasry suggested contacting a former acquaintance of his, Bob Warhover of Abrams Gleber Warhover Lithographers, who had an output bureau for storing physical images output from digital files. It was capable of generating positive films with a halftone dot that would duplicate the large halftone dot of the early commercial-process darkroom films. Zammiello's problem was then to get rid of the original large halftone dots in the film scans of the magazine pages, as these original dots would conflict with the new, smaller halftone dots and result in a moiré pattern. The original magazine pages were scanned and then manipulated on a computer, using a separate layer in Photoshop and with the application of a blur filter to a selected area (jut the images and not the type). By doing this, Zammiello was able to effectively reduce the original halftone pattern while not rendering the type out of focus. A photogravure plate was then made from the film and proofed on selected paper. For an image of *Bouffant Pride*, see the Two Palms website, http://www.twopalms.us/ (accessed September 26, 2011).

3. Made by the Bamana of central Mali, *boli* are "an unusual form of mixed-media sculpture . . . composed of a core of elements, including animal parts and other secret ingredients, which are said to symbolize the Bamana universe. String may be used to fill out the sculpture and help shape it. It is then regularly coated with a thick layer of sacrificial materials that gives it the appearance of caked mud. . . . They can be conceived of as reservoirs of spiritual force that function as objects of both science and ritual." Patrick R. McNaughton, "Bamana," *Grove Art Online, Oxford Art Online*, http://www.oxfordartonline.com/ (accessed September 29, 2011).

4. The lamination was carried out in a heat press using a heat-activated glue that comes in sheets called Fusion 4000. This is a dry-mount glue, or tissue, generally used for the archival mounting of photographs to supports such as museum board. The Fusion 4000 gave Zammiello and Gallagher the capability to create a bit more compression or "give" to the paper, enabling a smoother impression when printed with the offset blanket.

5. In intaglio printmaking, the paper is usually soaked before printing to give it the malleability necessary for pushing it into the incised lines of the copper plate, and to make it more accepting of the ink. The "dry" method developed in 1993 for the printing of Robert Rauschenberg's four-color photogravures *Street Sounds* involves replacing felt blankets—traditionally employed in this process to apply a cushioning pressure to the paper—with a compressible rubber blanket from an offset lithography press. This is wrapped around the top roller of the etching press and secured with tape. The inked plate is then printed with dry Japanese paper. The resulting impression is of the same quality as one printed with the paper dampened in the usual manner. The benefits of using this method are speed and the ability to use very thin Japanese papers (at times, weighing fifteen grams or less) without trying to handle them wet or dry them flat. Traditionally the chine collé method is used to laminate these papers to a support sheet of heavier paper during the printing process.

6. When Lasry traced Gallagher's cuts on the computer, he converted them to vector files. He was then able to use the laser to cut to different depths by changing the output power of the laser. Each incision was then peeled by hand and, according to the depth of the cut, would reveal the prescribed layer of paper.

7. Midway through the *DeLuxe* project, Zammiello introduced Gallagher to the tattoo machine as a way to directly engrave on the copper plate in a much more controllable and detailed manner than possible with conventional electric engravers or Vibro tools. This tattoo machine is the same apparatus used by tattoo artists. It functions by moving a needle in a reciprocating back and forth motion and by varying the speed with which it moves. Endless combinations of fine, coarse, and multiple (cluster) needles also make it a very useful tool for both line and tonal engraving.

8. This method, described earlier as being developed at ULAE in 1993 to print Robert Rauschenberg's *Street Sounds*, was brought back into use at Two Palms with work on Gallagher's *Bouffant Pride*. For *Coronet*, after the prints were dry, Gallagher handpainted the eyes of both the photogravured women and the googly eyes with white gouache.

9. Tatyana Grosman (known familiarly as Tanya) was the founder of ULAE.

10. *Cinco Continentes y una Ciudad* (Five Continents and a City) was held at the Museo de la Ciudad de México, in Mexico City, from November 26, 1998, to February 28, 1999.

11. When 16 mm film is enlarged, the negative is immersed in a solution that conceals scratches and graininess in the film as it is being rephotographed; this process is called wet-gate printing.

12. An optical bench is a system of lenses and cameras mounted on a rail. It is used to copy film or to blow it up, or for analogue animation. Scholten's bench is one of the last of its kind in use in Europe.

13. Ellen Gallagher's solo exhibition *Ellen Gallagher: eXelento* was held at the Gagosian Gallery in New York (Chelsea), from September 14 to October 23, 2004.

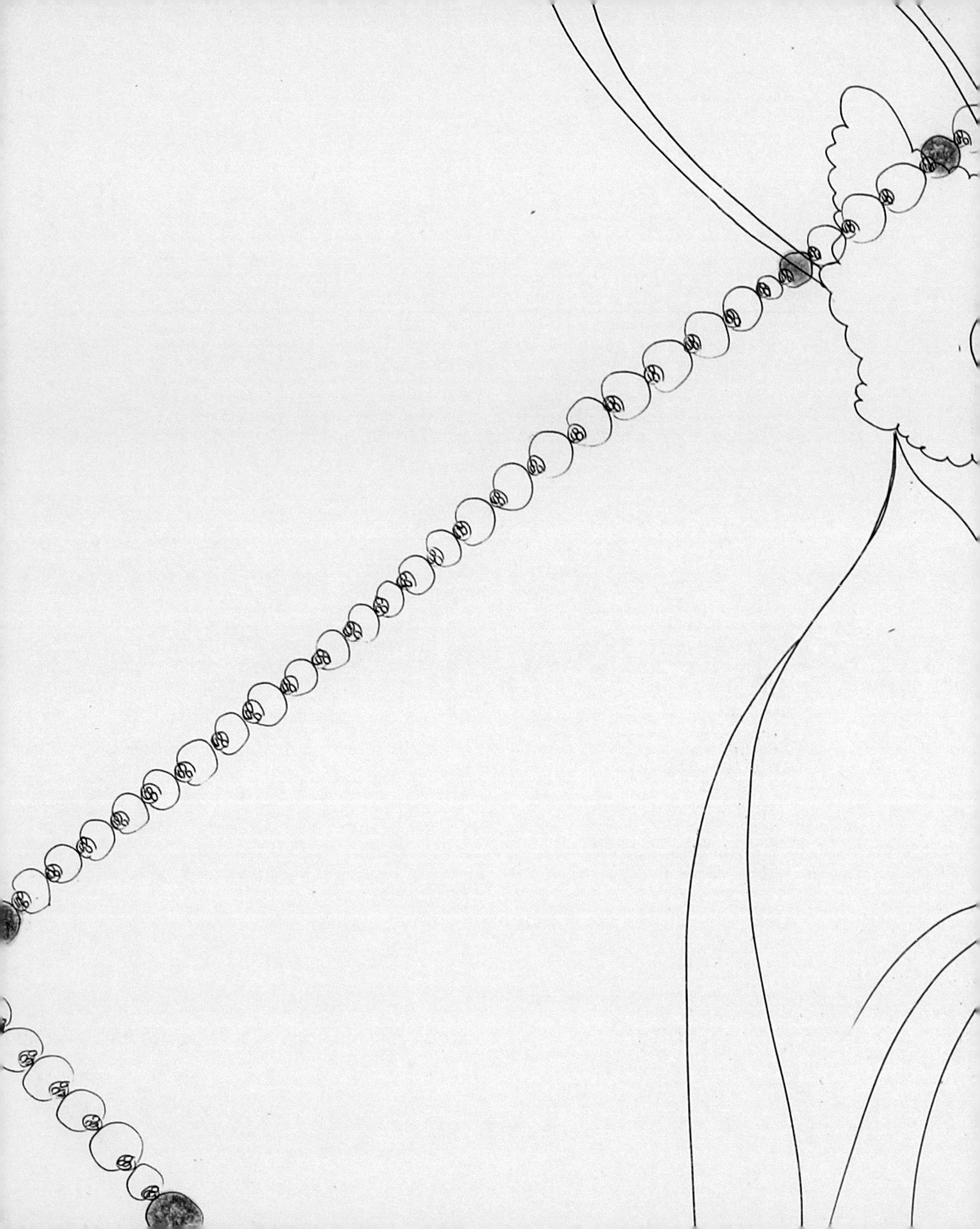

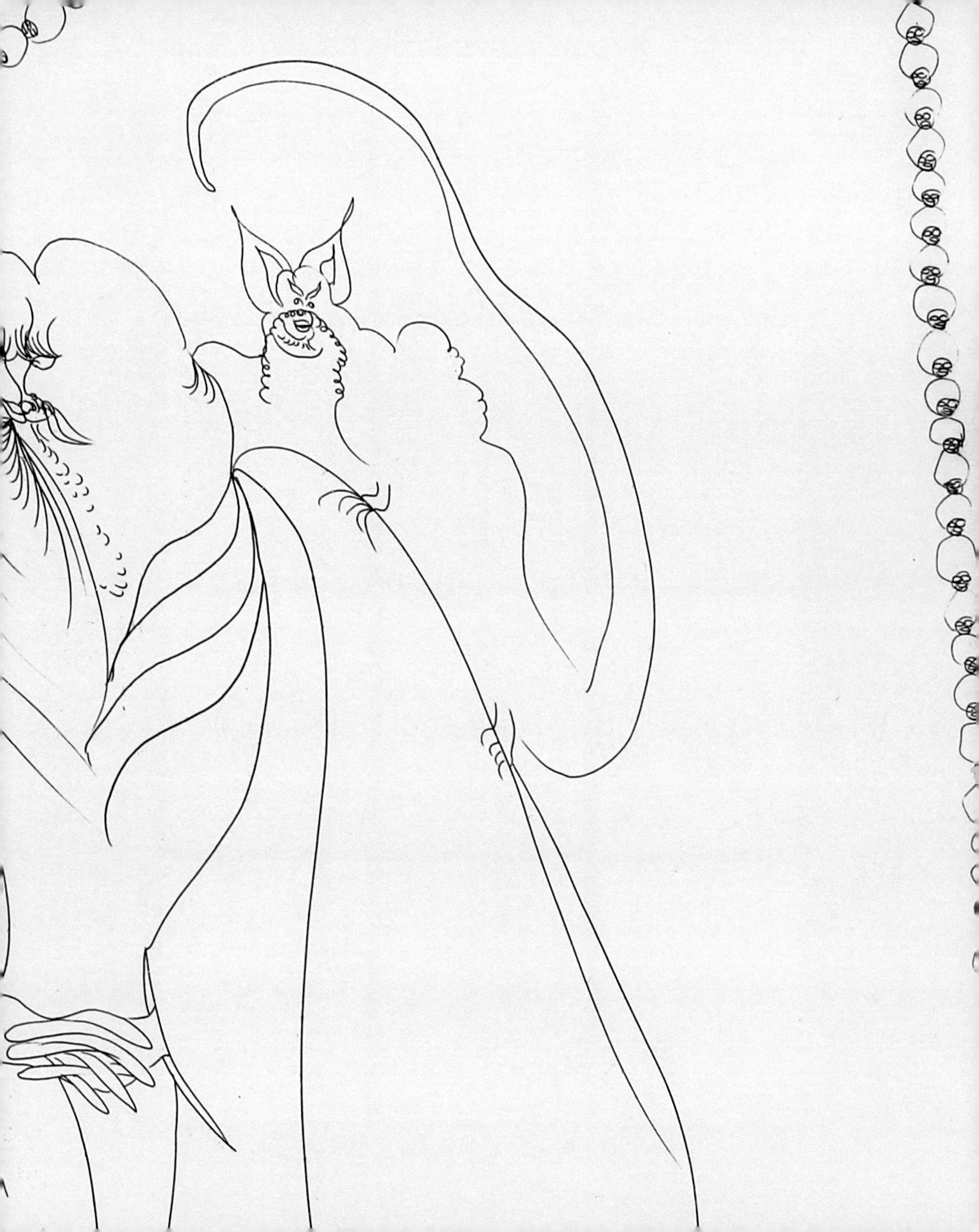

THE AGONY IN THE GARDEN

A SUITE OF 9 ETCHINGS WITH AQUATINT
EDITION OF 20 WITH 5 APS 4 PPS AND 1 BAT
PRINTED AND PUBLISHED BY TWO PALMS NYC

CHRIS OFILI
2006

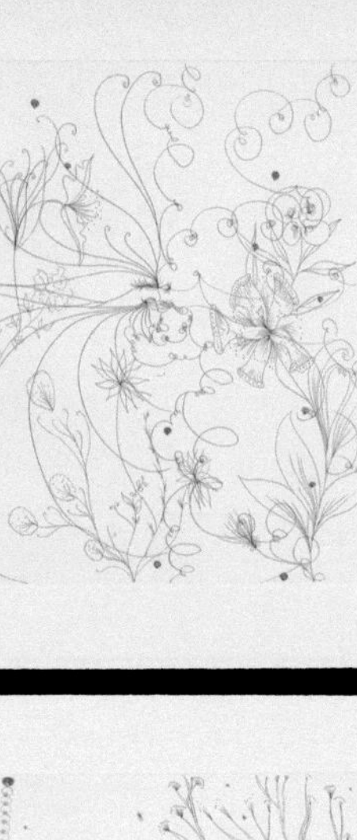

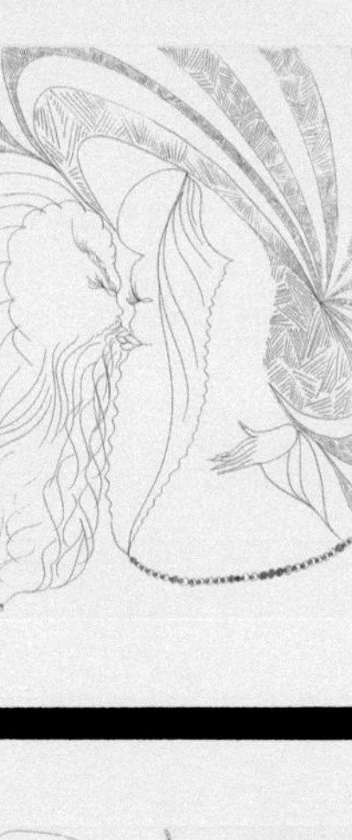

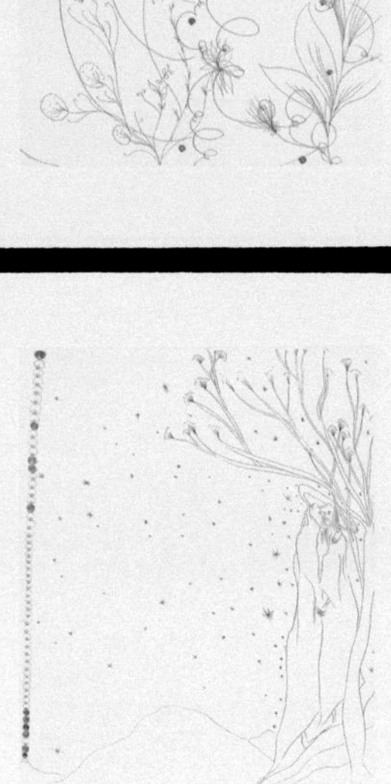

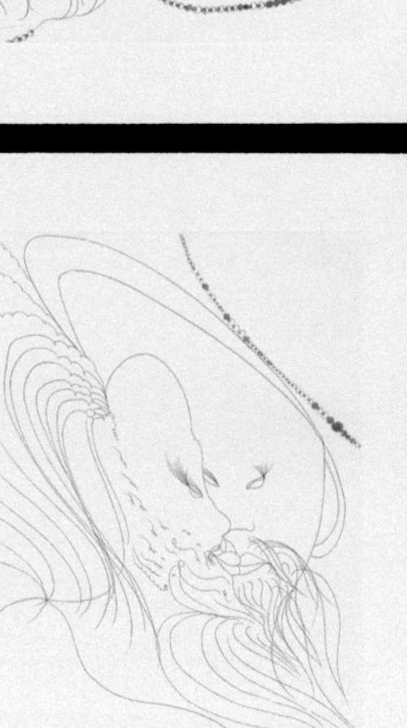

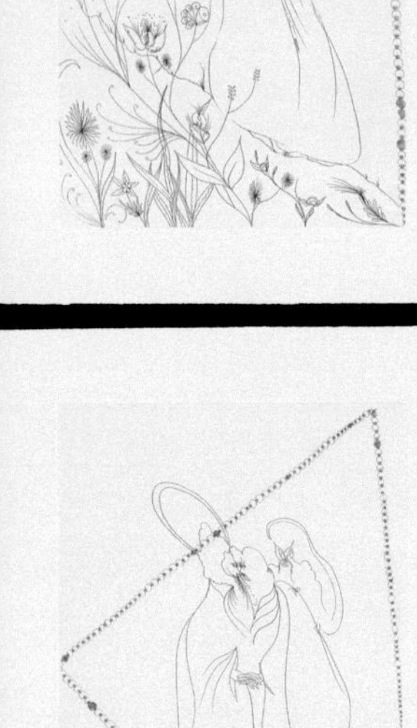

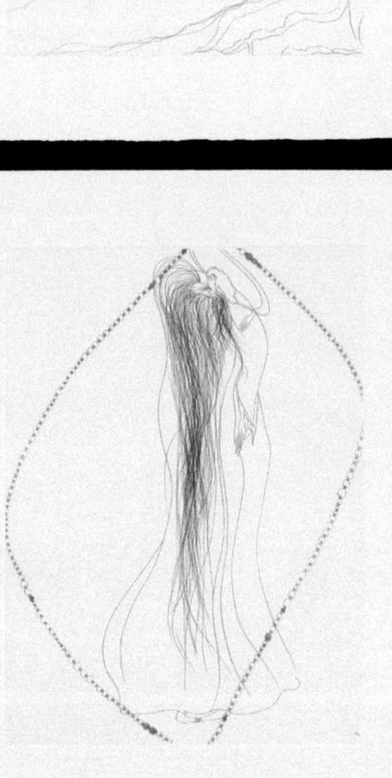

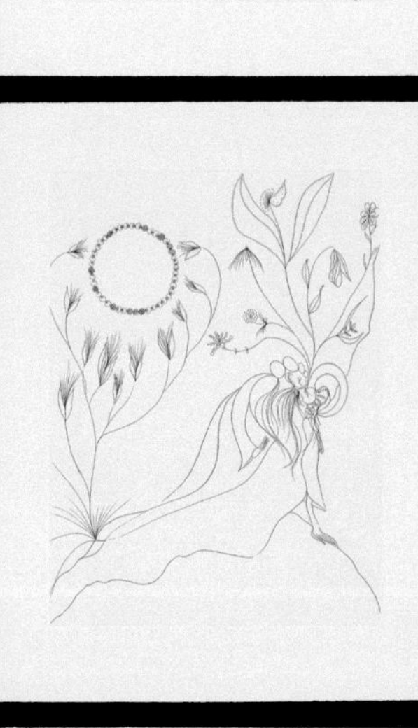

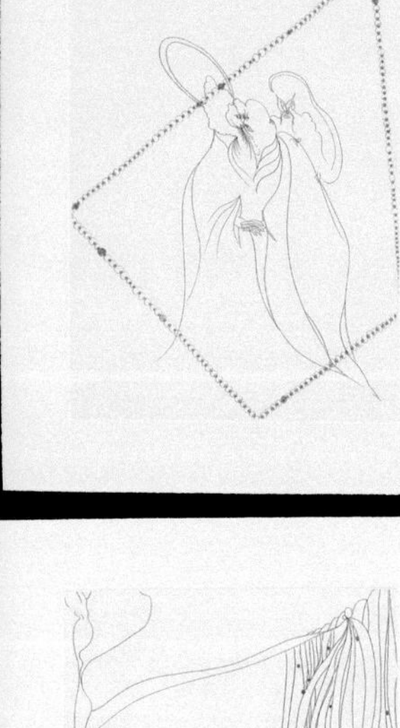

Chris Ofili arrived at Two Palms in 2006 at the invitation of David Lasry. He intended to make a series of screenprints derived from a suite of thirteen paintings he was working on titled *The Upper Room.*[1] The prints would be an ambitious undertaking for Two Palms, a highly complex project involving myriad technical processes and methods to mimic the feel and look of Ofili's multilayered paintings. It would employ metallic inks and varnishes and Two Palms's signature heavy embossment by way of acrylic plates and the hydraulic press. Six years later, these screenprints have yet to be produced.

As Ofili and Craig Zammiello describe in the conversation that follows, not too long into the process, Ofili became sidetracked when he began to make etchings with Zammiello in periods of inactivity between the *Upper Room* proofings, and *Agony in the Garden* (figs. 1–12) thus became Ofili's first suite of prints made at Two Palms. The subject matter—Christ's agony in the Garden of Gethsemane—is, as the next event in Christ's Passion, closely related to the Last Supper, which is explored in *The Upper Room.*

The word *agony* comes from the Greek word *agonia*, which at the time of Jesus's life had a second meaning, as a technical term applied to athletes warming up for the Olympic games. During their warm-up they would produce a certain sweat that would warm their muscles, and that sweat was called their "agonia." In the book of Luke, Luke describes how as Christ prayed "his sweat was as it were great drops of blood falling down to the ground."[2] Luke is explaining that Jesus is producing an agonia to prepare for his Passion. This concept of the agony resonates with the sort of angst often associated with an artist's creative process—the agony of creative revelation, and the self-doubt that occurs when an artist releases his work into the world—a struggle that Ofili describes more than once in this conversation. Zammiello also remarks on his own revelation: after a long career of developing increasingly complex intaglio methods, in working with Ofili he rediscovered the challenge presented in printing a pure etching and the beauty of the simple etched line.

Left to right, top to bottom: **FIGS. 1–12.** Chris Ofili, *Agony in the Garden*, 2007. Portfolio of eleven etchings with spitbite aquatint printed in one color on Somerset paper hand-torn to size, housed in a cloth-covered box with gold stamping, each 21 × 17 in. (53.3 × 43.2 cm). Edition of 20. Published by Two Palms

CHRIS OFILI: When you come into a print studio—especially one like Two Palms—it's empty. You go in, essentially, to create. And of course you can come with baggage, and with some ideas, but I've never really done that. I've just turned up, with some ability, and tried to work with possibilities. I wouldn't consider myself a great printmaker—because there's so much still out there to become more familiar with, perhaps never to master. But I like becoming more familiar with different techniques, and perhaps then to be able to abuse them, more than anything . . . so to combine my lack of knowledge with Craig's great knowledge, and somehow then make something completely fresh, I think—or I hope.

ELISABETH HODERMARSKY: I read that you made four suites of etchings in the mid-nineties at Hope (Sufferance) Press. Were those the first prints you had made?

CO: Yes. More or less, yes. They were pretty straightforward, linear etchings that were created by going to different places with the plates, and with almost a kind of set way of mark-making—and trying to respond to that place, to make drawings in relation to that place, but always using the same form of mark-making. So there was a set made in Barcelona, there was Berlin, and there was North Wales.

EH: Were they based on drawings you had made?

CO: No, just going there and looking at a place—like Mount Snowden, in North Wales, or the Sagrada Familia, in Barcelona—and making a drawing on the spot, on site. Oh, and actually there was a set made in New York, as well. I chose ten tourist sites—like the World Trade Center, in fact, which I was reminded of today [*this conversation took place on September 11, 2009*]. I went up to the Windows on the World bar to sit and look out at the view and just make an etching [*fig. 13*].

EH: Right on the plate?

CO: Yes, right on the plate.

CRAIG ZAMMIELLO: Fantastic!

CO: And then I'd just wrap up the plate and go. Those were in the days when people didn't pay that much attention to what you are doing in public. But that's really not the case anymore. Then I could travel with the plates and tools—no big deal. But I think that would be a little tricky now, certainly with the tools.

EH: And you came here to Two Palms in about 2006?

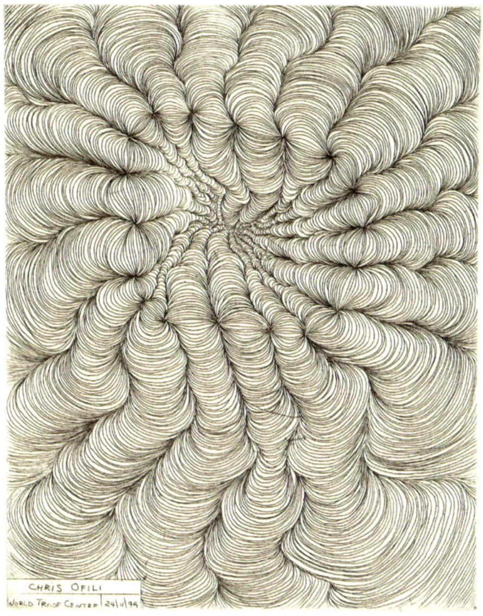

CO: I came here to do one thing, which I have not done yet: to work on a suite of prints based on the thirteen paintings in the *Upper Room* suite I finished in 2002. But then everything I've done since has kind of been "in the meantime . . ." [*looking sharply at CZ*]

[*laughter*]

CO: Everything!

CZ: Well, Chris, I wasn't prepared to work with you. Not at all. You came here to work with other printers to create a suite of screenprints, not to work with me on an etching. And that's why I refer to our experience of meeting and starting to work together as my "blind date."

CO: Really!

[*laughter*]

CZ: That's why, when you asked me if you could have an etching plate while you were waiting for a silkscreen to be printed or proofed, my heart was fluttering! "Oh, why of course, Chris, here you are!" [*pantomimes shyly yet excitedly handing a copper plate to CO*]

CO: You see, the strange thing is, when you come here, there's always a lot of hanging around between stages of making a piece. And I don't really like hanging around; I'd rather do something with my time. I could be here all day and only proof two silkscreen plates—and, well, what's the point? When I could make maybe ten etchings in the meantime.

When I began, I didn't really have any idea what I wanted to do. But then I started to make these etchings—and I think this is the first suite I made, right?

CZ: Yes, *Agony in the Garden* was the first.

CO: And that was the first drawing etched, in fact.

CZ: Well, there was actually one that we didn't use, but I think that one of these prints is from two plates, and one of them was the first plate that you made here. I mean, you can't get purer than that. That's sweet, pure etching.

CO: Yes. I think I just wanted to experiment with the quality of line. I hadn't done that for a while. And I think by then I had gone from working on zinc plates to working on copper plates in this suite, which I'm told gives a much cleaner line, a much finer line. And Craig had a whole load of tools that were quite enticing, with beetle needles and all sorts of tips.

EH: These prints are exquisite. To me, they look like engravings because they're so fine, so precise. They seem to simulate the way the burin sinks into the plate and then gradually tapers out. There's also something that resonates for me about the subject matter—the Agony—and its execution in intaglio. I can't help but be reminded of Old Master printmakers, like [Albrecht] Dürer, and their engraved Passion suites.

CO: Yes.

EH: How was it when you started working on copper?

CO: Oh, fantastic. And the tools were very precise—you know, I like a very clean, unhesitant line. A very clean motion, really. And that often has to do with how you're standing over the plate, how you're holding the tool.

EH: Do these prints have a particular order?

CO: I think they're sequenced in the order that I made them, essentially.

EH: But one could look at them in any order?

CO: You could, yes. Because they're a little bit like the movie *Rashomon*—the [Akira] Kurosawa film—where it's all the same scene. It's all the same story,

but it's narrated by several different characters. So this portfolio represents the viewpoints of all the apostles who were there at the time. So one
would say, "Oh, they were embracing"; another would say, "Oh, they were
clothed"; another, "Oh, they were very close together"; "Oh, there were lots
of flowers"; "Oh no, they were under a tree and it was a starry night"; "Oh,
I can see this particular constellation." So it's just the way stories are told
slightly differently according to the viewpoint or the memory or the slant
of the individual.

EH: Oh, I see—terrific!

CZ: Some are looser, some are more focused. Beautiful.
   Well, I also developed along with you, because we were trying to get more
depth and width to the line work, which is something you see more in engraving. As you were saying, Chris, where you flow with the line and then it kind of
licks off . . .

CO: Yes, because the drawing, for me, is really drawing on the plate. That
[*pointing to the print*] is a byproduct of that [*pointing to a copper plate*]. And
while I know that eventually the plate is going to be printed, the main
thrill is just the beauty, the peacefulness, of drawing through the hard
ground. Which later, of course, in some of the other prints became drawing
directly into the copper with a drypoint needle. Later we did away completely with the hard ground and just went right at it.
   And much of the drawing was done straight on the plate, but in certain
cases—for instance, the hands in this one [*see fig. 7*]—I remember I practiced
on a piece of paper.

CZ: Oh, really?

EH: They're beautiful, perfectly entwined.

CZ: Lisa and I were both commenting about this little figure [in fig. 7].

CO: Yes, the little demon on his back? That's a way of denoting which figure
is which. Often, you can identify by his halo which one is Christ. And this
one identifies Judas by the little demon on his back. It wasn't Judas that
betrayed Christ; someone or something was telling him to do it.

EH: You know, when I first saw this suite I made the immediate association with
that Bob Dylan song from 1963 called "With God on Our Side"?[3] Have you ever
heard that song?

CO: I don't think so.

EH: It's an antiwar ballad. And each stanza addresses a particular point of aggression in America's history. And today being September 11, of course, brings to mind America's current actions in the Middle East.

But there's a particular stanza in the song that raises the question of whether or not God was on Judas's side.

CO: That's really interesting. When was that written—you said 1963? Well, and I think that more recently they've discovered the Gospel according to Judas.[4] And so in some ways the role of Judas is being rethought, in that there has come to be some understanding that Judas knew, in some way, that Christ had to die in order to save mankind, had to go through this process of being murdered. And that somebody had to do the dirty work, somebody had to hand him over. So the "God on his side" idea here is that Judas had to do the dirty work, he had to somehow go through that process. So Judas's role has lately been completely rethought, in the sense that if he didn't betray, then things wouldn't have worked out.

CZ: If he didn't launch the mechanism. That's very interesting.

[*pause*]

CZ: This is where you really dug in, really engraved into the plate [*fig. 14*].

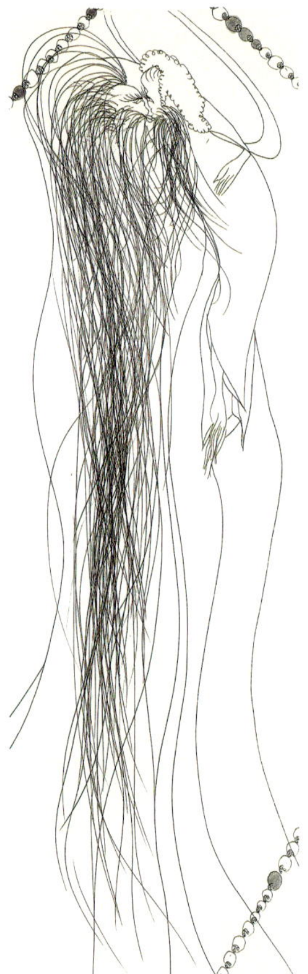

FIG. 14. Detail from *Agony #7*, from *Agony in the Garden*, 2007, showing the deeply engraved hair and beard

CO: That was actually a great passage to make. Where you couldn't tell the difference between the beard and the hair. Just the kind of freedom of the line, cascading down.

EH: And I love the feet, coming together [*see fig. 8*].

CO: And the little circles that are darkened in represent the apostles.

CZ: And that's just a little delicate spit bite.

But these are very straightforward, really. As simple as it gets and yet so elegant. After doing this for so many years, Chris, I forgot the pleasure that could be achieved by just a minimal line. And I want to thank you for that. For bringing me back to that. For years I've been so immersed in all the six billion pixels, high-tech, what have you—and yet, look at these, look at what you can do with just this [*picks up an etching needle*].

CO: Well, I think I was interested in just that. And I hadn't really made drawings—well, I had privately made drawings that were close to this, but doing this in etching, it's a form of exposure in a way. You expose what you enjoy—the joy of the line—but you also expose the limitations of your draftsmanship. The fact is that what you see here is what I drew. There are no corrections here. There's no rubbing out or burnishing.

CZ: Right.

CO: That's basically it. And doing that, for me, was quite a leap. So this was a very helpful suite of etchings to make because it made me realize that one's own insecurities about one's ability to actually make the drawing—all one's doubts—make the thing. All of the things that one worries about and tries to hide in painting actually give the thing its character. So the quality of line that I use actually makes it more distinctive.

EH: So you hadn't exhibited your drawings before this?

CO: Not ones as free-form as this, no.

EH: And now you are?

CO: Now I'm beginning to. I think the drawings you saw last night,[5] they're actually older than this. The earliest ones are from 2004, and I think the last one was from 2007. But this [*pointing to the* Agony in the Garden *suite*] is—dare I say—far more sophisticated. There's far more risk involved here, I think. And I'd like to get there with just straight pencil. I probably will, in fact.

CZ: Yes, and it's true, you didn't revisit anything—didn't make any revisions or corrections. And we lost nothing. Everything we did is what you see in this portfolio.

EH: I recently read an interview you did, Chris, with Brice Marden, in 2006—which is the same year you made these.

CO: It was probably when I was here in New York on the same trip.

EH: And there were a couple of sentences that I wanted to quote here: "But this idea of agony—this feeling of, Fuck, man, I fucked it up—is there a value to that in the making of the painting? Is the residue of that agony important to its character? What if there were no agony, after all?" [6] So obviously you were very much thinking about all of these concepts very deeply at that time.

CO: Yes, yes. Because, actually, the things that you leave out are just as important in giving the thing its character. The things that you consider to be impurities? And perhaps that's what I'm talking about—impurities in line, or just over-thinking something, or worrying about something, would lead you to omit the best, most important, most exciting aspects of the drawing. So the thing is ridden with doubt, really. I still remember thinking, "What the hell is *that*?" But then thinking, it's the "what" in "what the hell is that" that's important for me.

CZ: Well, in this room, you'd hand me these plates, and I too would have my little crises.

[*laughter*]

CZ: You know? I'd think, "Am I etching this deep enough? Is this going to have the effect that Chris needs?"

CO: I hadn't thought of that . . . you could lose it in here, you could lose the image.

CZ: Which I'm not used to. A lot of the things I do with artists are more mechanical-based. It's been literally years since I just worked on lines, simple lines!

EH: And such clean lines.

CZ: Yes, *so* clean. And you better be spot-on with it or . . . else. You can't hide any mistakes.

CO: So this is the original way one would make an etching, yes?

CZ: Yes, that's it. There were only two intaglio processes before this, and those were engraving and drypoint—just scratching and incising right into the plate.

But this is the idea of taking the labor out of making that line and letting the acid work for you. Let the acid cut the metal, and let the artist have the freedom and control over his line.

CO: A softer touch.

CZ: Right. So that's the difference between engraving and etching, where you start to see a more rhythmic line. Because the artist wasn't toiling away trying to displace metal, he was just drawing, as you say. Just drawing.

CO: I see.

CZ: And plus, I had never worked with you before, so I was really, really nervous.

CO: I was very excited, actually, because I thought, "Wow, this is actually becoming something." In the playfulness of the line. I was thinking, "This could be a subject." But really, I had no plan, no plan when I started this.

CZ: But how you work, Chris—and it's nice to hear it from your own mouth—is that you sort of open up, and just start to flow. And this came out of that [*pointing to a plate and the print from it*]. And while I was processing these, I remember I got you started on using Mylar—so as not to waste time [*fig. 15*].

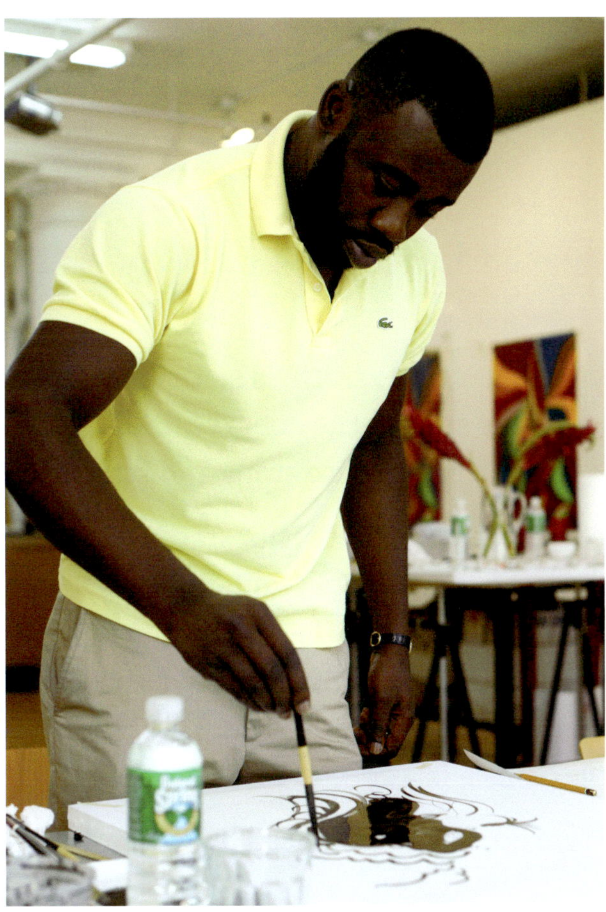

FIG. 15. Ofili painting on Mylar

CO: I remember that! I didn't know what the hell you were talking about. I thought, *"What?"*

[*laughter*]

CZ: And that was the beginning of the next portfolio, *Black Kiss* [*figs. 16 and 17*], and that was using a different technique, direct gravure.

CO: Right, right.

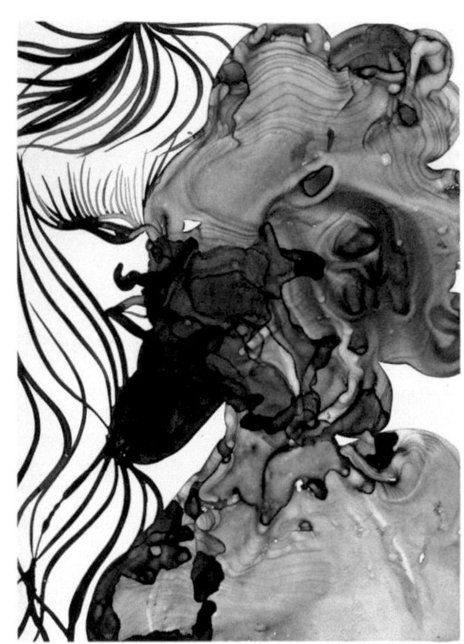
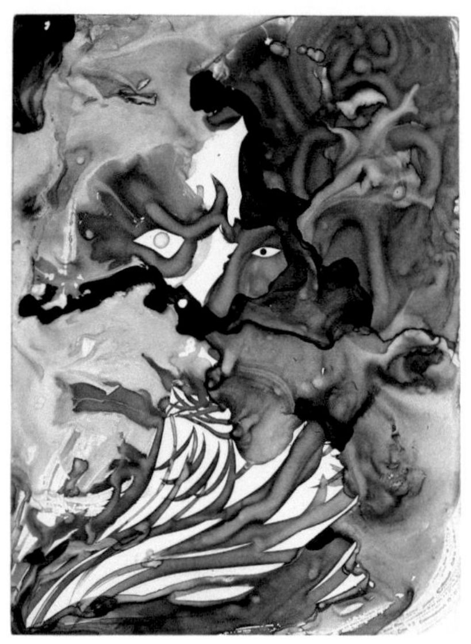

FIGS. 16–17. Chris Ofili, *Black Kiss #1* and *Black Kiss #2*, 2006. From a portfolio of thirteen direct gravures with *chine collé*, title page, and colophon on Somerset paper hand-torn to size, housed in a cloth-covered box with silver stamping, each 21 × 17 in. (53.3 × 43.2 cm). Edition of 20. Published by Two Palms

CZ: And that worked out really well. Because, as Chris said, it's nice to have two or three things going at the same time so that the energy that is created during the day continues steadily, and there are not these stops and starts.

CO: And for me, when I come here, I get into that state where I'm willing to accept all these doubts. So the last thing I want to do is take a break and risk snapping back and getting all neurotic again. I'd rather just keep going and go for a drink at the end of the day. So *Black Kiss* was actually quite different in that it was working with liquid, with ink. That's a very wet method, and this [in *Agony in the Garden*] is a very dry method.

EH: And so the qualities of the two portfolios produced by the two methods are completely different.

CO: Completely different. So it allowed me to completely shift gears. This was all very linear, very precise, and then I could just turn around and relax into the flow of the painting on Mylar.

EH: So you were literally working on both portfolios at the same time?

CO: Yes, it was great!

EH: And the latest portfolio that you're working on, what process are you using for those prints?

CZ: You mean *50 Dry Palms*? Those are drypoints [*figs. 18 and 19*]. Fifty drypoints. As Chris would finish one, the plate before it would just be finished being proofed, and the proof would be tacked to the wall. And they just flowed, one after the other—for two or three days?

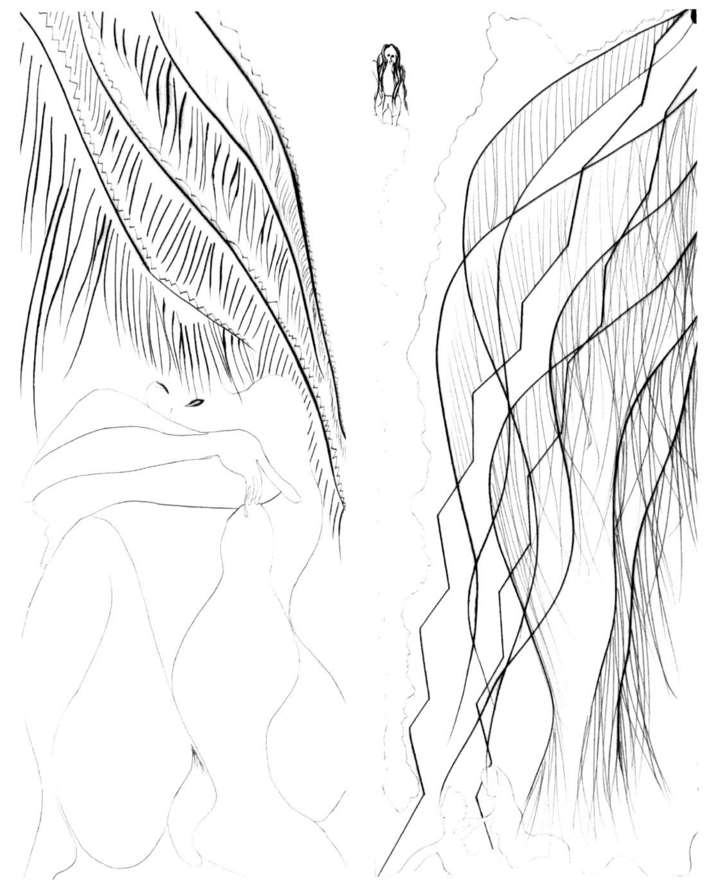

FIGS. 18–19. Two untitled prints from *50 Dry Palms*, 2009. From a portfolio of fifty drypoints, housed in a cloth-covered box with silver stamping, each 16¼ × 10⅝ in. (41.3 × 27 cm). Edition of 10. Published by Two Palms

CO: Something like that. One after the other, and quite small plates, and irregularly shaped.

EH: And what's the subject matter of those?

CO: Looking closer and closer into the tree, kind of abstracting it. But I would say that drypoint is the subject of those.

Chris Ofili

CZ: An excellent exploration of drypoint, of all of the different textures and feelings you can get with that medium. And this takes *me* out of the way. It's pure communication between Chris and the metal. Because what you do is what you get.

EH: But you can't print a large drypoint edition, because the lines collapse?

CZ: Well, we steel-faced them. That's the only thing we printers would do. We would take Chris's plates one by one and immediately steel face them before we printed so that we could capture every line. Because some of the lines were very fine.

CO: Very, very fine. Based on some of the tools I was using. The tools you were handing me were amazing. Many different types of points.

CZ: And made of different types of metals.

CO: And you made some of them yourself, right?

CZ: Yes. I make a lot of them.

EH: Has Craig got you going with the tattoo machine yet?

CO: No.

CZ: That's next.

EH: Uh-oh.

[laughter]

CO: Have you seen the box of beetle points or whatever they are?

CZ: Oh, that's right! Insect pins. You did a lot of work with those, Chris, that's right. Using insect pins as a scribe. Here they are. These are all various weights of insect pins that are inserted into hypodermic needle shafts and then put into the wood [*fig. 20*].

EH: Wow.

CZ: And you can make a really fine line with them.

CO: Like a whisper.

CZ: And it prints so finely—that's why we have to immediately steel face the plates, because a line made by one of these pins prints just like the finest pencil. Which is a beautiful result that you can get with drypoint.

CO: Oh, having that box! That box was such a find for me. And you asked about the subject of the *Dry Palms*—this is the subject. This box of quiet, quiet marks.

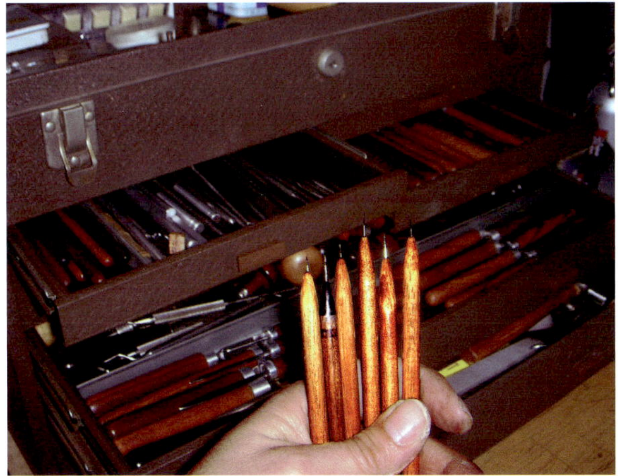

CZ: One of the many pleasures of working with Chris is his openness to new techniques.

EH: You know, Chris, looking at these . . . I would think you drew all the time. Your lines are so certain, and so fluid.

CO: I do draw a lot, I draw all the time.

EH: You just don't exhibit your drawings.

CO: No, no. But this opened things up, opened me up.

[*pause*]

EH: I don't want to end without talking a bit about color. Because your paintings are so much about color, but here you're obviously so comfortable working in monochrome.

CO: Well, essentially the paintings are line drawings—or they start that way—and then they build up from that. So this is not alien to me at all. But going so far as to exhibit these—that was a big step for me.

EH: I think these are incredibly successful. I'd love to see them up on a wall—perhaps, now that you've described them better, in a circular room, all of these witnesses.

CZ: Yes, I think both portfolios—*Agony in the Garden* and *Black Kiss*—are quite powerful. And these [*pointing to the* Agony in the Garden *prints*] were exhibited at David Zwirner gallery, right?

CO: Yes, these were shown at an exhibition I had at David Zwirner's in 2007.[7] And I think people found them interesting. It was a very successful show. Because they were in a room by themselves, but not a circular one—so they were almost like a complete surprise.

Chris Ofili

CZ: Yes. And it was very exciting to see them in context with your other work—and to see how everything communicates.

EH: I heard you were thinking of building a press at your home?

> CO: Yes.

EH: Are you still thinking of doing that?

> CO: Absolutely, absolutely. But at the same time, there's something exciting about coming away—here to Two Palms—and not having any of the baggage that you're used to having around you, and working in a very focused manner. This time it's been a week that I've been here, last time I think it was a couple of weeks? But just working on this, only on this. And sometimes, these long days—kind of forcing yourself to go a little further. Whereas ordinarily in your routine day, you'd think, "Oh, got to go home now and see my family," or do something else. But this is a very exclusive way of pushing ideas and experimenting, and also, of course, you have quite a lot of people on hand to help out. Which I think is very special.

EH: It's a really nice atmosphere here.

CZ: Well, that should be the case with all print studios. If they're successful, you'll get that type of a process happening.

> *[laughter from everyone as David Lasry inserts a note under the door that reads:*
> *"CHRIS, COUGH TWICE IF YOU NEED TO GET OUT."]*

EH: He thinks we're holding you hostage! Well, it's great that you're back and continuing to work.

> CO: Yes, yes. I can't see an end. And I must say that working here is really very exciting. Because it's freedom. Nobody's telling you that you have to produce, that you have to make a portfolio.

EH: Although you seem to like to work in series, series that become portfolios. Is that intentional?

> CO: I think it has to do with having an idea, and often working quite quickly—and that creates energy, and so I want to continue on. It's hard to think about doing something and that being the end of it. Because that might only be Monday . . .

> *[laughter]*

> CO: What am I going to do now?

EH: Are there any print media other than etching that you'd like to experiment with?

CO: Well, Craig and I have talked about color. Continuing on in etching but introducing color into it.

CZ: Right. That's our next step.

CO: Working with subtleties of color and seeing how that could bring more into the process.

EH: Although, you know, for me, these [*pointing to the* Agony in the Garden *etchings*] are full of color. They really are.

CO: I know! I think I'll always have some linear, copper-plate etchings on the go. Just as a kind of sketchbook. And a way of checking to see if I'm getting any better or worse. So whatever other projects we do, I think I'll always have a little box of plates with me to work on.

CZ: Well, Chris, the only other thing I'd like to say is that I've worked with lots of artists over the past thirty years, and sometimes it can be awkward. Watching somebody just toiling away over a plate and knowing that it's not going anywhere . . .

[*laughter*]

EH: Craig has told me horror stories . . .

CZ: But, again, it's been such a pleasure, such an exciting journey to have worked with you and to have this happen [*pointing to the* Agony in the Garden *etchings*].

CO: Oh, likewise, likewise.

CZ: And I can't wait for what the future holds. Thank you so much.

Notes

The preceding conversation was held on September 11, 2009, at Two Palms.

1. Chris Ofili's suite of thirteen paintings *The Upper Room* (2002) is based on the story of the Last Supper, Christ's final meal with his disciples, which was held in the upper room of an inn. This occasion directly preceded the Agony in the Garden in Christ's Passion.

2. Luke 22:44 (King James Version).

3. "With God on Our Side" was released on Bob Dylan's *The Times They Are A-Changin'* (Columbia, 1964).

4. See, e.g., John Noble Wilford and Laurie Goodstein, "'Gospel of Judas' Surfaces after 1,700 Years," *New York Times*, April 6, 2006, http://www.nytimes.com/ (accessed September 26, 2011).

5. Ofili is referring to Zammiello's attendance at the opening of the solo exhibition *Chris Ofili: Afro Margin*, at David Zwirner, in New York. The exhibition ran from September 10 to October 24, 2009.

6. "Painters' paintings: Brice Marden and Chris Ofili in Conversation," *Artforum International* 45, no. 2 (Oct. 2006): 223.

7. The solo exhibition *Chris Ofili: Devil's Pie* was held at David Zwirner from September 20 to November 3, 2007.

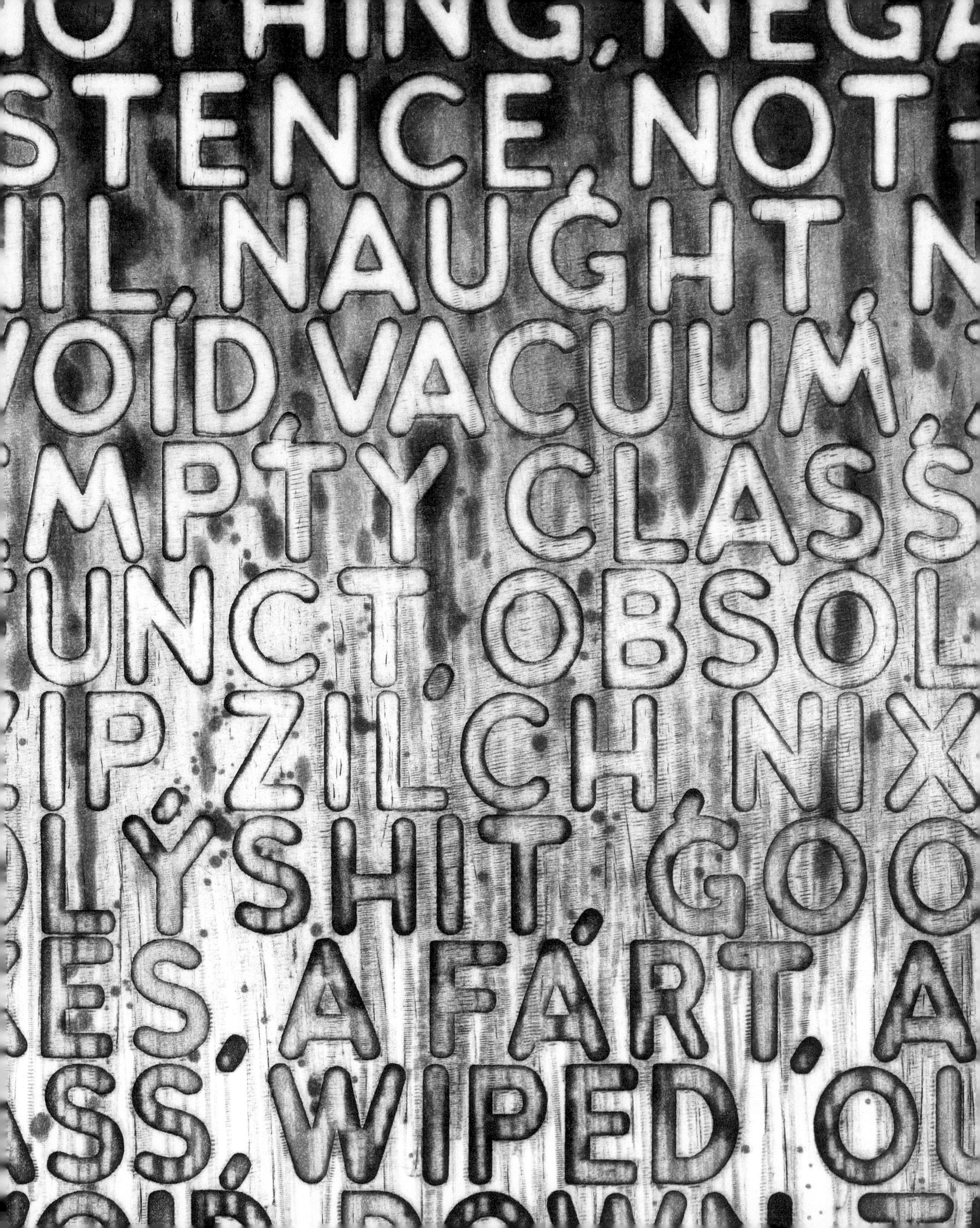

OTHING, NEGA
STENCE NOT
IL NAUGHT N
VOID VACUUM
MPTY CLASS
UNCT. OBSOL
IP ZILCH NIX
OLY SHIT. GOO
ES A FART. A
SS WIPED OU

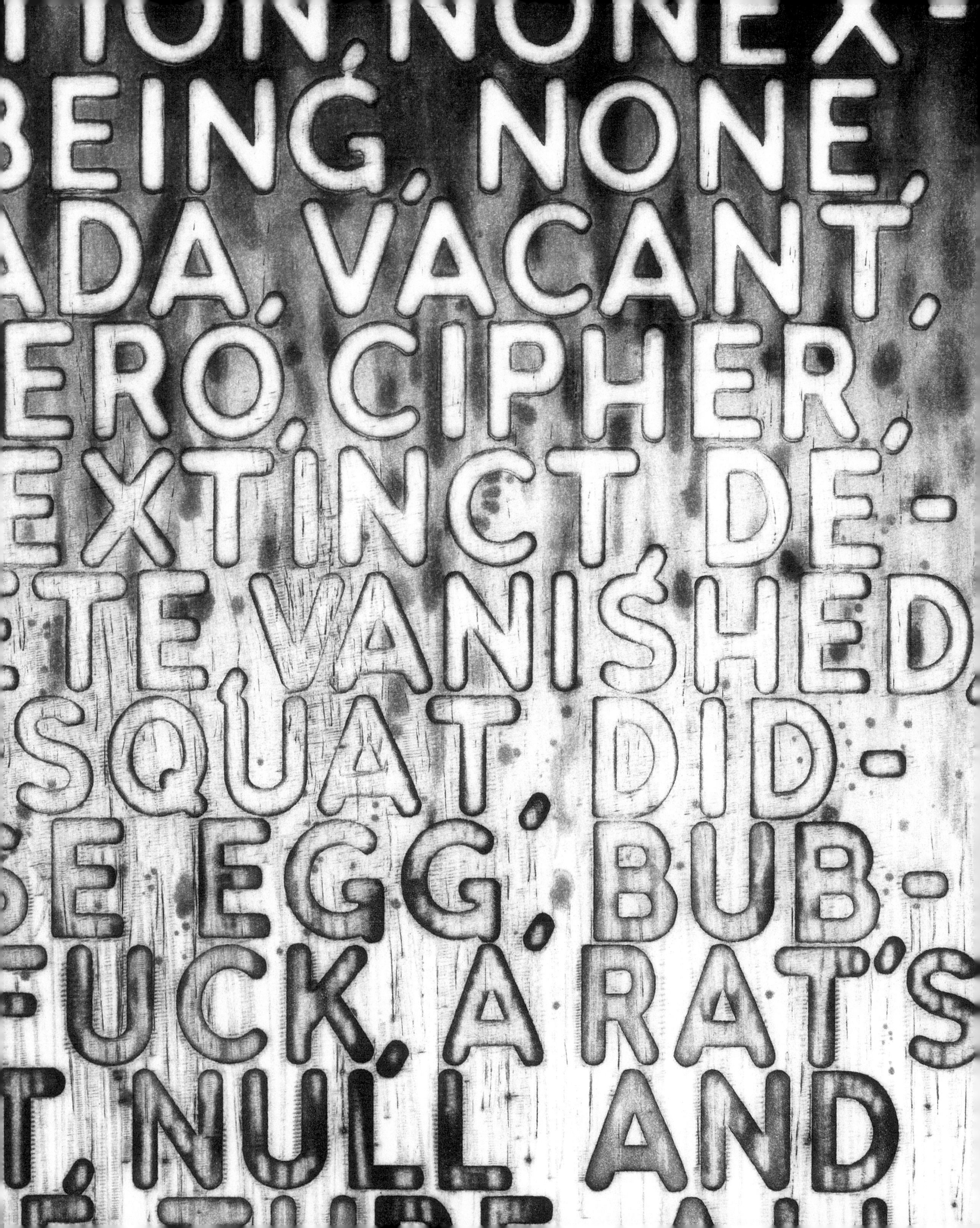

TION, NONE, EX-
BEING, NONE,
ADA, VACANT,
ERO, CIPHER,
EXTINCT, DE-
TE VANISHED,
SQUAT, DID-
BE EGG, BUB-
FUCK A RAT'S
NULL AND

NOTHING, NEGATION, NONEX-
ISTENCE, NOT-BEING, NONE,
NIL, NAUGHT, NADA, VACANT,
VOID, VACUUM, ZERO, CIPHER,
EMPTY CLASS, EXTINCT, DE-
FUNCT, OBSOLETE, VANISHED,
ZIP, ZILCH, NIX, SQUAT, DID-
DLY SHIT, GOOSE EGG, BUB-
KES, A FART, A FUCK, A RAT'S
ASS, WIPED OUT, NULL AND
VOID, DOWN THE TUBE, ALL
DONE, ALL GONE, NO MORE,
KAPUT, DEAD, FINISHED, PFFFT.

CRAZY, NUTTY, DAFFY, DIPPY,
DIZZY, LOOPY, GOOFY, KOOKY,
BATTY, BUGGY, BALMY, FLAKY,
SCREWY, SCHIZZY, SICKO, YOYO,
PSYCHO, WEIRDO, WACKO, LO-
CO, CUCKOO, BONKERS, BANAN-
AS, GAGA, MESHUGA, LOONY
TUNES, SPACE CADET, OUT TO
LUNCH, OFF THE WALL, OVER
THE TOP, AROUND THE BEND,
OUT OF YOUR GOURD, SPACED
OUT, FREAKED-OUT, FUCKED-
UP, FOAMING AT THE MOUTH.

OBSCENE, PORNOGRAPHIC,
PRURIENT, LEWD, LASCIVIOUS,
LECHEROUS, SCATOLOGICAL,
SMUTTY, DEBAUCHED, INDE-
CENT, RAW, RACY, RANDY, RAUN-
CHY, RIBALD, VULGAR, FILTHY,
VILE, GROSS, GOATISH, FETID,
OFF-COLOR, POTTY MOUTH,
GUTTER TALK, $#@!!!%?*&...,
FOUR-LETTER WORDS, DIRTY
PICTURES, EXPLICIT ACTION,
TRIPLE-X-RATED, HARD CORE,
ADULTS ONLY, HOT 'N HORNY.

MONEY, MOOLA, MAZUMA, GELT,
SCRATCH, SKINS, SIMOLEONS,
SHEKELS, DINERO, WAMPUM,
GREENBACKS, CHINK, BREAD,
DOUGH, PEANUTS, CABBAGE,
GRAVY, CHEDDAR, CHICKEN
FEED, DO-RE-MI, JACK, LOOT,
BOODLE, PENNY ANTE, SMALL
POTATOES, DEAD PRESIDENTS,
CHUMP CHANGE, BIG BUCKS,
ALMIGHTY DOLLAR, ROOT OF
ALL EVIL, HARD CASH, LIQUID
ASSETS, FILTHY LUCRE, $,$,$.

MEANINGLESS, SENSELESS, IR-
RELEVANT, POINTLESS, INSIGNIFI-
CANT, INCONSEQUENTIAL, EMP-
TY, FATUOUS, EMPHATIC, NULL, IN-
ANE, NONSENSE, MUMBO-JUMBO,
DOUBLE-TALK, JARGON, HOOEY,
HOKUM, HOGWASH, BUNK, BILGE,
BOSH, BLATHER, BLABBER, BAB-
BLE, BALONEY, BULLSHIT, CRAP-
OLA, JABBER, JIVE, GIBBERISH,
HOT AIR, DRIVEL...

IRASCIBLE, IRRITABLE, CAN-
TANKEROUS, SPLENETIC, AR-
GUMENTATIVE, BELLICOSE,
ABRASIVE, DYSPEPTIC, BEL-
LIGERENT, PETULANT, PRICK-
LY, PERVERSE, CAUSTIC, TES-
TY, CRABBY, CRANKY, GRUFF,
GROUCHY, BITCHY, BITTER,
DARK, DOUR, THIN-SKINNED,
TOUCHY, NASTY, SOUR, SURLY,
GRUMPY, PEEVISH, PISSED-
OFF, ORNERY, LOOKING FOR
TROUBLE, SON-OF-A-BITCH.

For more than fifteen years, Mel Bochner has been making lusciously colored, tactilely engaging monotypes and embossments at Two Palms. At midcareer, Bochner has become deeply invested in printmaking, and has come to consider it an integral part of his oeuvre. While some of his recent prints have incorporated intaglio techniques, the six etchings that *Strong Language* (2007; figs. 1–6) comprises were the first purely intaglio prints that Bochner had made since the early 1990s. As Bochner describes in the conversation that follows, that time lapse was not intentional; it was, rather, a case of his self-described "episodic" experiences making prints, coupled with Craig Zammiello's appearance "on the scene" at Two Palms in 2002.[1] Watching Zammiello collaborate with other artists reawakened Bochner's desire to make etchings.

Coincidentally, the year 2002—when Zammiello was hired as master intaglio printer at Two Palms—was also the year that Bochner began to make his *Thesaurus Paintings*. Bochner had discovered the markedly contemporized 150th-anniversary edition of *Roget's Thesaurus* (2002) and began to mine it for subject matter for his new series of paintings: "In 2002 I came across a new edition of *Roget's Thesaurus*. Not only did it include very up-to-date vernacular and slang, but outright obscenity as well. Because the thesaurus gets into the hands of fairly young children, that signaled a dramatic change in what is considered 'ordinary' language. Something had happened to the boundaries of public discourse—politically, conceptually, and morally—and I wanted to explore that."[2]

Those familiar with Bochner's *Thesaurus Paintings* will readily perceive how the prints that make up this suite vary from the paintings from which they derive, not only in their much-reduced size, but also in the artist's treatment of surface—the way he exploits the rich languages of intaglio printmaking (hard ground, soft ground, aquatint, spit bite, sugar lift) to create a wholly different family of objects. Another way in which the prints differ from the paintings is in their coloration, and that divergence from Bochner's palette of primaries is something that Bochner and Zammiello touch on in the following conversation. Despite this difference, color ultimately performs the same function in these prints that it does in Bochner's paintings: it is a tool that

FIGS. 1–6. *Strong Language*, 2007. Suite of six mixed-media intaglio prints, each 7¾ × 9¹³⁄₁₆ in. (19.7 × 24.9 cm). Edition of 20. Published by Two Palms. Yale University Art Gallery, Janet and Simeon Braguin Fund, 2008.28.1.1–.6. Left to right, top to bottom: **FIG. 1.** *Nothing*, etching with aquatint, open bite, spit bite, scraping, and burnishing; **FIG. 2.** *Crazy*, etching with aquatint, sugar lift, and *chine collé*; **FIG. 3.** *Obscene*, etching with aquatint, liquid aquatint, and open bite; **FIG. 4.** *Money*, etching, with aquatint, hard ground, open bite, spit bite, and burnishing; **FIG. 5.** *Meaningless*, etching with soft ground; **FIG. 6.** *Irascible*, etching with aquatint, direct gravure, and spit bite the artist employs to play with our perception of the meaning and content of language. Whether painted or printed, Bochner's *Thesaurus* pieces encourage the viewer to perceive how color affects one's response to language—how, for example, stronger or primary colors can transform a rather innocuous word into an aggressive one, how weaker colors can diffuse the offensiveness of a distasteful word, and how our ingrained associations with colors (black/white, pink/blue) predetermine our response to a subject. As Bochner has said, color "diverts the text from its duty to meaning."[3]

Perhaps the most extraordinary thing about this suite of prints is the mastery of their printing, their incredible depth (of surface, of color) that so beautifully flaunts the "telepathy" or "grace" of collaboration between two seasoned professionals: an artist well versed in intaglio techniques and a master printer completely open to pushing the envelope and taking on new challenges that sometimes render serendipitous surprises, engender new techniques for the printer's arsenal, or open new avenues for future artist-printer collaborations.

———————

MEL BOCHNER: I started making prints as a student, in the late fifties. I made etchings, engravings, aquatints, screenprints, lithographs, linoleum cuts, woodcuts, and also did some typography. So I had a very thorough and intense printmaking background. Printmaking was my favorite class, because of a great teacher, Robert Gardner, who had so much information at his fingertips. Unlike many of the other teachers, he never interfered with the content or the form of your work. He didn't care what it looked like, he was just there to help you facilitate it technically.

He would come in at about eleven PM with a six-pack of beer, lock the door to the print shop, and allow you to work there all night while he worked on his own prints. For me, the best thing about etching was that the acid would take over and do something that often made your print much better than what you had scratched into the ground. There were always bonuses to submitting to the process.

After I graduated, I had no access to a printmaking facility for another few years. It wasn't until the early seventies that Bob Feldman from Parasol Press called me up. He was publishing some prints out in California, with Sol [LeWitt] and Brice [Marden] and wanted to work with me. My first response was, "Why? Why make multiple copies of an image that you can't even sell one of?" And he answered, "Well, that's my problem." So I started going out to California and working—first with Kathan [Brown] and then with Gerald Parker, with whom I really enjoyed working. He was very adventurous, and a real technical wiz. He came up with some brilliant solutions to certain problems I was having with aquatint. Gerald came to New York in the mid-eighties and I did another project with him, which basically turned out to be a series of one-offs, monoprints, which I sometimes drew or painted over.

The next intaglios I did were in the early nineties. I met Maurice Payne, who had been at Petersburg [Press], and was another great printer. I had an idea for something I wanted to do, and nobody could figure out how to do it. But Maurice was willing to try. He had a really tiny, funky studio down on Warren Street, near City Hall. We finally figured it out, and I did a series of four rather large multi-plate prints—the *Quartets* [1988]. Then he moved out to California to become David Hockney's personal printer. So I suppose what I'm trying to say is that my printmaking ventures have been very episodic.

Then one day I was going to visit a shop that was printing an announcement for me in one of those printing buildings which used to be on Hudson Street, and I bumped into David Lasry, who was putting his key in the door . . .

ELISABETH HODERMARSKY: When was this?

MB: Ninety-one or Ninety-two? No, 1993. David had been a student of mine at Yale. He had just opened his own print shop and invited me in to see what he was up to. He had a vertical pressure [hydraulic] press, which I had never seen before, and he showed me what some artists were doing, which was basically drawing in oil paint on sheets of plastic and printing monoprints from those. But that process didn't really interest me. So I just said, "Thanks, I'll think about it and I'll get back to you . . ." And as I was walking out I noticed this thing hanging by the door, an embossed piece of pink rubber with type on it. And I asked, "What's this?" And David said, "Oh, that's what vertical presses were originally used for, to emboss offset litho plates that could then be put on a roller to print newspapers from." So I said, "Could we do something like that?" And he said, "Yeah, we could do that." And I said, "Do you have any free time next week?"

[laughter]

MB: So we began very primitively, by gouging out pieces of plywood . . .

EH: Manually?

MB: Yes. And experimenting with different ways to engrave and print, and eventually, seventeen years later, we arrived at where we are now,

using lasers and computers. Then a few years ago, David hired Craig.
I watched what Craig was doing and it reawakened in me the desire to
make some etchings.

EH: Because you had been making the embossed monotypes.

MB: Also because David didn't have the facilities to make etchings before
Craig appeared on the scene.

EH: But it still took you another six years to do something together?

MB: Well, everyone wanted to work with Craig, so I had to get in line!

CRAIG ZAMMIELLO: For years I was watching what Mel was doing and the wheels
[*pointing to his head*] were always turning, and I was thinking, "How can we turn
this into an etching?" And in the meantime, Mel was thinking, "Oh, I'd like to
do an etching." So there was this little dance that we did for a few years until we
finally made something.

EH: And you mentioned that there were certain technologies that didn't exist five
years ago that have subsequently come here [to Two Palms], that made what you
were thinking of doing with Mel possible? To respond to what he was doing?

CZ: Well, the main thing was the ability to quickly make a plate with Mel's language work, using the laser to burn through the hard ground. This way we could
have stencils of the words quickly and take it from there. Nobody would have to
either do it photographically—which takes a day or two—or paint out the letters
by hand, in a traditional way. These were plates that we could make in an hour,
and then Mel could take it from there, and utilize any intaglio technique. And
within a day of working with Mel, I learned that he was a master of all these traditional etching techniques. You have to realize that for the past few years I had
been working with artist/printmakers who really didn't know much about etching—which is something I really enjoy, to teach people—but with Mel it was kind
of like taking this liberating breath, this "oh, my God, this guy knows more than
I do! Yippee!"

MB: But at the same time I learned so much from you, Craig. It has definitely been reciprocal.

When I was doing the first prints at Crown Point [Press], I wanted a certain quality of aquatint—something that hadn't really been done before—an
absolutely flat aquatint on a really large scale. With no variations. In other
words, an anti-Goya aquatint. And it took over a year to figure out how to
make it. Each time they thought they had the aquatint on the plate I would

have to hand-paint the image, which would take a couple of days. Then they'd bite it, and it wouldn't come out and we'd have to start all over again. But with what Craig and David have developed, with the laser and with grounds that don't burn up under the laser, I'm able to start with the outline of the image already on the plate. So instead of starting at zero to get to sixty, you're starting at fifty-five.

CZ: Right.

EH: What interests me most about this set of six is that it's sort of an "everything but the kitchen sink" approach to intaglio—that among the six prints you've utilized every conceivable intaglio process. Was that something that was planned, or was that something that just happened over the course of making the six prints?

> MB: Well, I had it in the back of my mind. Over the years of making etchings, I felt I had gathered a lot of information about what each different technique could do—and I wanted the techniques themselves to become significant players in the image. What I tried to do was to approach each plate through a different technique and see how that would affect the meaning of the words.

EH: And, for me, there seems to be this relationship between "how many ways can I make a mark on a plate" and your thesaurus theme, the "how many ways can I convey this idea"? And I love the sort of marriage of the technical and the conceptual in this series.

> MB: I think of each particular technique as contributing a voice to the words. When you're using language, you're always dealing with the question of voice. What is the difference between the word as spoken and the word in your head—the so-called silent voice in your head? I wanted to try to visualize those competing voices, to somehow make sound part of the content.

EH: That's beautiful. So I think before we go on to discuss more about concept and content, we should first maybe focus on the prints—trace the technical aspects of their making. Was there one of these six that came first, that was the springboard for the rest? Or was work on them more or less simultaneous?

> MB: Well, the first sort of framing idea was to keep them small.

EH: I wanted to ask you about that. They're very modest.

> MB: Yes, I wanted to keep them small because etching, in the way that I wanted to think about it, is a very intimate activity. You basically do it on a table. Those big prints that I did with Maurice Payne, we put holes in

the copper and nailed the copper to the wall. And then I painted directly on those huge sheets of copper while they were on the wall. It was about the space between my body and the wall. I saw this project as more about the space between my face and the table.

EH: Did you think you were just going to do one print initially, or did you conceive of this project as a series?

MB: I just did them one at a time, really. And I think the first one in the set was *Nothing* [*see fig. 1*].

CZ: Yes. This one, and we really worked it.

EH: Take me through it. Oh, you have a lot of the states, great.

MB: Well, basically, this was done by just direct acid applied to the plate with a brush.

CZ: Yes, we started with the open bite. And that's how the first plate started—the one that's not part of this set. We tried it, thinking, would this be interesting? Can we do this? And it was, it had a beautiful look to it. And then the next step was to start this portfolio with *Nothing*. And we started in the same way. And I think . . . here it is, state one [*fig. 7*]. Then you started with spit biting the letters [*fig. 8*], which is applying acid with a brush directly to an aquatint. And the next step was Mel taking etching tools and burnishing and scraping—basically erasing the spit bite by hand [*fig. 9*]. From there we went to this one—state four [*fig. 10*]—where he really erased everything, and this is mainly scraping and a bit of burnishing, I believe. You can see the act of peeling away the copper with the knife and the marks it left.

FIG. 7. *Nothing*, state 1, with open bite

FIG. 8. *Nothing*, state 2, with aquatint and spitbite additions

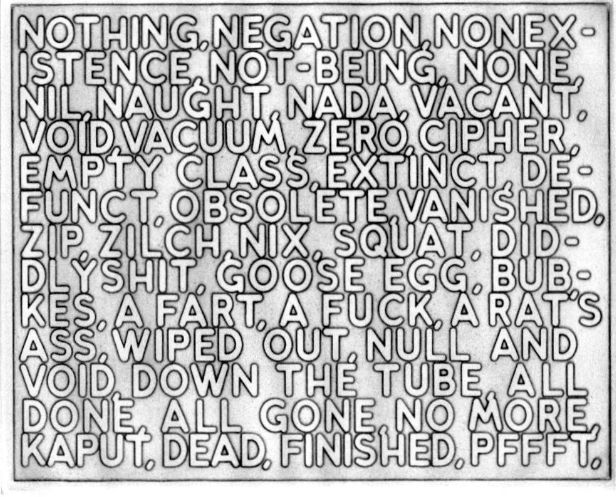

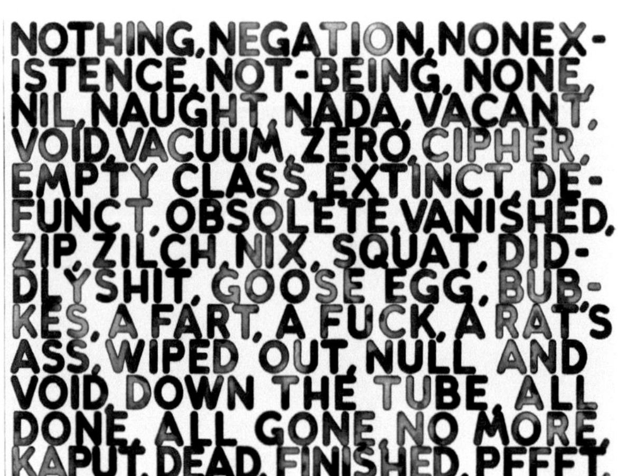

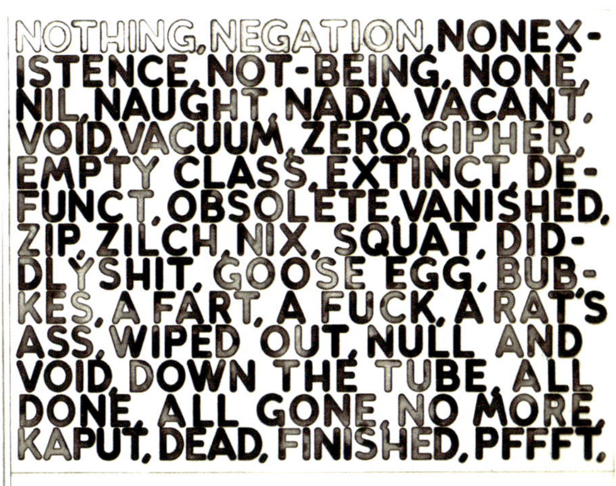

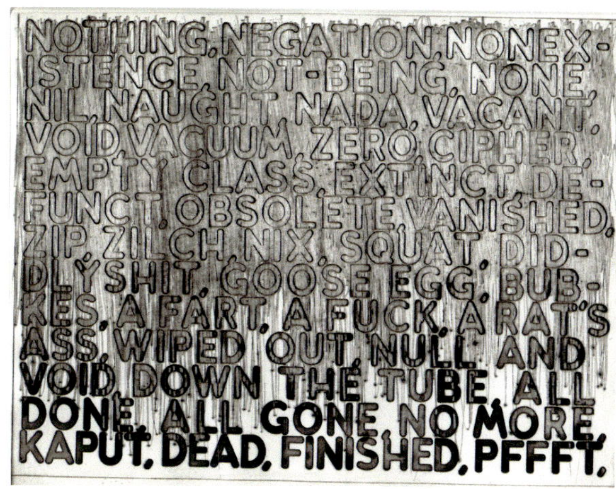

EH: So still one plate.

CZ: Still one plate. So that would be states one through four, and then we come to state five [*fig. 11*], which Mel has now started to scrape and burnish down more, so the plate holds less ink.

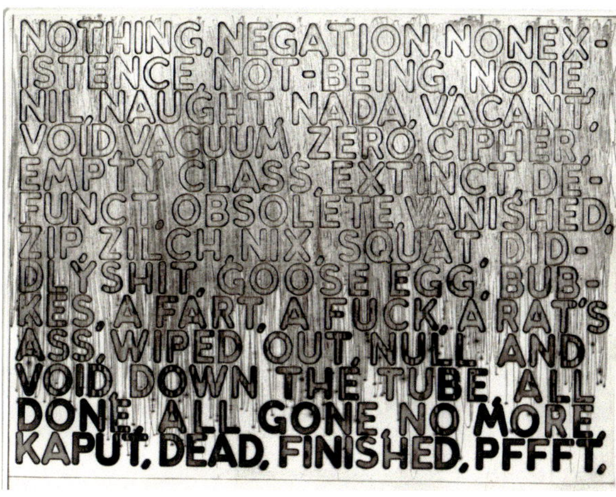

EH: To make it more legible?

MB: Yes.

CZ: Yes. We wanted to get some light in there.

MB: But, Lisa, you hit on one of the big issues in these . . . which is degrees of legibility. How you retrieve information from a background. And I was playing with this one to see how far we could push the legible/illegible aspects of it in a single work. And then, what did we do next, add another aquatint?

Mel Bochner

CZ: We put down another aquatint. And this is an airbrushed aquatint, with kind of an ukiyo-e fade down [*fig. 12*]. Because we were talking about how we could pop the letters, get them to the front. But it flattened it in a way too, didn't it? So taking it from there . . .

MB: It's nice that you saved all these states.

CZ: Well, it was the first time you and I were working together.
And so we went from there to here, which is adding a little bit more tone, evening out the middle [*fig. 13*]. And then Mel went in . . .

FIG. 12. *Nothing,* state 6, with airbrush aquatint additions

FIG. 13. *Nothing,* state 7, with more extensive airbrush aquatint additions

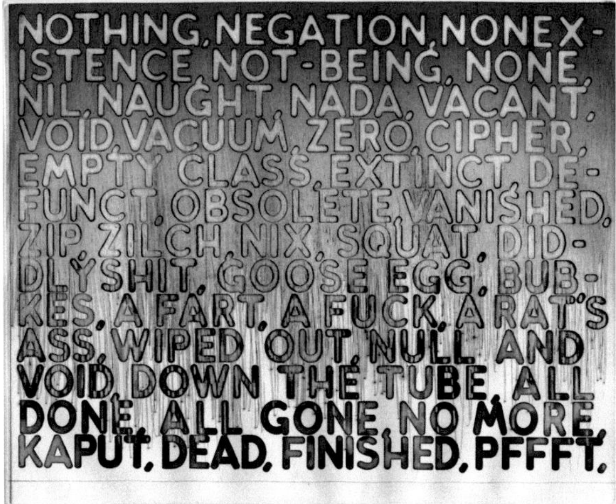

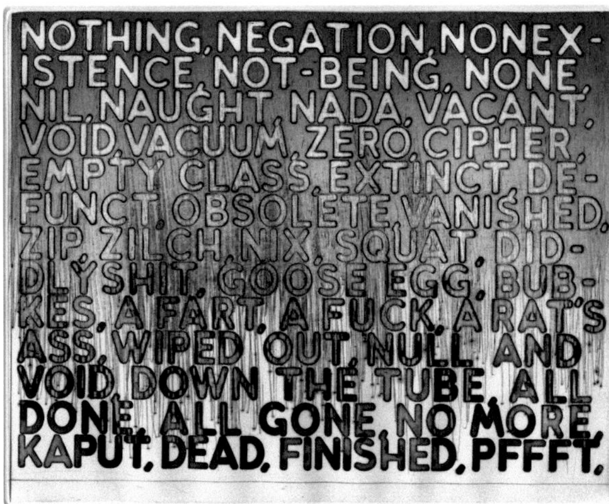

MB: Another open bite?

CZ: You burnished, mainly. I aquatinted the background and then you spit bit it, with acid, and that's when you start to see the drips, the brushwork, which really pops the front [*fig. 14*]. We decided to strengthen the top just a bit more, so Mel did a final spit bite over another aquatint [*see fig. 1*].

FIG. 14. *Nothing,* state 8, with spitbite additions

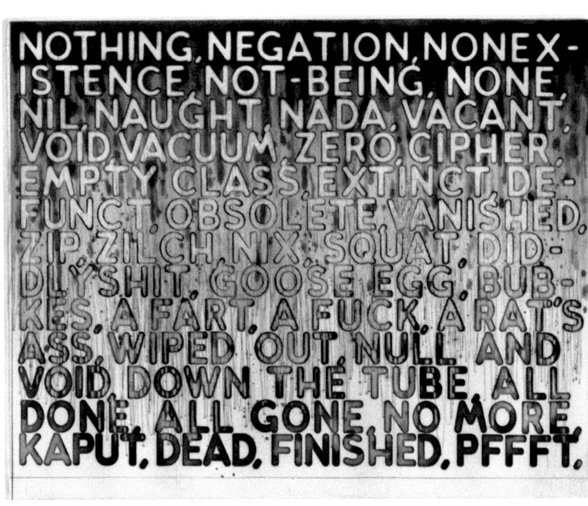

MB: Well, the interesting thing for me was that you could clean off the plate and then reapply the ground and protect anything you wanted to save. You could keep doing one thing after another, because you could clean it off and then come back and get a ground back on exactly where you wanted it. That was the secret.

CZ: Yes, that was the secret. The laser enabled a common stencil that could be applied and removed as needed. So we were able to keep registering and putting the letters right back where they belonged, to help save them. So that, at first, there was one spit bite that Mel did, and then we thought, "Oh, let's get it a little darker up here," and so in the next state we'd do that. And this is where I came to realize that "Wow, this is a breeze. This man knows exactly where this has to go, and he knows how to do it." And that's so much different from a situation in which the artist knows what they want but is not capable of achieving it yet.

EH: Or when they can't articulate . . . that it's hard for them to articulate what they want.

CZ: Yes, sometimes . . . in their mind they know what they want, but they aren't able to explain it. So, for me, this was really a birthday party.

MB: On the other hand, I've worked with printers where there is no flexibility in the relationship. In other words, if a printer has a number of favorite techniques in which he's very well versed, or a publisher has a thought that we should do such and such . . .

EH: It's very limiting?

MB: Yes, it's very limiting. And we know a lot of situations like that. For example, everyone I've ever known who worked with [Aldo] Crommelynck . . . you tell him what you want, you come back two days later, and he gives you a Picasso aquatint. If that's what you want, you work with Crommelynck. The thing with working with Craig is his ultimate flexibility and encyclopedic knowledge of the techniques, and his willingness to try anything: "What the hell, let's see what happens." And that's what made this project so interesting for me, because we had no idea what was going to happen next.

CZ: And the whole thing about that, Mel, is that there are no rules. It's as simple as that.

That's the way I look at it. If it doesn't work, it doesn't work. Which is the opposite of what you're talking about in those early aquatints you did with Kathan, which is more of a traditional approach.

EH: Well, it was also the 1970s, the period of the slick, flawless look.

MB: No, it wasn't about a "slick, flawless look," really. I wanted the thinnest layer of color possible deposited on the paper. The traditional aquatint was the "Goya effect," lots of lumps and bumps.

CZ: You mean the sack of rosin and the whole grainy thing.

MB: Yes. I don't have anything against Goya, I just didn't want to do that. An aquatint is a very beautiful, physical thing. Why not exploit it? But the technology to make it big and perfectly uniform didn't exist. Because it not only involved remaking the mentality of the print shop, it also involved problems in electrostatics, plus an enormous amount of time and investment. What everybody kept saying was, "You're crazy, why do you want to do this? If you want a flat tone, just do a silkscreen." But I said, "No, because with aquatint you're going to get 'air' in the color, and a silkscreen is just one solid layer of color spread flat." And—in those prints—there is a remarkable quality to that aquatint.

EH: They're absolutely gorgeous. Speaking of color . . . it looks like you really experimented with color in these [*Strong Language*] prints.

MB: We went through a lot of color proofs, which was the fun of it too, seeing how the color changed the meaning.

CZ: Mel would suggest colors, I would take it from there.

MB: My paintings have been within a certain range of color, and that's not a range of color that really translates to intaglio. In intaglio, you have all of the issues of the interactions between ink and copper and heat—which changes the color, so it's very hard to work in primaries. I wanted to explore another color range, but I wanted it to be a very offbeat color range. Because, except for those really weird portraits of Dora Maar that Picasso did in the thirties, there's very little that has been done in color etching that I find really interesting. Many artists have applied color to etching, but it rarely seems integral to the idea. I wanted color that felt integral to the process.

CZ: And I think that we went next to *Crazy* [*see fig. 2*]. One shot, very straightforward.

EH: That's surprising, because it looks like the most complicated one. It looks like a car wreck . . . crazy . . .

CZ: It's a traditional sugarlift technique. Mel painted the background with sugar after the letters were stenciled on. We aquatinted it, and then we dipped it in stages, which gives you different tones of aquatint. So what would happen would be that I would dip it for a minute, take it out, stop the etching and dry the aquatint. Mel would come in with a brush with varnish on it and block out areas. The process would then be repeated.

EH: By hand?

CZ: By hand. And using that kind of dry-brush technique. That's just the painting on the plate.

EH: It's beautiful.

CZ: And the color derived from a piece of Japanese paper. Echizen Shikibu Gampi, which is this orange color—and applied as a *chine collé*. So you have a blue, a Prussian blue I believe, printed on top of a laminated piece of orange Japanese paper. And that's it. Very straightforward. And we completed that very quickly.

MB: In a day.

CZ: Indeed.

MB: This one [*Nothing*] took weeks and weeks, and *Crazy* took a day.

CZ: So we were quite happy with it. Wow, look at all of that information.

MB: When I saw this second one, that's when I realized this could be a portfolio.

EH: I love how this goes right to the edge of legibility.

MB: A kind of self-erasing.

CZ: And the next one started as just an experiment [*showing the first proof of* Obscene; *fig. 15*].

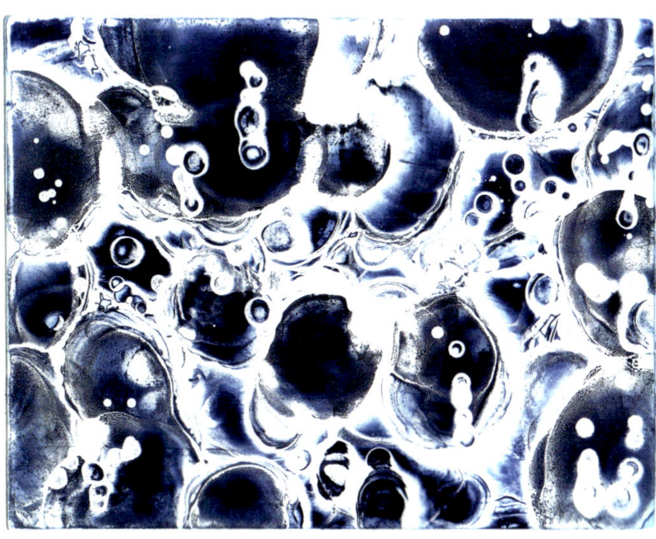

EH: Oh my God, that's exquisite.

CZ: And it started with me showing Mel something called "liquid aquatint," which is basically just rosin that is dissolved in brandy. There was a man in London at L. Cornelissen and Son, who has passed on now but used to make this stuff out of Courvoisier and really fine rosin. And I still have a few bottles of it. And [*gesturing at first proof of* Obscene; *fig. 15*] here's the mark of an artist who just takes a plate and just paints it. This was a one shot deal. I kind of explained to Mel how it worked . . . you puddle it, let it dry, and then puddle it some more. And then I took what Mel had done and etched it for maybe fifteen, twenty minutes. We printed it and were all excited about this look; it's a gorgeous look. So what was the next logical step? Well, put letters on top of it. So we put it in the laser, created a positive stencil, and etched away the background. And there you go [*fig. 16*]. So by open biting the background, you retain the letters with the original liquid-aquatint painting.

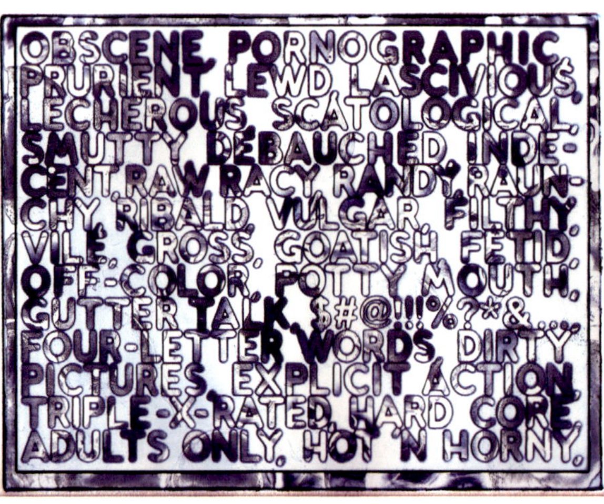

FIG. 16. *Obscene*, state 2, with openbite additions

I think then the next step was to clean that out. We removed the border around the image, the interior border inside the plate [*fig. 17*]. And then we made a couple of color proofs, and some chine collés, and then I think Mel ultimately decided that it should have a flat background. So I made a traditional flat-toned aquatint by dipping a rosin-coated plate in an acid bath, which would have given the print tone everywhere except the letters [*fig. 18*]. I thought that a cobalt blue would work nicely with the red letters, and Mel was happy with that, so as a print it was a fairly straightforward one that started as an experiment with a technique.

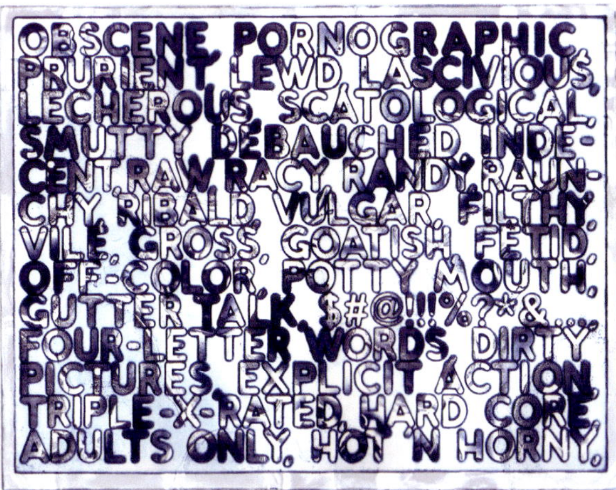
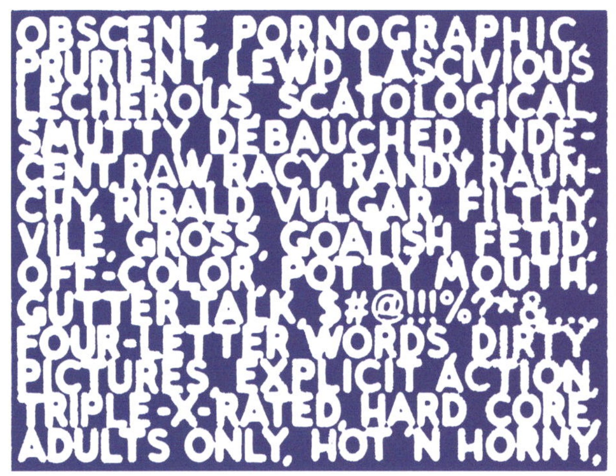

And then we went to *Money* next [*see fig. 4*], which was much more traditional, and a lot of work. Now, *Money* reminded me a lot of . . . well, Mel said,
"Let's go with a straight hard ground, and I'm going to do the lines." And that's
it. That's state one [*fig. 19*].

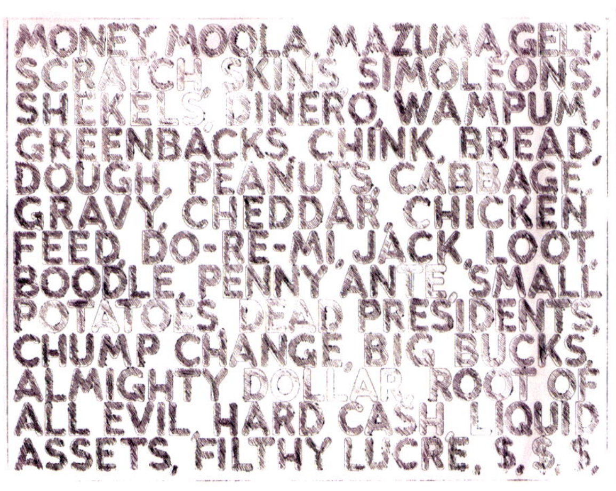

EH: Here you get that intimate feel, of sitting there at the table and working
the plate.

CZ: Yes. We added a second plate with the color [*fig. 20*]. And this is spit biting
[*fig. 21*], you went back in and spit bit around the letters.

MB: It's funny, looking back at these proofs . . . there are so many other
directions we might have gone.

CZ: I know, right? That's always the trouble with bringing out the working
proofs. And from there on it was just fine-tuning and adding to both plates, I
think. You can see them building and Mel going back in . . . See how the line
work here is kind of flat? [*gesturing to fig. 21*] We needed the letters to kind of pop
more. So he went back in to burnish and scrape some of the letters, take away

                                                                      Mel Bochner

some of those lines so they would pop [*fig. 22*]. And we went back in and brightened the colors a bit on the background letters. Mel went back in and also started to add some spit biting around the letters on the line plate, and what you end up with is this really rich, luscious thing. So this wasn't difficult, but it was labor intensive. You did a lot of work on this, Mel, right?

MB: Yes.

FIG. 20. *Money*, state 2, with aquatinted second plate added

FIG. 21. *Money*, state 3, with spitbite additions

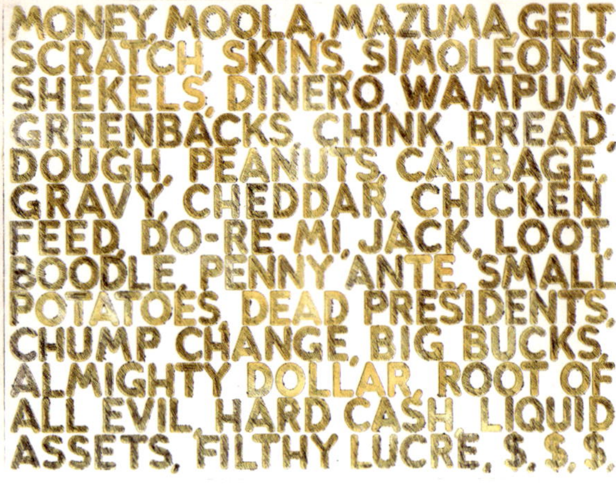

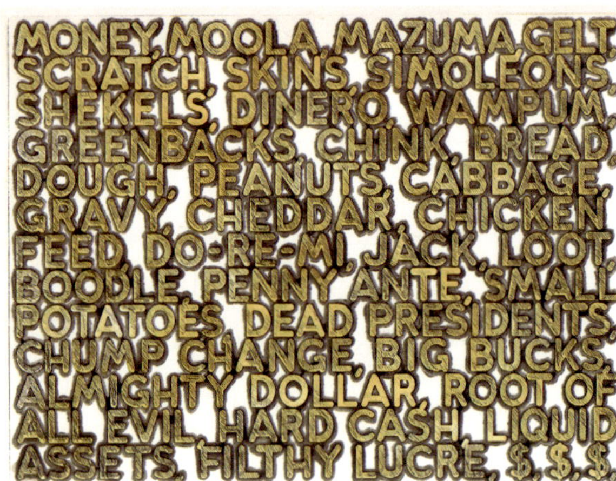

FIG. 22. *Money*, state 4, with burnishing additions

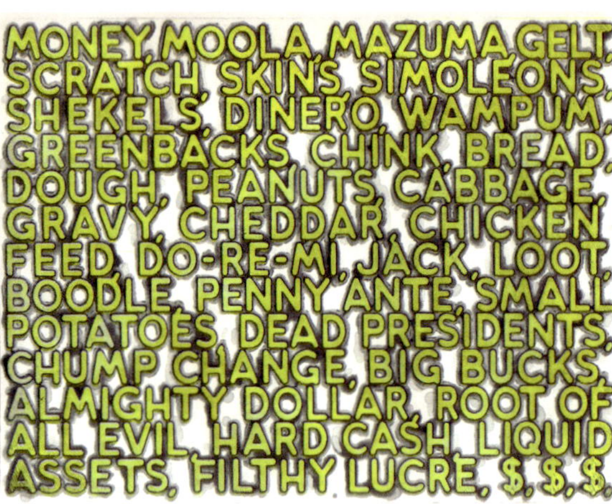

CZ: You were going back and forth with it. On this one I was just sort of facilitating. I was just giving it back to Mel.

MB: I wanted different kinds of relationships with each plate. Where my engagement with one might be very fast, and with another may be very slow—watch it evolve, watch it change, so that there would be this sense of—of reciprocity, a dialogue. I tell the plate something, and the plate tells me something—a sort of conversation which goes back and forth.

EH: But then there were surprises, right?

MB: Yes. There are always surprises.

CZ: And then I think the next one was *Meaningless* [*see fig. 5*].

MB: And it took forever.

CZ: That was the most difficult piece. It started as a very straightforward soft ground, a soft ground applied over the letters stencil from the laser.

You know, Mel came up with two things for this, as I look back at this. And they were, first, the hard ground for the letters, because we had to block out for Mel to go back to the lines. And Mel thought, "Well, instead of a typical asphaltum, that you paint on but that's hard to see through, how about a ball ground that you roll on, and that's almost transparent?" And I thought: bingo. Anything we threw at the stencil, the laser stencil ground, it held up to everything. And secondly, we had the same challenge again with the soft ground [*fig. 23*]. Hmmm. How are we going to get the soft ground on there? Well, let's try it. It requires heat for rolling on, and it is a solvent itself, you know, like shoe polish. But it didn't affect the laser stencil. Again, the laser gave us the ability to put on and block out letters, so Mel could draw around them, literally draw like that. And this one [*Meaningless*] contains two or three plates.

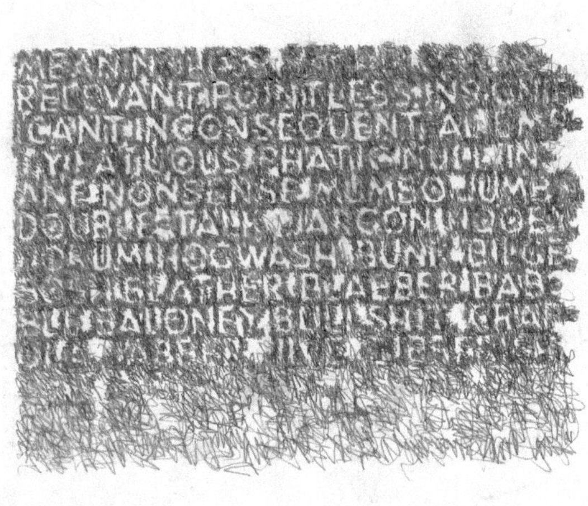

FIG. 23. Original drawing on tracing vellum used for soft ground on *Meaningless*

EH: So is that like a rubbing?

MB: Yes, in a way.

CZ: The vellum was laid on top of the softground plate and then Mel would draw with a pencil. And, as you see it, can be very selective.

EH: That is a nice drawing!

CZ: But the stenciled letters also afforded the possibility of complete randomness as shown here [*figs. 24–26*]. And this one became very difficult. And it kept going. And at some point we were up to three plates—here are proofs from two of them [*figs. 27–28*]. And we were starting to play with colors, and variations, and subtle things, like here [*fig. 29*]. And I think at some point, we decided to give it a dark background. And we pulled one of the three softground plates out of the group, leaving a graphite-y white, and then it's a straight silver on top of that.

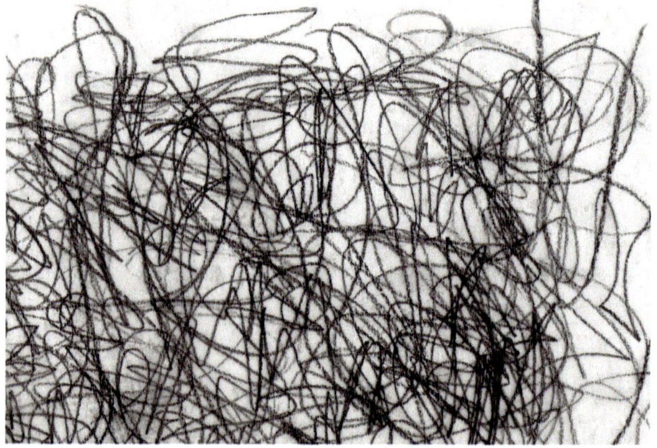

FIG. 24. Detail of drawing on tracing vellum for *Meaningless*

FIG. 25. Detail of computer-simulated rendering of *Meaningless,* showing where the laser stencil blocked the softground drawing

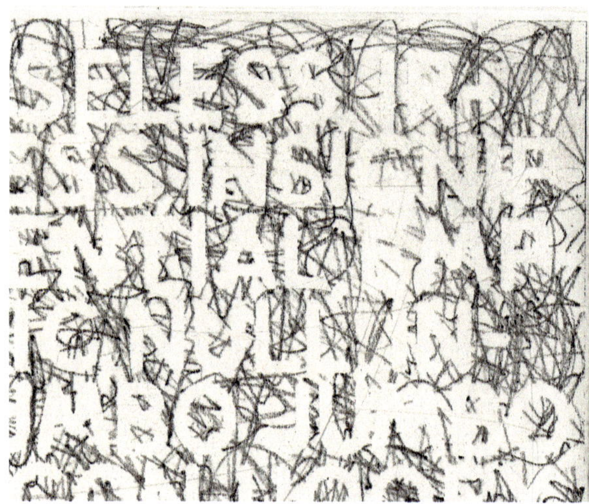

FIG. 26. Detail of final etched soft ground on *Meaningless* (showing same area as fig. 25)

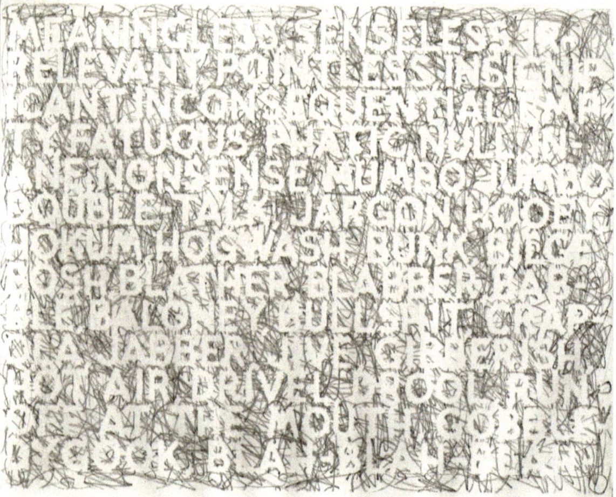

FIG. 27. *Meaningless,* plate 1, with soft ground

FIG. 28. *Meaningless,* plate 2, with soft ground

FIG. 29. *Meaningless*, color proof, with three softground plates

EH: So this [*indicating the final print; see fig. 5*] is two plates?

CZ: This is actually three plates: a background black plate and the two softground plates printed on top.

MB: I dumped one of the softground drawings, because there were getting to be too many lines and they were obscuring the image.

CZ: Right. But the thing that makes it a pleasure is that you can be working on a print literally for weeks, and then suddenly you pull a proof off the press and look at it and the light bulbs snap on above both people, the artist and the printer. "Yeah, that's it."

EH: You knew you were there.

MB: Well, we were close.

CZ: We were close. There was a lot of refining that then took place.

MB: "Do we want a more blue-black?" "Is there more silver in that?"

CZ: I mean, where the background was going back and forth . . . how much you could see . . . there is a history of that.

In the meantime, while we were working on *Meaningless*, we began the final print, *Irascible* [*see fig. 6*], which was based on a direct gravure. Direct gravure is a method where the artist will paint or draw on a sheet of Mylar plastic, and that Mylar becomes a stencil to block light, to utilize the photogravure technique. And so Mel made two paintings on Mylar plastic with ink wash, black ink wash. I made two gravure plates from those, which are basically aquatints. Those are the direct gravures. The nice thing is that you can go back and work on them with any traditional intaglio technique, because they are just aquatints.

EH: So here [in these two plates] you're dividing out—bisecting—the text [*figs. 30–31*].

Mel Bochner

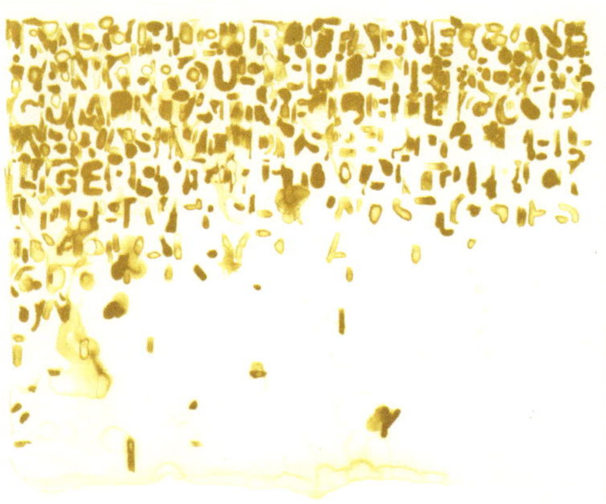

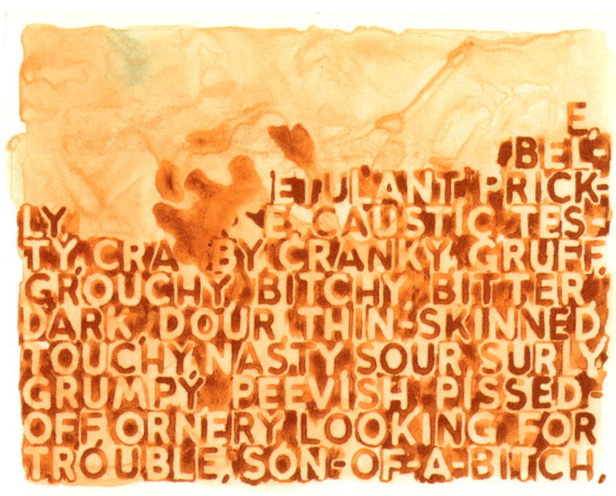

CZ: Right, you can kind of get an idea here of what's going to happen here. And originally, Mel, I think we were going to have a line plate, which was going to go on top of everything. And also a third plate, which was spit biting [*fig. 32*]. Again, this was an aquatint, and Mel selectively painted each letter with acid. But at some point Mel decided that the line plate made it . . . what is the word I'm looking for?

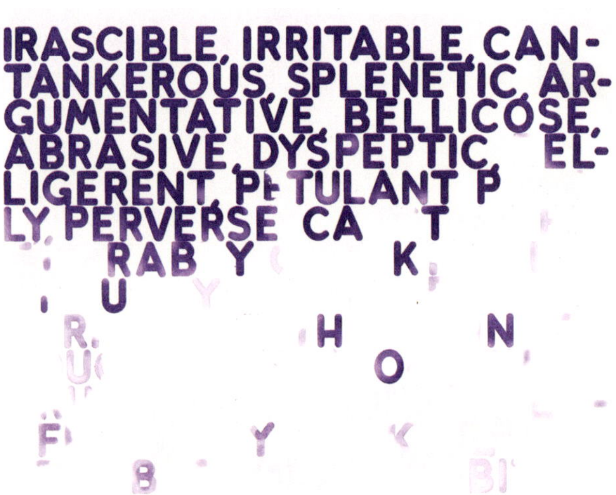

EH: Too much?

CZ: Yes, too literal. Because it kind of killed all of the mystery of the smokiness of Mel's painting. So we dropped that plate. And another thing was working out the colors . . .

MB: This one was very complex in terms of the color.

CZ: But when it finally came together, it was great. It has all the subtleties to it. It comes and goes and has the depth that we were looking for.

EH: So you were saying earlier, Mel, about the cropping—that you decided to trim them to the plate, which is interesting to me because it reminds me of the Old Master print concept. Did you want to hide the evidence of how they were done—the intaglio platemark—or did you just want them to pop more?

MB: The whole tradition of the borders around prints is something that annoys me. It's a sort of self-framing, a signifier of importance. And it's always so arbitrary.

So we were debating, "Should it be two inches? Should it be two-and-a-half inches? Three? How about bigger, how about smaller?" And finally David [Lasry] said, "Why do we need margins at all? Because all of the other prints we had been making—the direct embossments—have no margins. And now just because we're making etchings we're sort of retreating back into that conventional printmaking format. So we tried tearing it down, and it worked.

EH: They're incredibly mysterious.

CZ: David's description of it was that they ceased to be "just etchings" and now they're objects. And once they're framed, they're like . . . wow! Something different.

EH: [*to MB and CZ:*] So are you pleased with how these came out? I mean, you've both been saying, "Oh, we could have done this, we could have done that . . . " In retrospect, Craig, are there things that you feel you should have or could have suggested to Mel that would have . . .

CZ: No, quite the contrary. I'm very pleased with how this whole project came out.

MB: Me too, and hopefully we'll do another project together. But I think that as a print develops through each stage, it develops its own momentum. And there is that moment when all of the different strands of possibilities lead to something inevitable, the "well, that's the way that it had to be." At the same time, when you go back and look at the progressive proofs, you see that you could have taken another path. That doesn't negate what you did, but it offers you a place to start again. You don't want to repeat what you've done before, but you have to start there. So you're always looking for clues. It's the "what if . . ." question: "What if we had done this, where would it have taken us?"

EH: Were there any new techniques here? Or things that happened that you didn't expect to happen?

CZ: I think realizations of how rugged the laser stencil could be and how it would hold up to just about anything we threw at it.

EH: Because you worked these plates, and worked them, and worked them . . .

CZ: Yes, and that's something that's just . . . ammunition. That's a new weapon in our arsenal for the future. That we know that we can do just about anything over this stencil. So that's something new that developed out of this, for me.

And for myself, as a printer, it is so great to have the opportunity to be a part of creating something with an artist—especially an artist of Mel's stature. After all these years, it is still so surprising to me that someone like Mel allows you in and actually respects and listens to what you're saying. So that in the end, when something like this suite is completed, when you ask me, "How do you feel about this?" I have a sort of pride, a bit of the feeling that it's my child too.

MB: And it is. For me that's one of the great pleasures of printmaking. Because every print is a collaborative effort. And it's kind of a relief—and a release—from the studio, where the responsibility is always on your shoulders. You have no one to ask, "Is there another way to do this?" Printmaking is a unique experience. Because every print always has more than one voice in it.

As for the laser, well, the laser permitted us to create a stencil very quickly—basically a template. It gave us a mechanical way to achieve what previously could only be done by hand and very slowly. That enabled me to move forward and follow a line of thinking more quickly. Because you want to be able to capitalize on your thoughts as you're having them. Before you forget them . . .

EH: Well, that reminds me of this great quote from Jasper Johns about that kind of time lapse in printmaking. Something he said, I think in the early seventies, to the effect that by the time he saw the results of one action, he had already decided on taking the work in a completely different direction.[4] Which for a period, he said, really frustrated him. And he described the whole printmaking operation as "like a long distance call from an overseas operator."[5] So it's sort of interesting that with the laser you found a quicker way of getting from point A to B so that you could go from point B to C . . .

MB: It's a kind of time compression, yes. The thing that was interesting to me and stimulating about this project was that the laser facilitated following a train of thought. That involved taking the content that I'm dealing with now in my work and submitting it to all these classical intaglio techniques—none of which was invented after 1850—and finding a way to make something new out of them.

EH: I wanted to end with a quote from Craig . . . something that Craig wrote to me: "When we first started to actually work on these etchings, I was struck by Mel's seasoned ability and grasp of all the techniques of etching. In fact, after a few sessions I found a kind of grace or happiness, because I did not have to instruct (which I do enjoy, don't get me wrong), but just make suggestions, or comply with Mel's ideas. It then, by the third plate in the series, developed into a kind of telepathic relationship. We just kind of knew what to do: how dark, how long to etch, what color, et cetera. That's a great place to be in collaboration. Mel really trusted what I would do, and I could trust Mel with going directly to the finish with a print, not floundering or becoming lost." [6]

CZ: I said *that*?

EH: You did. And what I particularly love about this statement are the two words "grace" and "telepathy."

MB: I like "floundering."

[*laughter*]

Notes

The preceding conversation was held on September 18, 2007, at Two Palms.

1. *Roget's Thesaurus of English Words and Phrases*, 150th anniversary edition (London: Penguin, 2002). As Bochner describes in the conversation in this chapter, between the mid-seventies and mid-nineties, his printmaking experiences were rather few and far between. That changed in 1993, when he re-encountered his former student from Yale University David Lasry and began to make prints more regularly when he started to work on Two Palms's vertical hydraulic press. Until he began to work with Zammiello, however, his prints were mainly monotypes and embossments.

2. "Mel Bochner in Conversation with James Meyer," in *Mel Bochner: Language, 1966–2006*, by Johanna Burton (Chicago: Art Institute of Chicago, 2007), 141.

3. "Art in Conversation: Mel Bochner with Phong Bui," *Brooklyn Rail* (May 2006): 17.

4. Calvin Tomkins, "Profiles: The Moods of a Stone," *New Yorker* (9 Aug. 1982): 66.

5. Quoted in Joseph E. Young, "Jasper Johns: An Appraisal," *Art International* (Sept. 1969): 52.

6. Email from Zammiello to Hodermarsky, Sept. 13, 2007.

acid resist. *See* resist

acrylic plate: The matrix that allows for the most accurate laser engraving.

Adobe Flash: A multimedia platform used to add animation and interactivity to webpages.

Adobe Photoshop: A raster-based image-editing program that works by manipulating each individual pixel.

Adobe Streamline: A line-tracing program (now discontinued) by Adobe Systems Inc. The software is a conversion tool for importing scanned black-and-white or color raster images into editable vector-based line art.

à la poupée: A color print made by inking separate areas of a plate with different colors by hand, using rolls of felt or cotton daubs, known as "dollies" (*poupées,* in French). Unlike multiple-plate color printing, the *à la poupée* technique avoids problems with registration.

airbrush aquatint: An alternative to the traditional rosin aquatint method. In this process, an airbrush is used to spray a varnish that is resistant to acid directly onto the plate. This method allows for the manipulation of tone, because the varnish can be controlled directly by the density of shading, with an effect much like traditional painting.

aquatint: An intaglio printing technique used to create tone. Particles of a granular acid-resistant material, traditionally rosin, are distributed over all or part of a metal plate. Heat is then applied so that the rosin melts and adheres to the metal. The plate is then immersed in acid, which etches the metal in the gaps around the grains of rosin, forming a fine network of hills and valleys, which, when inked and printed, gives the effect of a soft, tonal grain or wash. *See also* liquid aquatint

artist's proof: An impression of the finished work printed specifically for the artist. Such proofs are pulled in addition to the numbered, editioned copies.

asphaltum: A substance made of tar used as an acid resist in etching. Also known as bitumen.

ballground hard ground: A traditional hard ground that usually contains asphaltum, beeswax, and rosin and is applied by rolling it directly onto a heated plate with a small brayer, or roller. After cooling, the ground can be drawn on as is or smoked with tapers to darken the finish, allowing the artist to see the drawing more clearly. It is typically sold in the form of a small ball, giving it the name.

BAT (*bon à tirer***) proof:** The final trial proof that has been approved by the artist as "good to print" and is used as a reference in printing the entire edition.

burin: A steel tool used for engraving, to incise lines or dots into a matrix.

burnish: A process in which a steel tool, called a burnisher, is rubbed on the copper plate to lighten dark areas or correct errors and scratches by polishing the metal surface.

CCD (charge-coupled device) scanning: A technology for image capture employed in scanners in which optic sensors convert light (photons) into an electrical charge (electrons) that can then be digitally manipulated.

chine collé: The process of using a press to laminate paper or other collage material to a backing sheet while at the same time printing on it.

copper plate. *See* matrix

CorelDRAW: A vector-based image-editing software for professional-quality graphics illustration, page layout, digital-image editing, tracing, Web graphics, and animation.

CO_2 laser: A gas laser that produces a beam of infrared light that is used commercially for engraving applications in various materials.

deletion fluid: A solution of benzyl alcohol, 1-methoxy-2-propanol, and ammonium hydrogen difluoride that removes all traces of drawing (grease) on an aluminum lithographic plate.

digital print: A print created through a digital camera or scanner, or through computer software. The print can be displayed, printed, stored, manipulated, transmitted, and archived using digital and computer techniques, without chemical processing.

direct gravure: A process similar to the photogravure process but which creates an image without photographic film, utilizing a handcrafted image in place of a photographic one. The image is typically drawn or painted on a translucent material, such as Mylar, that allows ultraviolet light to pass through.

drypoint: An intaglio printing technique in which the artist draws directly on a copper plate without using acid. The design is scratched onto the plate with a sharp point (drypoint needle), thereby displacing the metal alongside the line produced. This deposit of metal (or burr) holds ink and results in a print with a soft, velvety quality.

edition: The number of prints created from a matrix at approximately the same time, signed and numbered by the artist. As a verb, *edition* refers to the act of formalizing this relationship between several prints.

engraving: An intaglio technique in which lines are incised through direct carving with a steel tool, called a burin, rather than with acid. When the burin is driven into the plate, a strip of metal is removed, creating a trough for ink. In a finished print, lines drawn by engraving possess a crisp, even quality and taper at both ends. *See also* laser engraving

Epson printer: A brand of inkjet printer that reproduces a digital image by pushing droplets of ink onto a page.

etching: An image printed from a metal plate that has been incised by acid. The process involves coating the plate with an acid-resistant ground, removing the ground with an etching needle by scratching through it to create the image design, and then submerging the plate in a bath of diluted acid. The unprotected areas of the plate are corroded, forming troughs for ink. In the final print, lines ranging from very fine and sketchy to thick and dark can be achieved depending on the duration of time in the acid bath.

hardground etching: An intaglio printing technique in which the artist applies a ground of beeswax or asphaltum (the hard ground) to the surface of a metal plate. Lines are then drawn through the ground with a sharp tool, such as an etching needle, and the plate is etched with acid. Hardground lines are usually thin, wiry, and blunt at the ends.

hydraulic press: A machine consisting of a cylinder fitted with a piston that uses liquid under pressure to exert vertical compressive force on a stationary baseplate. In printmaking this type of press can be used to create embossment, to adhere images to the matrix, or to print intaglio, relief, or monotype.

intaglio printing: All metal-plate processes, including engraving, drypoint, and etching. Grooves are created within a matrix, then ink is forced into these grooves and transferred to paper with the aid of a printing press. Besides intaglio, the other three classes of printmaking are relief, stencil, and planographic.

laser engraving: An engraving method in which a laser machine is used to trace onto a planar surface patterns that are programmed into its computer (either in vector or raster modes). Since the process is computerized, drawings can be scanned, digitized, or even created using a computer and then engraved onto the matrix.

linoleum cut (linocut): A relief print cut in linoleum with a V-shaped chisel. Ink is applied to the surface of the linoleum, which is then impressed onto paper or fabric by hand or with a press. Linoleum-cut lines are usually more fluid than woodcut, due to the softness of material and lack of grain.

liquid aquatint: An aquatint using a form of rosin that is suspended in a liquid mixture of sugar and alcohol, usually cognac, which is painted on the bare plate surface and dried. As it dries, unique patterns are formed by the rosin. These are evident when the plate is etched, as it takes time for different areas to break down in the mordant, or acid.

lithography: A planographic method of printmaking based on the antipathy of oil and water. A greasy substance, typically grease crayon or wash (known as tusche), is used to draw on a lithographic stone or aluminum plate whose surface is then chemically treated and wetted with water. When applied to the stone, grease-based ink is attracted to the greased areas and, because water repels grease, is repelled by those areas that are wet. Lithography is perhaps the most painterly and autographic of printmaking techniques, achieving effects similar to drawing or paint on canvas.

matrix: The plate, stone, block, or other object on which an artist creates a design for a print. When the matrix is inked and put into contact with paper, a print is produced.

matte medium: An acrylic medium used to extend color, increase translucency, and decrease gloss.

mezzotint: A tonal technique of printmaking in which the entire printing plate is roughened by a curved, serrated tool called a mezzotint rocker. If the plate were to be inked and printed after this roughening process, it would produce an entirely black print. To obtain an image, the artist scrapes away the roughened areas. The surface retains ink according to the degree of roughness in any area; the image produced is one of light tones on a dark ground.

monoprint: A variation of monotype in which there is a partial matrix. After the matrix is inked and wiped, the artist adds nonrepeatable marks, and the matrix is then printed in a single pass through the press.

monotype: A process in which ink or paint is applied by hand to a flat, unworked surface. The printing of the image onto the sheet is achieved either by manual pressure or by a printing press. Each print produced is unique since there is no matrix to hold ink. Monotype impressions are characterized by their painterly and textured surfaces.

Mylar stencil: A sheet of plastic on which a design has been cut so that ink applied to the sheet will reproduce the pattern on the surface beneath it when printed.

offset lithography: A printmaking process in which a design applied to a lithographic stone or plate is picked up by a rubber roller. The roller is then rolled over a piece of paper to produce the print. Since the original image has been reversed twice in the process, it prints the right way round.

open bite: An etching technique in which acid is applied directly onto bare portions of the plate.

Pantone Matching System: A system by which specific colors can be matched regardless of the equipment used to produce the color. Pantone colors are reproduced from a set of fifteen base colors mixed in amounts specified in Pantone's color-swatch books. Pantone colors can also be approximated on computer screens, and matched using the four-color printing process, a method of printing the entire spectrum with four primary inks—cyan, magenta, yellow, and black (CMYK).

photogravure: A photomechanical method of applying an image to a copper plate using a light-sensitive gelatin mounted on paper, commonly called carbon tissue. After exposure to ultraviolet light, the carbon tissue adheres to the plate and dries, and then the plate is processed to remove all unhardened gelatin, leaving a gelatin resist on the plate surface. The plate is then etched in a series of ferric chloride baths, inked, and printed in the same manner as an intaglio plate.

planographic: A printmaking method, typically lithography, in which the image is printed from a single stone or plate that has been treated chemically so some areas hold ink and others refuse it.

plate. *See matrix*

pochoir: A method of adding color through a stencil.

portfolio: A set of prints typically of uniform format and size housed in a folder or box specifically designed for their presentation.

printer's proof: An impression of the finished work printed specifically for the printer who worked on the edition. Such proofs are pulled in addition to the numbered, editioned copies.

process blue: The blue from the four-color printing process used in offset lithography, also known as CMYK (cyan, magenta, yellow, and black), in which all colors are produced by a mixture of these four base colors. *Process blue, process red,* and *process yellow* are colloquial terms for the cyan, magenta, and yellow used in this process.

progressive proofs: Proofs made to provide a sequential record of the final printing. Proofs are pulled singly from each color plate and also in combination with each succeeding color. The final proof shows the finished color reproduction.

proof: A test print made during the printmaking process to monitor progress. *See also* artist's proof; BAT (*bon à tirer*) proof; printer's proof

raster graphics file format (bitmap): A data structure representing a grid of colored pixels viewable by a monitor, paper, or other display medium. The raster image size is based on the resolution (dots per inch) and the physical size of the image, and unlike a vector file graphic image it cannot be easily rescaled.

relief printing: One of the four basic printmaking methods in which the design to be inked is raised rather than incised. The process is found in woodcuts, linocuts, hand-set type, and rubber stamps, among other forms.

resist: A hard or soft ground applied to the metal plate during the etching process. Areas of the metal plate that are exposed by removing the ground are bitten or etched when treated with acid.

rosin: A translucent, amber-colored resin obtained from pine trees and pulverized into powder to be used in the aquatint process as an acid-resistant ground.

roulette: An engraving tool with a fine-toothed wheel that produces dotted lines when worked over a copper plate.

screenprint (silkscreen): A printmaking technique in which the design is imposed either manually or photochemically on a porous mesh stretched on a frame. Ink is forced through the fine-mesh openings onto the paper below using a squeegee that is drawn across the screen. Also known as a serigraph.

softground etching: A process that produces the effect of lines drawn with a soft pencil or chalk. An acid-resistant coating made of asphaltam, rosin, beeswax, and tallow is spread evenly over a heated copper plate. The design is then drawn onto paper laid over the cooled plate. The soft ground yields under pressure, revealing the plate for etching in the incised areas when the paper is lifted off the plate.

solvent-lift ground: A process that involves painting on top of a conventional hard ground with a substance traditionally made by mixing a mild, oily solvent, such as lithotine, with magnesium carbonate to achieve a paintlike consistency. This application is left to sit for a short period of time and then is wiped away with a soft towel in a quick motion. Afterward the plate is wiped again with cotton soaked in denatured alcohol, removing the hard ground with it and exposing the plate for open bite or aquatint.

spit bite: A process that involves painting acid directly over a prepared aquatint surface to create tones similar to a watercolor wash. Its name derives from the act of putting saliva into the mix to break the surface tension of the acid on the plate, thus preventing beading. Nowadays Kodak Photo-flo or soap is used.

state: Changes to the print matrix recorded in a proof.

steel facing: A technique wherein a thin layer of iron is electroplated onto a copper plate, both to protect the surface from oxidation and wear—thereby lengthening the printing life of the plate—and also for technical reasons, including the preservation of color pigments that can chemically react with the copper, changing the intended color. It also facilitates the wiping of the plate in preparation before printing.

sugar lift: A process used to etch a positive image onto the metal plate. A solution of sugar and black ink is painted onto the surface of the plate, which is then coated with an acid-resistant varnish. When placed in a bath of warm water, the sugar melts, lifting away the varnish where the sugar mixture was painted. The area can either be open bit or aquatinted to create a tone.

tarlatan: A heavily starched, sheer cotton fabric, similar to cheesecloth, that is used for wiping intaglio plates.

tattoo-machine engraving: A method of engraving using a handheld device traditionally used to create a tattoo. The machine uses alternating electromagnetic coils to move a needle bar back and forth, driving the needle tip into the matrix.

toluene: A common solvent used to dissolve printing ink, varnish, and grounds.

trial proof: An impression of the work made during the printmaking process to ascertain the progress of artwork.

vector file: A graphic file used in programs such as CorelDRAW and Adobe Illustrator so that images can be easily scaled and colors can be easily changed without distorting the integrity of the source image.

vertical pressure press. See hydraulic press

Wacom drawing tablet: A tool for artists who would rather draw with a pen than use a mouse to create cartoons and animations. This device is compatible with Adobe Photoshop, Illustrator, and Flash, as well as many other programs.

woodcut (woodblock) printing: A relief-printmaking technique in which the image is cut into wooden blocks and ink is applied to the top surface.

Xerox transfer: A method in which a typical Xerox printout is transferred to a printing matrix, such as a copper plate, or lithography plate or stone, by the use of various solvents. The material that is transferred is comprised of melted plastic, both an acid resist and an attractant for lacquer, or varnish in the case of lithography.

Mel Bochner

Mel Bochner was born in Pittsburgh in 1940. He received his B.F.A. in painting from the Carnegie Institute of Technology, also in Pittsburgh, in 1962. He currently lives and works in New York.

One of the pioneering Conceptual artists to emerge during the 1960s and 1970s, Bochner created word-drawings and experimented with number systems in his early work. Like many artists at this time, Bochner was reacting against the automatic gesture and improvisation of Abstract Expressionism. His installations and drawings, influenced by the analytic philosophy of Ludwig Wittgenstein, instead examine the ordered structure of mathematics and language, in addition to exploring visual perception. Bochner also played a principle role in theorizing Minimalism, particularly in his review of the Jewish Museum's exhibition *Primary Structures* of 1966. In that same year, Bochner curated the exhibition *Working Drawings and Other Visible Things on Paper Not Necessarily Meant to Be Viewed as Art* at the School of Visual Arts Gallery, which is regarded as one of the first conceptual art exhibitions. In recent years, Bochner's analytic and formal interests have been articulated in two public art projects: *The Joys of Yiddish*, at the Spertus Institute, in Chicago (2006), and *Kraus Campo*, at Carnegie Mellon University, in Pittsburgh (2005).

Bochner has been included in a number of solo and group exhibitions, including *Live/Work: Performance into Drawing*, at the Museum of Modern Art in New York (2007); *Open Systems: Rethinking Art* c. 1970, at the Tate Modern, in London (2005); and *Thought Made Visible: 1966–1973*, at the Yale University Art Gallery, in New Haven, Connecticut (1995). He was included in the Whitney Biennial in 2004, 1979, and 1977. Bochner made his first prints at Crown Point Press in 1973. His conceptually oriented prints have been featured in numerous exhibitions since then, including *Printmaking in America: 1960–1990*, at the Block Gallery at Northwestern University, in Evanston, Illinois (1995); *Marking the Decades: Prints 1960–1990*, at the Baltimore Museum of Art (1992); *The Unique Print*, at the Museum of Fine Arts, Boston (1990); *Projects and Portfolios: The Twenty-Fifth National Print Exhibition*, at the Brooklyn Museum (1989); and *Prints by Contemporary Sculptors*, at the Yale University Art Gallery (1982).

Bochner received an honorary doctorate of fine arts in 2005 from the School of Art at Carnegie Mellon University.

Beginning in 1965 he wrote art reviews for *Arts Magazine*, which, along with his theoretical texts and interviews, were published by the MIT Press in 2008 as *Solar System and Rest Rooms: Writings and Interviews, 1965–2007*. He has taught at the Yale School of Art, in New Haven, Connecticut, and the School of Visual Arts in New York. His work is included in major museum collections including the Metropolitan Museum of Art, the Art Institute of Chicago, and the Smithsonian American Art Museum. He is represented by Peter Freeman, Inc., in New York and Marc Selwyn Fine Art in Los Angeles.

Carroll Dunham

Carroll Dunham was born in New Haven, Connecticut, in 1949. He received his B.A. from Trinity College in Hartford, Connecticut, in 1972, and currently lives and works in New York and Connecticut.

Arriving in New York in the early 1970s at the peak of Minimalism and Process Art, Dunham eschewed the literalism of those movements in favor of automatism balanced by formal operations. By the mid-1980s, Dunham was known for his boldly colored, semi-abstract paintings on wood veneer. Since then, his vigorous, calligraphic line has moved between abstraction and figuration, inflected by a comically violent and often erotic sensibility. Whether paintings, drawings, or prints, Dunham's works are frequently described as explosive and expressive, which is likely a result of his innate sensitivity to the distinct attributes of each medium.

Dunham began creating prints in 1984 at Universal Limited Art Editions. Since then he has worked with a wide range of printmaking techniques, from traditional intaglio to screenprint to digital media, and has collaborated with numerous presses, including Grenfell Press, Two Palms, and Pace Editions, all in New York. Printmaking is an integral part of the way he thinks about art. Exploiting both the exacting nature of the printmaking process and the spontaneous, chance procedures that commonly result, Dunham is one of the most prolific and invested printmakers of his generation. His printed oeuvre received critical attention in the retrospective exhibition *Carroll Dunham Prints: A Survey*, organized by the Addison Gallery of American Art, in Andover, Massachusetts. He has also had numerous solo and group exhibitions of his paintings and drawings in the United States and abroad. Some of his most recent exhibitions include *Carroll Dunham Paintings*, at the Gladstone Gallery, New York (2009); *Paintings on Wood 1982–1987*, at the Skarstedt Gallery, in New York (2008); *Small Drawings*, at the Drammens Museum, in Norway; and *Urgent Painting*, at the Musée d'Art Moderne de la Ville de Paris (2002). In 2002 the New Museum of Contemporary Art, in New York, organized the first retrospective of Dunham's work. He was included in the Whitney Biennial in 1995, 1991, and 1985 and in Disparities and Deformations: Our Grotesque, SITE Santa Fe's fifth international biennial.

Dunham received the 2004 Skowhegan Medal for Distinction in Painting. Since 2001 Dunham has been a senior critic in painting at the Yale School of Art, in New Haven, Connecticut, and has taught painting at Columbia University, in New York. He is also a contributing writer to the magazine *Artforum*. His work is included in the collections of the Metropolitan Museum of Art; the Museum of Modern Art, New York; the Albertina Museum, in Vienna; the Tate Collection, England; and the Yale University Art Gallery, in New Haven, Connecticut, among other public and private collections. Dunham is represented by Gladston Gallery and David Nolan Gallery, both in New York.

Ellen Gallagher

Ellen Gallagher was born in Providence, Rhode Island, in 1965. She attended Oberlin College, in Ohio, from 1982 to 1984 and studied art in 1992 at the School of the Museum of Fine Arts, in Boston, and in 1993 at the Skowhegan School of Art, in Madison, Maine. Gallagher lives and works in Rotterdam, the Netherlands, and New York.

Gallagher builds her images from fragments of the past in order to recover lost narratives, specifically those related to the female, African American experience. She appropriates advertisements for hairstyling, skin-lightening, and feminine hygiene products from African American magazines dating from the 1930s through the 1970s, such as *Ebony*, *Our World*, and *Sepia*, yet alters them through handmade, labor-intensive processes, such as whiting out eyes, cutting out hair, and applying Plasticine clay and googly eyes. Gallagher employs a variety of formal devices—repetition, accumulation, grid structures, and fragmentation—that underscore her concerns with history, memory, and identity. Besides painting, drawing, and printmaking, Gallagher also creates sculpture and film. Most recently she has collaborated with the Dutch artist Edgar Cleijne on a number of environmental installations that feature 16 mm film and painted glass slide projections.

Since her first New York solo exhibition at the Mary Boone Gallery in 1996, Gallagher has had solo exhibitions in the United States and abroad, including *An Experiment of Unusual Opportunity*, at South London Gallery (2009); *Coral Cities*, at the Tate Liverpool (2007); and *Deluxe*, at the Whitney Museum of American Art, in New York (2005). Her work has been included in the Whitney Biennial (2010 and 1995); SITE Santa Fe's fifth international biennial, *Disparities and Deformations: Our Grotesque* (2004); and the Venice Biennale (2003). In 2005 Art21 featured Gallagher on the television series *Art in the Twenty-First Century*.

Gallagher has received several awards and fellowships throughout her career, including the American Academy Award in Art in 2000 and the Joan Mitchell Fellowship in 1997. Her work is included in public and private collections throughout the world, including the Broad Art Foundation, in Los Angeles; the Whitney Museum of American Art; and the Museum of Fine Arts. She is represented by the Gagosian Gallery in New York and Hauser and Wirth in London.

Jane Hammond

Jane Hammond was born in Bridgeport, Connecticut, in 1950. She earned her B.A. from Mount Holyoke College, in South Hadley, Massachusetts, and her M.F.A. from the University of Wisconsin, Madison. She currently lives and works in New York.

Operating with a fixed lexicon of 276 subjects—mined from magazines, board games, maps, science manuals, children's books, and the Internet, among other sources—Hammond combines and recombines imagery in her work, blurring the line between fact and fiction. By exploring the relationship between pictures and language through this menagerie of visual information, Hammond's images produce mental associations, often functioning along the lines of narrative.

Trained as a sculptor, Hammond now works primarily in two-dimensional media: painting, drawing, printmaking, and, most recently, photography. Hammond's first printmaking project resulted from a printmaking grant she received while teaching at the Maryland Institute College of Art, in Baltimore. She now collaborates with a variety of professional presses including Universal Limited Art Editions and Pace Editions in New York and Shark's Ink in Lyons, Colorado. The recombination and repeatability of images inherent in printmaking has played a key role in the development of her work within a fixed lexicon. Her paintings and drawing often include printed elements through the employment of rubber stamps, Xerox transfers, and linoleum block prints, among other printmaking techniques.

Hammond received her first solo exhibition at Exit Art, in New York, in 1989. Since then, she has had numerous such exhibitions, both nationally and abroad, and has been included in important thematic exhibitions including *Conjuring Houdini*, at the Jewish Museum, in New York (2010); *On the Margins*, at the Mildren Lane Kemper Art Museum, in St. Louis (2008); *Digital Printmaking Now*, at the Brooklyn Museum (2001); and *Picturing the Modern Amazon*, at the New Museum of Contemporary Art, in New York (2000). In 2006 the Mount Holyoke College Museum of Art organized *Jane Hammond: Paperwork*, a survey of her work on paper that has traveled throughout the United States. Her war memorial *Fallen* (2004–present), created with more than four thousand unique reproductions of leaves, each of which bears the name of a soldier killed in Iraq inscribed by the artist, has received critical attention and has toured museums nationally.

Hammond is the recipient of several distinguished awards, including the Joan Mitchell Foundation Award (2000), a National Endowment for the Arts Individual Fellowship in Painting (1989), and an Andrew W. Mellon Foundation Grant (1986). From 1980 to 1990, she taught sculpture at the Maryland Institute College of Art and was an artist-in-residence at the Skowhegan School of Painting and Sculpture, in Madison, Maine, in 1992. Her work can be found in several major public collections, including

the Metropolitan Museum of Art, the Detroit Institute of Arts, the Seattle Art Museum, and the Museum of Contemporary Art in San Diego. Hammond is represented by Galerie Lelong in New York.

Suzanne McClelland

Suzanne McClelland was born in Jacksonville, Florida, in 1959. She received her B.F.A. from the University of Michigan in 1981 and her M.F.A. from the School of Visual Arts in New York in 1989. McClelland lives and works in New York.

McClelland creates large-scale, gestural abstractions based on sound and the spoken word. She explores the multiple meanings of words, especially everyday language such as "forever," "more," "now," "would," "could," or "right," and overheard fragments of speech, such as "just relax" or "mama's boy," by manipulating their physical appearance through paint and other nontraditional materials. Her word-based compositions often have underlying political or social messages, and convey, as Roberta Smith has suggested, "a sensibility that is both feminine and feminist." While McClelland is best known for these large-scale paintings, she has also created a significant body of graphic work. The artist has made editioned prints and monotypes with presses including Universal Limited Art Editions and Two Palms. Her 2007 work STrAY consists of twelve portfolios containing drawings, photographs, and inkjet prints based on epistolary poems by George Garrett that draw from actual letters by two of the artist's relatives who were Civil War soldiers on opposing sides.

Among several gallery and museum shows, McClelland has had major solo exhibitions at the Orlando Museum of Art (2001), the Weatherspoon Art Gallery, at the University of North Carolina, Greensboro (1997), and the Whitney Museum of American Art at Phillip Morris, in New York (1992).

McClelland has received numerous awards and grants, including the Nancy Graves Grant for Visual Arts and the AXA Artist Award, both in 2006. She was also awarded a Pollock-Krasner Foundation grant in 2001. Since 2007 she has been a visiting professor at the Pratt Institute, in Brooklyn, and has been a faculty member of the School for Visual Arts in New York since 1997. Her work can be found in several major public collections, including the Brooklyn Museum, the Museum of Modern Art, and

the Whitney Museum of American Art, all in New York; the Walker
Art Center, in Minneapolis; the Grunwald Center for the Graphic
Arts at the Hammer Museum of the University of California, Los
Angeles; and the Museum of Art, Rhode Island School of Design,
in Providence, Rhode Island. McClelland is represented by Sue
Scott Gallery in New York.

Chris Ofili

Chris Ofili was born in Manchester, England, in 1968. He received
his B.A. in fine art in 1991 from the Chelsea School of Art and his
M.F.A. in fine art in 1993 from the Royal College of Art, both in
London. Ofili lives and works in Trinidad.

Ofili's paintings are concerned with issues of black
identity. His works from the 1990s, which were profoundly
influenced by his travels to Zimbabwe, have often been noted
for their ability to synthesize the incompatible. They are technically complex and meticulously executed, yet the richly colored
paint is peppered with nontraditional art materials such as
glitter, magazine cutouts, map pins, and elephant dung—indeed,
biblical and pornographic imagery often vie for space on the
canvas—and they are seemingly abstract, figurative, and deco-
rative at the same time. Formally and conceptually, this work
shares a dialogue with that of a range of artists including David
Hammons, William Blake, Philip Guston, Auguste Rodin, and
Jean-Michel Basquiat. After moving from London to Trinidad in
2004, a notable shift occurred in Ofili's art. He stopped using
elephant dung, his palette darkened, and overall his surfaces
became more nuanced, perhaps in response to the change in his
natural surroundings. Nevertheless, throughout his career he has
employed humor to undermine racial stereotypes.

Ofili has had solo exhibitions at the Studio Museum in
Harlem; the Kestnergesellschaft, in Hanover, Germany; the
Whitworth Art Gallery, in Manchester, England; and South-
ampton City Art Gallery, in England. In 2010 London's Tate
Britain organized the first traveling retrospective of his work.
He has also been included in a number of important thematic
exhibitions, most notably *Sensation: Young British Artists
from the Saatchi Collection* (1997), which opened at the Royal
Academy of Art in London and later traveled to the Brooklyn
Museum and the Hamburger Bahnhof, in Berlin. Ofili's prints
have been included in *The Compulsive Line: Etching 1990 to
Now*, at the Museum of Modern Art in New York (2006); *Prints
Now: Directions and Definitions*, at the Victoria and Albert
Museum, in London (2006); *Borderless Print* at the Rochdale Art
Gallery, in London (1993); and the Tokyo Print Biennial (1993),
where he won second prize. Ofili represented Britain in the
fiftieth Venice Biennale, in 2003.

In 2004 Ofili received an honorary fellowship from the
University of the Arts in London and the South Bank Show Award
in Visual Arts. He was awarded the distinguished Turner Prize in
1998 by the Tate Gallery in London and the Wingate Young Artist
Award in 1996. His work is in the permanent collections of the
Museum of Modern Art in New York, the British Museum, the San
Francisco Museum of Modern Art, and the Carnegie Museum
of Art, in Pittsburg, among others. Ofili is represented by David
Zwirner in New York and Victoria Miro in London.

Elizabeth Peyton

Elizabeth Peyton was born in Danbury, Connecticut, in 1965. In
1987 she received her B.F.A. from the School of Visual Arts in New
York, where she currently lives and works.

The artist is known for her small-scale yet lushly
painted and richly colored portraits of historical figures, such as
Napoléon Bonaparte and Ludwig II of Bavaria, and of contemporary cultural icons, including Kurt Cobain and Prince William,
as well as of her most intimate friends. While portraiture is one
of the oldest painting practices, Peyton has been widely credited
with bringing figurative painting to the center of the contemporary art discourse at a time when conceptualism was the
mainstream movement.

Peyton made her first prints at Derrière L'Étoile Studios,
in New York, in 1998, and for the past several years she has been
creating monotypes, woodcuts, and etchings at Two Palms. A
solo exhibition of her prints was organized by Guild Hall in East
Hampton in 2006. As is typically the case with her paintings,
Peyton's graphic work is based on photographs that she found or
took herself. Their cropping and angles lend an informality and
heightened sense of realism to her finished pieces.

The artist's first solo exhibition was held in New York at
the Althea Viafora Gallery in 1987. Since then she has had solo

exhibitions in the United States and abroad, including exhibitions at the Aldrich Contemporary Art Museum in Ridgefield, Connecticut (2008); the Royal Academy of Arts, in London (2002); and the Castello di Rivoli Museum of Contemporary Art, in Turin, Italy (1999). In 2008 the New Museum, in New York, organized a mid-career survey of her work, *Live Forever: Elizabeth Peyton*, which traveled to the Walker Art Center, in Minneapolis; the Whitechapel Gallery, in London; and the Bonnefantenmuseum, in Maastricht, the Netherlands. She was included in the Whitney Biennial in 2004 and was featured in *Drawing Now: Eight Propositions* (2002) and *Projects Sixty: John Currin, Elizabeth Peyton, Luc Tuymans* (1997), both at the Museum of Modern Art, New York.

In 2006 Peyton received the Larry Aldrich Award. Her work can be found in several major public collections, including those of the Museum of Modern Art, New York; the Kunstmuseum Wolfsburg, in Germany; the Seattle Art Museum; and the Centre Pompidou, in Paris. Peyton is represented by Gavin Brown's Enterprise in New York and Regen Projects in Los Angeles.

Matthew Ritchie

Matthew Ritchie was born in London in 1964. He received his B.F.A in 1986 from the Camberwell School of Art, in London. Ritchie lives and works in New York.

Drawing from science, theology, history, and philosophy, Ritchie employs the language of art to illustrate his personal creation myth in which everything happens at once in a continuum of space and time. His narrative, which includes forty-nine characters based on chemical, physical, or metaphorical properties, has been carried out in a series of chapters, or exhibitions, that consist of paintings, sculpture, drawing, and video. Ritchie employs this large-scale, multimedia format in a manner that creates the effect of cross-sections in order to convey the whole narrative picture. At times Ritchie inserts interactive features taken from video games, such as a joystick, allowing viewers to determine the projection of the narrative. Drawing is central to Ritchie's creative practice. Using these handmade images as his starting point, Ritchie often scans his drawings in order to digitally manipulate them, altering their scale, transforming them into sculpture or video, or layering one image over another.

Ritchie was included in the highly regarded *Drawing Now: Eight Propositions* at the Museum of Modern Art in New York (2002). His work was also exhibited at the International Biennial of Contemporary Art of Seville (2008), the Venice Architecture Biennale (2008), the São Paolo Biennial (2004), the Biennale of Sydney (2002), and the Whitney Biennial (1997). Ritchie has created permanent installations for the Massachusetts Institute of Technology, in Cambridge; the Shiodome City Center, in Tokyo; and the Wayne Lyman Morse United States Courthouse, in Eugene, Oregon. Ritchie has also produced web projects for the Walker Art Center, in Minneapolis; the San Francisco Museum of Art; and the Massachusetts Institute of Technology. In 2009 the artist wrote and directed a multimedia musical work, *The Long Count*, in collaboration with Bryce Dressner and Aaron Dressner for the New Wave Festival at the Brooklyn Academy of Music.

Additionally Ritchie has curated a number of exhibitions, including *Demonclownmonkey* at Artists Space, in New York (2002). His critical writings have been published in *Flash Art*, *Zing Magazine*, and elsewhere, and in 2005 Art 21 featured him on its third season of *Art in the Twenty-First Century*. His work is in the collections of the Museum of Modern Art in New York; the Massachusetts Museum of Contemporary Art, in North Adams; the Indianapolis Museum of Art; and the Goetz Collection in Munich, among other notable institutions. Ritchie is represented by Andrea Rosen Gallery in New York.

Kiki Smith

Kiki Smith was born in Nuremberg in 1954 and grew up in New Jersey. She attended the Hartford Art School, in Connecticut, from 1974 to 1976. Smith lives and works in New York.

Emerging in the 1980s at the height of gender and identity politics, Smith's early casts of hearts, wombs, and pelvises in various pliable materials such as beeswax and plaster focused on the abject body, evoking a sense of loss and trauma. As Helaine Posner has stated, Smith has revalidated the body as subject matter. Her unconventional depictions of women, moreover, have redefined the image of the female body in art. In recent years, Smith has expanded her representation of the female form to include mythology, religion, folklore, and nature. Whether working in bronze, plaster, or paper, Smith is inventive in her use of materials, and continues to seek out other methods that will afford her new possibilities. Most recently, Smith has begun to work in glass, collaborating with Steuben Glass on a collection of engraved pieces and creating a stained-glass window for the Eldridge Street Synagogue on the Lower East Side of Manhattan. Smith is also a prolific printmaker. Her printed oeuvre contains over 150 prints, books, and multiples, and the printmaking process is an integral component of her sculpture and drawing. She collaborates with professional presses such as Universal Limited Art Editions, Pace Editions, and Harlan and Weaver, all in New York, as well as with a host of smaller not-for-profit presses. She also publishes under her own imprint, Thirteen Moons.

In 2003 the Museum of Modern Art in New York organized the first retrospective of the artist's printed work, *Kiki Smith: Prints, Books, and Things*, and in 2005 the San Francisco Museum of Art organized a traveling retrospective of her painting and sculpture: *Kiki Smith: A Gathering*. Smith has also been included in a number of important group exhibitions, including the Whitney Biennial, in New York (1991, 1993, and 2002); Documenta 7, in Kassel, Germany (1982); and *Times Square Show*, at Collaborative Projects in New York (1980).

Smith received the fiftieth Edward MacDowell Medal from the MacDowell Colony in 2009; the Medal Award from the School of the Museum of Fine Arts, in Boston, in 2006; the Athena Award for Excellence in Printmaking from the Rhode Island School of Design in 2005; and the Skowhegan Medal for Sculpture in 2000. In 2006 she was awarded an honorary degree from Bowdoin College in Maine, and in 2005 she was elected to the American Academy of Arts and Letters in New York. Her work has been collected extensively by public collections both nationally and internationally, including the Metropolitan Museum of Art, and the Museum of Modern Art in New York; the Art Institute of Chicago; the Museum of Modern and Contemporary Art, in Trento, Italy; the Israel Museum, in Jerusalem; the Walker Art Center, in Minneapolis; and the Tate Collection, in England.

Smith has taught printmaking at the LeRoy Neiman Center for Print Studies at Columbia University, in New York; New York University; and Temple University, in Philadelphia. She has also taught at the Pilchuck Glass School, in Seattle. Smith is represented by the Pace Gallery, in New York.

Terry Winters
Terry Winters was born in Brooklyn in 1949. He earned his B.F.A. from Pratt Institute, in Brooklyn, in 1971. Winters currently lives and works in New York.

Since the 1980s Winters has created abstractions that are informed by his interest in biological forms, architecture, knot theory, and, most recently, information systems and digital technology. In respecifying existing imagery through the painting process, Winters opens up the possibility for multiple interpretations. He works equally in painting, drawing, and printmaking, with each medium often informing the others. Winters made his first prints in 1982 at Universal Limited Art Editions. Since then he has worked almost continuously, collaborating with various prints shops, including Solo Press, the LeRoy Neiman Center for Print Studies at Columbia University, Peter Blume Editions, Grenfell Press, and Two Palms, all in New York. Winters has long been interested in the connection between process and picture-making; thus, the systematic procedures, materials, and the opportunity for varied mark-making have drawn him to printmaking. Like his paintings and drawings, the surface of his prints have a lush materiality. His other projects include costume and set designs for the Merce Cunningham Dance Company and Trisha Brown Dance Company. In 2001 he collaborated with architect Rem Koolhaas on a site-specific installation at the Lehmann Maupin Gallery, in New York.

Winters has been widely recognized in exhibitions in the United States and Europe. His first solo exhibition was at the Sonnabend Gallery, in New York, in 1982. Since that time he has had solo exhibitions at the Irish Museum of Modern Art, in Dublin (2009); the San Jose Museum of Art, in California (2005); the Victoria and Albert Museum, in London (1998); and the Milwaukee Art Museum (1989), among other prominent institutions. The Detroit Institute of Art and the Metropolitan Museum of Art organized retrospective exhibitions of the artist's printed work in 1999 and 2001, respectively. His prints have also been included in a number of important group exhibitions, including *Artists and Prints: Part Three*, at the Museum of Modern Art in New York (2005); *Sets, Series, and Suites: Contemporary Prints*, at the Museum of Fine Arts, in Boston (2005); *Hard Pressed/Six Hundred Years of Prints and Process*, at the AXA Gallery, in New York

(2000); *Proof Positive: Forty Years of Contemporary American Printmaking at ULAE, 1957–1997,* at the Corcoran Gallery of Art, in Washington, D.C. (1997); *Postmodern Prints,* at the Victoria and Albert Museum, in London (1991); and *American Print Renaissance 1958–1988,* at the Whitney Museum of American Art, in New York (1988).

Winters received the Rosenthal Family Foundation Award in painting in 1982. His works are in many public institutions and collections, including the Metropolitan Museum of Art; the Museum of Fine Arts in Houston; Harvard University Art Museums, in Cambridge, Massachusetts; and the Reina Sofia National Museum, in Madrid, among others. Winters is represented by Matthew Marks Gallery in New York.

Index

of, 38–39; collaboration with B. Goldston of, 38, 46, 50; collaboration with Lund of, 38–40, 46; collaboration with Zammiello of, 39–40, 50; *Developmental Surface Model*, 41; direct-gravure use by, 40–42; early printmaking of, 38–41, 43–44, 53n.4; on editioned work, 51; *Face Boundary*, 41–42; *Folio*, 43–44; *Fourteen Etchings*, 39–40, 42, 53n.4; influence on Smith of, 27; *Monoprint/7*, 51; monotypes of, 51; *Multiple Visualization Technique*, 45; *Picture Cell*, 41; portfolios of, 40, 42–43; presses used by, 49; *Station*, 38–39; sugar lift use by, 44, 53n.9; suite of single-plate large etchings of, 41–44; *Systems Diagram*, 41, 44; at Two Palms, 49, 51; at ULAE, 38, 49–51; X-rays used by, 40. See also *Internal and External Values*

"With God on Our Side" (Dylan), 201–2

woodcut (woodblock) printing, 106–7; defined, 240

World Trade Center (Ofili), 198–99

Worm (Smith), 29–30

X

Xerox transfer, 168–70; defined, 240

X-rays, 95n.8; Hammond's use of, 79, 83–84, 95n.15; Winters's use of, 40

Z

Zammiello, Craig: airbrush techniques of, 37, 41–42, 48, 107; on the artist-printer relationship, 67, 73–75, 145–46; collaboration with Bochner of, 215, 220–35; collaboration with Dunham of, 127–32, 136–40, 144–47; collaboration with Gallagher of, 167, 171–84, 193n.2; collaboration with Hammond of, 79, 90, 95n.1, 95n.11; collaboration with McClelland of, 58–59, 61, 68–69, 72–73, 75n.3, 75n.7; collaboration with Ofili of, 197, 199–201, 203, 207–8, 211; collaboration with Peyton of, 153, 155; collaboration with Ritchie of, 104–5, 113–16, 122; collaboration with Smith of, 15–17, 28–29, 33n.5, 70; collaboration with Winters of, 39–40, 50; CO_2 laser etching by, 99, 105–8, 123n.6; direct-gravure work of, 40–42, 136, 145; etching tools of, 200, 208–9; hired by Lasry, 99, 218; innovations with Prussian blue of, 37, 46, 53n.8; photogravure work of, 131–32, 134–35; on pure etching, 197, 203–5; tattoo-engraving technique of, 176–77, 193n.7; tattoos of, 91–93

010101: Art in Technological Times (exh.), 101, 123n.1

Zig Zag (McClelland), 66–67

Credits

Tatyana Grosman: Photograph by C. Zammiello. Courtesy Universal Limited Art Editions: p. 5

Elizabeth Murray: Photograph by Lorena Salcedo-Watson. Courtesy Universal Limited Art Editions: p. 5

Robert Rauschenberg: Photograph by Elizabeth Zammiello, 1995: p. 5

Kiki Smith
© Kiki Smith/Universal Limited Art Editions, 1995. Photograph courtesy Universal Limited Art Editions: pp. 12–13 (detail), fig. 1; p. 14, fig. 1

© Kiki Smith, courtesy The Pace Gallery; Photograph by Ellen Page Wilson, courtesy The Pace Gallery: p. 17, fig. 2

Photograph by C. Zammiello: p. 18, fig. 3; p. 20, fig. 4

Photograph by C. Zammiello. Courtesy Universal Limited Art Editions: pp. 22–23, fig. 5

Photograph by Ivor Kerslake. Courtesy Universal Limited Art Editions: p. 24, fig. 6; p. 25, fig. 7

© Kiki Smith/Universal Limited Art Editions, 1992. Photograph courtesy Universal Limited Art Editions: p. 30, fig. 8

© Jo Fielder Photography. Courtesy Universal Limited Art Editions: p. 31, fig. 9

Terry Winters
© Terry Winters/Universal Limited Art Editions, 1998. Photograph courtesy Universal Limited Art Editions: pp. 34–35 (detail), fig. 1; p. 36, fig. 1; p. 45, figs. 9–10; p. 47, fig. 11

© Terry Winters/Universal Limited Art Editions, 1988. Photograph courtesy Universal Limited Art Editions: p. 38, fig. 2

© Terry Winters/Universal Limited Art Editions, 1989. Photograph courtesy Universal Limited Art Editions: p. 39, figs. 3–4

© Terry Winters/Universal Limited Art Editions, 1997. Photograph courtesy Universal Limited Art Editions: p. 41, fig. 5; p. 42, fig. 6

© Terry Winters/Universal Limited Art Editions, 1986: p. 43, figs. 7–8

© Terry Winters/Two Palms, 2004. Photograph courtesy Two Palms: p. 51, fig. 12

Photograph by C. Zammiello. Courtesy Universal Limited Art Editions: p. 52, fig. 13

Suzanne McClelland
© Suzanne McClelland/Universal Limited Art Editions, 2000: pp. 54–55 (detail), fig. 1; p. 56, fig. 1; pp. 61–63, figs. 4–6

© Suzanne McClelland/Universal Limited Art Editions, 1999. Photograph courtesy Universal Limited Art Editions: p. 60, figs. 2–3

© Suzanne McClelland/Universal Limited Art Editions, 2000. Photograph courtesy Universal Limited Art Editions: p. 64, fig. 7; pp. 70–71, fig. 9

© Suzanne McClelland/Universal Limited Art Editions, 1998. Photograph courtesy Universal Limited Art Editions: p. 66, fig. 8

Photograph by C. Zammiello. Courtesy Universal Limited Art Editions: p. 74, fig. 10

Jane Hammond
© Jane Hammond/Universal Limited Art Editions, 2001: pp. 76–77 (detail), fig. 1; p. 78, fig. 1; p. 88, fig. 8

Photograph by Brian Berry. Courtesy Universal Limited Art Editions: p. 83, fig. 2; p. 84, fig. 5

Photograph by C. Zammiello. Courtesy Universal Limited Art Editions: p. 83, figs. 3–4

Photograph by Vanessa Viola. Courtesy Universal Limited Art Editions: p. 85, fig. 6

© Jane Hammond. Courtesy Universal Limited Art Editions: p. 86, fig. 7; p. 90, fig. 9

© Jane Hammond/Universal Limited Art Editions, 2003: p. 92, fig. 10

© Jo Fielder Photography. Courtesy Universal Limited Art Editions: p. 94, fig. 11

Matthew Ritchie
© Matthew Ritchie/Two Palms, 2003: pp. 96–97 (detail), fig. 1; p. 98, figs. 1–5; p. 104, fig. 8

© Matthew Ritchie. Courtesy Two Palms: p. 101, fig. 6; p. 106, fig. 9; p. 109, figs. 11–17; p. 114, fig. 18

© Matthew Ritchie/Two Palms, 2002. Photograph courtesy Two Palms: p. 101, fig. 7; p. 116, fig. 19

Photograph by C. Zammiello. Courtesy Two Palms: p. 107, fig. 10

Photograph by David Lasry. Courtesy Two Palms: p. 117, fig. 20

Carroll Dunham
© Carroll Dunham/Two Palms, 2004: pp. 124–25 (detail), fig. 1; p. 126, figs. 1–5; p. 140, figs. 11–13; p. 141, fig. 14

© Carroll Dunham/Universal Limited Art Editions, 1995: p. 129, fig. 6

© Carroll Dunham/Universal Limited Art Editions, 1994. Photograph courtesy Universal Limited Art Editions: p. 131, fig. 7

© Carroll Dunham/Pace Prints, 2006. Photograph courtesy Pace Prints: p. 134, fig. 8

Photograph by David Lasry. Courtesy Two Palms: p. 136, fig. 9; p. 148, fig. 15

Photograph by C. Zammiello: p. 136, fig. 10

Elizabeth Peyton
© Elizabeth Peyton/Two Palms, 2004: pp. 150–51 (detail), fig. 1; p. 152, fig. 1

Photograph by David Lasry. Courtesy Two Palms: p. 154, fig. 2; p. 161, fig. 12

© Elizabeth Peyton/Two Palms, 2002. Photograph courtesy Two Palms: p. 155, fig. 3

© Elizabeth Peyton/Two Palms, 2003. Photograph courtesy Two Palms: p. 156, fig. 4

© Elizabeth Peyton/Two Palms, 2006. Photograph courtesy Two Palms: p. 158, fig. 5

© Elizabeth Peyton/Two Palms, 2005. Photograph courtesy Two Palms: p. 158, fig. 6

Photograph courtesy Two Palms: p. 160, figs. 7–11

Ellen Gallagher
© Ellen Gallagher/Two Palms, 2005. Photograph courtesy Two Palms: p. 6 (detail), fig. 1; pp. 164–65 (detail), fig. 2; p. 166, figs. 1–2; p. 174, fig. 5; p. 189, fig. 13

© Ellen Gallagher/Universal Limited Art Editions, 1997. Photograph courtesy of Universal Limited Art Editions: p. 171, fig. 3

© The Museum of Modern Art/Licensed by SCALA/Art Resource, NY: p. 173, fig. 4

Photograph by C. Zammiello. Courtesy Two Palms: p. 176, figs. 6–7; p. 177, figs. 8–9; p. 178, fig. 10; p. 188, fig. 12

© Ellen Gallagher/Two Palms, 2004. Photograph courtesy Two Palms: p. 186, fig. 11

Chris Ofili
© Chris Ofili/Two Palms, 2007: pp. 194–95 (detail), fig. 7; p. 196, figs. 1–12; p. 202, fig. 14

© Chris Ofili, 1995. Photograph courtesy the artist: p. 199, fig. 13

Photograph by David Lasry. Courtesy Two Palms: p. 205, fig. 15

© Chris Ofili/Two Palms, 2006. Photograph courtesy Two Palms: p. 206, figs. 16–17

© Chris Ofili/Two Palms, 2009. Photograph courtesy Two Palms: p. 207, figs. 18–19

Photograph by C. Zammiello. Courtesy Two Palms: p. 209, fig. 20

Mel Bochner
© Mel Bochner/Two Palms, 2007: pp. 212–13 (detail), fig. 1; p. 214, figs. 1–6

© Mel Bochner. Courtesy Two Palms: pp. 220–22, figs. 7–14; pp. 225–32, figs. 15–32